1973

book may be kept

Historical Perspectives in Psychology: Readings

Historical Perspectives in Psychology: Readings

edited by

VIRGINIA STAUDT SEXTON

Herbert H. Lehman College
of the City University
of New York

and

HENRYK MISIAK

Fordham University

BROOKS/COLE PUBLISHING COMPANY
Belmont, California

A Division of
Wadsworth Publishing Company, Inc.

L. C. Cat. Card No.: 77-155898
ISBN 0-8185-0012-3
Printed in the United States of America

1 2 3 4 5 6 7 8 9 10–1975 1974 1973 1972 1971

This book was edited by Micky Stay and designed by Linda Marcetti. It was typeset at Design Service, Fullerton, California, and printed and bound at Malloy Lithographing, Inc., Ann Arbor, Michigan.

Preface

Historical Perspectives in Psychology: Readings is a compilation of contemporary and significant articles gleaned from books and journals that are not readily available to the student. This book omits the traditional source materials already published in other collections and draws instead from the large body of literature that has appeared during the last two decades. Moreover, it is the only book of this type that focuses on trends rather than on isolated events in the history of psychology.

We have always been committed to the principle that students should be exposed to original sources and to considerably more detail and depth than most textbooks can provide. We also discern an eagerness among today's students to study original sources on their own. In addition, there are unavoidable limitations on library reserve facilities in most colleges and universities. This volume offers one means of coping with these vexing problems.

The readings are classified by theme into six parts. Each part is introduced by a general explanation of the topic, and each selection is prefixed by a brief summary about the author and his work. Original bibliographies have been retained so that the reader may, if he wishes, pursue the topics in greater depth.

Part I includes selections that expound the reasons for, and benefits of, studying the history of science in general and of psychology in particular. In Part II psychologists and sociologists examine psychology's relation to other sciences, its growth as a science and profession, and the factors—social, cultural, and intellectual—that have contributed to that growth. Part III presents the views of a distinguished group of contemporary psychologists on some significant theoretical issues in psychology. These issues, although frequently encountered by the student in various areas of psychology, are not usually treated formally except in history and systems courses. Part IV discusses some of the trends and special features of psychology's progress in the United States, and Part V deals with such trends in a selected group of other countries. Finally, in Part VI three selections project the course of psychology to the end of the 20th century.

This collection evolved from our teaching of undergraduate and graduate courses in history and systems of psychology, and it no doubt reflects our predilections as well as those of our students who have found these articles stimulating and provocative. Some of our colleagues may dispute the relevance or importance of one or another of our selections. Many readings are indeed controversial and undoubtedly contain conclusions or interpretations with which some psychologists may not agree. Such a state of affairs seems to us not only unavoidable but in many respects desirable. It is our hope that the study of these selections will encourage the student to discuss and explore psychology more deeply. Indeed, we are inclined to adopt the view of James Thurber that "it is better to know some of the questions than all of the answers."

An edited volume of this type represents the coordinated effort of many persons. We are grateful to the authors and publishers who, by granting their permissions, made our project possible. At the invitation of our publisher, the following of our colleagues critically but helpfully reviewed the manuscript: Robert B. MacLeod, Cornell University; Michael Wertheimer, University of Colorado; Robert G. Weyant, University of Calgary; Audrey Bohm, San Francisco State College; Judith A. Hunt, California State College at Hayward; and Vernon L. Kiker, California State College at Los Angeles. We likewise wish to acknowledge the inspiration and cooperation given to us by Charles T. Hendrix, Psychology Editor of Brooks/Cole. Above all, to our many students who have read, discussed, and evaluated these articles, we express our heartfelt thanks.

Virginia Staudt Sexton
Henryk Misiak

Contents

VI. PSYCHOLOGY'S FUTURE   399

INDEX   441

I

Why Study the History of Psychology?

In the last two decades the history of science has gained respectability and popularity, both as a specialty and as a subject of teaching. In 1950, according to a survey by the *New York Times*, there were five professional historians of science in North America, and only a few schools offered Ph.D.s in this area. But by 1970 there were at least 125 such scholars; 25 major universities were offering full degree programs and another 350 schools were teaching some courses in the field. The history of science has become one of the most sought-after courses of study in American universities. A similar rapid growth in respectability and popularity has been noted for the history of psychology. Almost every large department of psychology now offers a course or courses in the history of its science. What factors brought about this change?

The readings in this first section specify the numerous benefits that can be gained from studying the history of psychology. These readings lead to the conclusion that the history of psychology should be regarded not merely as a commendable scholarly pursuit, or as a specialty to be cultivated by a few, or as a sideline in the psychological academic curriculum, but as an essential part of psychological study—a valuable portion of the psychologist's intellectual equipment and an integral element in his scientific and professional formation. Some of the excerpts, especially those from Erwin A. Esper and Robert I. Watson, discuss the reasons for both the long neglect of this area of study and the recent upsurge of interest in it. They suggest how the history of psychology can be most profitably viewed and studied.

The Uses of History
Erwin A. Esper

The following selection is the introductory chapter of *A History of Psychology*, by Erwin A. Esper. The author is professor emeritus of psychology at the University of Washington. He received his Ph.D. from Ohio State University, where he studied under Albert P. Weiss, an early theoretician of behaviorism. Esper dedicated his *History* to Weiss and to another of his teachers, George M. Bolling. Esper taught briefly at the University of Illinois and then moved to the University of Washington, where he stayed from 1927 until his retirement.

Esper has written, as he said, a *selective* history of psychology as "the study of man as a biological organism." In this chapter Esper deplores the ahistoricism in American psychology that prevailed from about 1920 to 1960 but is now disappearing. The principal aim of the chapter is to show that historical orientation is useful—in fact, indispensable—for the science of psychology. He discusses three basic reasons for studying the history of psychology. The first reason is "to know what has been done, in order to avoid stupid repetition" and discover new research possibilities. Second, knowledge of the past, especially of the roots, may help to chart "our future course." The third reason is that understanding the historical and cultural background of science is an essential prerequisite to the "critical judgments in important areas of contemporary life," areas in which scientists are gaining increased influence.

This introductory chapter might perhaps have borne the title, "An Apology for the Study of the History of Psychology," although I would then have needed to explain that "apology" was used in its primary sense of "something said or written in defense or justification of what appears to others to be wrong." For that the study of the history of psychology is regarded as "wrong" by influential contemporary psychologists is evidenced by the inhospitality of journal editors, one of whom has arrestingly characterized historical writings as "the hashing over of old theories." In one of our oldest universities the subject disappeared from the curriculum

From Erwin A. Esper, *A history of psychology*. Philadelphia: Saunders, 1964. Pp. 1-19. Reprinted by permission of the author and publisher.

a few years ago amid expressions of distaste for historical studies by eminent experimentalists. But the era of ahistoricism in American psychology may perhaps in future history be temporally delimited as *circa* 1920-1960; for, as we shall see, there is much evidence of its passing. It has, of course, been a parochial American, not a universal, phenomenon.

In medicine, it is a common observation that there are differences not only of skills but also of personality between two classes of practitioners, the surgeons and the internists; these two classes might perhaps be characterized as the doers and the verbalizers, respectively. It is not always recognized that there is an analogous dichotomy of scientists. We live in an age of rapid expansion of experimental techniques, and it is not surprising that men selected for aptitudes in electronics, mathematics, or industrial and clinical applications should have little motivation to acquire a background in the history of science. To such men it may seem inconceivable that anything of relevance to contemporary research could have been done more than twenty years ago. In her witty presidential address to the International Society for Cell Biology, Fell (1960)* remarked:

> In science, as in the world of dress, fashions recur. . . . There is one form of recurrence that is wholly regrettable, and which is one of the unfortunate consequences of the vast expansion of research and the monstrous and unwieldy literature that it now produces. I will mention a small example of the sort of thing that I have in mind. In the 1920's some of my colleagues did a rather extensive series of experiments which they duly published. A few years ago, an account of an almost identical research with the same results appeared in one of the journals, but with no mention of the earlier study. One of my colleagues wrote and pointed this out to the author, who replied that he never quoted any literature prior to 1946 [p. 1625 f.].

A first basic reason, then, for studying the history of any science is to know what has been done, in order both to avoid stupid repetition and to take advantage of research possibilities

---

*The reference dates are those of the editions which I used; they are therefore merely code numbers which will enable the reader, if he wishes, to identify quotations in their contexts by page number. The reader need therefore not be startled by such a reference as "Kant (1951)." However, in the List of References I have added, where it seemed desirable, the dates of first and other editions.

that may have been suggested long ago but have lain dormant. Here two further quotations from Fell's address are pertinent:

> Sometimes information or an idea has been available for years before some astute and enterprising person realizes its significance and places it in the public eye. The history of research on the nucleic acids is an interesting example of this. According to Hughes's *History of Cytology*, nucleic acid was first discovered by Miescher in 1871. Work then proceeded steadily but without attracting very wide interest until the 1930's, when the subject rapidly became extremely popular [p. 1625].
>
> The motives that prompt us to follow fashions in research are various and not always estimable. . . . In general, the waves of interest in something fresh that constantly sweep through our world are vital to its well-being, and without them research would indeed be stagnant and dreary. But rushing after new things merely because they are new (or what is more commonly termed "jumping on the band wagon") is another matter; it leads to the abandonment of existing lines of work that ought to be carried much farther, and even to contempt for the realities of nature, as in the disdain for structure that was such a regrettable fashion in cell biology a few years ago [p. 1627].

In psychology, too, we have had fashions in research; e.g., there really is no good reason why psycholinguistics should not have burgeoned in the 1920's as it did in the 1950's, nor why it should now be so extensively taken up by psychologists ignorant of linguistic science; one technique in this area, that of word-association, has been turned on and off like a tap during the past eighty years. If a young psychologist were to read the history of his science he would be very likely to come upon a problem which, were he to begin exploiting it now, would bring him into prominence a decade or two hence.

In the last of the passages quoted above, Fell referred to "the disdain for structure that was such a regrettable fashion in cell biology a few years ago." In psychology, we have been passing through a period of similar disdain for biological structure. Skinner, with his concept of the "empty organism," has been a chief representative of this attitude. The attempt to analyze behavior in terms of biological structures has been stigmatized as "physiologizing" or as "reductionism." Two historical reasons for this posture may be mentioned: first, the neurophysiology available to psychologists in the early decades of our century was so inadequate to behavioral theorizing as to bring physiological speculations by psychologists into disrepute; and secondly, experimental psychology from its birth has felt a compulsion to demonstrate to others and to reassure itself that it is an independent science, with its own subject matter and laws. But history suggests that it was a historical accident that the founding of experimental psychology was credited to professors of philosophy, and that these founders and their successors therefore felt it necessary to assert their independence from philosophy on the one hand and from the ancient disciplines of medicine and biology on the other. Actually, when we survey the great names of the early days of modern psychology—Weber, Fechner, Helmholtz, Hering, J. Mueller, Donders, Exner, von Kries, Koenig, Preyer—we find that these men were either biologists or physicists with an interest in physiology; others, whom we think of as primarily biologists, made contributions which have had greater influence on psychology than those of most psychologists: von Haller, Galvani, Bell, Whytt, Marshall Hall, Pflueger, Sechenov, Gall, Flourens, Broca, Munk, Goltz, Fritsch, Hitzig, Bechterev, Pavlov, Loeb, Sherrington. And of course many of the men whom we reckon as psychologists received training as biologists and not a few entered psychology with a medical degree: e.g., Locke, Hartley, Cabanis, Lotze, Wundt, James, McDougall. Moreover, in the last decade of the nineteenth century a group of German biologists—Beer, Bethe, Uexküll, Ziegler, and Loeb—formulated a program for an objective physiology that anticipated everything of importance in American behaviorism, which has usually been regarded as a brilliant (or crassly sansculottic) innovation of John B. Watson. The term "objective psychology" was applied to the program by Arnhart (1899), and the program was outlined by Bethe (1898), Beer, Bethe, and Uexküll (1899), and Ziegler (1900). I regard it as an unfortunate historical accident that what we now call "behavioristics" did not develop from this beginning and under biological auspices.

Most of the history of what is nowadays called clinical psychology is to be found in the history of medicine, beginning with Hippocrates, and there is little in current therapy, other than the non-rational use of lobotomy and tranquilizing drugs, which does not have a medical history of at least several centuries. As for diagnostic tools, Meehl (1960) warns the "fledgling clinical psychologist" that if his "self-concept is mainly 'I am a (test oriented) psychodiagnostician' [he] may have to maintain his professional security over the next few years by not reading the professional literature" (p. 26).

Meehl further expresses the opinion that clinical psychology has neither a theory from which to predict behavior nor measuring instruments adequate for specifying it. A reading of such a history as that of Zilboorg (1941) might prompt a clinical student to ask the sobering question: what great advances have been made by psychologists in diagnosis or therapy in the last century? Particularly striking in this history from ancient to recent times are the alternating cycles of theological, organic, and functional interpretations, and of kind and punitive treatment. Very apposite is Zilboorg's quotation of Del Greco: *L'histoire nous rend modestes.*

In two areas, those of animal psychology and of behavioral correlates of brain damage, it seems possible that there might have been some advantage had the development occurred within biology and in continuity with the history of biology. Concerning animal psychology, Bitterman (1960) remarks:

> It is interesting to note . . . that the acceptance of the Darwinian hypothesis was accompanied by a growing disregard for the facts of brain-structure. After giving up their inquiry into animal consciousness, the early comparative psychologists were at some pains to establish that there still remained to them an area of investigation different from that of the zoologists, and that their methods and findings were as important as those of the zoologists. If some primitive experiments with a maze or a problem box suggested that the process of learning was the same in monkey and sparrow, why then perhaps the difference in brain development had no fundamental significance [p. 706].

And concerning the literature on the rat, Bitterman observes:

> It is significant, I think, that nothing much in the way of well-defined functional relations has been forthcoming even from those who have rejected the traditional questions and advocated a vacant empiricism; in the hands of the Skinnerians, for example, batteries of expensive automatic equipment have yielded little more than an idiosyncratic assortment of kymograph tracings scarcely capable of quantitative analysis [p. 708].

Concerning the behavioral correlates of experimental brain lesions, some psychologists have come to conclusions which practically deny any significance to the elaborate cytoarchitecture of the brain. Hebb (1949, p. xvii) quotes an anonymous anatomist "who claimed that psychologists think of the brain as having all the finer structure of a bowlful of porridge." It may be questioned whether the neglect of histology and physiology which has resulted from the separation of psychology from biology has not delayed the discovery of basic behavioral explanations in general. Hebb (1949, 1955) has pointed out the failure of psychological theorists to exploit recent physiological research in its possible applications to unsolved behavioral problems. For example, he states that "When the detailed evidence of neurophysiology and histology are considered, the conclusion becomes inevitable that the nonsensory factor in cerebral action must be more consistently present and of more dominating importance than reluctant psychological theory has ever recognized" (1949, p. 7). And elsewhere Hebb (1958, p. vii) has described psychology as "fundamentally a biological science"; even its applied fields "demand a solid understanding of the mechanisms of behavior in the individual subject"; the theories of learning, perception, emotion, etc. "are biological because they have always been profoundly influenced by neurophysiology, neuroanatomy, and evolutionary and genetic theory." A similar view has been expressed by Pratt (1939, p. ix f.):

> The principal task of theoretical psychology in making a scientific portrait of human nature is to discover the immediate antecedents of initial descriptive data. These antecedent conditions are located within the biological organism. All psychological explanation must therefore move in the direction of physiology. The theoretical importance of psychological descriptions, as contrasted with any practical significance they may conceivably possess, derives almost exclusively from the light they throw on physiological mechanisms.

From such opinions Mandler and Kessen (1959) demur. They express the view that "A theory of dreams, or of thinking, or of animal learning which makes confirmed predictions and which is the basis for the design of informative research is a good theory, regardless of whether it is possible to re-interpret its premises into statements consistent with current physiological theory" (p. 268). Their argument is the familiar one that on the one hand there is "a set of protocol sentences about behavior," and a theory which permits its deduction, and on the other hand there is "a set of statements about physiological functions," and a corresponding theory, and that it is a mistake in strategy to attempt to "reduce" the one to the other. They also state that

> It is well to recall . . . that the criteria for a scientific vocabulary do not demand that "actual existence" underlie terms in the sense that

tables and dogs exist. Rather, the basic requirements turn on the reliable usage of terms in particular observational circumstances and in the sentences of a theory. On the first criterion, there may be in the language of physiology a group of terms which, for reasons of their systematic history, have a high level of reliability of usage, but there seem to be no defensible reasons why "drive" may not come to be as reliably applied as "synapse," or "libido" as reliably applied as "association area" [p. 264].

But it should be observed that many of those who are most assiduously investigating "drive" are striving to "reduce" their behavioral sentences to the thing-language of reticular system, hypothalamus, and limbic lobe, or to that of blood composition, gastric conditions, etc. Moreover, in the convergent results of research on human isolation, early sensory deprivation in dogs and monkeys, and autistic children, on the one hand, and on the functions of neocortex, rhinencephalon, and brain stem reticular formation and lemnisci, on the other (cf., e.g., Sprague et al., 1961), physiological meaning and, it would seem, increased reliability of usage are being given to the ancient and nebulous concepts of "attention" and "affect." And though Mandler and Kessen express the hope that "in the rational scientific community . . . considerations of historical sources . . . would have little to do with research strategy and tactics" (p. 263), it seems legitimate to ask what history has to tell us about the sources and nature of our "protocol sentences." The language of conditioning comes to us from the physiologists Sechenov, Bechterev, and Pavlov. The language of animal psychology comes to us from the Darwinians, and contemporary animal psychologists are much preoccupied with neural and glandular structures. The language of sensation and perception was largely developed by physiologists and physiologically trained psychologists. Much of the history of personality analysis and most of the history of clinical diagnosis and therapy are to be found in the histories of medicine. What is there left? Social psychology? Or Freudian theory? It will hardly be argued that here are to be found the best examples of reliable protocol sentences or powerfully predictive theories. The hypothesis might be entertained that reliability of sentences is a decreasing function of distance from biological tissue.

The above discussion may suggest a second basic reason for studying the history of psychology; namely, that a knowledge of our historical roots may be relevant to charting our future course. It may then appear that the negative attitude of many contemporary psychologists toward physiological interpretations represents a passing phase, which increasing physiological knowledge will make untenable. Moreover, there has been a great deal of emphasis recently on the necessity of basic science research and theory; most psychologists, surveying the vast output of low-level data and high-level theories in their contemporary literature, probably share an uncomfortable feeling that psychology is still an immature science awaiting some future "break-through." It is hard to imagine a fundamental "break-through" in other than biological terms; so, for example, the researchers seem to think who are working so actively on computer models of the thinking process. In recent times, two interests, that in testing and that in social phenomena, have attracted relatively large numbers of psychologists with little or no training in biology. This phenomenon may turn out to have been a temporary perturbation of the curve of growth of our science, which will have been corrected perhaps by some future administrative reclassification.

Boring (1959) has denied the validity of the first two reasons which I have given for studying the history of science. He tells us that we should not study history with the expectation of projecting the future. "Specific prediction . . . almost always fails, or is right by mere chance, because the efficient antecedents are too numerous and too complexly related to be correctly understood." And, "The other wrong reason for studying the past of science is to protect oneself from rediscovering something already known." Scientific literature, Boring says, is so vast that it is hopeless for the investigator to catch possible anticipations of his projected work. There is left only one good reason for studying the history of science: "One finds that he needs to know about the past, not in order to predict the future, but in order to understand the present."

My comment on these views would be that in scientific research, as elsewhere in life, we are under the continual necessity of planning for the future, and there is no other basis for doing this than our knowledge of the past. And, as elsewhere in life, we do what we can; things are always too complex for perfectly reliable prediction, and yet we must predict, if not explicitly then implicitly. As for "understanding the present," what functional significance would this have if not to provide some preparation for the future? In the view of an eminent contemporary historian, "It is at once the justification and the explanation of history that the past throws light on the future, and the future throws light on the past" (Carr, 1962, p. 163).

Actually, the main point I would like to make is expressed very well by Boring in this same article: "Each individual effort is an eddy in the total stream of science; and we shall become much wiser, get much nearer the truth, if we remember to look at the stream as a whole and notice the eddies only as they contribute to the sweep of the main current." But I would apply this wise saying to the examples from the history of psychology which Boring gives as illustrations of the impossibility of predicting future trends in science. Karl Lashley, he says, "spent his life 'in search of the engram.' " "At one time it looked as if Lashley's skillful, ingenious, and indefatigable labor was destined to dissolve in failure." Then Boring goes on to say:

> But the face of nature was then changing under the combined attacks of physicists and psychologists. "Field theory" came into physics, the realization that causality often does not work between little bits of stuff, but only between large patterns of activity. The Gestalt psychologists, who were rebels against conventional psychological atomism, made comparable discoveries for human perception; they found that one can understand an optical illusion only by considering it as a whole. And that is just what Lashley had also been proving for the pattern of communal excitation in the brain: one can get useful laws for the brain only by considering the whole and ignoring the parts of which it is made up.

First, as to the "field theory" of physics: the history of psychology reveals over and over again the pathetic eagerness of psychologists to adopt *analogically* the current fashion in physics or chemistry; well-known historical examples are the psychical mechanics of Herbart and the mental mechanics and mental chemistry of the Mills. Unfortunately, psychologists, practitioners of an adolescent science, come in either of two dispositional varieties: mentalistic-vitalistic or physicalistic-objectivistic, and they are therefore predisposed to hail with enthusiasm any development in the physical or biological sciences which, however misunderstood, seems to bolster their postulates, by whatever analogical stretch. Notoriously, quantum theory was seized upon by some as an argument for free will or vitalism, an argument which has been cogently refuted, e.g., by Frank (1950, pp. 158-171). In the light of our history, psychologists might well have raised the question whether the field theory of the physicists had any relevance whatever to psychological theory or research; this matter has been well put by Spence (1941), in a review of Köhler's *Dynamics in Psychology*. As Köhler (1947, p. 42) himself said:

> If we wish to imitate the physical sciences, we must not imitate them in their highly developed contemporary form. Rather, we must imitate them in their historical youth, when their state of development was comparable to our own at the present time. Otherwise we should behave like boys who try to copy the imposing manners of full-grown men without understanding their *raison d'être*, also without seeing that intermediate phases of development cannot be skipped. In this respect, a survey of the history of physics is most illuminating. If we are to emulate the natural sciences, let us do so intelligently.

A sobering *reductio ad absurdum* of band wagon jumping is to be found in Scripture's (1936, pp. 258 ff.) account of his "four stages of mental development"; he was, he says, successively a Cartesian, a Wundtian, and a Freudian. And then—"The fourth stage began with a shock. Everything that I had ever believed in was swept away as soon as I managed to get some understanding of relativity. . . . I am now trying to revise my psychological and phonetic notions to accord with the new mode of thought." This traumatic shock, he tells us, resulted from his confrontation of the equations in Eddington's *Nature of the Physical World.* He foresees a "new psychology," in which an important role will be played by "the entropy clocks of the Great Unknown."

Secondly, as to gestalt theory: it has repeatedly been pointed out that this sectarian school produced neither a great innovation nor an acceptable general theory. For example, Commins (1932) listed the precursors of gestalt psychology: Herbart's theory of apperception, Wundt's principle of creative synthesis, Külpe's central factors, J. S. Mill's "mental chemistry," James's figured consciousness, conscious continuum, and experienced relations, and Dewey's organic wholeness. Wheeler (1936) wrote: "Scientific theory has had a strikingly cyclic history. At 1250, 1650, and 1820 and now at 1935 it is organismic in intent. . . . Between these peaks, the thought pattern swerved to an opposite extreme, that of mechanism, whose peaks fall at about 1400, 1775, and 1860." And Wheeler expressed the opinion that the cycles of emphasis have been shortening, that the peak of the then current organismic emphasis would be reached by 1940, and that a later swing to atomism, reaching a peak between 1950 and 1960, could be predicted. Line (1931), after tracing the historical antecedents of gestalt psychology and evaluating its contributions, concluded that it had made few positive accomplishments on which a distinctive general theory could be based. These were critiques written when gestalt psychology was young, and they used history both to evaluate the present and to guess the future. How reliable were the predictions? The statements that one finds in current literature are mostly to the effect that gestalt psychology had certain stimulating effects but that its doctrines about learning, neural functioning, and even perception are dubious or at least in need of a great deal of correction. Remarks of this sort are to be found, e.g., in the volume edited by Marx (1951). Thus Bergmann and Spence (p. 272) observe: "The extensive use of the term 'perception,' which the Gestalters advocate, makes it a weasel word that covers the whole of psychology only at the price of emptying it of any specific content. Historically speaking, this verbal preference is probably grounded in the intuitionistic philosophical background of the Gestalters." And Spence (1960), in his discussion of discrimination behavior, remarks: "The Gestalt theories have failed to furnish either a satisfactory explanation of these phenomena or an adequate experimental formulation of the problem" (p. 306).

As we have seen, such dubiety had already been expressed by historically sophisticated psychologists in the 1920's and 30's. As it happened, however, the Titchenerians were at this very time desperately defending themselves against the attempts of the behaviorists to deprive them of both their subject matter and their methodology. Many of them were therefore ready to sacrifice their mental atoms as the price of admission to a vigorous "new" school which practiced introspection and, although it did indeed reject "analysis," nevertheless made up for this by damning behaviorism. The gestalt school was thus a home away from home for those who could not tolerate behaviorism. These included the vitalists. As Lund (1929, p. 307) wrote:

> But the very intangibility of the gestalt concept is doubtless responsible for the sympathetic if not enthusiastic response received from the mystics, the vitalists, and those who feel that there *is*, or at least *ought* to be something the matter with certain mechanistic and naturalistic interpretations of today. Hence, the chorus of approval from the purposivists, the Bergsons, the McDougalls, and the Driesches. Indeed, with Koffka's insistence that "the universal Gestalt" is an original property of experience ... and Köhler's affirmation that "no experience is needed for a first formation of units in the visual field," we

again feel ourselves in the atmosphere of the Hegelian Universals and the Platonic Forms.

Thus gestalt psychology became another in the long line of "new" psychologies whose enthusiastic reception has not been wholly rational nor historically justified. From the point of view of the sociology of science, the gestalt "movement" was an importation into America of the German-style academic warfare between Berlin and Leipzig, and between the nativists and the empiricists. Boring (1929) has given a classic description of such a controversy, that between Stumpf and Wundt on "tonal distances." Since the American Wundtians collaborated with the invaders, the native behaviorists became substitute objects of aggression. The reception of gestalt psychology was no doubt facilitated by the well-known American hospitality to visitors from distant and more ancient shores; as the general populace cheered Einstein, so perhaps many psychologists hailed gestalt psychology as a scientific revelation which, like the theory of relativity in physics, was to usher in a new, if dimly seen, era in psychology. "New" psychologies are of course very stimulating and great fun for the young at heart, but they can lead to a great deal of wasteful effort; proponents and opponents tend, so to speak, to conduct a dialogue in falsetto, and to perform research in the same register. Perhaps the study of history might be recommended as a moderating influence in such situations.

And what about Lashley, the engram, and the doctrines of equipotentiality and mass action? Lashley's (1929) own review of the history of brain localization could, I think, have suggested the possibility that his conclusions represented another swing of the pendulum rather than a final approach to reality. This was all the more true because of the relative crudity, for his purpose, of the method—extirpation—which was then available to him, and also because of his reliance on rat material. Adrian (1932, p. 79 f.) expressed the view that the anti-reflex movement inspired by the work of Coghill and of Lashley was a pendular swing in physiological history; physiologists as teachers (rather than as specialists) emphasize whatever principles are in fashion at the moment, and then over-correct in the opposite direction. Hunter (1931, p. 233) pointed out that "the integrative action of the nervous system is a well-established fact," and declared *Lashley is now presenting no new theory of neural action*, unless he can show that integration is equipotential and that such a conception has meaning." Thus, at the time of Lashley's basic contribution, there were historical reasons for reserve in accepting his conclusions and for questioning whether his proposed doctrines represented any marked advance over the views expressed over the years between 1842 and 1906 by Flourens, Goltz, Loeb, and Sherrington. It is to be noted that Lashley himself later carried out ingenious research whose results he regarded as incompatible with Köhler's "electrical field theory" of cerebral integration; the weakness of this theory, he said, "is that it has been elaborated without sufficient attention to details of structure, and that it has stopped with the subjective phenomena of perception without following out the implications for the translation of perception into actions" (Lashley, Chow, and Semmes, 1951, p. 123). Or one might say, it has preferred physical analogy to biological correlation.

Thus to the historically sophisticated psychologist in the 1930's and to us in retrospect it could hardly appear that the gestalt psychologists had made revolutionary discoveries without historical antecedents, nor could they in any meaningful sense be said to have applied physical field theory to psychology. Lashley did not discover the engram, which is still undiscovered: "The detailed natures of the electric oscillations constituting consciousness and ephemeral memory, of the molecular patterns constituting permanent memory, and of the mechanism of their interaction are not known" (Pauling, 1961, p. 15). Nor was Lashley's view of neural function without precedent; it is not necessary to assert his historical unpredictability in order to pay proper homage to his contributions. Lashley himself, in summarizing his work (1960), said that "Innumerable studies have defined conditions under which learning is facilitated or retarded, but, in spite of such progress, we seem little nearer to an understanding of the nature of the memory trace than was Descartes." His own series of experiments "has yielded a good bit of information about what and where the memory trace is not. It has discovered nothing directly of the real nature of the engram. I sometimes feel, in reviewing the evidence on the localization of the memory trace, that the necessary conclusion is that learning just is not possible" (p. 500 f.). Here Lashley expresses very succinctly the impression left on a reader by the piling up of negative evidence. Lashley himself deprecated physiological inferences from anatomical data; it has seemed to me that similar difficulties arise from the functional interpretation of the results of extirpation procedures. Hebb (1949, pp. 38-59), after a most judicious review of the issues raised by

Köhler and Lashley, remarks, "It is important as psychology comes of age to avoid, if possible, the extreme positions that have often been adopted in the discussions of the past," and he likens the debate between gestalt and learning theory to "the running battle between the Left and the Right in governmental policy." Here again history shows us alternating cycles of thesis and antithesis, with overlapping periods of conflict. There has no doubt, as Hebb says, been some progress, stimulated in part by the configurationists, but basically I think the situation is this: Köhler and Lashley have rejected one physiological theory and proposed another on the basis of correlations between behavioral or introspective data on the one hand and anatomical (extirpation) procedures or physical analogies on the other; learning theorists have sought to construct theories based on correlations between external energy patterns and physical displacements (as of levers). If, as seems reasonable to suppose, learning and perception are functions of the central nervous system, then true progress toward explanation of these phenomena will have to be in terms of neurophysiological processes. It is my impression that the necessary techniques are in process of being developed in electron microscopy, electrophysiology, and biochemistry; the historical analogies which at once came to mind are the events which followed the invention of the microscope and the discovery by Galvani. That is, cycles of scientific controversy end when adequate techniques are invented; controversies which *never* end are "metaphysical"! For these reasons I think that Boring (1960, p. xvi) is speaking as a partisan rather than as a historian when he says that "The major movement is from mechanism to field theory, from *Undverbindungen* to *Gestalten*, from atomism to emergent wholes," and when he goes on to suggest an analogy between "the new physics" and "the latest psychology," which "would seem to have pulled neuropsychology along with them." Boring, it seems to me, has mistaken an eddy for the total stream.

And finally, a third basic justification for the study of the history of science—and of history in general—is related to the anxiety expressed by many writers lately about the state of American education in general and of the education of scientists in particular. It has been felt that our education has been lacking in the communication of cultural values and of the historical background necessary for critical judgments in important areas of contemporary life. For scientists this has been thought a particularly serious matter because of their greatly increased influence on the course of affairs in our times. We are all familiar with the opprobrious epithets which have been applied to the graduates of engineering colleges and military academies, derisively called "trade schools"; according to the semi-humorous stereotype, they are practitioners of the slide rule—culturally deficient, technological robots. There has been some question whether we in psychology have not been turning out a good many technicians of a similar stripe: persons skilled in mental testing, Rorschach interpretation, scale construction, analysis of variance, factor analysis, electronics, polygraph reading, etc., who neither know nor have any interest in the history or philosophy of science and who are also lacking in general cultural background. Beardslee and O'Dowd (1961) have reported that in the college student's image of the scientist, cultural deficiency is a prominent trait. The lack of interest of pupils can of course be attributed in large degree to the lack of interest on the part of their professors. Barzun (1945, p. 101), after quoting a professor who said, "You don't have to teach the history of science to make a man understand that water is H_2O," remarks, "It is precisely what you have to teach, unless you are willing to barter understanding for mere voodoo formulas." His remark is truer for psychology than it is for chemistry, for voodoo is more pervasive in psychology; as can be seen in the olla-podrida of the *Psychological Abstracts*, precise experiment and painful logic are intermixed with fantasies and autonomous verbalisms worthy of Pythagoras, Empedocles, and Plato, and with the Protagorean formulae of the "psychology of adjustment." A writer in the *American Scholar* (Hyman, 1960) has described psychologists as provincial, ignorant of the humanities and of the history of their own discipline, philosophically shallow, and possessed of "an amazing tolerance and even respect" for "necromancers" such as the parapsychologists.

The first American psychological laboratories were founded, in the last three decades of the nineteenth century, by men who had been trained in German universities, and who therefore had knowledge of the history both of philosophy in general and of psychology as—at that time—a branch of philosophy; they usually had training also in biology and in other natural sciences. In the second and third decades of the twentieth century, behaviorism burst upon the scene as what seemed to many at the time a rootless bolshevism of a philosophically backward America. The Titchenerians especially, disregarding their own very special and limited origins and purview, as well as the French and German origins of objective psychology, issued dire warnings that should this movement triumph, American psychology would lose its historical heritage and its international affiliations. It did in fact happen, as behaviorism evolved into behavioral science, that American psychology, preoccupied with techniques and with practical concerns, entered upon an ahistorical period, in which history courses disappeared from curricula and many psychologists expressed impatience with historical studies. Characteristic was the coldness with which the directors of the American Psychological Association received the proposal for the fourth volume of the *History of Psychology in Autobiography*. This attitude was reinforced by the anti-genetic movement led by Lewin.

In the past few years evidence has appeared of an awakening of interest in the history of psychology and of the behavioral sciences in general. Swartz (1958) urged that psychologists should encourage graduate dissertations in the history of psychology. "To insist upon an experimental type of dissertation . . . is a manifestation of our lack of a historical sense." R.I. Watson (1960) suggested that the lack of historical interest on the part of American psychologists may be due to immaturity and youthful exuberance, and very cogently pointed out that history is not written once for all time; that "each generation rewrites the history in terms of its own values"; that "we have not [as yet] looked back upon the past from the perspective of today"; and that "in the past writing of our history, material either ignored as irrelevant or simply not known at that time now can be utilized." Or, as Croce (1921, p. 12) said, "Every true history is contemporary history."

In July 1960 appeared the first number of the *History of the Behavioral Sciences Newsletter*, sponsored by several psychiatrists of the Payne Whitney Clinic. It notes that "Although the history of the development of the behavioral sciences is a relatively new research area, within recent years this study has attracted numerous workers throughout the world." It remarks that "As far as we know, the American Psychiatric Association is the only organization in the behavioral sciences to have a formal committee on history."

At the 1960 convention of the American Psychological Association a meeting was held "for informal discussion about work and interest in the history of psychology." Many projects, in considerable variety, were presented at this meeting. A letter was sent to the Board of Editors of the Association pointing out that the journals published by the Association do not adequately provide for articles on the history of psychology. Concern was expressed at the refusal of university psychology departments to accept doctoral dissertations on historical subjects. It was suggested that the Association appoint an archivist such as the British Association has, "to collect official archives and to encourage eminent psychologists to see that their personal papers go to a responsible archives." These interests were continued, and further meetings were held, under the chairmanship of Robert I. Watson, in 1961 and 1962.*

Thus it appears that ahistoricism in American psychology was another passing phase in the history of science. It is interesting to note the influence of psychology's biological and medical affiliations in the revival of historical interest, and to speculate that those psychologists who decry "physiologizing" tend also to disparage the study of history. In the history of medicine we may note interesting parallels to that of psychology. Sigerist (1951, pp. 4-6) tells us that "until about a hundred years ago the history of medicine was primarily medicine . . . part of the theory of medicine, the experience of the preceding generations that had to be assimilated if progress was to be achieved." But, "This attitude towards the past of medicine changed radically in the second half of the nineteenth century when a new medical science developed and progress was achieved such as never before. The past seemed dead. . . . Nothing could be learned from [the history of medicine]; to study it, to read the ancient writers, was a waste of time." But presently, collaborative work shared by historians, philologists, philosophers, and physicians began, and this eventuated in 1905 at Leipzig in the first research institute for the study of the history of medicine. The first such institute in America was founded at the Johns Hopkins University in 1929. Today the history of medicine is a generally recognized department of research and instruction. This development seems to be beginning in psychology, which might therefore, in this respect, be said to be following medicine at an interval of about fifty years.

*Since this was written there have appeared Robert I. Watson's *The Great Psychologists* (Philadelphia: Lippincott, 1963), and J.R. Kantor's *The Scientific Evolution of Psychology*, Vol. I (Chicago: Principia Press, 1963). The June 1963 (No. 6) issue of the *History of the Behavioral Sciences Newsletter* contains an extensive list of books and articles published in 1961; additional publications for 1961-1962 are listed in the "History & Biography" section of the *Psychological Abstracts*. Leo Postman has edited *Psychology in the Making: Histories of Selected Research Problems* (New York: Knopf, 1962), with more than 1100 references, which should be valuable in giving students the sense of historical continuity in research.

But though the historical specialty has been much better recognized in medicine than in psychology, some medical writers have remarked upon a certain neglect in recent times. Dr. Fred A. Mettler, in his editorial preface to Cecilia Mettler's (1947) *History of Medicine*, attributes this neglect in large part to the losses in war:

> It is one of the functions of the historian to preserve and explain the continuity of the present with the past. The greatest obstacle to medical progress, and indeed to all cultures, is the loss of this continuity with the past. The most fertile source of such discontinuities is war. War destroys scholars directly, it destroys their opportunity to work . . . and it destroys historical perspective.
>
> In the Editorial Preface of the supplementary volume [of the *Encyclopaedia Britannica*, 1922] Hugh Chisholm pointed out that a completely new twelfth edition "could not be made today so as to have anything like the scholarly value of the work produced before the war. . . ." He said that neither the minds nor wills were any longer obtainable, nor would they be for years to come. Pre-war authorities had died without leaving lineal successors, and a shifting of interest had occurred "among writers of the academic type, so that there is a disinclination to make the exertion needed for entering anew into old subjects—a necessary condition for just that stimulating, vital presentation of old issues in the light of all the accumulated knowledge about them, which was so valuable. . . ." (p. vii).

In a review of a recent book which is a "quite sophisticated exposition of biology," by an author whose "knowledge of the vast subject matter he covers is thorough and intimate," Graubard (1962, p. 276) wonders whether "so much precooked and ready-to-serve material can be consumed and digested by the beginning student," and continues:

> Moreover, should science be taught in this manner, without providing any historical perspective for the questions raised, the theories offered, discarded, accepted, modified, and challenged, or the controversies stirred up between such giants as Pasteur and Liebig, for example, which reveal the very essence and drama of growth and evolution in science as well as the meaning of theory and truth? Should the student memorize these thousands of facts with no motive, no evidence, no challenge, and above all, with no knowledge of how they came to be established and upon what foundations they rest?

It seems likely that the two world wars, and the threatened third, have had much to do with the neglect of history by psychologists, both because of the entrance of large numbers of young psychologists into applied fields, and because of the vast post-war increase in governmental and foundationary subvention of research which conforms to the patterns of "experimental design" or "statistical analysis" favored by selection committees. In recent times, a young psychologist without a numerically designated "project" and the "support" and prestige which this symbolizes has been at a grave professional disadvantage. Moreover, there have been the insistent demands of the military and of practical social problems arising from rapid social and political changes and from moral, intellectual, and artistic confusion. The times, in short, have not been favorable for quiet scholarship—for that historical scholarship which, as Mettler (1947) has observed, provides scientists with "a sense of perspective" and "a feeling of proportion among the component fields" of their sciences. One might be inclined to see the ahistoricism of recent psychology as a manifestation of the disenchantment with tradition which is characteristic of contemporary culture in general. As Bradbury (1962) says:

> Certainly one of the distinguishing features of what we like to call the modern dilemma is the degree to which we feel ourselves separated from the past, and the frenzy and energy with which we seek to annihilate the past. . . . There are scant signs that the creative artists of the twentieth century, at least in the West, are concerned for the cultural tradition to which they are the heirs. Indeed their sense is rather that this is a meaningless heritage.

There is perhaps this difference: that whereas the revolt of the artists is a reaction of revulsion, disillusionment, and pessimism, the neglect of history by psychologists is a result of the limitations imposed by their education and prevailing professional motivations; one cannot revolt against that of which one is not aware, although one is likely to avoid that in which one is unversed.

REFERENCES

Adrian, E. D. *The mechanism of nervous action.* Philadelphia: University of Pennsylvania Press, 1932.

Barzun, J. *Teacher in America.* Boston: Little, Brown, 1945.

Bitterman, M. E. Toward a comparative psychology of learning. *Amer. Psychologist*, 1960, **15**, 704-712.

Boring, E. G. Science and the meaning of its history. *The Key Reporter*, 1959, **24**(4), 2-3.

Boring, E. G. Introduction: Lashley and cortical integration. In F. A. Beach et al. (Eds.), *The neuropsychology of Lashley.* New York: McGraw-Hill, 1960. Pp. xi-xvi.

Bradbury, M. The taste for anarchy. *Saturday Review*, June 30, 1962.

Carr, E. H. *What is history?* New York: Knopf, 1962.

Croce, B. *Theory and history of historiography.* London, 1921.

Fell, H. B. Fashion in cell biology. *Science*, 1960, 132, 1625-1627.

Frank, P. *Modern science and its philosophy.* Cambridge, Mass.: Harvard University Press, 1950.

Graubard, M. Review of *Integrated basic science*, by S. M. Brooks. *Science*, 1962, **137**, 275-276.

Hebb. D. O. *The organization of behavior.* New York: Wiley, 1949.

Hebb, D. O. *A textbook of psychology.* Philadelphia: Saunders, 1958.

Hunter, W. S. Lashley on "Cerebral control versus reflexology." *J. gen. Psychol.*, 1931, **5**, 230-234.

Köhler, W. *Gestalt psychology.* New York: Liveright, 1947.

Lashley, K. S. In search of the engram. In F. A. Beach et al. (Eds.), *The neuropsychology of Lashley.* New York: McGraw-Hill, 1960. Pp. 478-505.

Lashley, K. S., Chow, K. L., & Semmes, J. An examination of the electrical field theory of cerebral integration. *Psychol. Rev.,* 1951, **58**, 123-136.

Lund, F. H. The phantom of the Gestalt. *J. gen. Psychol.,* 1929, **2**, 307-323.

Mandler, G., & Kessen, W. *The language of psychology.* New York: Wiley, 1959.

Marx, M. H. (Ed.) *Psychological theory.* New York: Macmillan, 1951.

Meehl, P. E. The cognitive activity of the clinician. *Amer. Psychologist*, 1960, **15**, 19-27.

Mettler, C. C. *History of medicine.* Philadelphia: Blakiston, 1947.

Pauling, L. A molecular theory of general anesthesia. *Science*, 1961, **134**, 15-21.

Pratt, C. C. *The logic of modern psychology.* New York: Macmillan, 1939.

Scripture, E. W. Autobiography. In C. Murchison (Ed.), *A history of psychology in autobiography,* Vol. III. Worcester, Mass.: Clark University Press, 1936. Pp. 231-261.

Sigerist, H. E. *A history of medicine, Vol. II: Early Greek, Hindu, and Persian medicine.* New York: Oxford, 1961.

Spence, K. W. *Behavior theory and learning.* Englewood Cliffs, N.J.: Prentice-Hall, 1960.

Some Guides to the Understanding of the History of Psychology
Richard S. Crutchfield
David Krech

Both professors of psychology at the University of California at Berkeley, Richard S. Crutchfield and David Krech have been active in experimental research and have made substantial contributions to social psychology, perception, and the neurological foundation of behavior. The second edition of their textbook *Elements of Psychology* appeared in 1969. In the following selection they present both general and specific reasons why the history of psychology is "to be commended to the student—whether he be a student who wants to know *about* psychology, or whether he be a student who wants to *do* psychology." Other sections of the chapter (not reprinted here) contain many helpful ideas and observations that can guide the student in his historical study, and we recommend them to the reader.

THE STUDY OF HISTORY OF PSYCHOLOGY

In the offerings of almost every large (and of many a small) psychology department there is a course called "History of Psychology" or some equivalent thereof. And there have been renowned psychologists whose eminence was almost entirely due to their scholarship as historians of psychology. There are numerous reasons why psychology is almost unique among the sciences in this respect. Let us briefly examine but three of them.

(1) Psychology is still close enough in time and in subject matter to its ancestral home—philosophy—to reflect the parental interests and predilections. And philosophy, as indeed all the humanities, has ever been concerned with history. In this sense, psychology's concern with its history might be termed vestigial.

(2) Psychology probably ranks above all other sciences in the persistence with which it has engaged the attention of mankind over the ages. Man, no matter what else he observed and wondered about,

From Richard S. Crutchfield and David Krech, Some guides to the understanding of the history of psychology. In L. Postman, (Ed.), *Psychology in the making.* New York: Knopf, 1962. Pp. 4-6. ©1962 by Alfred A. Knopf, Inc. Reprinted by permission of the authors and the publisher.

seems always to have observed and wondered about himself and his fellows. The accumulated lore about the behavior of man, passed down from generation to generation, sifted (somewhat) and tested (somewhat) by time, has in it a considerable number of fairly respectable generalizations and insights. All this has enabled man, long, long ago, to pose some fairly simple but basic questions about himself. And because the simple and basic questions are often the most difficult to answer in any science—and especially in so complex a science as psychology—many of these questions of the past are still with us. The concern of today's psychologists about the nurture of the creative process is a concern which probably antedated the first pedagogue and the first schoolboy's stylus. Today's psychologists are intrigued by the locus of the controlling mechanisms of emotions, of intellect, of wants and desires. So were the ancients—and the ancients before them. Already by the time of Aristotle this was a question of dispute among the physicians and philosophers (and one where Aristotle seemed to have pulled his greatest "boner" by placing the seat of the intellect in the heart). When animal psychologists today conduct experiments to determine whether the ability to perceive the spatial aspects of our environments is learned or innate, they are merely the latest entrants in a debate of many centuries' duration— . . .

It is probably true that problems persist longer in psychology than in most other sciences. When the psychologist reads the history of his science (perhaps the longest, uninterrupted intellectual history of any science) he reads of questions and attempted answers to questions with which he is struggling in his laboratory today. He finds very little of the "musty," the quaint, and the foolishly outmoded there. This may be why the history of psychology continues to attract the psychologist, more so, for example, than does the history of chemistry attract the chemist.

(3) Finally, nothing which is behavior can be foreign to the psychologist. Because psychology is concerned with all of man's behavior, it must not only *be* a science, but it must also *study* science as an important kind of human behavior. In the grammar of science, psychology must be in both the nominative and the accusative case. It must, in other words, study itself as it studies behavior. This means being self-conscious about the processes of science. It is therefore apparent why psychology seeks to study, carefully and analytically, the development and history of psychology. Psychology's concern

with scientific history can be understood as a concern with what is part of its own proper scientific subject matter.

But quite aside from these special considerations, there are a number of general reasons why students of psychology should (and sometimes do) study the history of their science. And these general reasons apply to students of other sciences with equal force. These general factors influence the vigor with which the scientist will pursue his science and the attitude he will adopt toward his science. Again we might look at three such factors.

It has often been said that a knowledge of the history of one's science teaches the scientist humility and tolerance for opposing views. The succeeding chapters of this book are replete with instances of scientists who, certain of the truth of their formulations, lived only to see these formulations abandoned by science; the succeeding chapters are filled, too, with instances of scientific hypotheses derided as silly, inane, and beyond the pale by the scientific authorities of the day—hypotheses which today live on in respectability while their authoritative detractors have been consigned to oblivion. One might draw the moral from this that error will out—eventually. But another moral would seem to be that truth *can* be and sometimes is suppressed for longer periods by the scientist who lacks humility and tolerance. Humility and tolerance, in other words, are not only good for the soul, but also good for the advancement of science. Studying history is not the only way to achieve these admirable attributes, but it can be a very effective way.

It has also been said that the history of science not only teaches one to be humble about his own achievements and scientific notions, but also teaches one to take pride in scientific endeavors, and to have courage in the face of immediate difficulties and frustrations. Each of the eleven narratives in this book tells a story of significant progress and of great achievement, but progress and achievement which are rarely without interruption, rarely without repeated and sometimes long and costly stumblings into blind alleys. The moral seems to be—science will get there, don't give up the ship! And so again, the history of science can help inculcate desirable traits, traits of pride, of courage, and of perseverance, which are not only good for the character, but also good for the progress of science.

And finally, of course, study of the history of one's science helps make the scientist a complete man. From what we can surmise about man's motivations and needs, he cannot live and function at his best except when he sees his life and his functions as an essential part of something of lasting value, except when he identifies himself with something greater, more durable than his mortal self. For a scientist to know the history of his science is to see his laboratory, and his tables of data, and his journal articles, and his scientific meetings as his participation and involvement in an ancient and honorable activity—an activity which has shaped and turned the world, which has engaged the great minds and noble men of countries and times distant from his own, and which will probably continue to do so for ages to come. He becomes a part of these eternal strivings. It may well be that, in studying the history of his own science, he will find therein the moral equivalent of religion, the moral equivalent of clan and national loyalty. And if this helps him function well, it helps science grow.

History of Psychology: What Benefits? A Review of Three Books
Jacob R. Kantor

Jacob R. Kantor, professor emeritus of psychology at Indiana University, has been known for his several volumes in theoretical psychology and for his concept of "interbehavioral psychology," which stresses the study of complex interactions between organisms and between organisms and inorganic objects. As a historian of psychology he has published several articles and the two-volume *Scientific Evolution of Psychology* (1963, 1969). In June 1970 he was awarded an honorary doctorate of letters by the University of Akron.

Kantor's article that is briefly excerpted here was prompted by the publication of three books: *The Neuropsychology of Lashley* (1960), edited by Beach, Hebb, Morgan, and Nissen; *Psychology in the Making* (1962), edited by Postman; and *A History of Psychology* (1964), by Esper. Excerpts from the last two books have just been presented. In this article Kantor warns against biases in historical writing and specifies the requirements that, in his opinion, historical writing must fulfill to be beneficial to the student of history.

Each of these volumes (*Psychology in the Making, The Neuro-psychology of Lashley,* and *A History of Psychology*) in its own way bears witness to the fact that the study of the history of psychology has become a conspicuous fashion. In the introduction to the Postman book, Crutchfield and Krech assert that a course called "History of Psychology" or some equivalent thereof is found among the offerings of almost every large (and of many a small) department of psychology. Esper, on the other hand, though he believes that the history of psychology still remains unappreciated, and that it is necessary to urge the study of the subject, argues most vigorously for it, as though he believed that no psychological curriculum can be adequate without a required course in history. And finally the Lashley book not only contains a thick slice of valuable history of one phase of psychology, but it is also proclaimed on its jacket that it is particularly helpful in courses in the history of experimental

From Jacob R. Kantor, History of psychology: What benefits? A review of three books. *The Psychological Record*, 1964, **14**, 433-443. Reprinted by permission of the author and publisher.

psychology, physiological psychology, comparative psychology, and learning theory. . . .

THE USES OF HISTORY

Now that we have seen how our three books present the History of Psychology we may paraphrase Peterkin and ask what good can come of it after all? What benefits are to be derived from studying history? What lessons does it teach? Unfortunately much historical writing suggests that history teaches us only that it does not teach us anything. And this despite the fact that every historical book is bound to contain some more or less reliable information (dates, names of writers, doctrinal comparisons and successions, and so on), besides its erroneous interpretations. A somewhat less discouraging conclusion is that the history of psychology does manage to flashback the doings and doctrines of ancient and modern psychologists.

Yet faulty historical writing should not obscure the fact that the proper writing of psychological history can provide an exceedingly important basis for the understanding of psychological events and for avoiding some of the outstanding errors that former writers have made about them. But like every intellectual endeavor there is required a proper postulational basis. The first requirement is that the historian should confront psychological events as directly and independently as possible. Historical events are not to be confused with traditional constructs about them. Traditional constructs whether presumed to be descriptions or interpretations must be examined carefully, and when found to be incongruous with original events they are to be rejected. As we know, science progresses in great part by the destruction of venerable and conventional axioms.

Again a history of psychology is better written when it is assumed that psychological events exist and are studied as independent data, howsoever closely they are associated with other kinds of events—whether biological, physiochemical, or anthropological. Specifically the historian may not assume that psychology is concerned with "phenomena" that are based on authentic or spurious biological processes, or are nothing but biological processes.

Another important requirement for historical study is that the views of various writers concerning psychological events be treated as phases of the cultural conditions in which they are formulated. Interpretations developed in later times are not to be imposed upon writers who lived under very different cultural conditions. For example, it is improper to impose upon Plato's dichotomy of sensing and rational knowledge the soul-flesh diremption that was invented in a non-Hellenic cultural period.

IN SUM

The writing and reading of history are in no sense valuable in themselves. Historical writings may be good or bad depending on their proximity to the events they portray. All the merits attributable to history writing are realizable only when historians are aware of and tell what actually happened in a particular time and place situation. But history writing may also perpetuate misleading institutions that cut off the view of things and events.

The History of Psychology: A Neglected Area
Robert I. Watson

The author of the next two articles, Robert I. Watson, is a professor of psychology at the University of New Hampshire. He received his Ph.D. at Columbia University. After teaching at various schools, he moved in 1953 to Northwestern University, where he became director of graduate training in clinical psychology. He remained at this post until 1967, when he accepted the professorship at New Hampshire. Watson has been a true champion of the cause of the history of psychology for many years. He is the author of *The Great Psychologists from Aristotle to Freud* (1963), the second edition of which appeared in 1968.

In the first article Watson analyzes the neglect—and its possible causes—of the history of psychology and makes a plea for greater attention on the part of psychologists to their history. That this plea has not passed unheeded has been shown by the creation of the Division of the History of Psychology within the American Psychological Association and the founding of the *Journal of the History of the Behavioral Sciences*—events in which Watson played a major role.

In the United States psychology is provincial, both geographically and temporally. While almost any European psychologist whom we meet surprises us by his knowledge of our work, we fall far short of equivalent familiarity with psychological activities in his country. Our relative ignorance of current psychological activities outside the United States is so well known and seemingly so complacently accepted as hardly to need exposition. It is not my intent to discuss our geographical provincialism except to point out that it seems to be similar to our historical provincialism, suggesting the possibility of common causal factors. Instead, I propose to document the extent of the current neglect of the history of our field, to suggest some of the factors which help to bring about this neglect, to answer certain possible criticisms of devoting one's time to advancing knowledge of

Robert I. Watson, The history of psychology: A neglected area. *American Psychologist,* 1960, **15**, 251-255. Reprinted by permission of the author and the American Psychological Association.

our history, and to try to show some positive values to be found by research in our history. I shall close with a few comments about the preparation for work in the history of psychology.

A variety of sources of evidence shows our neglect of the history of psychology. Some evidence may be found by examining the number of historical articles in our journals, by establishing the extent of expressions of interest in history by APA members, and by finding the number of psychologists who are members of the leading history of science society in the United States.

Three journals publish most of the historically oriented publication of psychologists in the United States: the *American Journal of Psychology*, the *Journal of General Psychology*, and the *Psychological Bulletin*. The contents of each of these journals for the last 20 years (1938-1957) were examined. Articles, excluding program descriptions, accounts of meetings, and obituaries, were classified as historical or nonhistorical. To be classified as historical the major theme of the article had to be placed in an historical perspective. Reviews, for example, which acknowledged they covered the work of 10, or 20, or some identified number of years, were not considered historical if they treated the research they discussed as more or less equally contemporaneous. In the *American Journal of Psychology* 12 out of 1,207 articles were historical in nature in this 20-year period. In the *Journal of General Psychology* only 13 historical articles appeared from a total of 937 articles. In the *Psychological Bulletin* 682 articles were published during this period of which 13 were historical in nature. It seems evident that psychologists publish only a handful of historical articles: 38 were primarily historical out of more than 2,800 articles over a 20-year period in the three journals examined.

An obvious source for the expression of interests by psychologists is the statement of their interests given by APA members in the *Directory*. Every tenth page of the 1958 *Directory* was searched for mention of interest in the history of psychology. In this way the stated interests of 1,638 psychologists were examined. Those mentioning an interest in history numbered 6. Extrapolating from the sample to the total membership of 16,644 gives only about 60 psychologists who consider the history of psychology among their interests, irrespective of whether or not they publish.

The History of Science Society is probably the leading organization in its field in the United States. We have some information about its membership. Using the 1951 APA *Directory* as the source, Daniel and Louttit (1953) listed the professional organizations to which a 12% sample of APA members belonged. They stopped listing by name of organization when they reached societies with five or less APA members. The History of Science Society was not listed. Moreover, not a single psychologist was found by a name-by-name check of about 5% of the organization's membership list.

On the basis of number of publications, expressed interest in the field, and membership in a specialty society, it seems appropriate to conclude that the history of psychology receives relatively little attention from psychologists in the United States at the present time.

Neglect of our history is an indication of a value judgment on the part of psychologists. Almost all psychologists simply have not been interested in it enough to be curious about it, let alone to work and to publish in this area. Probably there is a general distaste for historical matters among scientists in the United States, including psychologists. If this be true, psychologists as social beings share in a characteristic aberration of our times: a relative lack of curiosity about our past. Moreover, we have reached an age of specialization in psychology. The age of encyclopedists, if it ever existed, is certainly past. We must reconcile ourselves to limitation within our field. In short, we are specialists, not generalists.

It is one of the dubious fruits of specialization that one makes a sharp distinction between the historical development of his subject and the additive process by which he, himself, is developing it. The contemporary general lack of interest concerning the past and the age of specialism is shared by psychologists with other scientists. It is my impression that this neglect is even greater in psychology than in neighboring fields such as biology, medicine, and sociology. In these fields even a cursory acquaintance shows signs of considerably greater historical activity.

Specific to psychology, two related factors may accentuate our temporal provincialism, both stemming from psychology's relatively recent emergence as a science in its own right. First, we may be a bit ashamed of our past. The *nouveau riche* does not search his family tree. Second, self-conscious, as we are, of our recent hard-won victory of full-fledged scientific status, we may regard our heritage, as well as much European psychology, as somehow not quite respectable fields of interest simply because they smack of the unscientific. Interest in history is, save the mark, even scholarly!

In a somewhat more encouraging vein, still another reason for our relatively greater neglect of history is our sheer exuberance and what we have before us in the way of what appears to be limitless opportunities for research and service. Making history, we do not study what others have done in the past. There can be little question that our advances apparently are rapid, our expansion in numbers amazing.

The tremendous advances in scientific knowledge in our own and other fields lead to a feeling of exhilaration and satisfaction that should not be decried. The last 50 years has perhaps seen more scientific industry directed toward psychological problems than has all time before it. In the perspective of the future this optimistic judgment concerning the present half century may be shared by our successors, despite the doubt derived from the curious similarity of this remark to that made by many, many others concerning their own particular age. Be that as it may, I suspect many psychologists are influenced by some such unspoken opinion to the detriment of interest in the history of their field.

These speculations about the neglect of the history of psychology just presented may or may not be correct. Whatever their objective status as truth, they do not deal with the crucial question. One may still ask: "Assuming what you have said is correct, of what contemporary interest is the psychology of the past?" To put it baldly, why should serious attention and respect be given the history of psychology? It is necessary to inquire whether or not this lack of attention is precisely what the history of our field deserves. The question may be made more specific by asking whether this lack of attention to history does or does not reflect lack of significant material or lack of relevance of the material even if available.

It might be argued that the neglect of history that has been demonstrated is simply a reflection of the lack of significant material. Within the compass of this paper illustrations from only one temporal period may be given. The most unlikely period of all—the Middle Ages—is chosen for this purpose. Serious attention to the medieval period in our history has not been given since Brett published his *History of Psychology* nearly 50 years ago. In the meanwhile, as I propose to demonstrate, new sources have become available, and the number of workers in the general field of the history of science, who incidentally have touched upon matters of psychological interest, has increased considerably.

The basic source of my illustrations is to be found in the monumental *Introduction to the History of Science* by George Sarton. In connection with the medieval period he prepared a synopsis of about 2,000 pages in length. In these pages he made reference to what I consider to be psychological work on the part of 49 men. These references were to work either said to be psychological by Sarton or to psychological topics such as sensation and oneirology. For records of their accomplishments to appear in this survey of Sarton, they must have been preserved through the centuries of the medieval period and the 500 years since. One would expect that in view of this form of eminence the odds would be in favor that they should be known at least vaguely to psychologists. Selecting every fifth name from the list of 49 gives the following: Ibn Sirin, Al-Mas-Udi, Ibn Hibat Allah, Ibn Al-Jausi, Bahya Ben Joseph, Ibn Sabin, Peter of Spain, Thomas of York, and Witelo. I rather suspect that very, very few would be known to most psychologists.

It is relevant to compare the list of names of men found by reading Sarton to have worked in areas of psychology during the 900 years of the medieval period with those considered in Brett's history 50 years ago. Only 15 of the 49 are considered by Brett. A great majority of the Muslims and Jews found in Sarton were not mentioned at all by him. It would be a mistake to infer that Brett considered the workers he did not discuss as irrelevant because of lack of contact with Western intellectual development. Scholars in the Muslim world, including the Jewish workers among them, are acknowledged to be the intellectual leaders of the later centuries of the medieval period. Most of their works were translated into Latin in their own time or in the centuries that followed. Western commentaries on these works also appeared. Only at the end of the medieval period did their influence wane. It is quite plausible to believe that they were neglected by Brett because knowledge about them was either relatively inaccessible or even unknown at the time he was working.

It is difficult to classify medieval scholars into the neat categories demarcating the fields of knowledge of today. In any age the greater the man the more apt he is to range beyond the boundaries of one particular field. Yet it is possible by study of their contributions to classify them roughly into one or another field of knowledge. Sarton's description of the activities of these 49 medieval scholars was used as the basis of classification.

Contrary to expectation, less than one-half (21) were primarily philosophers and/or theologians. Nearly one-third (14) were physicians. The rest were scattered in a variety of other fields, none including more than two representatives. These fields were that of the chronologist, philologist, oneirologist, folklorist, traveler, physicist, astronomer, mathematician, historian, jurist, and oculist. Only one man, Isaac of Stella, was identified by Sarton as primarily a psychologist. In a broader sense he was a philosopher and was so classified by me. It will be remembered that 15 of these 49 workers were utilized by Brett in his history. Over half (8) of those to whom Brett referred were theologians and philosophers; while of those remaining, 6 were physicians and physicists. It is evident that only one of the 14 representatives of the other more peripheral fields, identified in Sarton, was utilized by him. Moreover, 10 philosophers and 10 physicians were found in Sarton that were not touched upon by Brett at all.

Two of the medieval psychologists are chosen for slightly more detailed exposition. One has been already mentioned—Peter of Spain, later John XXI. He had been trained as a physician (and in the classification was so placed) and had wide medical, zoological, logical, philosophical, and psychological interests. In psychology he wrote a volume on psychology, *De Anima*, which included an account of the historical development of psychological ideas found in Greek and Muslim works covering a *thousand years* of the history of psychology. Lest this work be dismissed as "mere" philosophy, it should be added that, according to Sarton, it stresses physiological and medical aspects! Elevated to the pontificate in 1276, he died in an accident eight months later. That there was a psychologist pope is probably not even known among most Catholic psychologists.

One of the greatest minds of the Middle Ages will serve as the second illustration—Moses Maimonides. He is best known for his *Guide for the Perplexed,* a monument of Jewish theology. Other than one relatively obscure reference, it never has been called to the attention of psychologists that this work contains material of psychological significance. For example, memory is discussed in Chapters 33-36 of Part I, and mind in Chapters 31-32 of Part I and Chapter 37 of Part II. Maimonides also wrote on medical matters, including descriptions of prophetic visions as psychological experiences; on the rules of psychotherapy; and various other psychological-medical matters. There is a strong probability that careful study of his works would reveal a theory of personality of some significance for us today.

These two men—Peter of Spain and Moses Maimonides—should have a special appeal to psychologists whose background of Catholic or Jewish scholarship makes them especially well prepared to evaluate their significance.

In general, there appears to be evidence that the 900 years from the sixth to the fifteenth centuries were not without their share of psychological speculation and observation. Scholars have examined this material in a philosophical perspective, but there has been an almost complete neglect of the psychological aspects.

It was following the medieval period that the revival of learning at the beginning of the modern period took place. This was the rebirth of Greek, particularly Aristotelian, ways of thinking in the twelfth and the thirteenth centuries, which gave us the origin of the empirical, especially experimental, ways of approaching nature. Out of the work of Renaissance man comes what we know about the origins of our present knowledge.

That greatest of modern historians of science, George Sarton, has shown that the "Dark Ages" transmitted the science of the Greek and the Hellenistic worlds. Transmission is, in itself, just as important as discovery and is sufficient reason to study the Middle Ages. But even more important, as Sarton puts it, medieval progress occurred not because of, but in spite of, its presumed crowning achievement of scholastic philosophy. Medievalists, he claimed, have stressed the scholastic aspects to the detriment of the real scientific advance especially in the Muslim world. In spite of scholastic and obscurantist tendencies which repel the modern mind, examination of the contributions of these men of the Middle Ages to psychology as psychology, separated from philosophical and theological preoccupation, would seem to be a worthwhile venture.

For the Middle Ages, and presumably even more cogently for other ages, we do not lack new material, and there would appear to be at least some contemporary relevance for its study. A more general statement of the values of historical study in psychology seems indicated.

It would be a serious mistake to consider the history of psychology to be limited to a mere chronology of events or biographical chitchat. It is a study of long-time cultural trends over time. Psychological contributions are embedded in the social context from which they emerge. Psychology has always responded in part to its social environment, but it also has been guided by an internal logic of its own. We cannot emphasize one of these trends at the expense of the other. Psychology neither reflects culture with passive compliance nor does it exist in a social vacuum. External and internal circumstances are present, and there is a constant interplay between them.

It is a truism of one approach to history that each generation rewrites the history in terms of its own values and attitudes. As yet, we have not looked back on the past from the perspective of today finding values for the present from the past. Old material is still to be seen in a new perspective. In the past writing of our history, material either ignored as irrelevant or simply not known at that time now can be utilized. The material from the Middle Ages commented upon earlier would illustrate the new material available. The presence of newly relevant material needs further comment. The field of psychology has expanded enormously in recent years. That it has re-extended beyond the limits of experimental psychology is a statement of fact on which there can be no disagreement. Consider the influence of the rapidly burgeoning fields of application, such as clinical psychology, and remember that the moment we expend our present concerns in psychology to that extent we have broadened and changed our past. The moment we embrace, even in the smallest degree, the traditions of others as, for example, we have done for some aspects of medicine, we have embraced some aspects of their past as well. Consider the importance in psychology today of personality theories and other influences of quasi- or nonexperimental nature. The history of experimental psychology is the solid core of our history, presumably less changed in this re-examination; but other aspects of its history do exist. In recent years no one has examined all major aspects of our history in the light of these changes.

An even more serious consequence of the neglect of history needs comment. To modify somewhat a statement from Croce via Beard: when we ignore history in the sense of the grand tradition of that field, narrowness and class, provincial and regional prejudices come in their stead to dominate or distort one's views without any necessary awareness of their influence. If psychologists are determined to remain ignorant of our history, are we not, at best, determined to have some of our labors take the form of discoveries which are truisms found independently and, at worst, to repeat the errors of the past? To embody a past of which they are ignorant is, at best, to be subject passively to it, at worst, to be distorted by a false conception of it. Ignorance does not necessarily mean lack of influence upon human conduct, including the human conduct of psychologists. Ignoring the study of the history of one's field through formal sources and published accounts does not result in lack of opinions about the past. Like the traditional man in the street who, too, refuses to read history, such psychologists inevitably have a picture of the past, by and large one which deprecates its importance. This inevitably influences their views just as does any other aspect of the "unverbalized." However little their ahistorical view of the past may correspond to reality, it still helps to determine their views of the present. To neglect history does not mean to escape its influence.

This has been a plea for greater attention on the part of psychologists to their history. With assumption of some knowledge and experience in contemporary psychology, the first stage of development of attention to history would be an interest in it and a conviction that it is a worthwhile field of endeavor. But knowledge, interest, and conviction are not enough for competence. It is not merely a matter of deciding to work in historical aspects of our field. With justice, professional historians have been indignant about the bland assumption, all too often made by scientists, that, because one knows something about a scientific field, the essential equipment for historical research automatically is available. Historical work does not consist of finding a few old books and copying this and that. Trained as he is in his own exacting techniques, the psychologist does not always realize that the technique of establishing the truth of the maximum probability of past events, in other words historical research, has its own complicated rules and methods.

There is a variety of areas with which more than a passing acquaintance is necessary if historical study is planned. Knowledge of the methodology of history—historiography—is essential for more than anecdotal familiarity with any area capable of being approached historically. Knowledge of the philosophy of history is also needed by the psychological historian as a defense against errors of procedure and of content. In psychology, as in similar disciplines, acquaintance with the history of science in general is demanded. Moreover, some appreciation of the influence of social and cultural factors in history is important if the findings are to be seen in broad context. I, for one, think it would be worth the trouble and time to secure this background in order to carry on the task of understanding and interpreting our past in the perspective of today.

REFERENCE

Daniel, R. S., & Louttit, C. M. *Professional problems in psychology.* New York: Prentice-Hall, 1953.

The Role and Use of History in the Psychology Curriculum
Robert I. Watson

In this article Watson addresses himself to the trained psychologist and presents reasons why the history of psychology should be studied and taught. Watson's arguments stem from the consideration of the meaning of history and of the advantage of its knowledge for a scientist. It is in the light of this consideration that the role and uses of the history of psychology are explained.

Lord Acton (1), the eminent British historian, has indicated that there are two ways in which a science may be studied—through its own particular methods, and through an examination of its history. The method of historical study adds a dimension to the science of psychology. As Collingwood (4) reminds us, history, as such, is concerned with human experiences, and to be more specific, with human thoughts. To an even greater extent than is the case in any of the physical sciences, psychology is in a position to profit from the study of history, since psychology in itself, is still another view of human behavior and experience. Both history and psychology are concerned with human behavior and experiences, but in characteristically different ways. Consequently, an appeal to history for understanding of human nature becomes all the more desirable.

Before presenting specific arguments on the role and use of history, the sheer inescapability of historical influences must be made evident. None of us can escape history. Each individual holds some attitude toward history, irrespective of whether or not his view is based on adequate knowledge. Our picture of the past influences our present decisions. History cannot be denied; the choice is

Robert I. Watson, The role and use of history in the psychology curriculum. *Journal of the History of the Behavioral Sciences*, 1966, 2, 66-69. Reprinted by permission of the author and the Psychology Press.

This paper was presented at the Annual Meeting of the American Psychological Association, St. Louis, Missouri, September, 1962, at a symposium entitled: "Strategies in the Teaching of Psychology."

between making it a conscious determinant of our behavior as psychologists, or allowing it to influence us unawares. There is no other alternative.

Denying history has stultifying consequences. An unarticulated view of the past results in being passively subject to it. Narrow provincial, class, and regional prejudices then substitute for a historically founded background. As psychologists, of all people, should realize, failure to take a verbalized position means subjugation to influences of which one is unaware. We have before us an example of the clinical psychologist or psychiatrist who endeavors to make his patient aware of unconscious influences upon his patterns of behavior so that he may be able to face them. Exploration of origins, that is to say, learning the history, before suggesting remedies, is a commonplace of clinical practice. Similarly, the historian by analyzing historical materials often tries to reveal unconscious social trends so that by facing them he may improve conditions through intelligent action (11). The desirability of vigilance in the uncovering of unverbalized sources of bias is further enhanced when it is recognized that history may aid us in that psychological problem of seeing the process by which an investigator comes to the conclusions that he does (2).

All of our classroom teaching is historical in that everything we say concerns the past in the strict sense of the term. Even though its historical character may be unperceived, since it is very recent past with which we are dealing, we find it impossible to teach research conclusions without discussing how they have been reached. A similar situation exists in our research endeavors. In most of our scientific papers there are references to previous papers. These cited papers, in turn, contain references to still earlier literature. Foreshortened though the historical setting of a particular paper may be, it is implicitly the whole history of its particular subject. However, since our present style of presenting research evidence calls for the barest mention of past work, it is quite possible for a researcher to be ignorant of the previous work except that on which his own immediately rests.

It has been remarked with invidious intent that the older the psychologist, the more he seems interested in history. I suspect that sometimes this is not so much a matter of interest in history *per se* as it is a matter of his widening his span of contemporaneity as the years roll on. For example, I must confess to a sense of shock to discover that the beginnings of clinical psychology after World War II, from the point of view of our present graduate students, all too often is "old stuff," and of no real interest. The older the psychologist, the longer the period which appears to him to be contemporaneous. To younger colleagues his particular span is not part of the contemporary scene, but history.

It is relevant to the theme to identify two points of view toward history. One may be interested in the past for its own sake or one may insist that history is of value only to the extent that it throws light on the present. One can expect that many scientists adopt the position of Croce that all history is contemporary history with all the rest being nothing more than chronicle. Croce's position is one which allows history to be a positive force in scientific advance; it admits we cannot escape history, for history is seen as surrounding us in the present. Principles and hypotheses are drawn from our knowledge of the past for use in the present. Historians advance arguments against adoption of this position that are relevant in other contexts, but those who disagree with Croce must admit that the position of insisting on seeing contemporary value is one which is reasonable for non-historians to take. This insistence on contemporaneity does not deny that others may approach history for its own sake. Indeed a historian, as historian, may be as truly following his vocation in trying to see his particular material from the perspective of its time and place as when he does so from the view of his own day. Nevertheless, demand for contemporaneity still allows a legitimate place for the history of psychology.

The history of a science has a characteristic which distinguishes it from all other history, artistic or military-political. The history of a science is cumulative. Indeed the outstanding difference between the arts and the sciences is that the latter are progressive while the former are not. Whether the history of political or military events shows progressive or cumulative historical development is a matter of controversy among historians, some insisting that they do, others arguing that they do not. It follows that scientists alone, of all scholars, may be in the exhilarating position of starting from the heights their predecessors have so laboriously climbed.

Ironically enough, this tremendous advantage of the history of a science can be turned into an argument against its study. Since science is cumulative, some scientists hold all that is of value from the past is to be found already available in the present state of knowledge of the field. They take the position that new achievements supersede previous ones and error drops away. One, they go on, can trust that which is of present scientific concern to supply all relevant scientific content. Bakan (2) refers to this view as the Darwinian theory of the evolution of ideas—natural selection among ideas occurs and those that work tend to survive.

Despite the cumulative character of the history of psychology, the view that all that is potentially valuable survives into the present is false on several counts. Errors committed in the past may drop out but this does not prevent their repetition. A remark of Santayana (9) becomes apposite—those who ignore the past repeat its errors. Moreover, a science is constantly developing with new points of view introduced every day; a point neglected in the immediate past context may become important in the present. As new ideas are introduced, a heretofore neglected, isolated point, not part of the contemporary picture, may need to be rescued from oblivion. A fact, not part of the present pattern, may take on new significance when seen in the context of a new theory (10). We cannot know of these points without historical knowledge.

To return to the analogy with Darwinian theory, it is true that a species, once extinct, cannot be resurrected. With ideas we are more fortunate; we can play Nature and revive an idea at will, and give it a second chance. Moreover, scrutiny of our history shows that there are recurring themes, although often couched under a different terminology. Their similarity or identity may not be recognized until time has passed, making it necessary for its historically based recovery. As an illustration, we are so enamored of the term, personality, that we forget there were theories of personality long before we began to call certain psychological phenomena by that particular catch word. From Homer onward, we have available records in every form from epics to funeral orations awaiting study to tease out the implicit theories of personality which they contain.

History is ever becoming; it is never finished. This creates a need for contemporary specialists in the history of psychology. Make no mistake, there is plenty of work for them. Several reasons may be given. If the history of psychology is to be rewritten in the light of contemporary interests, then in each age there must be those who sift the material again to bring out its value for that particular age. The selectivity of our interests demands this rewriting with every generation. Moreover, workers in history, both those within psychology and those in other areas, are unearthing material not known to earlier historians in psychology. In writing his monumental history of psychology over fifty years ago, Brett had to work without the aid of Jaeger's later careful work on Aristotle. Consequently, Brett knew nothing of Jaeger's findings on Aristotle's intellectual development, showing a progression away from Plato's teaching in the direction of a much greater naturalism in the mature Aristotle. Nor did Brett know that certain works of physiognomy on which he leaned would later be demonstrated to be Pseudo-Aristotle. In preparing a survey of the great psychologists, a certain number of relatively unknown findings come to light. An illustration on how knowledge of history deepens appreciation of the significance of events on which I wish to dwell is to be found in the work of Robert Harper published in 1949 and 1950.

There is no fragment of history on which there is more agreement among psychologists than that we can date the beginning of the experimental period of our science from the founding in 1879 of the laboratory of the University of Leipzig by Wilhelm Wundt. This date is as well known to us as, say, 1492, for the discovery of America. These two dates have something in common—they are both wrong! Actually, as Harper demonstrates, *two* laboratories were established in 1875, not one in 1879.

It has been customary to consider 1879 as the founding year for the first experimental laboratory in the world on the mistaken belief that it was in this year that Wundt's Leipzig Laboratory was given formal recognition by university authorities. According to Harper, formal recognition to a course in "experimental psychology" did not come from the University until the winter of 1883, while the laboratory, the "Institute for Experimental Psychology" was not listed by University authorities until 1894. So far as we can tell, 1879 is notable only for the appearance of the first student who was to do publishable psychological research under Wundt. Actually, before Wundt's arrival in Leipzig in October 1875, the Royal Ministry formally had set aside a room to be used by him for his experimental work and for demonstrations connected with his *Psychologische Ubungen* or Psychological Practicum. It is on this basis that 1875 is considered the founding year.

It was also in 1875, the same year as Wundt, that William James established at Harvard University the other of the first two psychological laboratories in the world. One especially compelling item Harper cited is the report of the Harvard Treasurer for 1875 which showed an appropriation to James of $300 for use in physiology. Other evidence, including knowledge of the nature of his 1875 course, shows that it was equipment for teaching physiological psychology. In retrospect, James himself was not sure whether it was 1874, 1875, or 1876. Parenthetically, I might mention this is not an entirely uncommon instance of historical research, leading to more accurate conclusions concerning a given point than was allowed an actual participant in the event in question.

Thus, 1875, not 1879, is the year most deserving of being honored by psychologists. Aside from a handful probably concentrated in this room, almost all other psychologists seem blithely unaware of this instance of the influence of later research upon past historical findings.

Time does not permit dwelling on other illustrations, but I cannot forebear throwing out two teasers—that, historically, the first recorded experiment was psychological in nature, and, that, except for someone's mistake, we might more properly have been called, thymotologists, not psychologists.

The study of the history of psychology may incite in us new ideas about human nature. We bring to history certain conceptions about human nature; we also revise our notions in the course of our historical readings (13). We start with certain criteria by which to judge behavior and experience; we may be induced to change these criteria when new possibilities are exposed to us. The case of history parallels that of literature—seeing a play or reading a novel teaches us about psychology even though we bring to the play or novel, already pre-existing beliefs.

Our knowledge of human nature, after all, does rest on experience. Revision of our knowledge by extra-laboratory experience is going on whether we wish it or not. Should it not occur on the basis of knowledge of our history as well?

One may question the utility of knowledge of history as a stimulus for current research by remarking that research data reports contain little, if any, mention of its inciting value. The reason is not far to seek; our conventions for reporting research to our colleagues give no place to our sources of inspiration. What happened *after* the problem occurred to us is all that we present. We report the psychology of the discovered with hardly any attention to that of the psychology of discovery.

Two closely related claims sometimes advanced for the utility of history will *not* be made. The study of the history of science does not seem to make a psychologist a better research man. Conant (5), who is not alone in expressing the view that study of the past is insignificant for an investigator *qua* investigator beyond the immediate background of his particular problem, sees the matter as follows: "The scientific investigator develops his skill as an investigator by a method closely akin to that by which masters of a craft trained apprentices in the past or the painters of the Renaissance developed in the studio of a great master. Continuous experience with experimentation from the advanced laboratory courses to the first independent work has kept the embryo research man in contact with the reality of his business. As compared with what he is learning and has learned in his laboratory, the chemist, physicist, or experimental biologist finds the past has little or nothing to tell him about the methods of research."

Nor does the cumulative character of psychological advance make history a predictive device. "A knowledge of history is not a crystal ball," as Boring (3) tersely put it. The antecedents of a psychological event are too numerous and too interrelated for correct specific prediction to be more than happenstance. Although theoretically demanded when one subscribes to causal determinism, in psychology we always seem to know too little about the present to predict the future and I see no reason to hope for an improvement in our ability to predict in the immediate future. So the study of history is not an aid in prediction.

To return to the positive uses of the history of psychology, it may serve to bring psychology to the laymen. According to Sarton (10), as well as many others, the historical approach is the ideal way to present science to unprepared individuals, this is to say, laymen, and to make it understandable.

Let us examine the state of laymanship with an eye to the various levels of unpreparedness. It is a truism that division of labor has entered every field of psychological research. A direct consequence of the subdivision is that the specialist in one branch of psychology becomes a layman in psychology in the other branches of the field, although at a relatively high level of sophistication. At the next level are the scientists in other fields who are therefore laymen so far as psychology is concerned. They are not as well prepared as the psychological specialists, but presumably many of them have some degree of preparation. At a still lower level there are the numbers of the general public who are even less conversant with the field.

The history of psychology may serve as the common meeting ground for individuals at these various levels. The utility of the history of psychology for colleagues in other fields will be singled out for more detailed comment. Through the medium of history we may be able to begin to progress with a task on which up to the present we can hardly be considered to have been conspicuously successful—that of supplying a view of human nature of use as an underpinning to other sciences concerned with human nature, *e.g.*, Walsh (13). From before Adam Smith to beyond Sigmund Freud our colleagues have complained that they have had to build a view of psychology on their own for use in their specialties. We share the method of history with these other fields with which, they too, are conversant. What would be more natural and fitting than that a serious effort be made to aid in this cross-field task through a historical approach?

At all levels of laymanship, among psychologists as well as others, if one does not introduce the historical approach, a survey often forces one to adopt the untenable position that a particular segment is, in fact, separated from the rest of the field. Experimental psychology divorced from abnormal psychology, child psychology isolated from physiological psychology and the even more narrow areas in which a research man works, have existence only of convenience and of specialization of the researcher-teacher. They are artificially separated segments. So, too, psychology, itself, may serve a separated-out-patch from the fabric of science. This is not a plea to give up specialization in research in favor of a more generalized approach which is quite a different matter. Rather, this is a plea that, in addition to research specialization, there be a cultivation of the historical method to help to supply that more generalized knowledge of psychology which we all need. Nor does acceptance of this argument require a conviction about the ultimate unity of the sciences. It merely requires that one go so far as to admit it is worthwhile to work toward seeing if a unity exists.

Knowledge of history can be part of our wider frame of reference. For each of us history could be a way of escaping the artificial partitioning of a science that specialization brings. To grasp the relative import of one's own work, to place it in perspective, a knowledge of history is invaluable. History demonstrates to us that the science of psychology is part of the human enterprise. There is a liberating influence to history (6). Bound by the realities of this life and hemmed in by circumstances as we are, through knowledge of history we can deepen and broaden our experience. To realize the richness of our inheritance, to know our kinship with times and places past, to see our own time and place as part of a grand progression, are a part of the role and use of history. The history of psychology is a means by which our knowledge of the field may be related to the main stream of our civilization by specification of points of contact between psychology and literature, the arts, philosophy and the other sciences.

I have addressed myself, not to the undergraduate or graduate student as the title of my paper might seem to call for, but to you, the trained psychologist. This has been a deliberate strategic maneuver. If you are not convinced of the value of history for yourself, you will not be convinced of its value for your students. Freedom from the unverbalized, the realization of the progression of scientific research, appreciation of the cumulative character of psychology, recovery of material from the past relevant to the present, the possibilities and implication to be followed up, the bringing of knowledge of psychology to our majors, to our students from related sciences and the remainder of our students, and the creation of an integrated frame of reference are possible values of the history in the psychology curriculum.

REFERENCES

1. Acton, J. Cited in H. Butterfield (Ed.) *Man and his past: the study of the history of historical scholarship.* New York: Cambridge University Press, 1955.

2. Bakan, D. *A standpoint for the study of the history of psychology.* Unpublished paper.

3. Boring, E. G. Science and the meaning of its history. *Key Reporter,* 1959, 20, No. 4, 2-3.

4. Collingwood, R. G. *The idea of history.* New York: Oxford University Press, 1946.

5. Conant, J. B. History in the education of scientists. *Harvard Libr. Bull.,* 1960, 14, 315-333.

6. Dilthey, W. The understanding of other persons and their life-expressions. In P. Gardiner (Ed.) *Theories of History.* Glencoe, Ill.: Free Press, 1959, 213-225.

7. Harper, R. S. The Laboratory of William James. *Harv. Alum. Bull.,* 1949, 52, 169-173.

8. Harper, R. D. The first psychological laboratory. *Isis*, 1950, 41, 158-161.

9. Santayana, G. *Interpretations of poetry and religion.* New York: Scribners, 1900.

10. Sarton, G. *The life of science: essays in the history of civilization.* Bloomington, Ind.: Indiana University Press, 1960.

11. Sigerist, H. *Medicine and human welfare.* New Haven, Conn.: Yale University Press, 1941.

12. Singer, C. *The story of living things.* New York: Harper, 1931.

13. Walsh, W. H. *Philosophy of history: an introduction.* New York: Harper, 1962.

The Relation of Psychology to Other Sciences

In studying the history of science, we are reminded of the words of Ralph Waldo Emerson: "There is properly no history, only biography." Science is a human enterprise, and it is both social and intellectual. It is the creation of scientists who work at a particular time in a particular place on a particular topic in a particular field. Although the sciences—physical, biological, behavioral—have much in common, each has its own distinctive features and its own particular interactions with the society in which it is cultivated.

The noted historian of psychology Edwin G. Boring repeatedly called attention to the prevailing climate of opinion, or *Zeitgeist*, at the period when a given scientist was working. In the first article in Part II, Boring discusses the dynamic character and dual role of the *Zeitgeist* as an aid and a hindrance to scientific progress. The scientist's need to know the thinking of others makes communication among scientists imperative. The history of science has repeatedly shown that developments in one science often stimulate progress in another.

Similarly, the eminent philosopher of science and psychologist Egon Brunswik frequently repeated the thesis that true progress in science has come from the various and imaginatively conceived different developments in the several disciplines. The case of

51

psychology, for example, illustrates clearly the confluence of multiple influences from developments in such diverse disciplines as physiology, biology, astronomy, psychiatry, statistics, and philosophy. In the second selection, Brunswik skillfully delineates the historical and thematic relations of psychology to other sciences. He calls for psychology's emancipation "from the suggestive power of those nomothetic-reductionist natural sciences in the shadow of which it began its development." In the history of psychology Brunswik discerns, as E. C. Tolman observed of him, "specific and to some degree logically sequential trends: away from dualism, away from sensationism, away from molecularism, away from encapsulated centralism, away from nomotheticism, but towards monism, towards distal-achievementism and towards molarity—that is toward his own doctrine of functionalism and probabilism." Admonishing psychology not to follow classical physics slavishly, Brunswik urges that psychology "demonstrate its structural affinity with disciplines already recognized as statistical in character."

Similarly, the third selection analyzes the similarities and differences between psychology and physics and challenges the traditional psychology that took physics as its model. The author, Robert Oppenheimer, warns that "the worst of all possible misunderstandings would be that psychology be influenced to model itself after a physics which is not there any more, which has been quite outdated." He cautions against excessive devotion to quantification and measurement, determinism, and objectification. Oppenheimer stresses the need for concern with individuality and insists that naturalistic methods and descriptive methods have a place in science.

Psychology has acquired a dual character: it has developed as a science and also as a profession. Its professional character grew out of the science, principally in the form of clinical psychology, and was fostered by psychiatry and psychoanalysis, especially by Freud. In the United States clinical psychology has received much social and cultural support. Psychology's dual character has posed numerous challenges and problems. Over the years several psychologists have tried to propose solutions to bridge the gap between psychology as science and as profession. In his article Rollo May, a distinguished clinical psychologist, has called for a new theoretical framework for psychology that could embrace both the scientific and the clinical, and he has specified the aspects to be included in such a theory. Despite proposals such as May's, it is difficult to preserve unity within the discipline and to meet the needs of psychological scientists and professional psychologists at the same time.

In studying the origins and growth of psychology as an independent discipline, historians have characteristically focused on intellectual factors, particularly the merger of philosophy and physiology aided by the contribution of discoveries in other sciences. Sociologists, however, have been reminding historians of science for some time that, because the development of science is in continuous interaction with other segments of a culture, the scientist's social and cultural milieu must be examined in studying his creations.

Recently two sociologists (Ben-David and Collins) and a historian (Ross) have debated the significance of social and intellectual factors in the origins of psychology. They differ in viewpoint from psychologists as well as from each other. Analyzing the social factors in psychology's origins, Ben-David and Collins have suggested that Germany—rather than England, France, or the United States—was the natural place for scientific psychology to originate, since only that country provided the opportunity for the new role of psychologist to emerge from a role hybridization, or merger, of the roles of philosopher and physiologist.

On the other hand, Ross, the historian, asserts that such role hybridization also occurred in the United States. She acknowledges the significance of such social factors as role, status, and competition, but she contends that they should be studied together with intellectual factors because social and intellectual factors are interdependent. Although her criticism and the rejoinder of Ben-David and Collins do not yield definitive answers, they do reaffirm that psychology, like all science, is subject to the influence of both social and intellectual factors. From the vantage points of sociology and history these three final articles in Part II furnish the reader with an interesting demonstration of scholarly disagreement and interaction. They also emphasize the value of the sociology of science and its possible contribution to understanding the history of science.

Dual Role of the Zeitgeist
in Scientific Creativity
Edwin G. Boring

A distinguished psychologist and noted historian of psychology, Edwin G. Boring (1886-1968) obtained his doctorate under Titchener at Cornell in 1914. After service in the armed forces during World War I he taught at Clark and Harvard. He was president of the American Psychological Association in 1928. Boring was well known for his numerous publications, including *A History of Experimental Psychology*, which he published in 1929 and revised in 1950. This volume long served as the main source of historical information for American psychologists. He also held several editorships, including *Contemporary Psychology* (1955-1961). In 1959 Boring was awarded the American Psychological Foundation Gold Medal in recognition of his varied and distinguished service to psychology as "investigator, teacher, historian, theorist, administrator and statesman, popular expositor, and editor."

As a historian, Boring was especially interested in the psychology of the history of scientific discovery. This interest led him to study the role of great men in science—their effects on science as well as the influences that operated on them in their time. Repeatedly Boring cited the effect of the *Zeitgeist*, or prevailing climate of opinion. In this selection Boring discusses the role of the *Zeitgeist* as a help and as a hindrance to scientific progress. He emphasizes that, since the thinking of every man is affected by the thinking of other men, effective communication in science is essential. (For a criticism of the *Zeitgeist* as a causal concept in historical explanation, the reader may consult Ross' selection "The 'Zeitgeist' and American Psychology" in Part IV.)

This "magic" term *Zeitgeist* means at any one time the climate of opinion as it affects thinking, yet it is also more than that, for the *Zeitgeist* is forever being altered, as if the thinker whom it affects were shifting latitude and longitude over sea and land so that his climate keeps changing in unpredictable ways. Goethe, who in 1827 may have been the first to use this word with explicit connotation, limited it to the unconscious, covert, and implicit effects of the climate of opinion, at the same time ruling out

Edwin G. Boring, Dual role of the *Zeitgeist* in scientific creativity. *Scientific Monthly*, 1955, **80**, 101-106. Reprinted by permission of the American Association for the Advancement of Science.

thought control by such explicit processes as persuasion and education (1).

Such a concept proves useful in those cases where plagiarism is clearly unconscious, as so often it is. No man clearly understands the sources of his own creativity, and it is only since Freud that we have begun to have an inkling of how general is this lack of understanding of one's own motives and of the sources of one's own ideas. On the other hand, this conception long antedates Freud, for it was the essence of Tolstoy's argument in 1869 that "a king is history's slave" whose conscious reasons for action are trivial and unimportant. Charles Darwin, Herbert Spencer, and Francis Galton all supported Tolstoy's view of the unconscious determination of the actions of great men, against the more voluntaristic views of Thomas Carlyle, William James, and some lesser writers.

Later the historians of science and of thought in general found themselves faced with the essential continuity of originality and discovery. Not only is a new discovery seldom made until the times are ready for it, but again and again it turns out to have been anticipated, inadequately perhaps but nevertheless explicitly, as the times were beginning to get ready for it. Thus the concept of a gradually changing *Zeitgeist* has been used to explain the historical continuity of thought and the observation that the novelty of a discovery, after the history of its anticipations has been worked out, appears often to be only a historian's artifact.

In addition to these anticipations there are, however, also the near-simultaneities and near-synchronisms that are clearly not plagiarisms. Napier and Briggs on logarithms. Leibnitz and Newton on the calculus. Boyle and Mariotte on the gas law. D'Alibard and Franklin on electricity. The sociologists Ogburn and Thomas have published a list of 148 contemporaneous but independent discoveries or inventions. Since you cannot in these pairs assume that one man got the crucial idea from the other, you are forced to assume that each had his novel insight independently by his ordinary processes of thought, except that each was doing his thinking in the same climate of opinion. Some such appeal to a maturing *Zeitgeist* is necessary to explain the coincidence (2).

Now how, we may ask, does the *Zeitgeist* of the present time interpret the generic concept of the *Zeitgeist*? Today the *Zeitgeist* is certainly *not* a superorganic soul, an immortal consciousness undergoing maturation with the centuries, an unextended substance interpenetrating the social structure. The *Zeitgeist* must be regarded simply as the sum total of social interaction as it is common to a particular period and a particular locale. One can say it is thought being affected by culture, and one would mean then that the thinking of every man is affected by the thinking of other men in so far as their thinking is communicated to him. Hence the importance of communication in science, which both helps and hinders progress. That is the thesis of this paper.

It is always hard to be original, to make progress in a minority thinking that goes against the majority. In science, moreover, even the dead help to make up the majority, for they communicate by the printed word and by the transmitted conventions of thought. Thus the majority, living and dead, may slow up originality. On the other hand, the chief effect of scientific communication and of the availability of past thought is facilitative. We all know how the invention of printing advanced science.

We shall not be far wrong—being prejudiced, of course, by the *Zeitgeist* of the present—if we regard the scientist as a nervous system, influenced by what it reads and hears as well as by what it observes in nature and in the conduct of other men—the smile of approbation, the sneer of contempt—and affected also by its own past experience, for the scientist is forever instructing himself as he proceeds toward discovery and is also forever being instructed by other men, both living and dead.

The single investigator works pretty much like a rat in a maze—by insight, hypothesis, trial, and then error or success. I am not trying to say that rats are known to prefer deduction to induction because they use hypotheses in learning a maze. The maze is set up to require learning by trial and error, which is to say, by hypothesis and test. The rat's insight, as it learns, may indeed be false: the rat looks down the alley, sees it is not immediately blind but later finds it is blind after all. An error for the rat. And its trial may be vicarious. The rat looks tentatively down an alley, entertains it as a hypothesis, rejects it, chooses to go the other way. Anybody's hypothesis can come as the brilliant perception of an unexpected relationship and yet be wrong. It may be a hunch. Rodent hypotheses begin as hunches—and by this I mean merely that the rat does not understand the ground of its motives.

The human investigator, on the other hand, may consciously base his new hypothesis on his own earlier experiment, or on something other persons did. For this reason erudition is important, and communication is vital in modern science. Nevertheless it remains possible to regard the single scientist as an organic system, as a discovery machine, with a certain input from the literature and from other forms of social communication and also—let the essential empiricism of science not be forgotten—from nature, which comes through to insights and a conclusion by that method of concomitant variation which is experiment. There we have the individual investigator, who, as he grows older, gains in erudition and wisdom and becomes more mature, with his past discoveries now available as part of his knowledge.

A broader and more interesting question, however, concerns, not the individual, but the maturation of scientific thought itself. The mechanics of one person applies to too small a system to throw much light on the history of science. The larger view substitutes social interaction and communication for an individual's input, thus exposing the whole dynamic process as it undergoes maturation down the years, the centuries, and the ages. This interaction *is* the *Zeitgeist*, which is not unlike a stream. It is bounded on its sides by the limits of communication, but it goes on forever unless, of course, some great cataclysm, one that would make Hitler's effect on German science seem tiny and trivial, should some day stall it.

Here we have a physicalistic conception of the *Zeitgeist*. The *Zeitgeist*, of course, inevitably influences the conception of the *Zeitgeist*. And the *Zeitgeist* ought to be the property of psychologists, for the psychologists have a proprietary right in all the *Geister*. Now the psychology of the 19th century was dualistic, mentalistic, spiritualistic. In those days the *Zeitgeist* would certainly have had to be the maturing superconsciousness of science, something comparable to the immediate private experience that everyone then believed he had. The 20th century, on the other hand, at least since 1925, is physicalistic and behavioristic. Nowadays the term *behavioral sciences* is on everyone's lips and there is no English equivalent for *Geisteswissenschaften*.

Between 1910 and 1930 the *Zeitgeist* changed. Mind gave way to behavior. This transition was eased by the positivists who supplied the transformation equations from the old to the new, transformations by way of the operational definitions of experience; but only a few bother to use these equations. It is enough for most persons that they are using the convenient language of the great majority. And truth in science, as S.S. Stevens has pointed out, is simply what competent opinion at the time in question does not dissent from (3). In a physicalistic era, we, physicalistically minded scientists, choose a physicalistic definition of the *Zeitgeist.* Our predecessors in 1900 would not so easily have accepted such nonchalance toward Cartesian dualism.

We are wise thus to accept the wisdom of the age. Nor is my personal history without interest in this respect, for I was brought up in the introspective school of E.B. Titchener and for 20 years believed firmly in the existence of my own private immediate consciousness. Then, about 1930, en route to Damascus, as it were, I had a great insight. I knew that I was unconscious and never had been conscious in the sense that to have experience is to know instantaneously that you have it. Introspection always takes time, and the most immediate conscious datum is, therefore, obtained retrospectively. Once this basic truth is assimilated, once one realizes that no system can include the report of itself and that to one's own introspection one's own consciousness is as much the consciousness of some "Other One" as is the consciousness of a different person, then it becomes clear that consciousness is not in any sense immediate, and then—just exactly then—the introspectionist gladly and sincerely joins the behavioristic school(4).

THE ZEITGEIST'S DUAL ROLE

The *Zeitgeist* has a dual role in scientific progress, sometimes helping and sometimes hindering. There can be nothing surprising in such a statement. Forces in themselves are not good or bad. Their effects can be, depending on what it is you want. Inevitably by definition the *Zeitgeist* favors conventionality, but conventionality itself keeps developing under the constant pressures of discoveries and novel insights. So the *Zeitgeist* works against originality; but is not originality, one asks quite properly, a good thing, something that promotes scientific progress? In the cases of Copernicus, Galileo, Newton, and other comparably great men of science, originality was good—good for what posterity has called progress. These are the men to emulate. The indubitably original

people are, however, the cranks, and close to them are the para-
noid enthusiasts. Velikovsky's conception of the collision of two
worlds is original. Does science advance under his stimulus?
Hubbard's dianetics is original. Is it good? Most of us right now
think not, yet these men point in self-defense to Galileo who also
resisted the *Zeitgeist* (5). This dilemma arises because it is well to
know and respect the wisdom of the ages and also to correct it
when the evidence for change is adequate. If men were logical
machines and evidence could be weighed in balances, we should
not be mentioning the *Zeitgeist* at all. The *Zeitgeist* comes into
consideration because it can on occasion work irrationally to distort the weight of the evidence.

When does the *Zeitgeist* help and when does it hinder the progress of science?

(1) It is plain that knowledge helps research, and knowledge,
whether it be explicit on the printed page of a handbook or
implicit in the unrecognized premises of a theory, is in the
Zeitgeist. There is no use trying to limit the *Zeitgeist* to that
knowledge which you have without knowing it, for the line simply
cannot be kept. One discovery leads to another, or one experiment
leads to a theory that leads to another experiment, and the history
of science tells the story. The law of multiple proportions, for
instance, validates the atomic theory, and then the atomic theory
leads off to all sorts of chemical research and discovery.

On the other hand, the *Zeitgeist* does not always help, for there
is bad knowledge as well as good, and it takes good knowledge to
get science ahead. It is useful to be ignorant of bad knowledge.

The idea that white is a simple color was a bit of bad knowledge
that was in the *Zeitgeist* in the middle of the 17th century. It is
not a silly idea. It was empirically based. You can see colors, can
you not? And white is a color. And you can see that it is simple
and not a mixture, can you not? It is not clear whether Newton
was lucky enough not to have absorbed this bit of false knowledge
from the *Zeitgeist* or whether he was just stubborn, when, having
bought his prism at the Stourbridge Fair, he concluded that white
is a mixture of other colors. He was probably consciously flouting
the *Zeitgeist*, for he sent his paper up to the Royal Society with
the remark that it was in his "judgment the oddest if not the most
considerable detection which hath hitherto been made into the
operations of nature." But Robert Hooke and the others at the

Royal Society would have none of it. They were restrained from belief by the *Zeitgeist*. White is obviously not colored, not a mixture. There was bitter controversy before the conventional scientists gave in, before the truth shifted over to Newton's side (*6*).

Helmholtz ran into a similar difficulty when in 1850 he measured the velocity of the nervous impulse. The *Zeitgeist* said: The soul is unitary; an act of will is not spread out over a period of time; you move your finger; you do not will first that the finger move with the finger not moving until the message gets to it. Thus Helmholtz' father had religious scruples against accepting his son's discovery. And Johannes Müller, then the dean of experimental physiology, doubted that the conduction times could be so slow. At the very least, he thought, the rate of the impulse must approximate the speed of light (*7*).

The persistence of the belief in phlogiston is still another example of the inertia that the *Zeitgeist* imposes on progress in thought. Here both Lavoisier and Priestley broke away from convention enough to discover oxygen, but Lavoisier, with the more negativistic temperament, made the greater break and came farther along toward the truth, whereas Priestley could not quite transcend his old habits of thought. His theory was a compromise, whereas we know now—insofar as we ever know truth in science—that that compromise was not the way to push science ahead then (*8*).

So it is. Good knowledge promotes progress, bad knowledge hinders, and both kinds make up the *Zeitgeist*. Ignorance of good knowledge and awareness of bad hinder; awareness of good and ignorance of bad help. The history of science is full of instances of all four.

(2) Not only do the discovery of fact and the invention of theory help progress when fact and theory are valid, but comparable principles apply to the discovery and invention of new scientific techniques. The telescope seems to have come out of the *Zeitgeist* for it was invented independently by half a dozen different persons in 1608, although lenses had been made and used for magnification for at least 300 years. But then Galileo's discovery of Jupiter's moons the next year created, as it were, a new phase in the *Zeitgeist*, one that promoted astronomical discovery. So it was with the invention of the simple microscope, the compound microscope, the Voltaic pile, the galvanic battery, the galvanometer, the electromagnet, and recently the electron tube—the

possibilities opened up by the availability of a new important instrument change the atmosphere within a field of science and lead quickly to a mass of valid research. Within psychology the experimental training of a rat in a maze in 1903, in order to measure its learning capacity, led at once to a long series of studies in the evolution of animal intelligence with the maze as the observational instrument.

It is true that the negative instances of this aspect of the *Zeitgeist* are not so frequent or obvious; yet they occur. For years the Galton whistle, used for the determination of the upper limit of hearing, was miscalibrated, because its second harmonic had been mistaken for its first. The highest audible pitch was thought to occur at about 40,000 cycles per second, whereas the correct figure is about 20,000. Did this error of an octave hold back science? Not much, but a little. For a couple of decades investigators reported facts about the octave above 20,000 cycles per second, an octave that is really inaudible. One experimenter even found a special vowel quality for it to resemble. Thus bad knowledge about the whistle led to confusion and hindered the advance of science.

(3) The *Zeitgeist* acts as inertia in human thinking. It makes thought slow but also surer. As a rule scientific thinking does not suddenly depart widely from contemporary opinion. In civilization, as in the individual, the progress of thought is sensibly continuous. Consider, for example, the history of the theory of sensory quality.

Empedocles believed that eidola of objects are transmitted by the nerves to the mind so that it may perceive the objects by their images. Later there arose the notion that there are animal spirits in the nerves to conduct the eidola. Then, under the influence of materialism, the animal spirits came to be regarded as a *vis viva* and presently a *vis nervosa*. Next Johannes Müller, seeing that every sensory nerve always produces its own quality, substituted for the *vis nervosa* five specific nerve energies, using the word *energy*, in the days before the theory of conservation of energy, as equivalent to *force* or *vis*. He said that the mind, being locked away in the skull, cannot perceive the objects themselves, or their images, but only the states of the nerves that the objects affect, and he fought a battle against the Empedoclean theory—as indeed had John Locke and Thomas Young and Charles Bell before him, and as still others were to do after him. After a while it was seen, however, that the specificity of the five kinds of nerves lies not in the peculiar energies that they conduct to the brain but in where they terminate in the brain. Thus there arose the concept of sensory centers in the cerebrum. Nowadays we see that a cerebral center is nothing more than a place where connections are made and that sensory quality must be understood in terms of the discriminatory response in which stimulation eventuates—or at least many of us see this fact while we fight a *Zeitgeist* that still supports the theory of centers (9).

Is there any reason why Galen in A.D. 180 or Albrecht von Haller in 1766 should not have invented the modern theory of sensory quality? None, except that most of the supporting evidence was lacking and, being contrary to the accepted notions of the time, it would have sounded silly. Yet each contributor to this strand of scientific maturation was original, and several contributors had to fight again the battle against the notion that the mind perceives an object by embracing it, or, if it cannot get at the object itself, by getting itself impressed by the object's eidolon or simulacrum. Nor has the *Zeitgeist* even yet been thoroughly disciplined in this affair, as you can tell whenever you hear the remark: "If the lens of the eye inverts the image of the external world on the retina, why do we not see upside down?"

The *Zeitgeist* was hindering progress in this piece of history. It made originality difficult and it made it necessary to repeat the same arguments in 1690 (John Locke) and in 1826 (Johannes Müller) and, if one may believe current advertisements of a scientific film, nowadays too. Yet let us remember that this *Zeitgeist* also helped progress. The continuity of development lay always within the *Zeitgeist*. It was a conservative force that demanded that originality remain responsible, that it be grounded on evidence and available knowledge. Had Galen espoused a connectionist's view of sensory quality in the second century, he would have been irresponsibly original, a second-century crank, disloyal to the truth as it existed then. Loyalty may be prejudice and sometimes it may be wrong, but it is nevertheless the stuff of which responsible continuous effort is made. Science needs responsibility as well as freedom, and the *Zeitgeist* supports the one virtue even though it may impede the other.

(4) What may be said of the big *Zeitgeist* may also be said of the little *Zeitgeister* of schools and of the leaders of schools and of

the egoist who has no following. They have their inflexible attitudes and beliefs, their loyalties that are prejudices, and their prejudices that are loyalties. Every scientific in-group with strong faith in a theory or a method is a microcosm, mirroring the macrocosm which is the larger world of science.

Take egoism. Is it bad? It accounts for a large part of the drive that produces research, for the dogged persistence that is so often the necessary condition of scientific success. So egoism yields truth. It accounts also for the hyperbole and exaggeration of the investigating enthusiast, and then it may yield untruth. When two incompatible egoisms come together, they account for the wasted time of scientific warfare, for the dethronement of reason by rationalization. Egoism is both good and bad.

Take loyalty. Think how it cements a group together and promotes hard work. Yet such in-groups tend to shut themselves off from other out-groups, to build up their special vocabularies, and so, while strengthening their own drives, to lessen communication with the outside, the communication that advances science. Loyalty is both good and bad, and with loyalty a person sometimes has to choose whether he will eat his cake or will keep it.

This dilemma posed by the little *Zeitgeister* of the in-groups and the scientific evangelists has its root in basic psychological law. Attention to this is inevitably inattention to that. Enthusiasm is the friend of action but the enemy of wisdom. Science needs to be both concentrated and diffuse, both narrow and broad, both thorough and inclusive. The individual investigator solves this problem as best he can, each according to his own values, as to when to sell breadth in order to purchase depth and when to reverse the transaction. He, the individual, has limited funds and he has to sell in order to buy, and he may never know whether he made the best investment. But posterity will know, at least better than he, provided that it troubles to assess the matter at all, for posterity, having only to understand without hard labor, can assess the effect of prejudice and loyalty and enthusiasm, of tolerance and intolerance, as no man ever can in himself.

CODA

This is a broad meaning for the word *Zeitgeist*—the total body of knowledge and opinion available at any time to a person living within a given culture. There is, certainly, no rigorous way of distinguishing between what is explicit to a scientist and what is implicit in the forms and patterns of communication, between what is clear conclusion and what is uncritically accepted premise. Available knowledge is communicated whenever it becomes effective, and this is the *Zeitgeist* working.

The *Zeitgeist* is a term from the language of dualism, while its definition is formally physicalistic. That paradox is for the sake of convenience in the present communication and is allowable because every statement can be transformed into physicalistic language when necessary. Dualism has the disadvantage of implying a mystery, the existence of a *Zeitgeist* as a vague supersoul pervading and controlling the immortal body of society. We need no such nonsense, even though this abstinence from mystery reduce us to so ordinary a concept as a *Zeitgeist* inclusive of all available knowledge that affects a thinker's thinking.

That such a *Zeitgeist* sometimes helps progress and sometimes hinders it should be clear by now. As a matter of fact, the distinction between help and hindrance can never be absolute but remains relative to some specific goal. The *Zeitgeist* hindered Copernicus, who, resisting it, helped scientific thought onward and presently changed the *Zeitgeist* on this matter to what it was in Newton's day. Did the *Zeitgeist* that Newton knew help relativity theory? No; relativity had to make its way against that *Zeitgeist*. The newest *Zeitgeist*, which will include the principles of relativity and uncertainty and complementarity, presumably exists today within the in-group of theoretical physicists. It will become general eventually, and then it will reinforce progress, and after that, much later, perhaps our posterity will find today's truth tomorrow's error. The one sure thing is that science needs all the communication it can get. The harm communication does to progress never nearly equals the good.

REFERENCES AND NOTES

1. The term *Zeitgeist* seems to have originated in this sense in 1827 with Goethe who, in discussing the way in which Homer had influenced thought, remarked in the last sentence of his essay, *Homer noch einmal*, "Und dies geschieht denn auch im Zeitgeiste, nicht verabredet noch überliefert, sondern *proprio motu,* der sich mehrfältig unter verschiedenen Himmelsstrichen hervortut." *Himmelsstrichen* can be translated "climates," thus justifying the figure of the text, but it must also be noted that Goethe meant to use the term *Zeitgeist* when the effect is "self-determined," brought about "neither by agreement nor fiat." See, for instance, *Goethes sämtliche Werke,* (I. J. Cotta, Berlin, 1902-07), vol. 38, p. 78.

2. The discussion of this paragraph and all the references will be found *in extenso* in E. G. Boring, "Great men and scientific progress," *Proc. Am. Phil. Soc.* **94**, 339 (1950). The reference to Tolstoy is, of course, to his *War and Peace*. For the longest list of nearly simultaneous inventions and discoveries, see W. F. Ogburn and D. Thomas, "Are inventions inevitable?" *Polit. Sci. Quart.* **37**, 83 (1922).

3. On the social criterion of truth, on scientific truth's being what scientists agree about, see S. S. Stevens, "The operational basis of psychology," *Am. J. Psychol.* **47**, 323 (1935), especially p. 327; "The operational definition of psychological concepts," *Psychol. Rev.* **42**, 517 (1935), especially p. 517; E. G. Boring, "The validation of scientific belief," *Proc. Am. Phil. Soc.* **96**, 535 (1952), especially pp. 537 f.

4. On the point that a self cannot observe itself, that in self-observation a person must regard himself as if he were another person, see M. Meyer, *Psychology of the Other One* (Missouri Book Co., Columbia, Mo., 1921); Stevens, *op. cit.,* especially pp. 328 f.; E. G. Boring, "A history of introspection," *Psychol. Bull.* **50**, 169 (1953), especially p. 183.

5. On the sincerity of cranks in science, see I. B. Cohen, J. L. Kennedy, C. Payne-Gaposchkin, T. M. Riddick, and E. G. Boring, "Some unorthodoxies of modern science," *Proc. Am. Phil. Soc.* **96**, 505 (1952).

6. On Newton's difficulty in changing the *Zeitgeist* with respect to the complexity of white, see E. G. Boring, *Sensation and Perception in the History of Experimental Psychology* (Appleton-Century, New York, 1942), pp. 101 f. This discovery of Newton's was exceptional in that it had no anticipations (unless my wisdom is at fault). In other words, the *Zeitgeist* was strongly fixed, and to break it Newton must have been very stubborn—as indeed other evidence indicates that he was.

7. On Helmholtz' trouble with the *Zeitgeist* with respect to the velocity of the nervous impulse, see E. G. Boring, *A History of Experimental Psychology* 2 ed. (Appleton-Century-Crofts, New York, 1950), pp. 41 f., 47 f.

8. On Priestley and Lavoisier and the *Zeitgeist's* support of the phlogiston theory, see J. B. Conant, *The Overthrow of the Phlogiston Theory,* Harvard Case Histories in Experimental Science, Case 2 (Harvard Univ. Press, Cambridge, Mass., 1950).

9. On the history of the physiological theories of sensory quality and the retardation of progress in thinking by successive phases of this *Zeitgeist,* see E. G. Boring, *Sensation and Perception (op. cit.),* pp. 68-83, 93-95.

Historical and Thematic Relations of Psychology to Other Sciences
Egon Brunswik

Budapest-born Egon Brunswik (1903-1955), a student of Karl Bühler's, taught for ten years at the University of Vienna and then became professor of psychology at the University of California at Berkeley, where he remained until his death. A philosopher of science with a special interest in perception, especially functionalism in perception, Brunswik proposed various approaches to methodology and theory. His theory of probabilistic functionalism holds that an individual's perceptions and especially the constancies he develops through experience work for him in practice but are never really accurate representations of the physical world of objects, shapes, sizes, and colors. Brunswik maintains that the individual sets up certain hypotheses or probabilities that he brings to perception unconsciously. Thus man never has perfect representation of the physical world and never achieves perfect constancy.

Among Brunswik's numerous publications are *The Conceptual Framework of Psychology* (1952) and *Perception and the Representative Design of Psychological Experiments* (1956), a volume published posthumously. In the following article, which Brunswik presented at the convention of the American Association for the Advancement of Science in 1954, he states that psychology should emancipate itself from the nomothetic-reductionist natural sciences and align itself with statistical disciplines, with which it seems to have a structural affinity.

Not quite a century has passed since experimental psychology began, in Gustav Theodor Fechner's treatise on the "psychophysics" of sensation in 1860, to emancipate itself as a science. The emancipation has taken place relative to the purely speculative approach of philosophy, on the one hand, and relative to the confinement to the human or animal body imposed within psychology's closest antecedent among the sciences, physiology, on the other. And not quite half a century has elapsed since John B. Watson, in 1913, suggested that psychology abandon its original subjectivistic or introspectionistic concern with sensation and other data of consciousness and concentrate on the "behavior" of the

Egon Brunswik, Historical and thematic relations of psychology to other sciences. *Scientific Monthly*, 1956, 83, 151-161. Reprinted by permission of the American Association for the Advancement of Science.

organism as a physical body in a physical environment. Thus psychology was to be placed fully under the auspices of the methodologically most rigorous of its older sister disciplines, physics.

In the light of a comparative science, psychology stands at the crossroads as perhaps none of the other disciplines does. I shall stress especially its relationships to the physical and biological sciences, including some of the relatively "lowbrow" cultural disciplines such as economics.

FROM PHYSIOLOGY TO PHYSIOLOGICAL PSYCHOLOGY

The emergence of what we may call the specific "thema" of psychology is best discussed by contrasting the physiological psychology of today with the physiology from which it has sprung. Some of the major physiological discoveries of the first half of the nineteenth century were more or less directly at the doorstep of psychology. Among these were the Bell-Magendie law, which asserts the structural and functional discreteness of the sensory and motor nerves, and the law of specific sense or nerve energies by Charles Bell, Johannes Müller, and Helmholtz, which recognizes the dependence of sensation on the receiving organism. Still another discovery, the establishment of the rate of nervous impulse by Müller and by Helmholtz, best represents the step-by-step tracing of internal processes, which is so characteristic of physiology; this is symbolized by the straight line in diagram A of Table 1.

Table 1.   The Emergence of Physiological Psychology from Physiology.

A. INTERNAL PROCESS TRACING		Specific nerve energies *(Bell, Müller 1834)* *Rate of nervous impulse *(Müller, Helmholtz 1850)*
B. PERIPHERAL ARC		Reaction time *(Bessel 1822, Wundt, Cattell 1893)* *Sensory-motor approach *(Watson 1913, Skinner)*
C. CENTRAL-DISTAL APPROACH		*Brain-and-achievement *(Lashley 1929, Halstead)* Hypothetical brain models *(Köhler 1920, McCulloch)*

Compare this pattern with the counterpart of rate of nervous impulse in psychology proper, reaction time. The distinguishing characteristic of problems of this latter kind is the concentration on the over-all functional correlation of sensory input and motor output without primary concern for the details of the mediating process. This correlational peripheralism is described by the bridgelike arc in schema B of Table 1. In line with its gross, achievement-oriented character, the study of reaction time received its first impetus from difficulties with observational error in astronomy raised by Bessel in the 1820's; later it became a favorite of Wilhelm Wundt, the founder of the first psychological laboratory at Leipzig in 1879, and of his American assistant, James McKeen Cattell, who applied it to his differential-psychological testing research at Columbia University.

The direct physical observability of both stimulus and response renders the study of reaction time a nineteenth century rudimentary anticipation of Watson's sensory-motor behaviorism and of Bekhterev's concurrent reflexology. Most importantly, Fechner's psychophysics shared with the study of reaction time a relational rather than a process-centered emphasis. This was manifested in the famous Weber-Fechner law, which expresses sensation as a direct mathematical function of the external stimulus. The fact that psychophysics is being considered almost unanimously the birth cry of psychology proper must be ascribed to this correlational feature.

Various conditioning and higher learning problems have recently been treated under the sensory-motor reflex schema by Skinner and others. Critics have bemoaned the fact that this approach, cutting short as it does from input to output, tends to bypass the brain; and the dean of historians of psychology, Edwin G. Boring, has criticized it as a "psychology of the empty organism" (Boring, 1949).

In the development of physiological psychology, the possibility of such an accusation is circumvented by the emergence of a third type of approach that at the same time does away with peripheralism in its various forms. It is described in Table 1 under diagram C. Occurrences in the brain—that is, "central" factors—are directly correlated with relatively remote, or "distal," results of behavior ("achievements"), such as the reaching of the end of mazes of varying intricacy by a rat (right arc; the arc to the left is shown to indicate that abstraction and related cognitive extrapolations into the causal ancestry of the stimulus impact are inseparably intertwined with all brain-and-achievement studies).

Foreshadowed by Gall's notorious "phrenology" in the early nineteenth century and by Flourens' pioneering of brain extirpation experiments soon thereafter, the central-distal approach reached its full scope in the brain-lesion study in rats by Lashley in 1929 (Lashley, 1929). The same year brought Berger's report on brain waves and thus the beginning of electroencephalography with its wide use in modern psychiatry. More recently, Halstead has applied the statistical tool of factor analysis to the study of brain and intelligence at the human level (Halstead, 1947). In contrast, the 1860's and 1870's witnessed the peripheralistically conceived brain-localization studies of Broca and of Fritsch and Hitzig in which the more narrowly sensory or motor aspects were stressed at the expense of organization and integration.

Of considerably shorter history than the empirical brain-and-achievement studies are the largely hypothetical studies of the brain, which began with Köhler's theory of dynamic brain fields or "physical Gestalten" in 1920 (Köhler, 1955). While the Gestalt-psychological approach is more purely central rather than genuinely central-distal, the distal, adjustmental aspects have come to share the limelight in the study of "teleological mechanisms" by McCulloch and other cyberneticists (Annu. N.Y. Acad. Sci., 1948).

PSYCHOLOGY AND THE ANCIENT SPECULATIVE UNITY OF SCIENCE

One of the most prominent problems of a comparative science of science is that of the unity of the sciences (Brunswik, 1952). Most scientists agree that there must be unity with respect to the objectivity of both observation and the procedural aspects of theory construction. Physiological psychology and the school of behaviorism are primarily dedicated to the unification of psychology with the natural sciences along these lines. Equally important as the procedural unification is the thematic diversification of the sciences, however. I have therefore made it a point to begin these considerations with an example of such diversification of psychology from a neighboring discipline.

Close inspection shows (Brunswik, 1952) the considerable inhibitions stemming from vested intellectual interests that must be overcome to achieve such differentiation among the sciences. We must be on guard against excessive thematic unity, especially if we are concerned with a younger discipline growing up in the shadow of overwhelming parent sciences.

Formidable and even grotesque examples of an excessive unity of a highly uncritical kind can be brought forth from ancient science. An example involving the psychology both of sensation and of personality along with physics and physiology is presented in Table 2. For the most part the schema is based on the pre-Socratic cosmology of Empedocles and on the humoral doctrine of four temperaments of Hippocrates and Galen; the last two columns are relatively modern elaborations (see Allport, 1937, pp. 63ff). The original dichotomies are developed into quadripartite systems either by doubling or by compounding so that a modicum of differentiation is achieved.

From the systematic point of view, two features must be especially emphasized in connection with Table 2. One is the arbitrariness of classification as revealed most drastically by the presence of alternative sets of columns for the same subject

Table 2. Simple and Compound Dichotomies and a Resultant Pervasive System of Corresponding Quadripartite Schemes in Ancient Physics and Physiology and in Personality Psychology.

Physics	Sensory Psychology	Physiology		Personality Psychology			
Cosmic elements	Dichotomies of qualities	Humors		Temperaments and their behavioral aspects		Compound dichotomies	
	(Alternatives:)					(Alternatives:)	
	Double Compound					Emotional response	Affective tone
(a)	(b)	(c)	(d)	(e)	(f)	(g)	(h)
Air	Dry	Warm-Moist	Blood	Sanguine	Hopeful	Weak-Strong	Pleasant-Excited
Earth	Cold	Cold-Dry	Black bile (Spleen)	Melancholic	Sad	Strong-Slow	Unpleasant-Calm
Fire	Warm	Warm-Dry	Yellow bile	Choleric	Irascible	Strong-Quick	Unpleasant-Excited
Water	Moist	Cold-Moist	Phlegm (Mucus)	Phlegmatic	Apathetic	Weak-Slow	Pleasant-Calm

matter—for example, a double dichotomy and a partly conflicting compound dichotomy for the sensory qualities. (We may add that another of the pre-Socratics, Anaximander, chose air to be cold rather than dry.)

The other feature noteworthy in Table 2 is the apparent ease of transfer of fourness from one area to another in the manner of an absolute one-to-one correspondence. Different areas of knowledge, capable of independent approach, are thus thrown together indiscriminately by means of vague analogy; this is comparable to what such child psychologists as Piaget or Heinz Werner have described as synocretic or diffuse modes of thought (for a recent summary, see M. Scheerer in *Handbook of Social Psychology,* G. Lindzey, Ed., 1954).

More specifically, Gestalt psychologists have criticized the ready assumption of a strict correspondence between physical stimuli and sensory qualities as an undue "constancy hypothesis." It is in this surreptitious manner that physics and sensory psychology (Table 2, columns a to c) become symmetrical and thus, in effect, merge into one. It is even difficult to reconstruct which of the two areas of knowledge has the observational primacy over the other, although it is evident that there is a good deal of give and take.

In philosophy, it is easily seen that the implied operational indistinguishability of matter and mind (in this case, sensation) constitutes, or at least reinforces, naïve realism; or else, by way of the horizontal dichotomy between columns, it helps to put dualism on an absolute basis. Once the constancy hypothesis of the coordination of the two realms has given rise to the accusation of "unnecessary duplication" (as in Occam's razor), this dualism in turn readily changes into either materialistic or idealistic monism. The regularity and symmetry, which result from easy transfer and carry with them the flavor of Pythagorean number mystics, may be criticized on the same grounds of subjectivism on which Schopenhauer criticized Kant's compulsive filling of all the plots in his 3x4 table of categories.

(In experimental psychology, the adoption of the constancy hypothesis in its radical form would lead to the obliteration of the stimulus-response problem of psychophysics which, as we have seen, lies at the roots of modern psychology; it would even lead to the at least theoretical impossibility of acknowledging any kind of illusion—as it has come close to doing in Locke's doctrine of primary qualities, such as size, shape or motion.)

Both the arbitrariness and the easy transfer that characterize early stages of science are further revealed in the fact that some systems are not dichotomous or fourfold but three-, five-, or seven-fold. In his capacity as a psychologist, Plato distinguished three major faculties (reason, emotion, and desire, the latter including the lowly sensation); he localized them in a corresponding hierarchy of physiological centers (brain, heart, and liver or "phern"—that is, diaphragm); and he further distinguished three corresponding sociopolitical personality types (philosopher, warrior, worker). The ancient Chinese favored a five-fold scheme. In the doctrine of cosmic elements, the air of the Greeks is replaced by metal, and wood is added as a fifth element; the scheme is syncretically generalized to five tastes, five intestines, five sentiments, five poisons, five planets, five dynasties, and so forth (Forke, 1925). The relative merits of the various base numbers are not discussed here, although it may be granted that some of them are not without a realistic basis in certain limited areas (such as twoness for sex, threeness for man between input and output or the healthy medium between extremes, and so forth).

RELATIVE LEVEL OF MATURITY OF PSYCHOLOGY

As has been noted in passing, the most distinctly psychological aspects of the doctrine of four temperaments have outlasted their counterparts in physics and physiology by centuries if not millenniums. Furthermore, this doctrine has flourished in much greater variety and thus is fraught with more ambiguity than its long-vanished correspondents in the natural sciences. Columns g and h of Table 2 show only two of the kinds of compound dichotomies usually suggested, both conceived in the Wundtian three-dimensional theory of emotion; Herbart used a combination of strong-weak and pleasant-unpleasant instead. There are at least sixteen major thinkers who expended their efforts on the four temperaments in a feast of arbitrary classification. Among the persons concerned were Kant and such serious experimental psychologists of the past as Ribot, Külpe, Ebbinghaus, Höffding, and Meumann; on the contemporary scene we find the well-known German typologist, Ludwig Klages (for further discussion and sources, see Allport, 1937, pp. 63ff). This suggests that the relative youth of psychology is matched, at least in the personality area concerned, by a backwardness in its categorical structure, or "modes of thought."

In investigating the question of the relative maturity of psychology further, we note that dichotomizing and related forms of absolute classification, as well as their formalistic-syncretic transfer to other areas, are but two of several aspects of a broader prescientific syndrome. Auguste Comte put his finger on this syndrome in his distinction between what he called the metaphysical and the positive stages of science; with an eye on the special situation in psychology, Kurt Lewin, somewhat similarly, distinguished between Aristotelian and Galilean modes of thought (Lewin, 1935). According to Lewin, progress from the former to the latter mode involves any or all of the following, partly overlapping shifts: from dichotomies to gradations, from qualitative appearance to quantitative reality, from subjective speculation to objectivism, from classification to causation, from phenotype to genotype, from static existence to dynamic flow, from surface to depth, and from disjointed description to the "nomothetic" search for laws.

We may try to assess the standing of psychology among the sciences by listing a few of the most crucial shifts in these respects (Table 3). Perhaps the earliest shift from phenotypical quality to genotypical quantity concerns physics. From Empedocles' qualitatively conceived four-fold scheme mentioned in a previous paragraph, the doctrine of elements moved on toward an essentially modern conception of physical reality in Democritus' atomic theory that stressed shape and size instead of sensation. This theory is far from free of subjective speculation or contamination by direct perceptual appearances (especially "synesthesia" from the tactile-kinesthetic sphere), to be sure, but the step from surface to underlying reality and from dichotomy to gradation is taken at least in intent. The step from perceptual appearances to an indirect, abstract construction of a much more dynamically conceived reality was next made in astronomy with the shift from the perceptually dominated geocentric to the nomothetically more economical Copernican system.

The biological sciences followed with the shift from static anatomy to dynamic physiology as epitomized by Harvey's discovery of the circulation of the blood, and with the shift from Linnaeus' phenotypical taxonomy to Darwin's genotypical evolutionary

Table 3. Shift in Modes of Classification and Outlook from the Subjective-Qualitative-Phenotypical-Static ("Aristotelian") to the Objective-Quantitative-Genotypical-Dynamic ("Galilean") Syndrome.

Physics (Elements)	Astronomy	Anatomy-Physiology	Biology	Psychiatry	Psychology
Empedocles 5th B.C. Democritus 4th B.C.					
	Ptolemy 2nd A.D. Copernicus 1530				
		Vesalius 1543 Harvey 1628			
			Linnaeus 1738 Darwin 1859		
				Kraepelin 1883 Freud 1900	
					Titchener 1901 Lewin 1935

classification in botany and zoology. Transitions between dichotomizing and gradations also occurred—for example, when in the Middle Ages the four humors were ranked according to their "degree" of aliveness (Leake, personal communication).

Confirming our suspicion, we note that corresponding steps in the psychological disciplines follow much later, mostly within the memory of ourselves or of our immediate elders. In psychiatry, there is a tradition of static description and cataloguing which began in the early seventeenth century with Robert Burton's revealingly titled *Anatomy of Melancholy,* which continued with Pinel—the man who freed the insane from prison during the French Revolution—and was still in evidence in Kraepelin until it was broken by Freud's "depth-psychological" revision of psychiatric classification, notably in the doctrine of neurosis. In psychology proper, there is the shift from Wundt's and Titchener's so-called "existential" inventory and description of sensory experiences to Lewin's more dispositionally conceived notions of the internal psychological "field." Instead of Lewin, I might have mentioned some of his older Gestalt-psychological colleagues, notably Wertheimer and Köhler. Beginning in the 1910's, these workers set out to work on the intrinsic central dynamics of perception, and of thinking and problem solving; by virtue of their introspectionistic orientation, they are more comparable to Wundt and Titchener than to the more behaviorally oriented Lewin. Indeed, the simile has sometimes been used that while Titchener tried to dissect consciousness analytically like an anatomist, and his "sensations" thus are no better than a carcass of experience, Gestaltists, with their "phenomenology" are more like physiologists in that they keep consciousness alive while studying it.

As in all structural interpretations of history, a table of examples can be no substitute for full documentation. Indeed, Hippocrates' humoral underpinning of the doctrine of temperaments may be set parallel to Democritus' geometric underpinning of the elements and offered as demonstration of the fact that at least part of psychology showed objectivistic intent as early as did physics. Yet humoral doctrine is physiology, not psychology; nor would the fact that much of ancient psychology was behavioristic from the outset change our impression that, in the handling of the actual problems in the area, relatively primitive patterns of thought were the rule. I have already mentioned in discussing Table 2 that syncretic dichotomizing persists much longer and flourishes more abundantly in the psychological doctrine of the four temperaments than it does in the corresponding doctrines of the four physical elements or of the four physiological humors. We may further remind ourselves of the fact that in the social sciences—in many ways still younger than psychology—elaborate dichotomous schemes are still in vogue in some quarters right under our eyes—for example, in the work of Talcott Parsons.

DEPENDENCE OF PSYCHOLOGY ON THE NATURAL SCIENCES

Next we turn to more direct cross-disciplinary comparisons that involve historical phase differences with respect to comparable categories and in which psychology appears at the receiving end. For chronologically arranged evidence, we may turn to Table 4. This table concentrates on the experimental and differential-psychological developments that constitute the core of modern psychology; developments in physiological and abnormal psychology which are incorporated in some of the preceding tables have been played down or omitted. Special emphasis is given to conceptual outlook and methodology.

Our first consideration concerns the law-stating or nomothetic approach; it is traced at the left side of the table. While the actual establishment of natural law as it has been able to stand the test of time was brought about in astronomy and physics during the seventeenth century, psychology had to wait until Fechner (1860) for the beginnings of the experimental-nomothetic treatment of sensation, and until Ebbinghaus (1885) for that of memory by association. Solid arrows indicating these cross-disciplinary infusions generally point downward in a telltale manner in the respective parts of the table. Thus axiomatization, or more generally what Feigl called higher-order theory (Feigl, 1949), was brought about in physics by Newton; much less impressive attempts in psychology—further preceded and indeed prompted by Hilbert's axiomatization of geometry and by Woodger's efforts toward an axiomatization of biology (as his contribution to the *International Encyclopedia of Unified Science*)—had to wait until the work of Hull and his associates in the 1940's (Hull, 1940, 1943). A perusal of the writings of such nomothetically oriented psychologists as Hull or Lewin reveals that the ostensible classic among physical laws, the law of falling bodies, is invoked as an exemplar with almost monotonous regularity.

The nomothetic ideal is paramount not only in the classical phase of experimental psychology in the nineteenth century and in the recent postulational behaviorism of Hull but also in Gestalt psychology and in the physiological theory of Gestalt referred to earlier in this article. Frequent reference to "dynamics" in a brain "field" suggests analogies to Maxwell's electromagnetic field theory. Warnings pointing out that gravitation also acts in a field, have been sounded against pressing this analogy; a broken, rather than solid, arrow has therefore been used in Table 4. The fact remains, however, that the revolutionary element in Gestalt psychology is the breaking

Table 4. Scientific Background and Cross-Disciplinary Relations of Psychology with Specific Emphasis on General Systematic Isomorphisms and on Methodology.

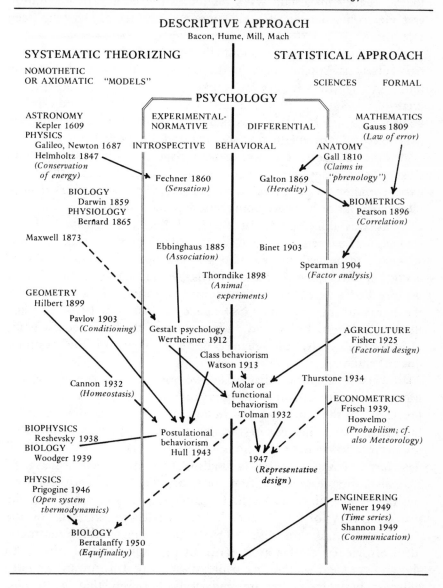

away from elementism and associationism and that the "machine-like" models to which these conceptions can be traced largely originated in classical mechanics. In addition, the coexistence of associationistic and of field-dynamic principles in modern psychological theory in certain ways resembles the duality of gravitation and electromagnetism of which modern physics has so long been tolerant.

The twenty-odd years about the turn of the century were a particularly turbulent phase in the development of psychology—so much so that Karl Bühler has spoken of them as the constructive crisis of psychology (Bühler, 1929). Gestalt psychology and classical behaviorism are but two especially clear-cut of at least four new psychological movements that sprang up in that period.

Another of these new movements is psychoanalysis. It shares with Gestalt psychology the insistence on the finding of regularities of a more complex scope. Freud, who had a distinguished active career in physiology prior to developing his dynamic theory of personality was, as was documented by Siegfried Bernfeld (Bernfeld, 1944), strongly influenced by the physical thinking of his time. He was strongly influenced by Helmholtz's principle of conservation of energy in developing his basic models. As was further demonstrated by Else Frenkel-Brunswik at the joint symposium of the AAAS with the Institute for the Unity of Science in Boston in 1954 (Frenkel-Brunswik, 1954), Freud had a keen sense of the basic requirements of the philosophy of science, popular belief to the contrary notwithstanding.

In Watson's classical behaviorism, we note that its primary concern was the fulfillment of the physicalistic ideal of observational precision. In the American psychology of this period, the desire for fact-finding and the fear of the dangers of speculation temporarily took precedence over the nomothetic aim and led to a form of descriptive empiricism or factualism that had the earmarks of Bacon's "simple enumeration" or of the early antitheoretical positivism of Comte or Mach. In stressing fact more than law, the prime urgency of the "general" was challenged in favor of the "particular," and thus a first inroad was made on the nomothetic ideal of science insofar as it concerns psychology. As I will try to show in the next section, psychology seems to drift toward a course halfway between factualism and nomotheticism—that is, toward probabilism.

Two lines of development issue from classical behaviorism. One is the formalized, nomothetic behaviorism of Hull and his associates at

Yale, which I have already mentioned. The other and more radical departure is the "purposive" behaviorism of Edward C. Tolman at the University of California (Tolman, 1932). It is best introduced by first referring to the fourth of the major crisis schools, frequently called American functionalism. Historically, this school precedes, parallels, and is about to outlive classical behaviorism. Under the influence of Darwin and other evolutionists, functionalism is characterized mainly by an emphasis on the readjustive value of behavior in coming to terms with the physical or social environment. An early representative was Thorndike with his problem-solving experiments with animals and his "trial-and-error" principle. In contrast to frequency of repetition, which played such a large part in the nonsense syllable experiments of Ebbinghaus and the "conditioning" experiments of the Russian physiologist, Pavlov, Thorndike stressed the importance of success and reward in learning ("law of effect").

Tolman's purposive behaviorism combines the constructive elements of classical behaviorism with those of functionalism and of Gestalt psychology in a program of animal and human experimentation and theory that is both "objective" and "molar." Its redefinition of purpose is operational, stressing the reaching of common end-stages from a set of differing initial or mediating stages. Thus it is not less or more "teleological" in the objectionable, vitalistic sense than Wiener's and McCulloch's cybernetics.

Convergence with a further type of influence from systematic theorizing in the physical sciences may develop if von Bertalanffy's attempted reduction of biological "equifinality," and thus of purposive behavior to Prigogine's new open-system thermodynamics (von Bertalanffy, 1950) should obtain the approval of physicists and biologists. It is one of the intrinsic limitations of high-complexity disciplines, such as psychology, that final judgment of reductive theory of this kind must remain outside its province. Since the verdict of history is not yet in, I have bracketed these developments in Table 4.

Claude Bernard's and Cannon's ideas on homeostasis have received increased attention in functional psychology, and Ashby has used them in his *Design for a Brain* (1952). Ashby's book is part of a current vogue in brain models which has developed out of the earlier examples I have mentioned in connection with physiological psychology and which has recently received a further impetus from the interest in the engineering problems of complex calculating machines. With a more distinctly nomothetic slant, Rashevsky and his associates at the University of Chicago (1948) have produced biophysical mathematical models that promise to be fruitful up to the level of social psychology and perhaps even in history.

Much of the work just mentioned, notably that on homeostasis and mathematical biophysics, proceeds under the assumption of a widespread isomorphy among outwardly diverse types of processes. Von Bertalanffy has, therefore, suggested the concerted development of a "general systems theory" (*Human Biology*, 1951). Such a theory could achieve a great deal toward the unification of the sciences under the auspices of the nomothetic-reductive approach that is so closely associated with the history of the natural sciences.

DIVERSIFICATION OF PSYCHOLOGY AS A PROBABILISTIC SCIENCE

At this point, we must pause and take a look at the foundations of our discipline. There is nothing in the development of science that will inspire paralyzing awe and induce adolescent dependence as much as will a headway in modes of conceptualization such as the natural sciences have been found to possess in relation to psychology. We must, therefore, be more on guard against the intrusion of policies that are alien to our basic problems. In particular, we must ask ourselves whether the following of the nomothetic lead is an unmixed blessing for psychology.

Let us fall back on the thema of psychology as we have tried to develop it in analyzing the differences between physiology and physiological psychology. We have conjectured that the emphasis on widespanning functional correlations at the expense of attention to the intervening technological detail is one of the major characteristics that distinguishes psychology from its predecessors (diagram C of Table 1). Tolman's molar behaviorism, and parallel developments in the study of perceptual "thing-constancy," can be shown to fall in essentially the same pattern, the fact notwithstanding that the focus in the central region remains hypothetical (Brunswik, 1952; Tolman, 1935).

On further analysis, we note that the functional arcs that span toward, and gain their feedback from, the remote, "distal" environment—and these are the really important arcs—become entangled with the exigencies and risks inherent in the environment. So long as the organism does not develop, or fails in a given context to utilize completely, the powers of a fullfledged physicist observer and analyst, his environment remains for all practical purposes a semierratic medium; it is no more than partially controlled and no more than probabilistically predictable. The functional approach in psychology must take cognizance of this basic limitation of the adjustive apparatus; it must link behavior and environment statistically in bivariate or multivariate correlation rather than with the predominant emphasis on strict law, which we have inherited from physics.

It is perhaps more accurate to say that the nomothetic ideology was influenced by a somewhat naïve and outdated high-school-type, thematic cliche of physics, which some of us have tacitly carried with us in the process of developing psychology into a science. As need not be reiterated here, physics itself has become statistical in the meantime. Yet we must not fall for easy analogy; we must make it clear that the statistical mechanics and quantum theory, being of a microscopic character, has little to do with the probabilism of functional psychology. Since the individual case or instance does not lose its identity in psychology, our form of probabilism is macroscopic rather than microscopic and thus of much greater consequence in the actual execution of our discipline.

The use of bivariate correlation statistics is most obviously inevitable in the study of individual differences. In reality, the two have developed in close contact with one another; I have, therefore, grouped them together on the right side of Table 4 rather than placing the statistical approach where it belongs—that is, halfway between the nomothetic and the purely fact-descriptive approach.

As long as correlation statistics were not available, problems of differential psychology were treated with an air of absoluteness that reminds one of the nomothetic approach. One of the most grotesque products of this would-be type of correlational study was the so-called "phrenology" of the anatomist, Gall, who tried to link mental faculties to the shape of the skull on the basis of the most casuistic evidence.

Psychology has from its beginnings been intertwined with statistics and its active development in a variety of ways. Classical psychophysics is closely linked to the study of unidimensional error distribution and thus to Laplace and Gauss, notably in such American psychophysicists as James McKeen Cattell. Bivariate correlation statistics was first introduced by Galton and Pearson and may even be considered to be a direct joint product of biometrics and psychometrics. The factor analysis of Spearman, of Thurstone, and of others is even more a distinctly differential-psychological development. Because of the partly mathematical character of most of these developments, I have placed them somewhere between differential psychology and formal statistics in Table 4. For the first time in this analysis, we witness a give-and-take between psychology and other disciplines (as brought out by the zig-zag course of arrows in the table); we may take this as an added omen of the inherently statistical character of psychology as a whole, briefly deduced in a preceding paragraph.

While statistical correlation and factoring, including the attendant representative sampling of individuals from a population, have traditionally been recognized as necessary in the area of individual differences as they occur in intelligence or personality testing, the possibility of studying the broader functional organism-environment relationships by these statistical methods has long been ignored. In certain essential respects, this even holds true for R. A. Fisher's factorial design and analysis of variance (1935). The variables and their levels of strength are still arbitrarily selected rather than naturally sampled; hence the results are subject to severe limitations of generalizability. By allowing multivariate analysis, however, Fisher's methods are definitely superior to the older univariate designs, especially in the study of problems of higher complexity. It is, therefore, not astonishing that their first transfer from their original domain, agriculture, to psychology (Crutchfield and Tolman, 1940) fell within the framework of Tolman's molar-functional study of behavior; their use has since rapidly expanded over wide areas of experimental psychology.

To obviate the intrinsic shortcomings of the artificial, "systematic" designs of which factorial design is but an elaborate case, I have advocated that in psychological research not only individuals be representatively sampled from well-defined "populations," but also stimulus situations from well-defined natural-cultural "ecologies" (Brunswik, 1947; 1949); only by such "representative design" of experiments can ecological generalizability of functional regularities of behavior and adaptation be ascertained. Representative sampling of situations from the ecology allows us to take cognizance of the occasional major failures that result from the fallibility of perceptual cues or behavioral means while at the same time fully recognizing the favorable cases also. Generalization of the achieved degree of success to the ecology as a whole becomes possible with the use of the routine technical criteria for sampling statistics hitherto confined to differential psychology. Since representative design has so far been used only in a limited set of contexts, it has been bracketed in Table 4.

As was pointed out by Hammond (1951; 1954), certain parallels can be drawn between the situation created in psychology by representative design and the situation created in physics by relativity theory. In both cases, an earlier overgeneralization of classical results obtained within a limited type of universe is corrected. As has been pointed out by Hammond in a different context, factorial design is geared to the manufacturing type of problem situation that prevails in agriculture, while the organically developed natural-cultural range of generalization to which psychology must aspire demands other methods. As in the example from antiquity, which was discussed in the second section, we are faced with a warning against the uncritical transplantation of content-alien themas or instrumental scaffoldings, at least as long as we wish to prize and uphold our indigenous thematic identity above all else.

Perhaps the first to see that psychology was not a "fundamental" discipline in the sense of the standard natural sciences was the Columbia psychologist, Woodworth (1918). Representative design and the resultant probabilistic functionalism are nothing but the consistent projection of such a belief onto the plane of methodology and explicit theorizing. Since the statistical macroprobabilism of representative design would move psychology away from physics and other fundamental natural sciences with their nomothetic thema, considerable resistances must be expected along the way. (A recent symposium in which I defended my views against such advocates of the nomothetic-reductionist point of view in psychology as L. Postman, E. R. Hilgard, D. Krech, and H. Feigl has been published in *Psychol. Rev.*, 1955.)

Our thematic submissiveness to the physical sciences may be more readily overcome if we can show that the proposed reorientation would bring psychology closer to other, perhaps less glamorous but no less urgent or real, natural and social sciences in which macroprobabilism has long been recognized as a legitimate attitude. Prominent among these admittedly and recognizably statistical disciplines are meteorology (for an outline of statistical procedures in meteorology, see H. R. Byers, *General Meteorology*, 1944, pp. 486ff.) and economics insofar as they use autocorrelation and intercorrelation, as theoretically stressed especially by Wiener (1949), for probability prediction. Economics deserves special attention in view of the reinforcement that the statistical conception has received in the Norwegian school of econometrics, notably by Haavelmo (1944). Within still another discipline, communication theory—as cast into mathematical form by Claude Shannon, with psychologically cogent commentary by Warren Weaver (1949)—the study of message transmission through semierratic external media comes very close to the psychological problem of the anticipation of, and adjustment to, a distant world. Communication and psychological functioning also have in common the use of redundancy as a means of overcoming the low predictive probability of single signals of these instrumentalities (Brunswik, 1952, Chapter 2, and Section 23). In probabilistic functionalism this low predictive probability finds its counterpart in the limited "ecological validity" of cues or means, and the place of redundancy is taken by intersubstitutability or "vicarious functioning."

CONCLUSION

The growing strength of behaviorism has long assured that the core of a procedural physicalism and thus of the essential operational aspects of the unity of science are rapidly becoming a matter of course in psychology. The time has come when unity of science is best served by stressing the thematic differentiation among the sciences within the overall unity. In carrying this diversification to its logical conclusion, psychology emerges as a macrostatistical discipline, thus acquiring not only distinct thematic identity but also internal methodological unity. The acceptance of this probabilistic functionalism and of the attendant representative design of research may be facilitated, both inside and outside psychology, by a comparative methodology involving sciences of all shadings. The best way to emancipate psychology from the suggestive power of those nomothetic-reductionist natural sciences in the shadow of which it began its development is to demonstrate its structural affinity with disciplines already recognized as statistical in character.

REFERENCES

Allport, G. W. *Personality.* New York: Holt, 1937.

Ashby, W. R. *Design for a brain.* New York: Wiley, 1952.

Boring, E. G. *History of experimental psychology.* (2nd ed.) New York: Appleton, 1950.

Brunswik, E. *The conceptual framework of psychology.* Chicago: University of Chicago Press, 1952.

Brunswik, E. *Perception and the representative design of experiments.* Berkeley, Calif: University of California Press, 1956.

Brunswik, Else F. Psychoanalysis and the unity of science. *Proc. Am. Acad. Arts and Sci.,* 1954, No. 80.

Bühler, K. *Die drise der psychologie.* (2nd ed.) Jena, Germany: Gustave Fischer Verlagbuchhandlung, 1929.

Byers, H. R. *General meterology.* New York: McGraw-Hill, 1944.

Crutchfield, R. S., and E. C. Tolman. Multiple—variable design for experiments involving interaction of behavior. *Psychol. Rev.,* 1940, **47**, 38-42.

Feigl, H. Some remarks on the meaning of scientific explanation. In H. Feigl and W. Sellars (Eds.), *Readings in philosophical analysis.* New York: Appleton, 1949. Pp. 510-514.

Fisher, R. A. *Design of experiments.* Edinburgh: Oliver & Boyd, 1935.

Forke, A. *The world conception of the Chinese.* London: *Probathain,* 1925.

Haavelmo, T. Probability approach in econometrics. *Econometrica,* Suppl., 1944.

Halstead, W. C. *Brain and intelligence.* Chicago: University of Chicago Press, 1947.

Hammond, K. R. Relativity and representativeness. *Phil. Sci.,* 1951, **18**, 208-211.

Hammond, K. R. Representative vs. systematic design in clinical psychology. *Psychol. Bull.,* 1954, **51**, 150-159.

Hull, C. L., *et al. Mathematico-deductive theory of rate learning.* New Haven, Conn.: Yale University Press, 1940.

Hull, C. L. *Principles of behavior.* New York: D. Appleton-Century Company, Inc., 1943.

Köhler, W. *Gestalt psychology.* New York: Liveright, 1947.

Lashley, K. S. *Brain mechanisms and intelligence.* Chicago: University of Chicago Press, 1929.

Leake, C. D. Personal communication.

Lewin, K. *Dynamic theory of personality.* New York: McGraw-Hill, 1935.

Rashevsky, N. *Mathematical biophysics.* Chicago: University of Chicago Press, 1948.

Scheerer, M. Cognitive theory. In G. Lindzey (Ed.), *Handbook of social psychology.* Vol. 1. New York: Addison-Wesley, 1954.

Shannon, C. E., and W. Weaver, *Mathematical theory of communication.* Urbana, Ill.: University of Illinois Press, 1949.

Symposium on the probability approach in psychology. *Psychol. Rev.,* 1955, 62, 193-242.

Tolman, E. C. *Purposive behavior in animals and men.* New York: Century, 1932.

Tolman, E. C., and E. Brunswik. The organism and the causal texture of the environment. *Psychol. Rev.,* 1935, 42, 43-77.

Von Bertalanffy, L., *et al.* General systems theory. *Human Biology,* 1951, 23, 302

Wiener, N. *Extrapolation, interpolation, and smoothing of stationary time series.* New York: Wiley, 1949.

Woodworth, R. S. *Dynamic psychology.* New York: Columbia University Press, 1918.

Analogy in Science
Robert Oppenheimer

It has been the practice of the American Psychological Association to invite prominent representatives of other sciences and disciplines to address its annual meetings. Since physics had been the ideal model for psychology for a long time, the APA in 1955 invited the noted theoretical physicist Robert Oppenheimer to present his view on the relation between physics and psychology. Oppenheimer (1904-1967), recognized as one of the brightest minds of American science and one whose interests extended far beyond physics, examined the parallels and contrasts between physics and psychology. His address has evoked comments and discussions and has often been quoted.

One would think that the two sciences (physics and psychology) could hardly be further apart. In all hierarchical schemes they are put far apart. Psychology, to everyone who works in the field, is felt to be a new subject in which real progress and real objectivity are recent. Physics is, perhaps, as old as the sciences come; physics is reputed to have a large, coherent, connected corpus of certitudes. This does not exist in psychology, and only the beginnings of it, the beginnings of things that are later going to be tied together, are now before us.

But I have always had a feeling that there were ways in which the two sciences had a community; in some sense, of course, all sciences do. One very simple one is that each is responsive to a primitive, permanent, pervasive, human curiosity: What material bodies are and how they behave, on the one hand, and how people and the people-like animals behave and feel and think and learn. These are the curiosities of common life and they will never be abated. Both, for this reason, can hardly make important pronouncements of a technical sort which do not appear to have some bearing on our views of reality, on metaphysics. Both manifestly have, and continue

From Robert Oppenheimer, Analogy in science. *American Psychologist*, 1956, **11**, 127-135. Reprinted by permission of the American Psychological Association.

to have, a fresh and inspiriting effect on the theory of knowledge, on epistemology.

There are other ways in which we are brothers. In the last ten years the physicists have been extraordinarily noisy about the immense powers which, largely through their efforts, but through other efforts as well, have come into the possession of man, powers notably and strikingly for very large-scale and dreadful destruction. We have spoken of our responsibilities and of our obligations to society in terms that sound to me very provincial, because the psychologist can hardly do anything without realizing that for him the acquisition of knowledge opens up the most terrifying prospects of controlling what people do and how they think and how they behave and how they feel. This is true for all of you who are engaged in practice, and as the corpus of psychology gains in certitude and subtlety and skill, I can see that the physicist's pleas that what he discovers be used with humanity and be used wisely will seem rather trivial compared to those pleas which you will have to make and for which you will have to be responsible.

The point, of course, is that as the relevance of what we find to human welfare and human destiny becomes sharper and more manifest, our responsibilities for explication, for explanation, for communication, for teaching grow. These are rather our responsibilities for being sure that we are understood than responsibilities for making decisions; they are our responsibilities for laying the basis in understanding for those decisions.

There are other ways in which we are alike. The practical usefulness of our professions gives us often the impression that we are right for the wrong reasons, and that our true nature is very different from our public presence. We are both faced with the problem of the need to keep intact the purity of academic and abstract research and, at the same time, to nourish and be nourished by practice. In physics, of course, our debt to technology and engineering is unlimited. I think it would be so in psychology as well.

Both sciences, all sciences, arise as refinements, corrections, and adaptations of common sense. There are no unique, simple, scientific methods that one can prescribe; but there are certainly traits that any science must have before it pretends to be one. One is the quest for objectivity. I mean that not in a metaphysical sense; but in a very practical sense, as the quest to be sure that we understand one another, and that all qualified practitioners mean essentially the same thing. Common-sense language is inherently ambiguous; when the poet uses it, or the rhetorician, he exploits the ambiguity, and even when we talk in ordinary life we almost need ambiguity in order to get by. But in science we try to get rid of that, we try to talk in such simple terms, and match our talk with deeds in such a way that we may differ as to facts, but we can resolve the differences. This is, of course, the first step in the quest for certitude. But certitude is not the whole story. When we move from common sense into scientific things, we also move toward generality using analysis, using observation and, in the end, using experiment. And we also do something which is even more characteristic; we look for novelty, we look for transcendence, we look for features of experience that are not available in ordinary life. Characteristic in physics are the instruments that enable us to transcend elementary, daily experience: the telescope that lets us look deep into the sky, the enormous accelerators which are, today, the logical extension of the microscope, enabling us to look on a finer and finer scale into the structure of matter.

I need to be cautious in citing parallels in psychology; but certainly the use of hypnosis, the use of drugs, are typical extensions into unfamiliar realms of human experience which just bring out characteristics of psychological phenomena that are largely lost in day-to-day experience. There is an example which may be only a physicist's idea of a perfect experiment. It is the work that was done at McGill in the last years on the effects of reducing sensory stimuli, with very simple arrangements to change the level of stimulation; these produce most striking and almost frighteningly great, though essentially temporary, changes in memory, in the intellectual and cognitive life of the subjects. This is again an example of carrying to an extreme something which is indeed encountered in ordinary experience but which only the patience and the abstractness of experimental enquiry is likely to make manifest.

We come from common sense; we work for a long time; then we give back to common sense refined, original, and strange notions, and enrich what men know and how they live. And here, I suppose, the real hero is the teacher. . . .

But for all of that I would like to say something about what physics has to give back to common sense that it seemed to have lost from it, not because I am clear that these ideas are important tools in psychological research, but because it seems to me that the worst of all possible misunderstandings would be that psychology be influenced to model itself after a physics which is not there any more, which has been quite outdated.

We inherited, say at the beginning of this century, a notion of the physical world as a causal one, in which every event could be accounted for if we were ingenious, a world characterized by number, where everything interesting could be measured and quantified, a determinist world, a world in which there was no use or room for individuality, in which the object of study was simply there and how you studied it did not affect the object, it did not affect the kind of description you gave of it, a world in which objectifiability went far beyond merely our own agreement on what we meant by words and what we are talking about, in which objectification was meaningful irrespective of any attempt to study the system under consideration. It was just the given real object; there it was, and there was nothing for you to worry about of an epistemological character. This extremely rigid picture left out a great deal of common sense. I do not know whether these missing elements will prove helpful; but at least their return may widen the resources that one can bring to any science.

What are these ideas? In our natural, unschooled talk, and above all in unschooled talk about psychological problems, we have five or six things which we have got back into physics with complete rigor, with complete objectivity, in the sense that we understand one another, with a complete lack of ambiguity and with a perfectly phenomenal technical success. One of them is just this notion that the physical world is not completely determinate. There are predictions you can make about it but they are statistical; and any event has in it the nature of the surprise, of the miracle, of something that you could not figure out. Physics is predictive, but within limits; its world is ordered, but not completely causal.

Another of these ideas is the discovery of the limits on how much we can objectify without reference to what we are really talking about in an operational, practical sense. We can say the electron has a certain charge and we do not have to argue as to whether we are looking at it to say that; it always does. We cannot say it has a place or a motion. If we say that we imply something about what we ourselves—I do not mean as people but as physicists—are doing about it.

A third point is very closely related to this; it is the inseparability of what we are studying and the means that are used to study it, the organic connection of the object with the observer. Again, the observer is not in this case a human; but in psychology the observer sometimes is a human.

And then, as logical consequences of this, there is the idea of totality, or wholeness. Newtonian physics, classical science, was differential; anything that went on could be broken up into finer and finer elements and analyzed so. If one looks at an atomic phenomenon between the beginning and the end, the end will not be there; it will be a different phenomenon. Every pair of observations taking the form "we know this, we then predict that" is a global thing; it cannot be broken down.

Finally, every atomic event is individual. It is not, in its essentials, reproducible.

This is quite a pack of ideas that we always use: individuality, wholeness, the subtle relations of what is seen with how it is seen, the indeterminacy and the acausality of experience. And I would only say that if physics could take all these away for three centuries and then give them back in ten years, we may well say that all ideas that occur in common sense are fair as starting points, not guaranteed to work but perfectly valid as the material of the analogies with which we start.

The whole business of science does not lie in getting into realms which are unfamiliar in normal experience. There is an enormous work of analyzing, of recognizing similarities and analogies, of getting the feel of the landscape, an enormous qualitative sense of family relations, of taxonomy. It is not always tactful to try to quantify; it is not always clear that by measuring one has found something very much worth measuring. It is true that for the Babylonians it was worth measuring—noting—the first appearances of the moon because it had a practical value. Their predictions, their prophecies, and their magic would not work without it; and I know that many psychologists have the same kind of reason for wanting to measure. It is a real property of the real world that you are measuring, but it is not necessarily the best way to advance true understanding of what is going on; and I would make this very strong plea for pluralism with regard to methods that, in the necessarily early stages of sorting out an immensely vast experience, may be fruitful and may be helpful. They may be helpful not so much for attaining objectivity, nor for a quest for certitude which will never be quite completely attained. But there is a place for the use of naturalistic methods, the use of descriptive methods. I have been immensely impressed by the work of one man who visited us last year at the Institute, Jean Piaget. When you look at his work, his statistics really consist of one or two cases. It is just a start; and yet I think he has added greatly to our understanding. It is not that I am sure he is right, but he has given us something worthy of which to enquire whether it is right; and I make this plea not to treat too harshly those who tell a story, having observed carefully without having established that they are sure that the story is the whole story and the general story.

It is of course in that light that I look at the immense discipline of practice, that with all its pitfalls, with all the danger that it leads to premature and incorrect solutions, does give an incredible amount of experience. Physics would not be where it is, psychology would not be where it is if there were not a great many people willing to pay us for thinking and working on their problems.

If any of this is true there is another thing that physicists and psychologists have in common: we are going to have quite a complicated life. The plea for a plural approach to exploration, the plea for a minimal definition of objectivity that I have made, means that we are going to learn a terrible lot; there are going to be many different ways of talking about things; the range from almost un-understood practice to recondite and abstract thought is going to be enormous. It means there are going to have to be a lot of psychologists, as there are getting to be a lot of physicists. When we work alone trying to get something straight it is right that we be lonely; and I think in the really decisive thoughts that advance a science loneliness is an essential part. When we are trying to do something practical it is nice to have an excess of talent, to have more sailors than are needed to sail the ship and more cooks than are needed to cook the meal; the reason is that in this way a certain elegance, a certain proper weighing of alternatives, guides the execution of the practical task.

We are, for all kinds of reasons, worrying about how our scientific community is to be nourished and enough people who are good enough are to come and work with us. And then on the other side we are worried about how we are to continue to understand one another, and not get totally frustrated by the complexity and immensity of our enterprises.

I think there are good reasons of an inherent kind, beside the competitive compulsion to the communist world, why we would do well to have more and better scientists. I know that exhortation, money, patronage, will do something about this; but I do not think that is all that will be needed. I think that if we are to have some success it must be because, as a part of our culture, the understanding, the life of the mind, the life of science, in itself, as an end as well as a means, is appreciated, is enjoyed, and is cherished. I think that has to be a very much wider thing in the community as a whole, if we are to enjoy with the community as a whole the healthy relations without which the developing powers of scientific understanding, prediction, and control are really monstrous things.

It may not be so simple, to have in the community at large some genuine experience of the pleasures of understanding and discovery. It may not be simple because what this requires is not merely that this experience be agreeable, but that it have a touch of virtue; that not only the consideration of ends, of products, of accomplishments and status, but the texture of life itself, its momentary beauty and its nobility, be worth some attention; and that among the things that contribute to these be the life of the mind and the life of science. Let us try to make it so.

The Historical Meaning of Psychology as a Science and Profession
Rollo May

A prominent analyst, teacher, editor, and author, Rollo May has contributed significantly to psychotherapy, personality theory, and psychoanalysis. He is an ardent proponent of the view that psychology should scrutinize its philosophical presuppositions. Among his well-known publications are *The Meaning of Anxiety* (1950) and *Love and Will: Sex, Eros, Machines* (1969). He has edited *Existence: A New Dimension in Psychiatry and Psychology* (1958) and *Existential Psychology* (1961, rev. ed. 1969).

In this article, originally presented at the New York Academy of Sciences in 1955, May examines the emergence of psychology's dual character as science and as profession and states that new psychological theory must be developed to bring together clinical and traditional scientific psychology. May outlines the aspects to be included in this new theory for psychology, which will serve also as a basis for psychotherapy.

Psychology, until about 100 years ago, was part of philosophy and ethics. The great psychological insights before the time of Freud are to be found in the writings of philosophers and religious teachers such as Socrates, Plato, Augustine, Pascal, Spinoza, Kierkegaard, and Nietzsche. The first emergence of psychology in the experimental scientific sense was relatively late; Wundt established his psychological laboratory in Leipzig in 1879 for the exploration of physiological psychology.

To understand the meaning and development of contemporary psychology, we need to see briefly what has happened in man's relation to nature and to himself in the modern period. Since the Renaissance, as is well known, a new view of the objectivity of man arose. For complex reasons that we shall not discuss here, natural science in its modern mathematical form was founded on a career to be marked by tremendous progress. When Descartes made

Rollo May, The historical meaning of psychology as a science and profession. *Transactions of the N.Y. Academy of Sciences*, 1955, **17**, 312-314. Copyright 1955 by The New York Academy of Sciences. Reprinted by permission of the author and the New York Academy of Sciences.

his famous dichotomy in the 17th century between extension—matter which can be measured—and thought, which cannot be measured, modern man was given a methodology by means of which he thereupon devoted himself, with great emphasis, to the measuring and control of physical nature. The sciences which best fit this method made the greatest strides: physics, for example; later, chemistry; and so on. Thus, medicine made greater strides than psychology and, in the psychological field itself, psychophysics was the most advanced until the last few years. The Newtonian classical physical view that went along with this development is well known. I wish only to emphasize that the philosophical concomitants during this period were, understandably, a great emphasis on rationalism and, later, a devotion of philosophy to an elucidation of scientific method.

During the last part of the 19th century, radical changes occurred in the social systems of Western man. These changes are portrayed in the work of Freud, Marx, Nietzsche, and others, who pointed out that the inherited ways of understanding experience no longer had the same validity. The disunity that became evident during that period in the various sciences is graphically presented by Ernst Cassirer in his lectures at Yale, published under the title *An Essay on Man.* These basic changes and evidences of disunity in modern society had a great deal to do with the emergence of psychology as a centrally important science in its own right.

As is well known, psychology, in this country, when it broke off from theology and philosophy in the last half of the 19th century, devoted itself largely to laboratory and experimental work. Though it was kept broad by such leaders as William James, nonetheless, psychology, predominantly in America, has followed until recently the emphasis upon experimental laboratory methods.

The importance of Freud and the later development of clinical and therapeutic psychology can be seen when we realize that Freud sought to find some bases for psychological unity amid the progressively disunified tendencies characterizing persons of the Victorian culture. In essence, Freud pointed out that the rationalistic view of man—that is, man trying to live his life solely by reason and repressing the irrational, unpredictable, and unmeasurable tendencies—was not only unsatisfactory but led to the breakdown of personality.

There is no doubt that clinical psychology and the more intensive forms of psychotherapy are here to stay in our civilization chiefly because of the great and pressing social need for these psychological services.

The bringing together of clinical and traditional scientific psychology presents a number of problems, some of which remain unsolved. I believe that the development of new theory is necessary. This theory in psychology may well be parallel to the new theory in physics as elaborated by Heisenberg, Einstein, Bohr, and others. The essence of the new physical theory is that objective nature can no longer be understood as detached from man. The human being is actor as well as spectator. The parallel to this in psychology would be that we must view man as subject as well as object. I see the new development in physics as symptomatic of far-reaching and necessary changes in our attitude toward man and nature in the Western World. The changes in psychology will occur not because physics now gives us "permission," but rather because of changes running through the basic concepts of Western society.

Psychology needs to work out the theory and method which will be most fruitful for its particular subject matter and aims. The new theory for psychology, which will also serve as a basis for psychotherapy, will include at least the following five aspects:

First, it will preserve the careful methods of experimental psychology. But it will put these methods in a broader understanding of the nature of man. The experimentalist will be aware that, whenever we experiment on a person, we are necessarily leaving out some elements of the whole autonomous human being.

Second, the new theory will include human self-awareness. For we can never see man whole except as we see him, including ourselves, as the mammal who has a distinctive capacity for awareness of himself and his world. Herein lie the roots of man's capacity to reason and deal in symbols and abstract meanings, and herein lies also the basis for a sound view of human freedom.

Third, the new theory will include some concept of the dynamism of the self. It is not satisfactory to assume the person "grows" like a plant or that the self merely is characterized by a "thrust towards health" like the body. We need some understanding of the aspect of the human being which Allport sought to describe in his term "functional autonomy" and which Goldstein characterizes as "self-actualization."

Fourth, it will include the aspect of culture. For man always lives, moves, and has his being in a social, interpersonal world.

Fifth, the new theory will include the historical dimension of the human being. For man is the mammal who, unlike other animals, can have self-awareness of his past, can transcend the present moment of time, can project himself into the future, thus can learn from the past and, to some extent, can mold his future. It is not generally realized that scientific psychology has treated man almost entirely as an ahistorical unit and, to my mind, this has meant a considerable truncation of understanding.

The sixth aspect of the new theory should be the relation of psychology to ethics. For it is clear from the implications above that man's behavior always influences his own future and impinges upon the rest of the community.

Social Factors in the Origins of a New Science: The Case of Psychology
Joseph Ben-David
Randall Collins

Here two sociologists, Joseph Ben-David of Hebrew University, Jerusalem, and Randall Collins of the University of California at Berkeley, examine the social factors that were influential in the development of scientific psychology. They argue that these factors—status, competition, and role—have usually been ignored by historians of psychology in favor of intellectual factors in accounting for the origin of scientific psychology. The innovation of experimental psychology was effected, according to these sociologist-authors, by the merger of the roles of philosophers and physiologists. Only in Germany did the following requisite factors for that merger of roles, or role hybridization, exist: "(a) an academic rather than an amateur role for both philosophers and physiologists; (b) a better competitive situation in philosophy than in physiology encouraging the mobility of men and methods into philosophy; (c) an academic standing of philosophy below that of physiology, requiring the physiologist to maintain his scientific standards by applying his empirical methods to the materials of philosophy." This article is based partly on Collins' master's thesis.

THE PROBLEM

The growth of scientific disciplines, as of many other phenomena, can be represented by an S-shaped curve.[1] First there is a long period, going back to prehistory, during which there are various ups and downs but no continuous growth; this is followed by a spurt of accelerated growth; eventually the development slows down and approaches a ceiling.[2] This typical pattern is obtained whether one

Joseph Ben-David and Randall Collins, Social factors in the origin of a new science: The case of psychology. *American Sociological Review*, 1966, 31, 451-465. Reprinted by permission of the authors and the American Sociological Association.

The authors are indebted to Professors David Krech and Harold Wilensky for their comments and suggestions, and to the Comparative National Development Project of the Institute of International Studies of the University of California at Berkeley for financial support.

[1] Derek de Solla Price, *Little Science, Big Science*, New York: Columbia University Press, 1963, pp. 1-32; Gerald Holton, "Scientific Research and Scholarship: Notes Toward the Design of Proper Scales," *Daedalus*, 91 (Spring, 1962), pp. 362-99.

[2] Although this may be followed by escalation into further growth, it is unnecessary for the purpose of the present paper to consider this possibility.

uses as the index of growth the numbers of publications, discoveries, or people doing research in the subject; the pattern corresponds well with the intuitive picture one obtains from the histories of the different sciences.

The process, as presented in the accounts of scientific development, can be presented schematically as follows. Ideas beget ideas until the time is ripe for a new and coherent system of thought and research to arise. Thenceforth the system possesses a life of its own. It is identified as a new field of science, is eventually given a name of its own (such as chemistry or psychology), and grows rapidly into maturity. This still leaves open the question of beginnings. If the whole story consisted of ideas begetting ideas, then growth would have to start at an exponentially accelerating rate (to a point of saturation) right from the first relevant idea. Since this does not happen, it has to be assumed either that only a few ideas are capable of generating new ones—the rest simply being sterile—or that ideas are not self-generating, and, even if potentially fertile, have to be carried from person to person and implanted in some special way in order to give rise to new generation.

Common sense indicates that both statements are true. Not all original ideas are fertile, and some potentially fertile ideas are lost or left unused because they are not communicated effectively. Nevertheless histories of science have concentrated on the first type of explanation. If an idea has no historical consequences, the historian of ideas will take it for granted that something must have been at fault with the idea. Conversely, when an idea with a seemingly not-so-brilliant beginning proves capable of further growth, he will assume that it must have had hidden qualities which ensured its success. Obviously he will find no difficulty after the fact in demonstrating the correctness of his hunches.

In this paper, we shall pursue the other tack. Instead of trying to show what inherent qualities made one idea fertile and another infertile, we shall ask how it happened that at a certain point in time the transmission and diffusion of ideas relating to a given field became strikingly increased in effectiveness. Instead of contemplating the internal structure of intellectual mutations,[3] we shall concentrate on the environmental mechanisms which determine the

[3] This is not to say that such contemplation is necessarily useless. Its potential utility depends on finding identifiable characteristics which predict what is and what is not a "fertile" idea.

selection of mutations. Specifically, we postulate that: (1) the ideas necessary for the creation of a new discipline are usually available over a relatively prolonged period of time and in several places;[4] (2) only a few of these potential beginnings lead to further growth; (3) such growth occurs where and when persons become interested in the new idea, not only as intellectual content but also as a potential means of establishing a new intellectual identity and particularly a new occupational role; and (4) the conditions under which such interest arises can be identified and used as the basis for eventually building a predictive theory.

THE CASE OF PSYCHOLOGY: THE TAKE-OFF INTO ACCELERATED GROWTH

The earliest beginnings of psychology reach back into prehistory. Explanations of human thought and behavior are inherent in every language; with the rise of philosophies, more abstract and systematic formulations came into being. Finally, in the nineteenth century, the methods of natural science were applied to the subject. Using publications in experimental and physiological psychology as an index of the growth of modern scientific psychology, we find that the acceleration started about 1870, and that the period of rapid growth was reached about 1890 (Table 1).[5]

The place where accelerated growth began can be ascertained from comparisons of the growth in different countries. The pattern is similar to that found in other nineteenth century sciences. The main development occurs in Germany, to be continued in the twentieth century in the United States, with a much more modest growth in Britain. For a while France also seems to develop strongly, but production there declines soon after the initial spurt around the turn

[4] This accords with the oft-noted phenomenon of multiple discoveries in science. Cf. Robert K. Merton, "Singletons and Multiples in Scientific Discovery: A Chapter in the Sociology of Science," *Proceedings of the American Philosophical Society*, 105 (1961), pp. 471-486.

[5] These publications do not represent the total number of reports of experimental and physiological researches in psychology, but rather review articles, books, and papers dealing with the theory and methodology of experimental and physiological psychology. Complete tables of research reports are not available for this period; however, this particular bibliography may be more useful for our purposes than they would have been. It represents a set of self-conscious summaries of scientific work in the field; therefore it indicates the rise of interest in scientific psychology better than would a collection of researches which may not at the time have been considered relevant to psychology.

Table 1. Number of Publications in Experimental and Physiological Psychology, by Nationality and Decade, 1797-1896

Decade	Nationality					
	German	French	British	American	Other	Total
1797-1806	1	1	—	—	—	2
1807-1816	2	1	—	—	—	3
1817-1826	1	—	3	—	—	4
1827-1836	4	3	2	—	—	9
1837-1846	11	4	2	—	1	18
1847-1856	15	2	6	1	—	24
1857-1866	16	8	7	—	3	34
1867-1876	38	11	15	1	4	69
1877-1886	57	22	17	9	12	117
1887-1896	84	50	13	78	21	246

Source: J. Mark Baldwin (ed.), *Dictionary of Philosophy and Psychology*, New York: Macmillan, 1905, vol. III, Part 2, pp. 950-64.

of the century (Table 2). Moreover, French development seems to have been isolated from the mainstream; it has been quoted in major textbooks less than its relative share in production of publications would indicate (Table 3).

These are the data to be explained. Since the conditions under which something new is created are not necessarily the same as the conditions under which the innovation is effectively received somewhere else, we shall confine ourselves to the explanation of the take-off, and leave the analysis of the diffusion of the new field for another discussion.

PROCEDURE

Originally the subject matter of psychology was divided between speculative philosophy and physiology. Towards 1880, specialized psychological publications came to constitute the bulk of the work in the field, and philosophical psychology was widely disparaged by the "new psychologists."[6] The acceleration of production was associated with a growing consciousness among these men of the existence of a distinct field of psychology, and of the need for

[6] Richard Müller-Freienfels, *Die Hauptrichtung der gegenwärtigen Psychologie*, Leipzig: Quelle & Meyer, 1929, pp. 3-6.

Table 2. Annual Average Number of Publications in Psychology, by Language, 1896-1955

Years	German	English Total	American	British	French	Other	Total
1896-1900	764	745	....	...	709	270	2494
1901-1905	1119	747	....	...	660	210	2781
1906-1910	1508	941	....	...	478	158	3185
1911-1915	1356	1090	....	...	376	160	2982
1916-1920	386	1639	....	...	159	191	2395
1921-1925	1163	1850	....	...	326	315	3653
1926-1930	1761	2654	....	...	428	913	5951
1931-1935	1362	3371	....	...	472	975	6376
1936-1940	1160	....	3238	328	299	747	6330
1941-1945	216	....	3411	296	72	299	4465
1946-1950	203	....	4257	346	246	560	5662
1951-1955	459	....	5955	557	502	572	8385

Source: Samuel W. Fernberger, "Number of Psychological Publications in Different Languages," *American Journal of Psychology,* 30 (1917), 141-50; 39 (1926), 578-80; 49 (1936), 680-84; 59 (1946), 284-90; 69 (1956), 304-09.

Table 3. Per Cent Distribution of References in Psychology Texts by Language

Text	Language Total	English	German	French	Other
Ladd, *Elements of Physio-logical Psychology,* 1887.	100.0 (420)	21.1	70.0	7.4	0.5
Ladd & Woodworth, 2nd edition, 1911.	100.0 (581)	45.6	47.0	5.2	2.2
Woodworth, *Experimental Psychology,* 1938.	100.0 (1735)	70.9	24.5	3.1	1.5
Woodworth & Schlosberg, 2nd edition, 1954.	100.0 (2359)	86.1	10.9	2.5	0.5

distinguishing their work from traditional fields. It is usually assumed that the emergence of a new group devoting itself to a new specialty is an effect of intellectual growth. As knowledge in a field increases, no one is able to master all of it any more, and specialization is the necessary result. We shall try to show, however, that the new scientific identity may precede and indeed make possible the growth in scientific production. At least in the rise of the new psychology, social factors played an important role, independently of intellectual content.

The first step is to determine the persons who consciously identified themselves as practitioners of a new science investigating mental phenomena by means of empirical methods such as experimentation, systematical observation, and measurement, (irrespective of whether they called themselves "psychologists" or "experimental philosophers"). Operationally, there are three conditions for the existence of such a new scientific identity: (1) the person must do empirical work in the subject matter of psychology; (2) he must not have some other clearly established scientific identity, such as physiologist; (3) he must be a part of an on-going group of scientific psychologists, rather than an isolated individual.

Taking these points in order: (1) The first group to be excluded are speculative philosophers such as Descartes, Locke, Hartley, Herbart, and even Lotze as well as various "social philosophers." However much they may have theorized about the use of empirical methods, they are not classified as scientific psychologists if they did not actually use such methods. (2) Also excluded are those natural scientists, principally physiologists, whose experiments can be retrospectively included in psychology, but whose identification was clearly with the natural sciences. Psychiatrists are also excluded: at the time in question, they belonged to a medical discipline which was quite independent of philosophy, and thus of psychology. Moreover, their theories were rather self-consciously based on the views of nineteenth-century medical science.[7]

(3) Finally, we must make an operational distinction among three categories of persons: *forerunners, founders,* and *followers.* The first two are distinguished by whether or not they had students who became psychologists. An example of a forerunner would be the scientific dilettante—such as Francis Galton. These men did not consider themselves psychologists, nor were they so identified by their contemporaries. Generally they remained isolated from any specific discipline until historians of the science—which was created by other forces—offered them a posthumous home.

[7]Gregory Zilboorg, *A History of Medical Psychology,* New York: Norton, 1941, pp. 400, 411-12, 434-35, 441. Breuer and Freud were developing a psychological psychiatry at the end of the nineteenth century, but there was no contact (except of the most negative kind) between Freudianism and German academic psychology for many decades thereafter.

Those who were not themselves the students of psychologists, but who trained their own disciples as psychologists, are the *founders* of the new discipline of psychology. Their disciples are the *followers.* The latter two classes can be considered psychologists proper. What we have referred to as "discipleship"—the fact of having studied under a man, or having worked under him as a laboratory assistant— is, we believe, an adequate measure of the existence of a consciously self-perpetuating identity, a "movement" or discipline. The use of purely objective criteria in establishing such lines of descent has the disadvantage that we may misjudge the extent of actual influence and identification, but the overall picture should be accurate.

The names to be classified are taken from five histories of psychology, including ones written in each of the countries to be examined.[8] For Germany and the United States, all names between 1800 and 1910 were taken. Beyond the latter date, the numbers of psychologists in these countries become so great that the histories are necessarily selective; moreover, scientific psychology was well into its second and third generations in these countries by this point. For Britain and France, all names between 1800 and 1940 were taken, since the numbers of names involved were much smaller than for either Germany or the United States. Scientific psychology became established in Britain or France considerably later than in the other two countries.[9]

[8] Germany: Müller-Freienfels, *op. cit.;* France: Fernand-Lucian Mueller, *Histoire de la Psychologie,* Paris: Payot, 1960; Britain: John C. Flugel, *A Hundred Years of Psychology,* 2nd edition, London: Duckworth, 1951; United States: Edwin G. Boring, *A History of Experimental Psychology,* 2nd ed., New York: Appleton-Century-Crofts, 1950; Robert I. Watson, *The Great Psychologists,* Philadelphia: Lippincott, 1963. Russia has not been treated in this analysis. The number of its contributions to psychological literature until recent years has been very small; its great innovators, Sechenov, Pavlov and Bekhterev, were all physiologists and would therefore have been excluded from the population of psychologists. They provide good examples of persons whose work could be integrated into scientific psychology only because subsequent developments elsewhere created such a discipline.

[9] Information about biographies and careers has been drawn from the five histories of psychology cited above (especially Boring) and from: Mollie D. Boring and Edwin G. Boring, "Masters and Pupils Among American Psychologists," *American Journal of Psychology,* 61 (1948) 527-34; Carl Murchison (ed.), *A History of Psychology in Autobiography,* Vols. I-IV, Worcester, Massachusetts: Clark University Press, 1930-1952; Carl Murchison (ed.), *Psychological Register,* Vols. II and III, Worcester, Massachusetts: Clark University Press, 1929-1933; *Minerva: Jahrbuch der Gelehrten Welt,* Leipzig: 1892–. "Germany" is taken to include Austria and the German-speaking universities of Switzerland and Central Europe; "France" includes French-speaking Switzerland and Belgium.

RESULTS

Figures 1-4 show the population of scientific psychologists for each country in the form of genealogical charts.[10] A great many names of physiologists and philosophers had to be excluded from the histories of German psychology, among them many of the most eminent men in those fields in the nineteenth century. In Germany our population includes 32 names, five of which have no predecessors on the chart (Figure 1). Two names do not appear in the figure. Gustav Fechner has all of the characteristics of an innovator save one: he gave rise to no personal school of followers, although, as will be seen, he influenced some of the founders. On balance, he was probably more of a forerunner than a founder, as one cannot say that his innovation of psychophysics would have been developed into a discipline of experimental psychology if an institutionally-based movement had not been founded subsequently.[11] Karl Groos appears rather late to be an indigenous developer, having habilitated in 1889, nine years after Ebbinghaus, who was the last of other self-starters. In any case, he cannot be considered a founder, as he gave rise to no following. This brings us down to five men who can be regarded as the founders of scientific psychology in Germany: Wilhelm Wundt, Franz Brentano, G.E. Müller, Carl Stumpf, and Hermann Ebbinghaus.

In Britain, the biologists C. Lloyd Morgan and George Romanes were excluded, as well as the statistician Karl Pearson. Francis Galton, who instigated psychological testing in Britain but whose

[10]Clearly, those charts do not represent the total population of such psychologists for this period, and men may appear to have no psychological followers only because they are not listed in the texts from which the names are drawn. Nevertheless, we feel justified in using this form of measurement of the rise of a discipline, because the visibility of the men who form such a movement is an important factor in its existence.

[11]Fechner was a retired physicist who devoted many years to writing pantheistic, anti-materialistic philosophical works. His writings met with little success, due to the reaction against Idealism that had developed by the mid-nineteenth century. In 1850, he took up the physiologist E.H. Weber's experiments on touch and muscle sense, in an attempt to establish mathematical laws of perception. This research, however, was an integral part of Fechner's pantheistic system; the laws of psychophysics were intended to give a demonstrable proof to his belief that mind and matter were aspects of the same thing, and he went on to propose an explanation of the entire physical world as composed of souls related to each other by material bodies. Cf. Robert I. Watson, *The Great Psychologists*, Philadelphia: Lippincott, 1963, p. 215, and E.G. Boring, "Fechner: Inadvertent Founder of Psychophysics," in E.G. Boring, *History, Psychology, and Science: Selected Papers*, New York: Wiley, 1963, pp. 126-131.

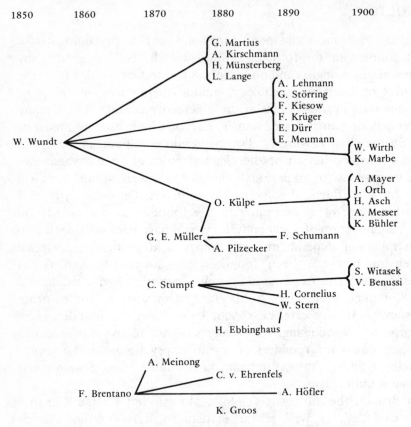

Figure 1. Founders and Followers among German Experimental Psychologists, by Decade of Habilitation, 1850-1909.

scientific interests extended from geographical exploration to chemistry, photography, and statistics, and who left no school of psychologists to carry on is also omitted. This leaves 9 names in British psychology, virtually all of whom go back to the German innovators, Wundt and Müller (Figure 2). The exceptions are G.H. Thomson who is not shown in the figure, who took his degree at Strassburg (a German university at the time) in 1906; and W.H.R. Rivers, who studied with Ewald Hering, a physiologist closely identified with the "new psychology" in Germany. But by the 1890's, one could hardly study in Germany without becoming aware of the new developments, and Rivers cannot be called an originator of experimental methods in the field of psychology.

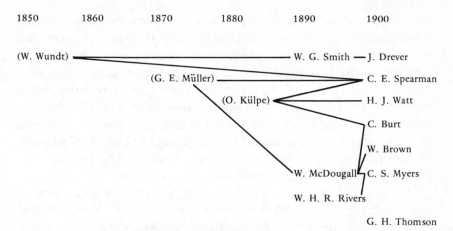

Figure 2. Founders and Followers among British Experimental Psychologists, by Decade of Highest Degree, 1850-1909

In France, the names of numerous psychiatrists and some physiologists and biologists were excluded, leaving 10 names (Figure 3). Two men comprising the Swiss school can be traced back to Wundt; one—Victor Henri—worked with Müller, although he had previously worked with Alfred Binet. The self-starters appear to be Théodule-Armand Ribot, Henri Beaunis, Pierre Janet. Ribot cannot be considered a major innovator, as he made his reputation by

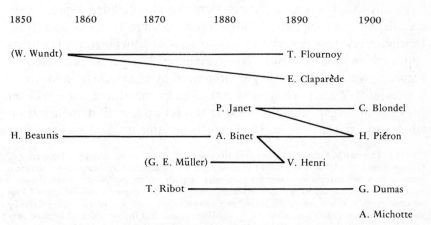

Figure 3. Founders and Followers among French Experimental Psychologists, by Decade of Highest Degree, 1850-1909.

publicizing German psychology, and was given the first chair of Experimental Psychology in France in 1889 as a result; he remained by and large a speculative philosopher. Beaunis was a physiologist who set up the first psychological laboratory in France in the same year; again, it is difficult to assign Beaunis a role as an independent innovator since a rash of laboratory-foundings had already been going on in Germany and the United States for a decade. Janet was an M.D. who succeeded to Ribot's chair in 1902 at the College de France; he was primarily a psychiatrist, however, and maintained a private practice throughout his career.

In France, then, there appear to be a number of figures without direct antecedents among the German psychologists. Some of them were obviously influenced by the Germans, others had ideas of their own. Had ideas been enough, the French school might have become an effective rival to the German school. But the French development came from the German in that there was no continuity in France. Ribot and Beaunis each had but one important follower and Janet had two. This relative lack of descent resulted from a lack of interest in creating new roles for the new ideas. As will be shown later, those working in the new field were content to remain philosophers, psychiatrists, or broad-gauged scientific intellectuals, often interested in finding a scientific solution to some practical problem, like Binet. They did not attempt, therefore, to create a coherent and systematic "paradigm," and to transmit it to the next generation.[12]

Finally, in the United States virtually all excluded figures were speculative philosophers, among them George T. Ladd and John Dewey. Very few American physiologists or other natural scientists appeared in the histories. The remaining 37 figures, presented in Figure 4, were overwhelmingly influenced by the German innovators, particularly Wundt. Only one name lacks an antecedent: William James, who began as a physiologist and set up a small demonstration laboratory at Harvard in 1875 which he later claimed was the first

---

[12]Cf. Thomas S. Kuhn, *The Structure of Scientific Revolutions*, Chicago: University of Chicago Press, 1963, for a discussion of how sciences are able to make cumulative advances because they are integrated around a particular "paradigm" or model of scientific reality, with its implied methodology and research directions. Of course, it can be argued that psychology even today still lacks overwhelming consensus around a central, reality-defining theory of the sort that Kuhn means by a "paradigm," and that the term should be used only in such fields as physics which do have such a theory. We have used the term here more broadly, to refer to the necessity of a new discipline to have at least minimal consensus on the boundaries of the subject matter upon which its practitioners will focus their attention, and on an acceptable range of research methods.

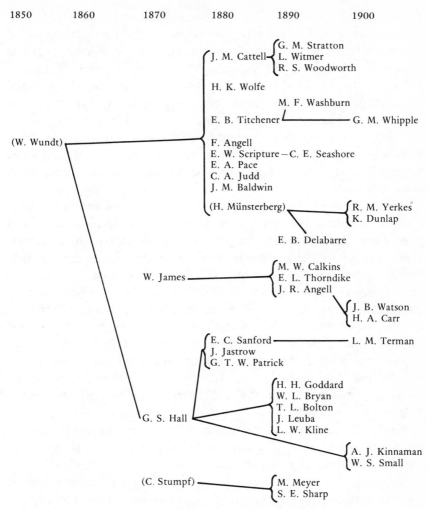

Figure 4. Founders and Followers among American Experimental Psychologists, by Decade of Highest Degree, 1850-1909.

psychological laboratory in the world. He became Professor of Philosophy at Harvard in 1885, and had his title changed to Professor of Psychology only in 1889. James is the closest America comes to an indigenous development in psychology, but his work was largely an exposition of European ideas and discoveries (he had visited Germany in 1869, while preparing to teach physiology); he himself became increasingly interested in philosophy during the time that experimental psychology was developing in America. (All of James' major philosophical works date from 1897, when his title was changed back to Professor of Philosophy.) The first generation of experimentalists were almost entirely students of Wundt, including G. Stanley Hall, who did not take his degree with Wundt. Hall in 1881 set up the first functioning psychological laboratory in the U.S. at Johns Hopkins after returning from a visit with the German psychologists, and the lines to succeeding generations can be clearly traced. Without any important contributions from American philosophers or natural scientists, experimental psychology suddenly sprang up in the United States, transplanted from Germany.

Germany, then, is where the crucial conditions for the innovation of scientific psychology are to be sought. Ideas which could have given rise to a cumulative tradition could be found outside of Germany. In fact, towards the end of the nineteenth century, France nearly rivalled Germany as a center for such ideas. But as shown in Table 2, French production declined rapidly after a momentary peak around 1900, while German, American, and, to a much lesser extent, British work continued to grow. Figures 1-4 indicate that only in Germany had there developed an autonomous network for the regular transmission and reception of the new ideas. Subsequently the U.S. and later Britain linked up with this network, and the U.S. eventually became its center. France only partially linked up with it and it did not develop a network of its own. In the absence of such a network, innovations remained isolated events; only the existence of networks could make them into a cumulative process.[13]

We shall not here follow the entire story of the creation of communication networks and their diffusion from country to country, but shall confine ourselves to the original establishment of the German network. For this purpose, all the other countries will be treated as negative instances, with Germany as the sole positive case. The question to be answered is: Why did an effective network for the communication of these new ideas develop only in Germany?

[13] A further indication of the weakness of the French system is the relatively greater mortality of French psychological journals. Between 1850 and 1950, 70 per cent of the psychological journals begun in France had ceased, as compared to 50 per cent for the United States, 51 per cent for Germany (before 1934, excluding the many stoppages during the Nazi era), and 21 per cent for Britain. Cf. Robert S. Daniel and Chauncey M. Louttit, *Professional Problems in Psychology*, New York: Prentice-Hall, 1953, pp. 25, 358-74.

ROLE-HYBRIDIZATION

The answer is that the conditions for the establishment of a new professional role variety, committed to the new field, existed only in Germany. Ideas which are not cultivated by people whose regular jobs are to cultivate them are like souls hovering in a mythological limbo before entering a body. They can light upon the dreams or the imagination of one person here and another one there, of someone who lives today or of someone else who will be born in a thousand years. If, however, ideas become the end-products of scientific roles, they can be likened to genes which are transmitted from generation to generation through a reliable and natural process; under normal conditions, they will not only survive but increase.

There are several ways in which new scientific role varieties arise. The present instance is a case of role-hybridization: the individual moving from one role to another, such as from one profession or academic field to another, may be placed at least momentarily in a position of role conflict.[14] This conflict can be resolved by giving up the attitudes and behaviors appropriate to the old role and adopting those of the new role; in this case, identification with the old reference group must be withdrawn. However, the individual may be unwilling to give up his identification with his old reference group, as it may carry higher status (intellectual as well as perhaps social) than his new group. In this case, he may attempt to resolve the conflict by innovating, i.e. fitting the methods and techniques of the old role to the materials of the new one, with the deliberate purpose of creating a new role.

Examples of scientific roles created by this process are psychoanalysis, which was created by a man who moved from the

[14]Joseph Ben-David, "Roles and Innovations in Medicine," *American Journal of Sociology*, 65 (1960), pp. 557-68. John T. Gullahorn and Jeanne E. Gullahorn, "Role Conflict and its Resolution," *Sociological Quarterly*, 4 (1963), pp. 32-48, have distinguished between two kinds of role conflict: "status-produced role conflict," in which the occupant of a single status position is subjected to conflicting expectations by the different persons with whom he deals, and "contingent role conflict," in which the conflicts arise from the simultaneous occupancy of two statuses. Most of the discussions in the literature have dealt with the first variety, e.g., Robert K. Merton, "The Role-Set: Problems in Sociological Theory," *British Journal of Sociology*, 8 (1957), pp. 106-120; and Neal Gross, Ward S. Mason, and Alexander W. MacEachern, *Explorations in Role Analysis*, New York: Wiley & Sons, 1958. We are distinguishing a third kind of role conflict, resulting from mobility rather than from the "static" situations indicated above. See Peter M. Blau, "Social Mobility and Interpersonal Relations," *American Sociological Review*, 21 (1956), pp. 290-95. For a discussion of why scientists would tend to identify with a traditional discipline rather than with an emerging specialty of lower prestige, see Warren O. Hagstrom, *The Scientific Community*, New York: Basic Books, 1965, pp. 53, 209.

prestigious profession of scientific research to the relatively lower-status occupation of German medical practice; Freud attempted to maintain his status by trying to raise medical practice into a form of scientific research, and as a result created psychoanalysis. Similarly, Pasteur gave rise to bacteriology by maintaining his theoretical perspectives after moving into research on wine fermentation, and elaborated his discovery into a new specialty.

Mobility of scholars from one field to another will occur when the chances of success (i.e., getting recognition, gaining a full chair at a relatively early age, making an outstanding contribution) in one discipline are poor, often as a result of overcrowding in a field in which the number of positions is stable. In such cases, many scholars will be likely to move into any related fields in which the conditions of competition are better. In some cases, this will mean that they move into a field with a standing relatively lower than their original field.[15] This creates the conditions for role conflict. Of course, not everyone placed in such a position will choose to or be able to innovate a new role, nor is it possible to predict exactly which individuals will do so. It is possible, however, to say that the chances of such a major innovation occurring in a discipline into which there is mobility from a higher-status discipline are considerably greater than in a discipline into which there is no such mobility, or which stands higher in status than the discipline from which mobility takes place. For example, if physiology has higher standing in an academic system than philosophy, but competitive conditions are better in the latter than in the former, one might expect a role-hybridization in which physiological methods will be applied to the material of philosophy (at their most adjacent point, psychology) in order to differentiate the innovator from the more traditional practitioners of the less respected discipline. This would not be expected if philosophy's status were equal or higher, or if the competitive conditions in philosophy were equal or worse than those in physiology.

Moreover, since a major academic innovation has a chance of success only if it can attract a sizable following, it is usually not

---

[15]For the scholar or scientist, this is not simply a matter of social status or prestige, but rather of the effectiveness or ability of the field to make progress as judged by its own intellectual standards. Cf. Hagstrom, *op. cit.*, pp. 9-104, for a theoretical exposition of science as a form of social organization in which competition for recognition by the colleague group is a prime mechanism of control; see also pp. 208-220 for a general discussion of disciplinary differentiation.

enough (except perhaps in cases of striking utility, such as bacteriology), that an individual innovator be placed in a situation of role conflict. The conditions have to be general so as to ensure a widespread response to the innovation. The motivation of the man who merely joins such a movement is quite similar to that of the man who begins it—moving into a discipline of lower standing than his old one, he is likely to welcome the opportunity to raise his status through adopting the innovation. Even more importantly, the existence of such relationships between disciplines may have a vicarious effect upon individuals within the system who do not personally move from the high-status discipline to the low-status discipline. For example, the younger men in the low-status field may attempt to upgrade themselves by borrowing the methods of a high-status field. The simplest way to upgrade themselves would be to move to the other field, but they are restrained from doing this by the differences in competitive conditions. If they do not make the innovation themselves, they may be very receptive to an innovation by a migrating scientist. Even young scholars who have not yet chosen a field, knowing the relative prestige and conditions of competition in the several fields, will be attracted to the new hybridized role.

It is important to distinguish role-hybridization from what might be termed "idea-hybridization," the combination of ideas taken from different fields into a new intellectual synthesis. The latter does not attempt to bring about a new academic or professional role, nor does it generally give rise to a coherent and sustained movement with a permanent tradition.

Antecedents of modern psychology as far back as Descartes had discussed psychological functioning in a physiological perspective, but without giving rise to any movement to extend these ideas as other sciences were doing with their respective materials. Similar connections were made by the British associationists, from John Locke and David Hartley up to Alexander Bain, James Ward, and James Sully at the end of the 19th century, but without giving any indication that a continuous scientific tradition would ever result from these theories. In Germany, Herbart and Lotze certainly fall into this category, along with Fechner, who introduced experimental methods into philosophical psychology in the 1850's with his psychophysics, but who did not thereby create any movement to reform the role of the psychologist-philosopher. Galton in England,

and in France, such men as Ribot, Beaunis, and Binet must be considered more "idea-hybrids" than "role-hybrids"; rather than creating a new role, they merely added another facet to the established role of the multi-purpose intellectual such as had existed in these countries since the seventeenth century. Finally, William James in the United States would fall into the category of an "idea-hybrid," particularly since he finally decided on the traditional role of philosopher rather than the new role of scientific psychologist.

THE POSITIVE CASE

In the German universities of the 19th century, physiology was a highly productive, expanding science. One of its greatest periods of productivity took place between 1850 and 1870, when most of the chairs of physiology were first split off from anatomy. Fifteen chairs were created between 1850 and 1864. After that date, the field rapidly reached a limit of approximately one chair per university in a system comprising 19 universities before 1870 and 20 after 1870.[16] Table 4 shows that physiology, with approximately half as many chairs as philosophy, added only two full chairs from 1873-1910, whereas philosophy, already the largest field in the universities, added eight. The number of Extraordinary Professors and Privat-dozents in physiology grew much more rapidly during this period than in philosophy. But these were poorly paid and largely honorific positions; their number indicates something of the competitive pressures in these fields for the truly desirable positions, the full professorships. Advancement was particularly difficult in physiology, since most of its full chairs, having been created at about the same time, were filled with men of about the same age who held them for decades.[17] Table 5 shows that in the 1850's, the chances of becoming a full professor were better for those habilitating in the medical sciences than in the philosophical disciplines. In the next decade, however, the situation was reversed and the relative competitive situation within the medical sciences steadily worsened through the rest of the century. Clearly, from about 1860 on,

[16] Awraham Zloczower, *Career Opportunities and the Growth of Scientific Discovery in Nineteenth Century Germany with Special Reference to Physiology,* unpublished M.A. thesis, Department of Sociology, Hebrew University, 1960.
[17] *Ibid.*

Table 4.   Number of Academic Positions in Philosophy and Physiology in the German University System, 1864-1938

Field and Academic Position	1864	1873	1880	1890	1900	1910	1920	1931	1938
Philosophy									
Ordinary Professor	36	40	43	44	42	48	56	56	36
Extraordinary Professor	21	16	12	14	14	23	30	51	34
Dozents	23	21	18	19	25	43	45	32	21
Total	81	79	75	81	85	117	140	163	117
Physiology									
Ordinary Professor	15	19	20	20	20	21	24	27	21
Extraordinary Professor	3	3	4	6	9	12	15	24	18
Dozents	9	1	2	7	20	27	22	23	15
Total	27	23	27	33	49	61	66	80	67

Note: In the German university system, the rank of Ordinary Professor is equivalent to Full Professor and Extraordinary Professor to Associate Professor. Dozents are private lecturers.

Source: Christian von Ferber, *Die Entwicklung des Lehrkörpers der deutschen Universitäten und Hochschulen,* 1864-1954, vol. III in Helmut Plessner (ed.), *Untersuchungen zur Lage der deutschen Hochschullehrer,* Göttingen: Van den Hoeck, 1953-56, pp. 204, 207.

philosophy offered much more favorable competitive conditions than did physiology. The first condition for the occurrence of role-hybridization was thus present.

The second condition was provided by the trend of the prestige conflict that raged between philosophy and the natural sciences throughout the nineteenth century in Germany. Before 1830, the great systems of Idealism claimed for philosophy the position of a super-science, deriving by speculation all that might be painstakingly discovered by empirical methods. But these pretensions were shattered by the rapidly expanding natural sciences, led first by the chemists, then by the physiologists. Paulsen notes the contempt in which speculative philosophy came to be held after the rise of the sciences in the 1830's, a contempt which was receding only at the end of the century.[18]   Hermann von Helmholtz, the physicist and physiologist, was the leading propagandist for the scientific attack on

[18] Friedrich Paulsen, *The German Universities and University Study,* New York: Longmans Green, 1906.

Table 5.   Highest Rank Reached by Scholars in the German University System Who Habilitated in the Medical Faculty and Philosophical Faculty (Natural Sciences Excluded), 1850-1909

Year and Faculty	Rank				Per cent remaining dozents
	Ordinary Professors	Extra-ordinary Professors	Privat-dozents	Total	
1850-59					
Medicine	57	19	15	91	16.5
Philosophy	53	13	15	81	18.1
1860-69					
Medicine	72	44	37	153	24.2
Philosophy	68	24	22	114	19.3
1870-79					
Medicine	94	74	53	221	24.0
Philosophy	138	24	26	188	13.8
1880-89					
Medicine	89	59	64	212	30.2
Philosophy	118	25	36	179	20.1
1890-99					
Medicine	131	57	138	326	42.3
Philosophy	162	33	66	261	25.3
1900-09					
Medicine	184	48	249	481	51.8
Philosophy	142	25	75	242	31.0

Source: von Ferber, op cit., p. 81.

philosophical speculation; in his student days in 1845 in Berlin, he banded together with a group of young scientists (including Emil Du Bois-Reymond, Ernst Brücke, and Carl Ludwig), who swore to uphold the principle: "No other forces than common physical chemical ones are active in the organism."[19]   By the 1860's, the scientists were near to extinguishing the academic reputation of philosophy and its "super-science" pretensions.[20]

Wundt began his career as a physiologist in 1857, at the height of the competition for the new chairs being created in physiology. He remained a Dozent for 17 years, however, and after being passed over

[19] Edwin G. Boring, op. cit., p. 708.
[20] G. Stanley Hall, Founders of Modern Psychology, New York: Appleton, 1912, p. 138.

for the chair of physiology at Heidelberg in 1871, made the transition to philosophy.[21] This transition was made in 1874 with the chair at the University of Zurich, which served as something of a "waiting-room" for appointments to one of the great universities in Germany proper. On the strength of his *Physiological Psychology* in that year, he won a first-class chair of philosophy at Leipzig in 1875.

Before Wundt began to take philosophy as a second reference group, he was doing the same kind of things that Helmholtz, Hering, Frans Donders, and many other physiologists were doing— experimenting on the functions of the sense-organs and the nervous system, and occasionally pointing out that their work made speculative philosophy a superfluous anachronism. Wundt had once been an assistant to Helmholtz, the leader of the anti-philosophical movement; Wundt's move into philosophy must have been an acute identity crisis for him, which could be resolved only by innovating a new philosophical method.[22] Using Fechner's empirical methods of studying perception, Wundt proposed to build metaphysics on a solid basis, thus making philosophy a science.[23] To preserve his scientific status, he was forced not only to carry out a revolution in philosophy by replacing logical speculation with empirical research, but also to widely advertise the fact that he was in a different kind of enterprise than the traditional philosophers.

Brentano, Stumpf, Müller, and Ebbinghaus were all philosophers who became interested in using empirical methods in their field. Apparently, they were aware of the onslaught physiology was making into the territory of philosophy; rather than accept its deteriorating position, they in effect "went over to the enemy." It is known that Stumpf met Fechner and E.H. Weber in his days as a Dozent;[24] Müller also corresponded with Fechner;[25] and Ebbinghaus apparently decided to re-enter the academic world after accidentally encountering a copy of Fechner's *Elements.*[26] Brentano, although he makes reference to Helmholtz, Fechner, and Wundt in his first major work, *Psychology from an Empirical*

[21] Edwin G. Boring, *op. cit.*, p. 319.

[22] Helmholtz may well have seen it as a kind of treason; there are reports that it was Helmholtz's antagonism to his former assistant that blocked the appointment of the latter to Berlin in 1894. Cf. *Ibid.*, p. 389.

[23] Hall, *op. cit.*, pp. 323-326.

[24] Edwin G. Boring, *op. cit.*, p. 363.

[25] *Ibid.*, p. 374.

[26] *Ibid.*, p. 387.

Standpoint (1874), was considerably less influenced by them than were the others. He also remained the least experimental of this group of founders. Wundt is undoubtedly the central figure. He had the largest following and he articulated the ideology of the "philosophical revolution" most clearly. The others, originally philosophers, put the position less strongly and had smaller personal followings. Yet they were role-hybrids to some extent, as clearly appears when one compares them with Fechner. The latter had the decisive idea, but was content to write about it and submit it to what Derek de Solla Price calls "the general archives of science." The philosophers, however, influenced by the example of Wundt, used it for the creation of a new role variety.

THE NEGATIVE CASES

In France, there was no innovation of using experimental methods in philosophy. There was heavy competition in the French academic system for positions in all the natural sciences; the physiologists were fairly hard-pressed, having fewer than one chair per university even at the turn of the century (Table 6). The number of available positions in philosophy was a little better. However, the relative situation was nothing like in Germany, where physiology had been filling up for several decades, whereas in France it was still expanding into all of the universities for the first time.

Table 6. Number of Academic Positions in Philosophy and Physiology in the French University System, 1892-1923

	Philosophy		*Physiology*		
Year	*Full chairs*	*Total*	*Full chairs*	*Total*	*Number of Universities[a]*
1892	17	27	10	17	15
1900	20	28	12	20	15
1910	22	30	14	27	15
1923	22	*	17	*	16

[a]Includes Collège de France.

*Figures on positions below the level of full professor are not available for 1923.

Source: *Minerva, Jahrbuch der Gelehrten Welt*, 2 (1892), 10 (1900), 20 (1910), 27 (1923).

Besides, in France a central intellectual elite existed whose status was dependent on a diffuse evaluation of excellence rather than on regular university appointments and specialized attainment.[27] The lines of demarcation between disciplines were too amorphous to mean anything for a man like Binet, who could afford to dabble in law, entomology, psychiatry, experimental psychology, and educational testing. He could expect that some kind of facilities would be created for his particular needs, and that his achievements would be recognized without the need for justifying them in the terms of a specific academic discipline.

Existing positions allowed a broad range of possible activities for their holders; Lucien Levy-Bruhl, the anthropologist, for example, held a chair of philosophy; Emile Durkheim, the sociologist, held a chair of education, and the few chairs of experimental psychology were likely to be turned over to men who were primarily psychiatrists such as Pierre Janet or Charles Blondel. The Collège de France, the most prestigious institution in France, rewarded unique individual accomplishments, but did not provide much opportunity for those following an established career, nor did it allow the training of "disciples," since its positions were for research rather than teaching. Ribot, by proselytizing German psychology, could have a new chair in Experimental Psychology established for himself at the Collège de France, but this personal recognition probably prevented him from developing a school of followers. The purely individual basis of recognition is indicated by the fact that Henri Piéron could have a new chair created for himself at the Collège de France (in the Physiology of Sensation) because the Professor of Archeology died without a suitably eminent successor.[28]

Unlike in the German system, disciplines were not differentiated sharply enough to create serious role conflicts among men with ideas. The elite comprised a single reference group of relatively nonspecialized intellectuals and "philosophers" in the old eighteenth century tradition, and prestige adhered to the individual, not to the discipline. The French system, in short, was suited to picking up intellectual innovations by specific individuals, but was not at all

[27]Joseph Ben-David and Awraham Zloczower, "Universities and Academic Systems in Modern Societies," *European Journal of Sociology*, 3 (1962), pp. 45-85.

[28]Henri Piéron, "Autobiography," in Carl Murchison (ed.), *A History of Psychology in Autobiography*, vol. IV, Worcester, Mass.: Clark University Press, 1952.

suited for giving rise to movements attempting to create a new discipline.

The same conditions which prevented the development of a reference group conflict in France existed to an even greater extent in Britain. The relative number of chairs in philosophy and physiology was similar to that in France (Table 7). Both were about one per university, with chairs in philosophy in a slight lead over those in physiology, but with the latter expanding. The necessity of gaining an academic position was even less important than in France. In the latter country, one eventually had to obtain some kind of official position. In England, even this was unnecessary.

Before 1832, there were only two universities in all England and four in Scotland, and they were little more than an upper-class intellectual backwater. Four provincial universities were founded throughout the remainder of the century and another half dozen in the first decade of the twentieth century. Under the threat of being left behind by these technologically-minded, "lower-class" universities, Oxford and Cambridge began to take in the new sciences, and in the process, to recover intellectual as well as merely social pre-eminence.[29]

This process was still going on in the late nineteenth century; both philosophy and physiology were still centered to a considerable

Table 7.   Number of Academic Positions in Philosophy and Physiology in the British University System, 1892-1923

	Philosophy		Physiology		
Year	Full chairs	Total	Full chairs	Total	Number of Universities
1892	13	15	9	20	10
1900	16	20	12	21	11
1910	19	38	14	29	16
1923	22	*	16	*	16

*Figures on positions below the level of full professor are not available for 1923.

Source: Minerva, Jahrbuch der Gelehrten Welt, 2 (1892), 10 (1900), 20 (1910), 27 (1923).

[29]Walter H. B. Armytage, Civic Universities, London: Ernest Benn, 1955, pp. 178, 206.

extent outside of the British universities.[30] From the point of view of the physiologist fighting for entrance into the conservative strongholds, the academic philosophy taught there must have seemed a somewhat outdated and unduly privileged field. But the mobility factor was missing; it was still possible to attain the highest prestige in philosophy or in physiology outside of the universities. This non-university tradition provided a safety-valve which let off the pressure which might have led to the innovation of a new psychology.

In the United States as well, an indigenous innovation of experimental psychology failed to appear; however, a large and successful movement of followers of the German psychology did spring up in the 1880's, a full decade or two before such movements (on a smaller scale) appeared in France and Britain. Before this period, there had been a very large number of small colleges in the country.[31] In these colleges, psychology was a branch of philosophy of the eighteenth-century Scottish variety, with heavily religious overtones. It was taught by the college presidents, 90 per cent of whom were clergymen.[32] Philosophy occupied the same dominant position as in Germany in the early part of the century, but in other respects the colleges resembled the philosophical faculties (the lower, "undergraduate" section) of the German universities before von Humboldt's reforms in 1810. Learning was by rote, salaries were low, and there were no facilities for research. Teaching positions were merely sinecures for unsuccessful clergymen.[33] Under these conditions, there could be no movements to innovate new disciplines: there were no positions worth competing for, the institutions were too small for specialization, and research was not a function of the academic community at all. A vigorous movement in experimental psychology, clearly derivative of the German movements, grew up only after the foundings of the first graduate schools beginning in 1876.

[30]Both Herbert Spencer and J.S. Mill, for example, held no academic positions. Physiological research was largely carried on by medical practitioners in the independent hospitals. Cf. Abraham Flexner, *Medical Education: A Comparative Study*, New York: Macmillan, 1925.

[31]There were 182 colleges in 1861, averaging six faculty members each. Cf. Richard Hofstadter and Wolfgang Metzger, *The Development of Academic Freedom in The United States*, New York: Columbia University Press, 1955, pp. 211, 233.

[32]That is, the "faculty psychology" of Thomas Reid, Dugald Stewart and Thomas Brown; for the role of the president, see Hofstadter and Metzger, *op. cit.*, p. 297.

[33]Bernard Berelson, *Graduate Education in the United States*, New York: McGraw-Hill, 1960, p. 14.

SUMMARY

The innovation of experimental psychology was brought about by the mechanism of role-hybridization. Excluding the independently originated practical traditions in Britain and France which only later became attached to the movement in experimental psychology, this innovation took place only in Germany. Three factors were required: (a) an academic rather than an amateur role for both philosophers and physiologists; (b) a better competitive situation in philosophy than in physiology encouraging the mobility of men and methods into philosophy; (c) an academic standing of philosophy below that of physiology, requiring the physiologist to maintain his scientific standing by applying his empirical methods to the materials of philosophy.

Germany had all three factors. France had a measure of the first. All the persons involved eventually acquired full-time scientific appointments, but their careers had often started outside the academic framework, and their official positions were little standardized. The second factor was present to an insignificant degree, and the latter not at all, as prestige was attached to the individual and the formal honors he received rather than to the discipline. Britain was similar to France concerning the last two factors and the first was present to an even more limited extent than in France, since the amateur pattern still prevailed widely among philosophers and physiologists. The United States before 1880 lacked even the rudiments of an academic system in which these factors could operate.

This explains why the take-off occurred in Germany. The reason France never linked up with the mainstream of the development while the United States, and eventually Britain, did, remains to be investigated.

On the Origins of Psychology
Dorothy Ross

Dorothy Ross, a former fellow in history and psychiatry at the Cornell University Medical College in New York, did her undergraduate work at Smith College. In 1965 she received her Ph.D. from Columbia University, where she wrote a thesis on G. Stanley Hall under the late Richard Hofstadter, an eminent historian. Her biography of Hall was published by the University of Chicago Press in 1971. Ross is a specialist in the history of American psychology.

In this article Ross agrees with Ben-David and Collins that social factors should be considered, but she objects to the isolation of the operation of social factors from intellectual factors. "Ideas and social phenomena generally operate in the closest interdependence." She also argues that role hybridization, which helped create scientific psychology in Germany, occurred more widely and under more varied status and competitive conditions than Ben-David and Collins suggest.

Ben-David and Collins present a stimulating synthesis of socio-logical insight and historical materials in their study of the origins of psychology as an independent scientific discipline in the late nine-teenth century (*American Sociological Review*, August, 1966). Historians of the subject, as the authors complain, do tend to pay more attention to the intellectual factors involved than to such factors as status, competition and role, with which the sociologist is more familiar. The authors have in turn, however, paid insufficient attention to the complexity of the historical situation they discuss. A more accurate reading of the facts could suggest different socio-logical conclusions.

Contary to the authors' analysis, the professional "take-off" that began in the 1870's occurred in both Germany and America, and was largely the product of the fruition and interaction of two lines of professional development: the development within philosophy of a

Dorothy Ross, On the origins of psychology. *American Sociological Review*, 1967, **32**, 466-469. Reprinted by permission of the author and the American Sociological Association.

special field of empirical psychology, which was based on physiological, psychiatric and biological data and, in part, on empirical methods; and the development within physiology of a special field devoted to the study of the physiological basis of sensation, perception and movement, using laboratory and experimental methods.

The authors' suggestion that what occurred early in the 1870's to catalyze this "take-off" was a role-hybridization by people in philosophy and physiology is a very interesting idea and, so far as I can judge, a sound one. Their attempt to make Wundt's forging of a new role the single decisive case is, however, not sound. It is based, apparently, on a dismissal of the development within philosophy itself as somehow too tainted with "speculative philosophy" to deserve independent status, and an over-emphasis on the experimental strain within scientific psychology.[1] The result of this skewed interpretation is a failure to take adequate account of the contemporaneous innovation of scientific psychology by Brentano, Stumpf and G.E. Müller in Germany, and by William James in America.[2]

Although the authors claim that Brentano, Stumpf and Müller followed Wundt's example into scientific psychology, a claim which is made on the basis of no evidence whatsoever, these three men made the commitment to scientific psychology under the influence of their mentor, Hermann Lotze, a philosopher at Göttingen who was one of the chief framers of an empirical psychology within philosophy, through his writings in the 1840's and 1850's and through teaching empirical psychology as his principal course for nearly forty years, from 1842 to 1881.[3] The publications and

---

[1] The authors may have been misled by E.G. Boring's standard text, *A History of Experimental Psychology,* which often unconsciously equates experimental and scientific psychology. Although Boring's comprehensive scholarship provides the materials for my own, contrary, analysis, below, his interpretation is shaped by his vantage point as a student of a disciple of Wundt. The authors were further misled by their superficial analysis of the literature of scientific psychology. By taking their figures only from the theoretical subsection "Experimental and Physiological Psychology" in Baldwin's *Dictionary,* Vol. III, Pt. 2, instead of from all of those subsections that comprised scientific psychology, they obscured the development in America of an indigenous psychological tradition. Had they studied the section on space and time perception, for example, they would have discovered studies by James, Hall and Bowditch, Jastrow and Ladd in the 1870's and 1880's that were clearly a part of the new scientific psychology.

[2] I limit my comments to Germany and America chiefly because of incompetence to analyze the French and British developments. I suspect, particularly in the French case, that a different analysis could be made, for the authors' bias has also obscured the considerable interaction between psychology and psychiatry in the formative decades.

[3] Having eliminated Lotze at the outset as a "speculative philosopher," the authors missed the importance of this line of development. See Wallace A. Russell, "A Note on

university appointments of Brentano, Stumpf and Müller in the early 1870's marked the fruition of the empirical philosophical tradition carried by Lotze and the point of its catalyzing into a distinct scientific psychology. What influence the new laboratory methods in psychology had on this innovation was apparently exercised by Fechner rather than by Wundt.

The importance of this development is obscured by the bias of the authors' diagram; it can be seen more clearly in the recent study by Wesley, tracing the professional antecedents of about half of the current psychological teaching force in German and Austrian universities. Wesley found that the network largely divided into "three almost equally large clusters of masters": the Lotze cluster, which developed through Brentano, Stumpf and Müller; the Wundt cluster; and the Külpe cluster, Külpe having been influenced by both Wundt and Lotze through Müller. Wesley concludes that Wundt's influence in Germany "was shared with two other great masters. As a whole the German psychology shows more historical diversification in its stem as well as in its side roots [than the American]."[4]

It is not clear, moreover, that the sociological conditions influencing Wundt to move from physiology to psychology were similar to those influencing Lotze's disciples to branch out from their parent discipline. The status and competitive situation in philosophy should not be seen only relative to physiology. Had not the prestige of generic philosophy, rooted in the tradition of *Geisteswissenschaft*, remained high, despite the decline in prestige of metaphysics, these young philosophers may have had little desire to rejuvenate the field. Had not philosophy remained a highly competitive field, they may have had little incentive to seek the advantage their competence in a distinct scientific specialty gave them.

The kinds of, and conditions for, role-hybridization were also more complex than the authors indicate in the United States. The authors conclude that no indigenous innovation of scientific psychology occurred in America, and hence fail to examine it thoroughly, on the grounds that William James was really more of a philosopher than a psychologist (although not so much of one as to exclude him from their network, which presumably includes only genuine

---

Lotze's Teaching of Psychology, 1842-1881," *Journal of the History of the Behavioral Sciences* 2 (January, 1966), pp. 74-75.

[4] Frank Wesley, "Masters and Pupils Among the German Psychologists," 1 (July, 1965), pp. 252-255.

scientific psychologists), and that his work was chiefly an exposition of European ideas and discoveries.

The latter is a bit puzzling when the authors elsewhere are so reluctant to take ideas into consideration. Their conception of intellectual activity as the result of the selection through "environmental mechanisms" of ideas "available over a relatively prolonged period of time and in several places," would seem to preclude such a criterion. Indeed, if the national origin of ideas is to be taken seriously as a criterion, it would be difficult to find *any* indigenous development of psychology. Wundt himself can appear as the expositor of English and French ideas.

James combined the empirical-philosophical and laboratory-physiological traditions which developed separately in Germany. Initially a physiologist by training and vocation, he was also, by personal inclination and study, a philosopher. Contemporaneously with Wundt, in the mid-1870's, he moved decisively into scientific psychology and for the next two decades his work bears every index of role-hybridization that does Wundt's, from the nature of his research, writing and teaching to his activity in founding some of the institutional bases of the discipline.

It is difficult to see how James' turn to philosophy in the late 1890's can alter the fact that for two crucial decades he operated as a scientific psychologist and propagated the role. The authors could have felt that James's early commitment to philosophy and his later return to it suggest that he thought of himself as a philosopher and did not "consciously identify himself as a practitioner of a new science." James did think of himself as a philosopher; he also thought of himself as a scientist, however, and he quite consciously conceived of making psychology into a science. At a time when psychology was still thought of as a part of philosophy, Wundt and G. Stanley Hall, as well as James, thought of themselves as both philosophers and scientific psychologists, with "philosopher" being the larger term, and Wundt, as well as James, turned to philosophy in his later years.

James's precedence becomes even clearer when it is recognized that Stanley Hall should be placed in the network as a student of James rather than Wundt. This fact is not easy to establish from the standard literature on the subject, which relies heavily on Hall's own *Life and Confessions,* which is often inaccurate and distorted. While Ben-David and Collins say only that Hall "did not take his degree with Wundt," even the standard literature reports, however, that Hall did take his degree with James in 1878, the first Ph.D. in the subject of psychology to be awarded in this country.[5] My own research on Hall makes it clear that while his intellectual development was leading him toward scientific psychology, he owed his adoption of the field as a professional identity to his two years of study under James. His subsequent studies in Germany brought him into far less contact with and influence by Wundt than is ordinarily supposed.[6]

The careers of James and Hall indicate the error of the authors' contention that there were no academic institutions in America advanced enough to allow specialization. The academic scene was dismal enough without its being reduced to caricature. Advanced scientific training existed at Harvard and Yale since 1847. Yale had awarded the Ph.D. degree in arts and sciences since 1860, Harvard after 1872. In his studies and teaching at Harvard, and in his work in H.P. Bowditch's new physiological laboratory in the Harvard Medical School after 1871, James was participating in the early development of advanced university work in the country.

Nor should the generally elementary and theological tone of most higher education in America automatically eliminate it from consideration. Many strains of religious opinion in America remained hospitable to the advance of various aspects of natural science, and many professors managed to carry on independent advanced work despite the institutional pressures against it. A number of minister-philosophers of the old regime, like Ladd at Yale and McCosh at Princeton, were receptive to all or some of the new work in scientific psychology, studied it, and led a number of their students into the new field.

The American case, then, presents the picture of an indigenous development of psychology which is very early reinforced by the German development. And, as it happens, the social conditions influencing the American innovation were very different from those in Germany. In America during the 1870's, philosophy still held a higher status than natural science, a situation that reflected its traditional ties with theology. Both James's and Hall's early commitment to the pursuit of philosophy reflected that prestige. Natural science was already rising in status in intellectual and academic circles in the

---

[5] E.g., Boring, *Experimental Psychology*, p. 519.

[6] Dorothy Ross, "G. Stanley Hall, 1844-1895: Aspects of Science and Culture in the Nineteenth Century," Doctoral Dissertation, Columbia University, 1965.

1870's, however, and both James and Hall, in turning to scientific work, reflected that fact, as well. In the society at large, as in their own minds, the status judgments of the older American culture and of the newer scientific professions coexisted uneasily.

Moreover, the competitive situation in philosophy in the 1870's was very difficult for a young man. James found philosophy pre-empted at Harvard by mature men and had little chance of receiving an appointment in the department until his reputation and religious standing were more secure. Hall, trying to make his way in the smaller colleges of the Midwest, found an opening in philosophy only by the chance of a college temporarily without its minister-president, and when one was found, he had to leave. To the extent this com-petitive situation influenced James's choice of career, it influenced him towards taking an academic appointment in physiology, a field which was just beginning to expand in America and which presented fewer obstacles to the appointment of a young man.[7]

James, then, presents the case of a physiologist moving over the course of his career towards philosophy, the field of high prestige and difficult access, by means of specializing in scientific psychology, a field which allowed him to use the scientific methods which were rising in prestige. Hall, in turn, grasped James's innovation in the hope it would give him the access to academic philosophy he sought. In the 1880's Hall did eventually find a place in the Johns Hopkins philosophy department on the basis of his distinct scientific specialty within philosophy, and promptly used his position and the rising prestige of science to vanquish the other philosophers in the depart-ment and turn it into the first chair specifically for scientific psychol-ogy in the country, in 1884.

If my reading of the historical situation is correct, the role-hybridization that helped create psychology as an independent discipline occurred more widely and under more varied status and competitive conditions than Ben-David and Collins suggest. As a member of that berated guild of "historians of ideas," I must admit that I am tempted to see the authors' failure to recognize this complexity as a result of a more pervasive predilection for simplicity,

[7] R.B. Perry, *The Thought and Character of William James*, I, p. 325, comments that "Physiology, psychology, and philosophy all attracted [James], and he ended by teaching them all; physiology coming first, not because his interest was greatest, but because the first opportunity came to him in that field."

a simplicity which is suggested as well by their desire to prove by this study that "social factors played an important role, independently of intellectual content." In this case, as in most historical cases, social factors do play an important role, but how can they be said to operate "independently of intellectual content"? Could the social situation in Germany have created scientific psychology without the existence of the ideas that animated Lotze, Wundt and their colleagues? Is it an accident that the physiological profession in Germany was prestigious, crowded and highly competitive at a time when physiological knowledge had advanced to the point of penetrating psychoneurological functioning? Is it possible for a scientific profession of psychology to have been established except on the basis of ideas conducive to scientific institutionalization?[8] Ideas and social phenomena generally operate in the closest interdependence. I hardly think the scientific status of sociology will be advanced by attempting to raise the dignity of the social dimension of reality at the expense of the integrity of the whole social fabric.

[8] The authors are surely ingenuous to remark that earlier attempts to apply physiological understanding to psychology, like that of Descartes and the British associationists, did not of themselves create a "continuous scientific tradition." The state of physiological knowledge before the nineteenth century hardly permitted the continuous productivity required for institutionalization. When physiological precision, among other factors, permitted such a development, James, in fact, brought the British tradition into scientific psychology.

Reply to Ross
Joseph Ben-David
Randall Collins

In this final article of Part II, Ben-David and Collins respond to Ross' criticisms and reaffirm their original position—namely, that "only by defining social factors independently and by trying to isolate their effects from those of intellectual content shall we ever be able to learn anything worthwhile about the interdependence of ideas and social phenomena."

We welcome the detailed comment of Dr. Dorothy Ross, and are especially gratified by the fact that she is a historian, since collaboration—which includes mutual criticism—between historians and sociologists can greatly advance research in both fields. At the same time, however, it should be pointed out that much of her criticism is due to a failure to appreciate the difference between what we called "idea hybridization" on the one hand and "role hybridization" on the other. The former is a cross-fertilization of ideas from different fields, which occurs quite often. Its effects are usually not far-reaching, because this kind of innovation does not create new research techniques. Role hybridization, on the other hand, does involve the development of new techniques. It is, therefore, a difficult and rare achievement which usually leads to rapid developments.

If we understand it correctly the main criticism of Dr. Ross concerns our neglect of the speculative and our "over-emphasis on the experimental strain" in psychology. This is an important issue, but before trying to explain the rationale of our position, we have to deal first with her criticism of our alleged mistakes about facts and their interpretations. She accuses us of not having taken adequate account of the contemporaneous innovation of scientific psychology

Joseph Ben-David and Randall Collins, Reply to Ross. *American Sociological Review*, 1967, **32**, 469-472. Reprinted by permission of the authors and the American Sociological Association.

by Brentano, Stumpf and G.E. Müller in Germany and by William James in America.

Concerning Wundt's contemporaries in Germany, we have clearly said that independent beginnings were made by Brentano, Stumpf, Müller and Ebbinghaus and that these beginnings were made under the influence of Fechner, Weber and Helmholtz. Following this we explicitly stated that "they were role-hybrids to some extent" (p. 463). It is nowhere implied that these men were followers of Wundt into scientific psychology, only that Wundt was "the central figure. He had the largest following and he articulated the 'philosophical revolution' most clearly"; the others were influenced by his example in the "creation of a new role variety." The basis of this last statement was that Wundt was older, a full professor and the author of the programmatic *"Physiological Philosophy"* before Stumpf and Müller even got their *Habilitations,* and the evidence for this is shown in Figure 1 (p. 456).

None of this is contradicted by Wesley's data (only by his conclusion). Even though Wesley uses a different population (members of the *Deutsche Gesellschaft f. Psychologie* in 1962 who were, or had been regular teachers at German or Austrian universities), and a different criterion of influence (he asked his population who had the greatest influence on them, while our criterion was whether a person was actually a student or an assistant of a teacher), his lines of influence, when counted, show, like ours, the overwhelming influence of Wundt. The only "bias" in our diagram is the omission of Lotze, for which we gave sufficient reasons, namely, that he was not an experimental psychologist.

The position of Külpe as a student of both Wundt and Müller is clearly shown in our diagram, and it is misleading to quote this from Wesley, implying thereby that this was something we missed. What Dr. Ross fails to see here—as well as in Wesley's account—is that Külpe, who was also a student of Wundt, was the only one who had a significant following among Müller's students. And this is the crucial point since it shows better than anything else that the Wundt "strain" proved the strongest as far as scientific succession is concerned. For the evolution of experimental psychology as a growing field of activity (though not for the evolution of scientific ideas) this reduces the three clusters of masters to two, and not two "almost equally" large ones, but an overwhelmingly large, and a very small one. Even this small one can hardly be called the "Lotze cluster," since Brentano had little following among psychologists apart from Stumpf, who must have read Wundt and known of his methods of work even before he completed his *Habilitationsschrift.*

There is, on the other hand, a great deal of interest in what Dr. Ross says about William James, and the United States in general. Her comment contains relevant information and important considerations which we hope to deal with in a later publication. There is certainly more to be said about the rapidity with which psychology was developed in the United States—much beyond anything that had existed in Germany. But as far as the first creation of the role of experimental psychologist is concerned, we see no reason to change our interpretation. James was not a founder in this field of equal importance with Wundt for two reasons. (1) Unlike Wundt, he did not introduce regular laboratory work and instruction on any significant scale. Physiology for him—even though he was trained in it—was a source of ideas rather than of methods. His physiological training was also much more deficient than that of Wundt. The latter had been a *Privatdozent* in physiology and the assistant of Helmholtz for several years, while James had despaired of doing serious experimental work as soon as he got the first taste of it, nor did he change his mind subsequently.[1] But the role innovation which eventually turned the psychologist into an entirely different intellectual type than the philosopher, or even other social scientists, was laboratory work. James had some sympathy for the new role, at one time played with the idea of taking it up himself, and had as much understanding of it as anyone not really prepared to practice it could have had. But—in contrast with Wundt—he was not himself a practitioner. We are indebted to Dr. Ross for providing us with the opportunity to repeat this more unequivocally than in the original paper. She is perfectly right that our remarks on James' lack of originality and eventual turning to philosophy, as phrased in the paper, were irrelevant. We should have been more explicit and said that the idea of taking up experimental psychology occurred to James in Germany while studying with DuBois-Reymond and under the influence of the work of Wundt and Helmholtz. He knew about the latter two and intended at one time to work with them, but his

---

[1] Cf. R.B. Perry, *The Thought and Character of William James,* Cambridge: Harvard University Press, 1948, pp. 84-85, 106-107, and 180-185; and R.I. Watson, *The Great Psychologists,* Philadelphia: Lippincott, 1963, p. 326.

state of health and—it would seem—lack of real motivation prevented him from carrying out his intention.[2]

(2) Whatever advances had occurred in the 1860's, only in the 1880's and the 1890's, with the return of an increasing number of American students from Germany, did the ideas of systematic research and strict scientific discipline become regular functions of the American university. The career of William James and his moves from subject to subject within the same university had been still a reflection of the semi-amateur teaching and research pattern of American colleges and universities and not the deliberate creation of a new kind of scientific role. This is why we accepted Hall's account of the influence of his stay in Germany. Even if his reminiscences are inaccurate, the evidence that only in Europe and especially in Germany did American scholars at that time obtain a conception of professional science is corroborated from so many other sources that we have no reason to doubt the importance of his stay in Germany in this respect, even if he was less influenced by Wundt than was generally assumed.[3] Incidentally, we pointed out that he did not take his degree with Wundt in order not to overstate Hall's link with the latter. We notice, however, that, due to a mistake in the copying of Figure 4 (on p. 458), the link between Hall and James was omitted. We use this opportunity to correct this error, but it should be emphasized that this does not affect our conclusions. Hall's case is an exact parallel with that of Külpe. As was the case among the students of Lotze, the only student of James with a large following was the one who also studied with Wundt. This, in fact, to a certain extent makes controlled cases of Külpe and Hall, similar to others in that they were students of masters other than Wundt, but differing from them by studying also with Wundt and in the result one would expect from this latter circumstance, namely, the number of their successors.

On this basis we decided to treat the American case as originally a transplantation from Germany, but pointed out without going into details that the transplant found extremely fertile soil on which to grow in the new country. This is only one shade different from Dr. Ross's position according to which "the American case . . .

---

[2] Perry, *op. cit.*, pp. 85 and 106-107.
[3] Cf. F.M. Albrecht, *The New Psychology in America, 1880-1895*, unpublished Ph.D. dissertation, Baltimore: Johns Hopkins University, 1960.

presents the picture of an indigenous development of psychology which is very early reinforced by the German development." What Dr. Ross had to say about the relationship between philosophy, physiology and psychology at the American universities was interesting and we believe that it is highly relevant to the spread of the new discipline in the U.S.[4] But the conditions were not ripe for role hybridization. This latter involves the existence of clearly defined roles and the conscious and competent application of the methods of the one role to the problems of the other. It has not been demonstrated that this ever occurred in American psychology independently of Germany.

This brings us back to the main difference between our approach and that of Dr. Ross. We have chosen to emphasize the emergence of experimental psychology, and not the other types of more or less empirically oriented branches of psychology, because experimentalism lent to psychology its distinctive and unique character. Psychology, in common with the other social sciences, has recently been differentiated from philosophy. But unlike economics, sociology, anthropology and political science, all of which are intellectual crossbreeds between philosophy and some kind of exact or empirical scientific approach, psychology is the only one which has actually become a laboratory science. It is true that experimentalists are not the only psychologists, but they are central enough to have implanted into the practice of scientific psychology customs and institutional forms which have made it into a uniquely fast-growing cooperative enterprise among the social sciences, reminiscent of the natural sciences. Investigations in psychology are repeated and there are broad fronts of interlinked research on specialized topics published in specialized journals.

Dr. Ross is correct in stating that the development of an empirically oriented psychology within philosophy, using all kinds of observational data, was an important element in the growth of modern psychology. However, without the actual entrance into the field by people who grew up in a physiological laboratory and for whom experimentation was a habit rather than something requiring a special effort, and without such people consciously and deliberately attempting to persevere in their old methods in attacking the new objects, psychology would have been an entirely different discipline.

[4] For further details on this, cf. R. Collins' M.A. thesis quoted in our original paper.

In order to identify the point and the circumstances in which it assumed its present characteristics, we had to use a clear definition to distinguish experimental psychology from other types of empirically oriented psychologies. We were not misled into doing this by any of our sources, but made a deliberate decision, and stated our reasons for it.

All that we intended to do was to find the conditions in which psychology turned into an experimental science (without taking a stand on whether this development was desirable by some external criterion). The conditions were optimal in Germany, and Wundt (for whom otherwise we hold no brief either as a psychologist or as a philosopher) happened to play a key role in the events. Others might have had better ideas than his, but he—or someone like him—was necessary to turn psychology into a cumulative experimental activity in fact and not only as an ideal. This explains his importance as a "father" of the next psychological generation which was out of all proportion to the importance of his psychological ideas relative to those of his contemporaries.

Our attempt to define the problem and to isolate the conditions does not represent any predilection for simplicity. Nor do we disregard the role of ideas. On the contrary, we believe that only by defining social factors independently and by trying to isolate their effects from those of intellectual content shall we ever be able to learn anything worthwhile about the interdependence of ideas and social phenomena. "The integrity of the whole social fabric" is a beautiful phrase, but if we refrain from dissecting it we shall know as little about it as our ancestors knew about the human body before the days of Vesalius.

III

Theoretical
Issues in
Psychology

Webster's dictionary lists more than a dozen definitions of the word *issue*. One of them is "a matter that is in dispute between two or more parties: a point of debate or controversy." It is in this sense that the word is used here. The theoretical issues of psychology are diverse. Some are basic and general and pertain to the very nature of psychology—its goals and methods. Others are related to various specific aspects of psychology, such as learning, perception, and emotion. Some, such as the body-mind problem, are perennial; others, such as the issue of mental chronometry or attributes of sensation in the past, are temporary and ephemeral. Many of the problems, both past and present, had their roots in psychology's philosophical ancestry. However, it must be realized that cultural, socioeconomic, and political conditions also influence the appearance, sharpness, and urgency of psychological issues.

The readings in Part III illustrate how theoretical issues are formulated and discussed. With the exception of Skinner, the authors of these articles are principally historians or theoreticians. Boring and Skinner discuss behaviorism. Correnti discusses an entirely new orientation in American psychology—existentialism—and contrasts it with behaviorism and psychoanalysis. Watson identifies the theoretical formulas or prescriptions that have guided psychology. Koch examines an intriguing and vital issue for our time, the relationship between science and the humanities. Royce points out the need and benefits of theorizing in psychology. Finally, Coan tells us how we can objectively analyze and evaluate theories. These issues will probably continue to be discussed for some time. Other issues will continually emerge as each era and each generation create and encounter new problems.

The Trend toward Mechanism
Edwin G. Boring

This article represents one of Boring's last works. It is an introduction to a symposium held on April 24, 1964, and chaired by Boring. The symposium was organized to review the position of operant behaviorism with regard to certain traditional topics of psychology. In this introduction Boring, as a historian, traces the path of psychology from Descartes to the "new psychology" of operant behaviorism. This form of behaviorism, in Boring's view, has successfully emerged as "a new phase of the understanding of the conduct of men and animals." It is to be noted, however, that not only the mechanistic tradition but also the antimechanistic tradition derived from the Cartesian dualism. The latter tradition has led to an orientation that is opposed to behaviorism: the "Third Force" in American psychology—that is, another theoretical framework in addition to behaviorism and psychoanalysis.

The contributions to the symposium are summarized by Boring. The reader who is interested can read them in their entirety in the *Proceedings of the American Philosophical Society*, 1964, **108**(6). A criticism of the symposium was written by philosopher Brand Blanshard and was published in the *Proceedings*, 1965, **109**, 22-28.

The belief in a fundamental dualistic dichotomy between the corporeal and the mental is very old, but it was Descartes who impressed this distinction upon philosophy and common sense, the absolute difference between matter and mind, or, as Descartes put it, between extended substance and unextended substance. Ever since then the mental philosophers have been offered a Procrustean bed. Should subjectivism be decapitated to rid it of its protruding epiphenomenal consciousness, or should objectivism be stretched to include immediate awareness, which is the basis of all scientific observation?[1]

Edwin G. Boring, The trend toward mechanism. *Proceedings of the American Philosophical Society*, 1964, **108**, 451-454. Reprinted by permission of the American Philosophical Society.

[1] On the history of behavioristics and the trend toward mechanism, see Edwin G. Boring, *A History of Experimental Psychology* (2nd ed., New York, 1950), pp. 620-633; also "A History of Introspection," *Psychol. Bull.* **50** (1953): pp. 169-189; reprinted in Boring, *Psychologist at Large* (New York, 1961), pp. 210-245.

At first the subjectivists won, at least in respect of man, though not for animals, for even Descartes regarded infrahuman organisms as automata. But how could anyone deny the reality of immediate experience in man? William James eventually summed the matter up:

> *Introspective Observation is what we have to rely on first and foremost and always.* The word introspection hardly needs to be defined—it means, of course, looking into our own minds and reporting what we there discover. *Everyone agrees that we there discover states of consciousness.* So far as I know, the existence of such states has never been doubted by any critic, however critical in other respects he may have been. That we have *cogitations* of some sort is the *inconcussum* in a world most of whose other facts have at some time tottered in the breath of philosophical doubt.[2]

This faith, which established dualism as fundamental to an understanding of the nature of man, dominated psychology from Descartes almost to the present, or at any rate from John Locke in 1690 to William James in 1890. The British empiricists, Locke and David Hume (1740), were dualists, metaphysical dualists, as was also David Hartley (1749), although not Bishop Berkeley (1709), who was so sure of the existence of immediate experience that he regarded physical objects as formed out of ideas by inference. The later philosophers in this school were epistemological dualists, like John Stuart Mill (1843), who believed that the distinction lies in the point of view from which experience is viewed. This faith set the epistemological beliefs of the new experimental psychologists, Fechner (1860), Helmholtz (1867), and Wundt (1874), who based their systematic positions upon psychophysical parallelism, the notion that certain events in a closed physical system, which is partly neural and partly environmental, are accompanied by psychic events that parallel them. Introspection, the principal reliance of the mental philosophers, was taken over as the primary psychological method by these new psychologists, and psychology itself seemed to be firmly established as dualistic even as late as 1910.

Nevertheless, through the years, dualistic subjectivism was constantly being invaded by physicalistic objectivism. Dualism

---

[2]William James, *Principles of Psychology* (2 v., New York, 1890) 1: p. 185.

presented a baffling mystery. How could so immaterial an event as an awareness cause a material neural process or be caused by one under the theory of mind-body interaction, or how could certain physical processes in some nerves, yet not in others, always generate extra immaterial events under the theory of psychophysical parallelism, the events that are peculiarly available to observation by introspection? This mystery was increased when it became apparent that these psychic events were often perceived as purposive in nature and also as subject to the action of a will which enjoyed a certain amount of freedom. Science needed more positive concepts than such vague and indeterminate relations.

The resistance to dualism began with the French materialists—J. O. de La Mettrie in 1748 and P. J. G. Cabanis in 1802, who were thinking in the tradition of Descartes that animal activity is reflex and automatic and extended the view to man. There was Auguste Comte (1830-1842) who denied the possibility of introspection. Objection was so natural that it sprang up without persuasion from the logic of the situation. There were the Russian reflexologists, with I. M. Sechenov who wrote on thinking as "reflexes of the brain" in 1863, and his two distinguished disciples, I. P. Pavlov and V. M. Bekhterev who, perhaps not uninfluenced by dialectical materialism, turned Russian psychology firmly away from subjectivism, presenting it as a branch of physiology and so preparing a way for American behaviorism.

Meanwhile, under the influence of Darwin, animal psychology was starting up, at first in England and on the Continent and then in America. Interest in the continuity of mind from animals to man established a special interest in the levels of animal intelligence, but the anecdotes of the dog, cat and horse lovers soon fell into disrepute with C. Lloyd Morgan's establishment of his canon of parsimony (1894), the rule that the inference from behavior to consciousness must always be as simple as possible. For the simpler species, first plants and then the lower organisms, Jacques Loeb (1899) showed that behavior can be explained on mechanistic principles, the tropism. He was still writing about forced movements and animal conduct after the behavioristic movement was well under way.

John B. Watson is regarded as having started the behavioristic movement in 1913 because he was an entrepreneur and invented the term, although, as we have seen, the movement was old and continuous and the birth of behaviorism was simply one event in a genetic process.[3] Watson no more than Loeb denied the existence of consciousness, but he felt that it could be regarded as scientifically irrelevant and recommended that it be ignored. His systematic text of 1919, attempting, as it did, to cover the conventional field of psychology, is considered to have been epistemologically naive because it sought principally to substitute physiological events for mental instead of undertaking to explain the inescapable connection between them. In this volume for the facts of learning he took over from Pavlov the concept of the conditioned reflex. For sensory phenomena he substituted the discriminatory response. Introspection became verbal report, and in that respect he spoke more wisely than he knew, for introspection involves report, and report, if its data are to get into science, is behavior. Later in the hands of the positivists and the operationists it became obvious that the behavioristic view is invulnerable, since any report of conscious phenomena can be reduced to the behavior that is the report.

Edwin B. Holt (1915) was the first person to give philosophical sophistication to Watson's view.[4] He showed how cognition can be understood as discrimination which is behavioral and he undertook in his discussion of the Freudian wish to bring purpose back into an objective psychology. Edward C. Tolman, his follower, systematized this purposive behaviorism further, and that contribution is discussed by Herrnstein in this Symposium.[5] Other outstanding behaviorists of the period 1920 to 1950 were Max Meyer, Karl S. Lashley, Albert P. Weiss, Walter S. Hunter, and B. F. Skinner. Lashley and Hunter were content for the most part to promote research that showed how the problems of psychology can be solved in behavioral terms without reference to consciousness, but Skinner also made systematic proposals which eventually changed the nature of behaviorism and extended its applicability.

Meanwhile the logical positivists had been discovered by American psychologists, perhaps more through P. W. Bridgman's argument for

[3] John B. Watson, "Psychology as the Behaviorist Views It," *Psychol. Rev.* **20** (1913): pp. 158-177. Watson's systematic text is *Psychology from the Standpoint of a Behaviorist* (Philadelphia, 1919).

[4] Edwin B. Holt, *The Freudian Wish and Its Place in Ethics* (New York 1915), which reprints as a supplement Holt's "Response and Cognition," *Jour. Philos.* **12** (1915): pp. 365-373, 393-409.

[5] Edward C. Tolman, *Purposive Behavior in Animals and Men* (New York, 1932).

the operational definition of concepts than by direct acquaintance with the work of the Vienna Circle itself.[6] Herbert Feigl was the emissary from Vienna who patiently explained the new operational positivism to American psychologists; and in the 1930's they took over this epistemological schema with enthusiasm. Skinner was one of them.

At first Skinner was concerned to rule out of psychology the events in the nervous system as well as those alleged to be in consciousness. Behavior, he held, is to be understood in terms of reflexes, but a reflex is a correlation between stimulus and response and concern with any neural connection between the two is irrelevant. That was a new kind of pure reflexology and, although Skinner could make use of the Pavlovian conditioned reflexes in which a secondary stimulus is substituted for the original one, he regarded these functional relations as mere observed correlations, ignoring the physiological connection between them. In this conception of a causal relation between stimulus and response he was following Ernst Mach more than the logical positivists, and perhaps also Hume: cause is correlation.[7]

Skinner, however, soon went much further. He introduced the important concepts of reinforcement and operant conditioning. The classical conception was that learning takes place by the continued repetition of contiguous associations: the more frequent the previous concurrence, the more likely the present realization of one associate when the other is given. Thorndike had shown nevertheless that associations and trains of conduct become reinforced when they lead to success, that is to say, to the realization of the learner's intent as in obtaining food or being rewarded in some other way. Thorndike called this reinforcement by success or reward the law of effect, and Skinner adopted this principle, showing how such reinforcement again and again shapes behavior into the pattern which has proved to lead to reward.[8]

The Pavlovian conception of the conditioned reflex was never satisfactory. It was that inherited (unconditioned) reflexes can be

---

[6] Percy W. Bridgman, *The Logic of Modern Physics* (New York, 1927).

[7] B. F. Skinner, "The Concept of the Reflex in the Description of Behavior," *Jour. General Psychol.* 5 (1931): pp. 427-458—the original discussion of the reflex as a correlation without specified neural connection.

[8] B. F. Skinner, *The Behavior of Organisms* (New York, 1938); *Science and Human Behavior* (New York, 1953); *Cumulative Record* (2nd ed., New York, 1961), which reprints 33 of Skinner's publications from 1931 to 1961.

changed by learning so that a new (conditioned) stimulus can be substituted for the original one. The animal, having always salivated when the food stimulus is in its mouth, now by conditioning salivates at the sight of food, and later by another conditioning when it hears the dinner bell. What Skinner saw was that it is not necessary to consider the unconditioned stimulus at all. If you reinforce with a proper reward any chance movement of a subject, the movement is likely to be repeated, when it can be reinforced again, and so on as behavior is shaped. Herrnstein describes this process. This is what Skinner has called operant conditioning. Its introduction into behavioral psychology has radically altered the Watsonian conception of how an organism learns its repertoire of behaviors.

While Skinner's views have by no means received universal acceptance in America and even less abroad, he has a constantly increasing number of enthusiastic followers, who by their research are reinterpreting the old concepts into the new behavioral terms with such success that it is not far wrong to say that there has emerged in psychology a new phase of the understanding of the conduct of men and animals, a new phase that is, nevertheless, the natural part of the long history of the understanding of mind from Descartes on down to the present. There is still a belief in the necessity for the concept of consciousness, especially among the phenomenologists and existentialists on the Continent, as well as with many philosophers, but in America just now the new psychology is this operant behaviorism. For that reason some of us planned this symposium in order to present to the intellectually élite a picture of the new movement and its significance. We chose for our titles ancient psychological terms in order to emphasize the continuity of psychology in the face of constant change. The papers themselves show what the new view is, even though the six authors have not sought to curb their idiosyncrasies in order to achieve consistency.

Herrnstein comes first with "will" and the concept of motivation. By describing operant conditioning and a situation in which one pigeon shapes the behavior of another, with the conduct of each pigeon reinforced by food when the behavior fits the experimenter's intent, he shows how both learning and purpose are handled in the new psychology. He discusses the relation of purpose to cause, and thus the relation of reinforcement in operant conditioning to selection in evolution, two situations in which apparent purposiveness has been reduced to the more scientific causal relation, the substitution of a push for a pull.

Guttman comes next with the topic of "experience," that is to say, an account of the way in which the new behaviorism determines with animals the form of sensory functions which have hitherto been established by introspective psychophysics. He shows how the rate of a rat's pressing a bar to get food, the rate of its drinking, and the rate of its heart beat are direct functions of sugar concentration in the stimulus, and also how one can demonstrate in an animal the degree of similarity and difference in the perceived wavelength of monochromatic light, in the brightness of light, in the inclination of a vertical illuminated bar, and in the pitch of a tone. Thus we see how sense-differences can be measured by operant procedures.

Teitelbaum, with the topic of "appetite," considers hunger, appetite, and the regulation of food intake. He describes research on the physiology of feeding and its internal regulation. The unfed animal ordinarily eats. The fed animal presently stops eating. These drives at first appear under regulation by the hypothalamus, but it turns out in due course that gustatory stimulus also plays an important role. An animal with hypothalamic damage may starve to death in the presence of nutritious tasteless food, but return to adequate eating if the food be sweetened. Teitelbaum remarks that the history of belief on this matter has now gone the full circle, starting from von Haller's belief that taste is a motivator inciting eating (1763), moving on to the view that the phageal drive is under control of the hypothalamus and is not sensory, and returning now to von Haller's belief again. This circle does not mean, however, that the psychophysiologist is returning to introspection. Von Haller thought functionally about sensation. For him sensory stimulation and sensory events, having the purpose of preserving the organism, were motivators.

Dews, under the heading "humors," discusses the relation of current to traditional psychopharmacology. He shows how Skinner's new concept of scheduling reinforcements turns the problems of motivation into studies of learning and how the psychopharmacological problem can be attacked in this way. He also notes how split-second electronic automation in these researches makes possible greater quantities of more precise observation than could be achieved under the older method of observation by eye and recording by hand.

Sidman, speaking of "anxiety," deplores the vague use of the concept, showing how it can be given exact specification in experimentally specific situations in which rats and monkeys are placed. He shows how compulsions can be set up in monkeys and discusses the implications of these techniques for animal and human coercion. He also gives the inverse view of the way in which reinforcement can control behavior without coercion, as occurs with the teaching machines that induce education without counter-aggression. Like all new powerful agents the new psychology needs to be used in social control with discrimination, wisdom, and grace.

Finally Skinner turns to the topic of "man" to defend man's dignity, as it were. The scientific view of man pictures him as the site of the interaction of external forces from heredity and environment. By the manipulation of external variables behavior can be shaped. The child can be taught self-control and also to want to do the right things. A science of man moves away from the consideration of covert inner activities to experimentation with variables accessible to observation, variables which are proving in practice to be adequate. Does this new knowledge of the causes of man's conduct lessen his dignity? Skinner asks this question, and notes that man, a product of so many complex variables, still remains individually unique. As such he could remain worthy of admiration, but it can be questioned whether this support of man's vanity is necessary or good. At any rate, Skinner remarks that the new psychology has not changed the nature of man. It has merely increased his understanding of himself. Science cannot rob a fact.

Behaviorism at Fifty
B. F. Skinner

In 1913, in the March issue of the *Psychological Review*, John B. Watson announced a new psychology, behaviorism—that is, psychology redone and rewritten in terms of behavior or, as he put it, "stimulus and response . . . habit formation, habit integration and the like." Fifty years later, in 1963, B.F. Skinner, the acknowledged most distinguished representative and most successful champion of behavioristic psychology, reexamined the behavioristic thesis, confronted it again with mentalistic psychology, and reviewed the issues and studies that occupy behaviorism now. This endeavor, reprinted here, was originally an address at a symposium on behaviorism and phenomenology at Rice University in 1963.

Skinner received his Ph.D. in psychology from Harvard in 1931. He taught at the Universities of Minnesota and Indiana and in 1948 joined the faculty of Harvard, where he is now Edgar Pierce Professor of Psychology. His first book was *The Behavior of Organisms* (1938). His other works include *Walden Two* (1948), *Science and Human Behavior* (1953), *Verbal Behavior* (1957), *Schedules of Reinforcement* (1957), and *The Technology of Teaching* (1968). Thirty-three articles by Skinner were reprinted in *Cumulative Record* (1958, rev. ed. 1961).

Since Skinner is one of the most influential psychologists, the following article is of particular interest because it reveals his scientific creed and behaviorism's ambition not merely as a psychological school but as a philosophy of science. The article tells us what the behavioristic program is half a century after its inception and at the same time attests to the persistence of the behavioristic thesis—a thesis that has met with increasing opposition in recent years.

Behaviorism, with an accent on the last syllable, is not the scientific study of behavior but a philosophy of science concerned with the subject matter and methods of psychology. If psychology is a science of mental life—of the mind, of conscious experience—then it must develop and defend a special methodology, which it has not yet done successfully. If it is, on the other hand, a science of the behavior of organisms, human or otherwise, then it is part of biology,

B.F. Skinner, Behaviorism at fifty. *Science*, 1963, **140**, 951-958. Reprinted by permission of the author and the American Association for the Advancement of Science. © 1963 by the American Association for the Advancement of Science.

a natural science for which tested and highly successful methods are available. The basic issue is not the nature of the stuff of which the world is made, or whether it is made of one stuff or two, but rather the dimensions of the things studied by psychology and the methods relevant to them.

Mentalistic or psychic explanations of human behavior almost certainly originated in primitive animism. When a man dreamed of being at a distant place in spite of incontrovertible evidence that he had stayed in his bed, it was easy to conclude that some part of him had actually left his body. A particularly vivid memory or a hallucination could be explained in the same way. The theory of an invisible, detachable self eventually proved useful for other purposes. It seemed to explain unexpected or abnormal episodes, even to the person behaving in an exceptional way because he was thus "possessed." It also served to explain the inexplicable. An organism as complex as man often seems to behave capriciously. It is tempting to attribute the visible behavior to another organism inside—to a little man or homunculus. The wishes of the little man become the acts of the man observed by his fellows. The inner idea is put into outer words. Inner feelings find outward expression. The explanation is satisfying, of course, only so long as the behavior of the homunculus can be neglected.

Primitive origins are not necessarily to be held against an explanatory principle, but the little man is still with us in relatively primitive form. He was recently the hero of a television program called "Gateways to the Mind," one of a series of educational films sponsored by Bell Telephone Laboratories and written with the help of a distinguished panel of scientists. The viewer learned, from animated cartoons, that when a man's finger is pricked, electrical impulses resembling flashes of lightning run up the afferent nerves and appear on a television screen in the brain. The little man wakes up, sees the flashing screen, reaches out, and pulls a lever. More flashes of lightning go down the nerves to the muscles, which then contract, as the finger is pulled away from the threatening stimulus. The behavior of the homunculus was, of course, not explained. An explanation would presumably require another film. And it, in turn, another.

The same pattern of explanation is invoked when we are told that the behavior of a delinquent is the result of a disordered personality, or that the vagaries of a man under analysis are due to conflicts among his superego, ego, and id. Nor can we escape from primitive features by breaking the little man into pieces and dealing with his wishes, cognitions, motives, and so on, bit by bit. The objection is not that these things are mental but that they offer no real explanation and stand in the way of a more effective analysis.

It has been about 50 years since the behavioristic objection to this practice was first clearly stated, and it has been about 30 years since it has been very much discussed. A whole generation of psychologists has grown up without really coming into contact with the issue. Almost all current textbooks compromise: rather than risk a loss of adoptions, they define psychology as the science of behavior *and* mental life. Meanwhile the older view has continued to receive strong support from areas in which there has been no comparable attempt at methodological reform. During this period, however, an effective experimental science of behavior has emerged. Much of what it has discovered bears on the basic issue. A restatement of radical behaviorism would therefore seem to be in order.

EXPLAINING THE MIND

A rough history of the idea is not hard to trace. An occasional phrase in classic Greek authors which seemed to foreshadow the point of view need not be taken seriously. We may also pass over the early bravado of a La Mettrie who could shock the philosophical bourgeoisie by asserting that man was only a machine. Nor were those who, for practical reasons, simply preferred to deal with behavior rather than with less accessible, but nevertheless acknowledged, mental activities close to what is meant by behaviorism today.

The entering wedge appears to have been Darwin's preoccupation with the continuity of species. In supporting the theory of evolution, it was important to show that man was not essentially different from the lower animals—that every human characteristic, including consciousness and reasoning powers, could be found in other species. Naturalists like Romanes began to collect stories which seemed to show that dogs, cats, elephants, and many other species were conscious and showed signs of reasoning. It was Lloyd Morgan, of course, who questioned this evidence with his Canon of Parsimony. Were there not other ways of accounting for what looked like signs of consciousness or rational powers? Thorndike's experiments, at the end of the 19th century, were in this vein. They showed that the behavior of a cat in escaping from a puzzle box might seem to show reasoning but could be explained instead as the result of simpler processes. Thorndike remained a mentalist, but he greatly advanced the objective study of behavior which had been attributed to mental processes.

The next step was inevitable: if evidence of consciousness and reasoning could be explained in other ways in animals, why not also in man? And in that case, what became of psychology as a science of mental life? It was John B. Watson who made the first clear, if rather noisy, proposal that psychology be regarded simply as a science of behavior. He was not in a very good position to defend the proposal. He had little scientific material to use in his reconstruction. He was forced to pad his textbook with discussions of the physiology of receptor systems and muscles, and with physiological theories which were at the time no more susceptible to proof than the mentalistic theories they were intended to replace. A need for "mediators" of behavior which might serve as objective alternatives to thought processes led him to emphasize subaudible speech. The notion was intriguing because one can usually observe oneself thinking in this way, but it was by no means an adequate or comprehensive explanation. He tangled with introspective psychologists by denying the existence of images. He may well have been acting in good faith, for it has been said that he himself did not have visual imagery, but his arguments caused unnecessary trouble. The relative importance of a genetic endowment in explaining behavior proved to be another disturbing digression.

All this made it easy to lose sight of the central argument—that behavior which seemed to be the product of mental activity could be explained in other ways. In any case, the introspectionists were prepared to challenge it. As late as 1883 Francis Galton could write (1): "Many persons, especially women and intelligent children, take pleasure in introspection, and strive their very best to explain their mental processes." But introspection was already being taken seriously. The concept of a science of mind in which mental events obeyed mental laws had led to the development of psychophysical methods and to the accumulation of facts which seemed to bar the extension of the principle of parsimony. What might hold for animals did not hold for men, because men could *see* their mental processes.

Curiously enough, part of the answer was supplied by the psychoanalysts, who insisted that although a man might be able to see some of his mental life, he could not see all of it. The kind of thoughts

Freud called unconscious took place without the knowledge of the thinker. From an association, verbal slip, or dream it could be shown that a person must have responded to a passing stimulus although he could not tell you that he had done so. More complex thought processes, including problem solving and verbal play, could also go on without the thinker's knowledge. Freud had devised, and he never abandoned faith in, one of the most elaborate mental apparatuses of all time. He nevertheless contributed to the behavioristic argument by showing that mental activity did not, at least, *require* consciousness. His proofs that thinking had occurred without introspective recognition were, indeed, clearly in the spirit of Lloyd Morgan. They were operational analyses of mental life—even though, for Freud, only the unconscious part of it. Experimental evidence pointing in the same direction soon began to accumulate.

But that was not the whole answer. What about the part of mental life which a man can see? It is a difficult question, no matter what one's point of view, partly because it raises the question of what "seeing" means and partly because the events seen are private. The fact of privacy cannot, of course, be questioned. Each person is in special contact with a small part of the universe enclosed within his own skin. To take a noncontroversial example, he is uniquely subject to certain kinds of proprioceptive and interoceptive stimulation. Though two people may in some sense be said to see the same light or hear the same sound, they cannot feel the same distension of a bile duct or the same bruised muscle. (When privacy is invaded with scientific instruments, the form of stimulation is changed; the scales read by the scientist are not the private events themselves.)

Mentalistic psychologists insist that there are other kinds of events uniquely accessible to the owner of the skin within which they occur which lack the physical dimensions of proprioceptive or interoceptive stimuli. They are as different from physical events as colors are from wavelengths of light. There are even better reasons, therefore, why two people cannot suffer each other's toothaches, recall each other's memories, or share each other's happiness. The importance assigned to this kind of world varies. For some, it is the only world there is. For others, it is the only part of the world which can be directly known. For still others, it is a special part of what can be known. In any case, the problem of how one knows about the subjective world of another must be faced. Apart from the question of what "knowing" means, the problem is one of accessibility.

PUBLIC AND PRIVATE EVENTS

One solution, often regarded as behavioristic, is to grant the distinction between public and private events and rule the latter out of scientific consideration. This is a congenial solution for those to whom scientific truth is a matter of convention or agreement among observers. It is essentially the line taken by logical positivism and physical operationism. Hogben (2) has recently redefined "behaviorist" in this spirit. The subtitle of his *Statistical Theory* is, "an examination of the contemporary crises in statistical theory from a behaviorist viewpoint," and this is amplified in the following way: "The behaviorist, as I here use the term, does not deny the convenience of classifying *processes* as mental or material. He recognizes the distinction between personality and corpse: but he has not yet had the privilege of attending an identity parade in which human minds without bodies are by common recognition distinguishable from living human bodies without minds. Till then, he is content to discuss probability in the vocabulary of *events*, including audible or visibly recorded assertions of human beings as such . . ." The behavioristic position, so defined, is simply that of the publicist and "has no concern with structure and mechanism."

The point of view is often called operational, and it is significant that P.W. Bridgman's physical operationism could not save him from an extreme solipsism even within physical science itself. Though he insisted that he was not a solipsist, he was never able to reconcile seemingly public physical knowledge with the private world of the scientist (3). Applied to psychological problems, operationism has been no more successful. We may recognize the restrictions imposed by the operations through which we can know of the existence of properties of subjective events, but the operations cannot be identified with the events themselves. S.S. Stevens has applied Bridgman's principle to psychology, not to decide whether subjective events exist, but to determine the extent to which we can deal with them scientifically (4).

Behaviorists have from time to time examined the problem of privacy, and some of them have excluded so-called sensations, images, thought processes, and so on, from their deliberations. When they have done so not because such things do not exist but because they are out of reach of their methods, the charge is justified that they have neglected the facts of consciousness. The strategy is, however, quite unwise. It is particularly important that a science of behavior face the problem of privacy. It may do so without abandoning the basic position of behaviorism. Science often talks about things it cannot see or measure. When a man tosses a penny into the air, it must be assumed that he tosses the earth beneath him downward. It is quite out of the question to see or measure the effect on the earth, but an effect must be assumed for the sake of a consistent account. An adequate science of behavior must consider events taking place within the skin of the organism, not as physiological mediators of behavior but as part of behavior itself. It can deal with these events without assuming that they have any special nature or must be known in any special way. The skin is not that important as a boundary. Private and public events have the same kinds of physical dimensions.

SELF-DESCRIPTIVE BEHAVIOR

In the 50 years which have passed since a behavioristic philosophy was first stated, facts and principles bearing on the basic issues have steadily accumulated. For one thing, a scientific analysis of behavior has yielded a sort of empirical epistemology. The subject matter of a science of behavior includes the behavior of scientists and other knowers. The techniques available to such a science give an empirical theory of knowledge certain advantages over theories derived from philosophy and logic. The problem of privacy may be approached in a fresh direction by starting with behavior rather than with immediate experience. The strategy is certainly no more arbitrary or circular than the earlier practice, and it has a surprising result. Instead of concluding that man can know only his subjective experiences—that he is bound forever to his private world and that the external world is only a construct—a behavioral theory of knowledge suggests that it is the private world which, if not entirely unknowable, is at least not likely to be known well. The relations between organism and environment involved in knowing are of such a sort that the privacy of the world within the skin imposes more serious limitations on personal knowledge than on scientific accessibility.

An organism learns to react discriminatively to the world around it under certain contingencies of reinforcement. Thus, a child learns to name a color correctly when a given response is reinforced in the presence of the color and extinguished in its absence. The verbal community may make the reinforcement of an extensive repertoire of responses contingent on subtle properties of colored stimuli. We have reason to believe that the child will not discriminate among colors—that he will not see two colors as different—until exposed to such contingencies. So far as we know, the same process of differential reinforcement is required if a child is to distinguish among the events occurring within his own skin.

Many contingencies involving private stimuli need not be arranged by a verbal community, for they follow from simple mechanical relations among stimuli, responses, and reinforcing consequences. The various motions which comprise turning a handspring, for example, are under the control of external and internal stimuli and are subject to external and internal reinforcing consequences. But the performer is not necessarily "aware" of the stimuli controlling his behavior, no matter how appropriate and skillful it may be. "Knowing" or "being aware of" what is happening in turning a handspring involves discriminative responses, such as naming or describing, which arise from contingencies necessarily arranged by a verbal environment. Such environments are common. The community is generally interested in what a man is doing, has done, or is planning to do, and why, and it arranges contingencies which generate verbal responses which name and describe the external and internal stimuli associated with these events. It challenges his verbal behavior by asking, "How do you know?" and the speaker answers, if at all, by describing some of the variables of which his verbal behavior was a function. The "awareness" resulting from all this is a social product.

In attempting to set up such a repertoire, however, the verbal community works under a severe handicap. It cannot always arrange the contingencies required for subtle discriminations. It cannot teach a child to call one pattern of private stimuli "diffidence" and another "embarrassment" as effectively as it teaches him to call one stimulus "red" and another "orange," for it cannot be sure of the presence or absence of the private patterns of stimuli appropriate to reinforcement or lack of reinforcement. Privacy thus causes trouble first of all for the verbal community. The individual suffers in turn. Because the community cannot reinforce self-descriptive responses consistently, a person cannot describe or otherwise "know" events occurring within his own skin as subtly and precisely as he knows events in the world at large.

There are, of course, differences between external and internal stimuli which are not mere differences in location. Proprioceptive and interoceptive stimuli may have a certain intimacy. They are likely to be especially familiar. They are very much with us: we cannot escape from a toothache as easily as from a deafening noise. They may well be of a special kind: the stimuli we feel in pride or sorrow may not closely resemble those we feel in sandpaper or satin. But this does not mean that they differ in physical status. In particular, it does not mean that they can be more easily or more directly known. What is particularly clear and familiar to the potential knower may be strange and distant to the verbal community responsible for his knowing.

CONSCIOUS CONTENT

What *are* the private events which, at least in a limited way, a man may come to respond to in ways we call knowing? Let us begin with the oldest and in many ways the most difficult kind, represented by "the stubborn fact of consciousness." What is happening when a person observes the conscious content of his mind, when he looks at his sensations or images? Western philosophy and science have been handicapped in answering these questions by an unfortunate metaphor. The Greeks could not explain how a man could have knowledge of something with which he was not in immediate contact. How could he know an object on the other side of the room, for example? Did he reach out and touch it with some sort of invisible probe? Or did he never actually come into contact with the object at all but only with a copy of it inside his body? Plato supported the copy theory with his metaphor of the cave. Perhaps a man never sees the real world at all but only shadows of it on the wall of the cave in which he is imprisoned. (The "shadows" may well have been the much more accurate copies of the outside world in a camera obscura. Did Plato know of a cave at the entrance of which a happy superposition of objects admitted only the thin pencils of light needed for a camera obscura?) Copies of the real world projected into the body could compose the experience which a man directly knows. A similar theory could also explain how one can see objects which are "not really there," as in hallucinations, after-images, and memories. Neither explanation is, of course, satisfactory. How a copy may arise at a distance is at least as puzzling as how a man may know an object at a distance. Seeing things which are not really there is no harder to explain than the occurrence of copies of things not there to be copied.

The search for copies of the world within the body, particularly in the nervous system, still goes on, but with discouraging results. If the retina could suddenly be developed, like a photographic plate, it would yield a poor picture. The nerve impulses in the optic tract must have an even more tenuous resemblance to "what is seen." The patterns of vibrations which strike our ear when we listen to music are quickly lost in transmission. The bodily reactions to substances tasted, smelled, and touched would scarcely qualify as faithful reproductions. These facts are discouraging for those who are looking for copies of the real world within the body, but they are fortunate for psychophysiology as a whole. At some point the organism must do more than create duplicates. It must see, hear, smell, and so on, and the seeing, hearing, and smelling must be forms of action rather than of reproduction. It must do some of the things it is differentially reinforced for doing when it learns to respond discriminatively. The sooner the pattern of the external world disappears after impinging on the organism, the sooner the organism may get on with these other functions.

The need for something beyond, and quite different from, copying is not widely understood. Suppose someone were to coat the occipital lobes of the brain with a special photographic emulsion which, when developed, yielded a reasonable copy of a current visual stimulus. In many quarters this would be regarded as a triumph in the physiology of vision. Yet nothing could be more disastrous, for we should have to start all over again and ask how the organism sees a picture in its occipital cortex, and we should now have much less of the brain available in which to seek an answer. It adds nothing to an explanation of how an organism reacts to a stimulus to trace the pattern of the stimulus into the body. It is most convenient for both organism and psychophysiologist, if the external world is never copied—if the world we know is simply the world around us. The same may be said of theories according to which the brain interprets signals sent to it and in some sense reconstructs external stimuli. If the real world is, indeed, scrambled in transmission but later reconstructed in the brain, we must then start all over again and explain how the organism sees the reconstruction.

An adequate treatment of this point would require a thorough analysis of the behavior of seeing and of the conditions under which we see (to continue with vision as a convenient modality). It would be unwise to exaggerate our success to date. Discriminative visual behavior arises from contingencies involving external stimuli and overt responses, but possible private accompaniments must not be overlooked. Some of the consequences of such contingencies seem well established. It is usually easiest for us to see a friend when we are looking at him, because visual stimuli similar to those present when the behavior was acquired exert maximal control over the response. But mere visual stimulation is not enough; even after having been exposed to the necessary reinforcement, we may not see a friend who is present unless we have reason to do so. On the other hand, if the reasons are strong enough, we may see him in someone bearing only a superficial resemblance to him, or when no one like him is present at all. If conditions favor seeing something else, we may behave accordingly. If, on a hunting trip, it is important to see a deer, we may glance toward our friend at a distance, see him as a deer, and shoot.

It is not, however, seeing our friend which raises the question of conscious content but "seeing that we are seeing him." There are no natural contingencies for such behavior. We learn to see that we are seeing only because a verbal community arranges for us to do so. We usually acquire the behavior when we are under appropriate visual stimulation, but it does not follow that the thing seen must be present when we see that we are seeing it. The contingencies arranged by the verbal environment may set up self-descriptive responses describing the *behavior* of seeing even when the thing seen is not present.

If seeing does not require the presence of things seen, we need not be concerned about certain mental processes said to be involved in the construction of such things—images, memories, and dreams, for example. We may regard a dream not as a display of things seen by the dreamer but simply as the behavior of seeing. At no time during a day-dream, for example, should we expect to find within the organism anything which corresponds to the external stimuli present when the dreamer first acquired the behavior in which he is now engaged. In simple recall we need not suppose that we wander through some storehouse of memory until we find an object which we then contemplate. Instead of assuming that we begin with a tendency to *recognize* such an object once it is found, it is simpler to assume that we begin with a tendency to *see* it. Techniques of self-management which facilitate recall—for example, the use of mnemonic devices—can be formulated as ways of strengthening behavior rather than of creating objects to be seen. Freud dramatized the issue with respect to dreaming when asleep in his concept of dreamwork—an activity in which some part of the dreamer played the role of a theatrical producer while another part sat in the audience. If a dream is, indeed, something seen, then we must suppose that it is wrought as such, but if it is simply the behavior of seeing, the dreamwork may be dropped from the analysis. It took man a long time to understand that when he dreamed of a wolf, no wolf was actually there. It has taken him much longer to understand that not even a representation of a wolf is there.

Eye movements which appear to be associated with dreaming are in accord with this interpretation, since it is not likely that the dreamer is actually watching a dream on the undersides of his eyelids. When memories are aroused by electrical stimulation of the brain, as in the work of Wilder Penfield, it is also simpler to assume that it is the behavior of seeing, hearing, and so on which is aroused than that it is some copy of early environmental events which the subject then looks at or listens to. Behavior similar to the responses to the original events must be assumed in both cases—the subject sees or hears—but the reproduction of the events seen or heard is a needless complication. The familiar process of response chaining is available to account for the serial character of the behavior of remembering, but the serial linkage of stored experiences (suggesting engrams in the form of sound films) demands a new mechanism.

The heart of the behavioristic position on conscious experience may be summed up in this way: seeing does not imply something seen. We acquire the behavior of seeing under stimulation from actual objects, but it may occur in the absence of these objects under the control of other variables. (So far as the world within the skin is concerned, it always occurs in the absence of such objects.) We also acquire the behavior of seeing-that-we-are-seeing when we are seeing actual objects, but it may also occur in their absence.

To question the reality or the nature of the things seen in conscious experience is not to question the value of introspective psychology or its methods. Current problems in sensation are mainly concerned with the physiological function of receptors and associated neural mechanisms. Problems in perception are, at the moment, less intimately related to specific mechanisms, but the trend appears to be in the same direction. So far as behavior is concerned, both sensation and perception may be analyzed as forms of stimulus control. The subject need not be regarded as observing or evaluating conscious experiences. Apparent anomalies of stimulus control which are now explained by appealing to a psychophysical relation or to the laws of perception may be studied in their own right. It is, after all, no real solution to attribute them to the slippage inherent in converting a physical stimulus into a subjective experience.

The experimental analysis of behavior has a little more to say on this subject. Its techniques have recently been extended to what might be called the psychophysics of lower organisms. Blough's adaptation of the Békésy technique—for example, in determining the spectral sensitivity of pigeons and monkeys—yields sensory data comparable with the reports of a trained observer (5). Herrnstein and van Sommers have recently developed a procedure in which pigeons "bisect sensory intervals" (6). It is tempting to describe these procedures by saying that investigators have found ways to get nonverbal organisms to describe their sensations. The fact is that a form of stimulus control has been investigated without using a repertoire of self-observation or, rather, by constructing a special repertoire the nature and origin of which are clearly understood. Rather than describe such experiments with the terminology of introspection, we may formulate them in their proper place in an experimental analysis. The behavior of the observer in the traditional psychophysical experiment may then be reinterpreted accordingly.

MENTAL WAY STATIONS

So much for "conscious content," the classical problem in mentalistic philosophies. There are other mental states or processes to be taken into account. Moods, cognitions, and expectancies, for example, are also examined introspectively, and descriptions are used in psychological formulations. The conditions under which descriptive repertoires are set up are much less successfully controlled. Terms describing sensations and images are taught by manipulating discriminative stimuli—a relatively amenable class of variables. The remaining kinds of mental events are related to such operations as deprivation and satiation, emotional stimulation, and various schedules of reinforcement. The difficulties they present to the verbal community are suggested by the fact that there is no psychophysics of mental states of this sort. That fact has not inhibited their use in explanatory systems.

In an experimental analysis, the relation between a property of behavior and an operation performed upon the organism is studied directly. Traditional mentalistic formulations, however, emphasize certain way stations. Where an experimental analysis might examine the effect of punishment on behavior, a mentalistic psychology will be concerned first with the effect of punishment in generating feelings of anxiety and then with the effect of anxiety on behavior. The mental state seems to bridge the gap between dependent and independent variables, and a mentalistic interpretation is particularly attractive when these are separated by long periods of time—when, for example, the punishment occurs in childhood and the effect appears in the behavior of the adult.

Mentalistic way stations are popular. In a demonstration experiment, a hungry pigeon was conditioned to turn around in a clockwise direction. A final, smoothly executed pattern of behavior was shaped by reinforcing successive approximations with food. Students who had watched the demonstration were asked to write an account of what they had seen. Their responses included the following: (i) the organism was conditioned to *expect* reinforcement for the right kind of behavior; (ii) the pigeon walked around *hoping* that something would bring the food back again; (iii) the pigeon *observed* that a certain behavior seemed to produce a particular result; (iv) the pigeon *felt* that food would be given it because of its action; and (v) the bird came to *associate* his action with the click of the food-dispenser. The observed facts could be stated, respectively, as follows: (i) the organism was reinforced *when* its behavior was of a given kind; (ii) the pigeon walked around *until* the food container again appeared; (iii) a certain behavior *produced* a particular result; (iv) food was given to the pigeon *when* it acted in a given way; and (v) the click of the food-dispenser *was temporally related* to the bird's action. These statements describe the contingencies of reinforcement. The expressions "expect," "hope," "observe," "feel," and "associate" go beyond them to identify effects on the pigeon. The effect actually observed was clear enough: the pigeon turned more skillfully and more frequently. But that was not the effect reported by the students. (If pressed, they would doubtless have said that the pigeon turned more skillfully and more frequently *because* it expected, hoped, and felt that if it did so food would appear.)

The events reported by the students were observed, if at all, in their own behavior. They were describing what *they* would have expected, felt, and hoped for under similar circumstances. But they were able to do so only because a verbal community had brought relevant terms under the control of certain stimuli, and this had been done when the community had access only to the kinds of public information available to the students in the demonstration. Whatever the students knew about themselves which permitted them to infer comparable events in the pigeon must have been learned from a verbal community which saw no more of their behavior than they had seen of the pigeon's. Private stimuli may have entered into the control of their self-descriptive repertoires, but the readiness with which they applied these repertoires to the pigeon indicates that external stimuli had remained important. The extraordinary strength of a mentalistic interpretation is really a sort of proof that, in describing a private way station, one is to a considerable extent making use of public information.

The mental way station is often accepted as a terminal datum, however. When a man must be trained to discriminate between different planes, ships, and so on, it is tempting to stop at the point at which he can be said to *identify* such objects. It is implied that if he can identify an object he can name it, label it, describe it, or act appropriately in some other way. In the training process he always behaves in one of these ways; no way station called "identification" appears in practice or need appear in theory. (Any discussion of the discriminative behavior generated by the verbal environment to permit a person to examine the content of his consciousness must be qualified accordingly.)

Cognitive theories stop at way stations where the mental action is usually somewhat more complex than identification. For example, a subject is said to *know* who and where he is, what something is, or what has happened or is going to happen, regardless of the forms of behavior through which this knowledge was set up or which may now testify to its existence. Similarly, in accounting for verbal behavior, a listener or reader is said to understand the *meaning* of a passage although the actual changes brought about by listening to or reading the passage are not specified. In the same way, schedules of reinforcement are sometimes studied simply for their effects on the *expectations* of the organism exposed to them, without discussion of the implied relation between expectation and action. Recall, inference, and reasoning may be formulated only to the point at which an experience is remembered or a conclusion is reached, behavioral manifestations being ignored. In practice the investigator always carries through to some response, if only a response of self-description.

On the other hand, mental states are often studied as causes of action. A speaker thinks of something to say before saying it, and this explains what he says, although the sources of his thoughts may not be examined. An unusual act is called "impulsive," without further inquiry into the origin of the unusual impulse. A behavioral maladjustment shows anxiety, but the source of the anxiety is neglected. One salivates upon seeing a lemon because it reminds one of a sour taste, but why it does so is not specified. The formulation leads directly to a technology based on the manipulation of mental states. To change a man's voting behavior we change his opinions, to induce him to act we strengthen his beliefs, to make him eat we make him feel hungry, to prevent wars we reduce warlike tensions in the minds of men, to effect psychotherapy we alter troublesome mental states, and so on. In practice, all these ways of changing a man's mind reduce to manipulating his environment, verbal or otherwise.

In many cases we can reconstruct a complete causal chain by identifying the mental state which is the effect of an environmental variable with the mental state which is the cause of action. But this is not always enough. In traditional mentalistic philosophies various things happen at the way station which alter the relation between the terminal events. The effect of the psychophysical function and the laws of perception in distorting the physical stimulus before it reaches the way station has already been mentioned. Once the mental stage is reached, other effects are said to occur. Mental states alter each other. A painful memory may never affect behavior, or it may affect it an unexpected way if another mental state succeeds in repressing it. Conflicting variables may be reconciled before they have an effect on behavior if the subject engages in mental action called "making a decision." Dissonant cognitions generated by conflicting conditions of reinforcement will not be reflected in behavior if the subject can "persuade himself" that one condition was actually of a different magnitude or kind. These disturbances in simple causal linkages between environment and behavior can be formulated and studied experimentally as interactions among variables, but the possibility has not been fully exploited, and the effects still provide a formidable stronghold for mentalistic theories designed to bridge the gap between dependent and independent variables.

METHODOLOGICAL OBJECTIONS

The behavioristic argument is nevertheless still valid. We may object, first, to the predilection for unfinished causal sequences. A disturbance in behavior is not explained by relating it to felt anxiety until the anxiety has in turn been explained. An action is not explained by attributing it to expectations until the expectations have in turn been accounted for. Complete causal sequences might, of course, include references to way stations, but the fact is that the way station generally interrupts the account in one direction or the other. For example, there must be thousands of instances in the psychoanalytic literature in which a thought or memory is said to have been relegated to the unconscious because it was painful or intolerable, but the percentage of instances in which even the most casual suggestion is offered as to why it was painful or intolerable must be very small. Perhaps explanations *could* have been offered, but the practice has discouraged the completion of the causal sequence.

A second objection is that a preoccupation with mental way stations burdens a science of behavior with all the problems raised by the limitations and inaccuracies of self-descriptive repertoires. We need not take the extreme position that mediating events or any data about them obtained through introspection must be ruled out of consideration, but we should certainly welcome other ways of treating the data more satisfactorily. Independent variables change the behaving organism, often in ways which persist for many years, and such changes affect subsequent behavior. The subject may be able to describe some of these intervening states in useful ways, either before or after they have affected behavior. On the other hand, behavior may be extensively modified by variables of which, and of the effect of which, the subject is never aware. So far as we know, self-descriptive responses do not alter controlling relationships. If a severe punishment is less effective than a mild one, this is not because it cannot be "kept in mind." (Certain behaviors involved in self-management, such as reviewing a history of punishment, may alter behavior, but they do so by introducing other variables rather than by changing a given relation.)

Perhaps the most serious objection concerns the order of events. Observation of one's own behavior necessarily follows the behavior. Responses which seem to be describing intervening states alone may embrace behavioral effects. "I am hungry" may describe, in part, the strength of the speaker's ongoing ingestive behavior. "I was hungrier than I thought" seems particularly to describe behavior rather than an intervening, possibly causal, state. More serious examples of a possibly mistaken order are to be found in theories of psycho-therapy. Before asserting that the release of a repressed wish has a therapeutic effect on behavior, or that when one knows why he is neurotically ill he will recover, we should consider the plausible alternative that a change in behavior resulting from therapy has made it possible for the subject to recall a repressed wish or to understand his illness.

A final objection is that way stations are so often simply invented. It is too easy to say that someone does something "because he likes to do it," or that he does one thing rather than another "because he has made a choice."

The importance of behaviorism as a philosophy of science naturally declines as a scientific analysis becomes more powerful because there is then less need to use data in the form of self-description. The mentalism which survives in the fields of sensation and perception will disappear as alternative techniques prove their value in analyzing stimulus control, and similar changes may be anticipated elsewhere. Cognitive psychologists and others still try to circumvent the explicit control of variables by describing con-tingencies of reinforcement to their subjects in "instructions." They also try to dispense with recording behavior in a form from which probability of response can be estimated by asking their subjects to evaluate their tendencies to respond. But a person rarely responds to a description of contingencies as he would respond under direct exposure to them, nor can he accurately predict his rate of respond-ing, particularly the course of the subtle changes in rate which are a commonplace in the experimental analysis of behavior. These attempts to short-circuit an experimental analysis can no longer be justified on grounds of expedience, and there are many reasons for abandoning them. Much remains to be done, however, before the facts to which they are currently applied can be said to be adequately understood.

BEHAVIORISM AND BIOLOGY

Elsewhere, the scientific study of man has scarcely recognized the need for reform. The biologist, for example, begins with a certain advantage in studying the behaving organism, for the structures he analyzes have an evident physical status. The nervous system is somehow earthier than the behavior for which it is largely responsible. Philosophers and psychologists alike have from time to time sought escape from mentalism in physiology. When a man sees red, he may be seeing the physiological effect of a red stimulus; when he merely imagines red, he may be seeing the same effect re-aroused. Psychophysical and perceptual distortions may be wrought by physiological processes. What a man feels as anxiety may be autonomic reactions to threatening stimuli. And so on. This may solve the minor problem of the nature of subjective experience, but it does not solve any of the methodological problems with which behaviorism is most seriously concerned. A physiological translation of mentalistic terms may reassure those who want to avoid dualism, but inadequacies in the formulation survive translation.

When writing about the behavior of organisms, biologists tend to be more mentalistic than psychologists. Adrian could not understand how a nerve impulse could cause a thought. The author of a recent article on the visual space sense in *Science* (7) asserts that "the final event in the chain from the retina to the brain is a psychic experience." Another investigator reports research on "the brain and its contained mind." Pharmacologists study the "psychotropic" drugs. Psychosomatic medicine insists on the influence of mind over matter. And psychologists join their physiological colleagues in looking for feelings, emotions, drives, and the pleasurable aspects of positive reinforcement in the brain.

The facts uncovered in such research are important, both for their own sake and for their bearing on behavior. The physiologist studies structures and processes without which behavior could not occur. He is in a position to supply a "reductionist" explanation beyond the reach of an analysis which confines itself to terminal variables. He cannot do this well, however, so long as he accepts traditional mentalistic formulations. Only an experimental analysis of behavior will define his task in optimal terms. The point is demonstrated by recent research in psychopharmacology. When the behavioral drugs first began to attract attention, they were studied with impromptu techniques based on self-observation, usually designed to quantify subjective reports. Eventually the methods of an experimental analysis proved their value in generating reproducible segments of behavior upon which the effects of drugs could be observed and in terms of which they could be effectively defined and classified. For the same reasons, brain physiology will move forward more rapidly when it recognizes that its role is to account for the mediation of behavior rather than of mind.

BEHAVIORISM IN THE SOCIAL SCIENCES

There is also still a need for behaviorism in the social sciences, where psychology has long been used for purposes of explanation. Economics has had its economic man. Political science has considered man as a political animal. Parts of anthropology and sociology have found a place for psychoanalysis. The relevance of psychology in linguistics has been debated for more than half a century. Studies of scientific method have oscillated between logical and empirical analyses. In all these fields, "psychologizing" has often had disappointing results and has frequently been rejected in favor of an extreme formalism which emphasizes objective facts. Economics confines itself to its own abundant data. Political scientists limit themselves to whatever may be studied with a few empirical tools and techniques, and confine themselves, when they deal with theory, to formalistic analyses of political structures. A strong structuralist movement is evident in sociology. Linguistics emphasizes formal analyses of semantics and grammar.

Straight-laced commitments to pure description and formal analysis appear to leave no place for explanatory principles, and the shortcoming is often blamed on the exclusion of mental activities. For example, participants at a recent symposium on "The Limits of Behavioralism in Political Science" (8) complained of a neglect of subjective experience, ideas, motives, feelings, attitudes, values, and so on. This is reminiscent of attacks on behaviorism. In any case, it shows the same misunderstanding of the scope of a behavioral analysis. In its extension to the social sciences, as in psychology proper, behaviorism means more than a commitment to objective measurement. No entity or process which has any useful explanatory force is to be rejected on the ground that it is subjective or mental. The data which have made it important must, however, be studied and formulated in effective ways. The assignment is well within the scope of an experimental analysis of behavior, which thus offers a promising alternative to a commitment to pure description on the one hand and an appeal to mentalistic theories on the other. To extend behaviorism as a philosophy of science to the study of political and economic behavior, of the behavior of people in groups, of people speaking and listening, teaching and learning—this is not "psychologizing" in the traditional sense. It is simply the application of a tested formula to important parts of the field of human behavior.

REFERENCES AND NOTES

1. F. Galton, *Inquiries into Human Faculty* (London, 1883), Everyman ed., p. 60.

2. L. Hogben, *Statistical Theory* (Allen and Unwin, London, 1957).

3. P.W. Bridgman, *The Way Things Are* (Harvard Univ. Press, Cambridge, Mass., 1959).

4. S.S. Stevens, *Am. J. Psychol.* **47**, 323 (1935).

5. D.S. Blough, *J. Comp. Physiol. Psychol.* **49**, 425 (1956); ―― and A.M. Schrier, *Science* **139**, 493 (1963).

6. R.J. Herrnstein and P. van Sommers, *Science* **135**, 40 (1962).

7. K.N. Ogle, *ibid.*, p. 763.

8. *The Limits of Behavioralism in Political Science* (Am. Acad. Political and Social Sci., Philadelphia, 1962).

A Comparison of Behaviorism and Psychoanalysis with Existentialism
Samuel Correnti

Existence, a book edited by Rollo May and published in 1958, presented existentialism for the first time as a relevant movement for American psychiatrists and psychologists. Since then numerous books, articles, and symposia have been published on existential psychology, and the new edition of May's *Existential Psychology* (1st ed. 1961, 2nd ed. 1969) is a concrete indication of the continued interest in this movement in the United States. The theoretical underpinning and ideas of existential psychology have significantly influenced and nourished a new psychological stream, which has been called humanistic psychology.

Every new systematic concept or approach that appears in American psychology begins by stating its position with reference to psychoanalysis and behaviorism—particularly to behaviorism because of its dominance in the United States. In this selection Samuel Correnti compares existentialism, which he calls "a third psychological frame of reference," with behaviorism and psychoanalysis, the two "historical pillars of psychology" and "the most widely accepted explanatory systems of behavior." Such a comparison renders the character and claims of the new movement clearer and easier to comprehend.

The author, Samuel Correnti, had considerable teaching and clinical experience before he received his Ph.D. from the University of Denver in 1958. He has since been in private practice. His interests are psychotherapy, existential psychology, and personality theory.

Two psychological frames of reference—behaviorism and psychoanalysis—are the historical pillars of psychology, the most widely accepted explanatory systems of behavior. A third psychological frame of reference, existentialism, now claims our attention. As a general term, it summarizes numerous, divergent, and often independently attained but similar points of view. As a frame of reference, it enters American psychology in the wake of the advent of the epistemology of phenomenology.

Samuel Correnti, A comparison of behaviorism and psychoanalysis with existentialism. *Journal of Existentialism*, 1965, **5**, 379-388. Reprinted by permission of the author and Libra Publishers.

In the past decade, the experiential empiricism of phenomenology has become increasingly accepted and the utility of the inferential rationalism of behaviorism and psychoanalysis has been increasingly questioned. With the wane of the explanatory power of behaviorism and psychoanalysis and the clear need for a broader, more humanistic, and more useful conception of man, the phenomenologically based existential position has attracted scores of clinical and social psychologists and psychiatrists.

Admittedly, the procedures, clinical techniques, and theory of this new frame of reference are not yet as synthesized or systematized as are the behavioristic or psychoanalytic psychologies. From the contemporary cultural situation, however, one gets the impression that a synthesis may occur, pressured in large part by the relevance of the existential position to mankind's need for a utilitarian way-of-life philosophy to assist us in our constant struggle with meaninglessness, despair, and freedom.

This paper presents first, a cursory review of behaviorism and psychoanalysis, and a more elaborate summary of existentialism; and, second, the fundamental, comparable aspects of the three frames of reference.

BEHAVIORISM

As a frame of reference, behaviorism stresses observation of overt, peripheral behavior. Being solely objective, it derides the method of introspection. It clearly rules out the phenomenon of consciousness. As in mechanistic theory, it emphasizes the machine-like qualities in animal and human activities. Behaviorism limits its concepts and symbols to observable facts, and in this sense, is positivistic. In defining personality in terms of action *qua* action, its conceptual schemes are mechanistic and elementaristic. Stimulus-response connections are generally considered the basic functional unit of all behavior; behaviorism regards personality as the sum total of these stimulus-response connections. It concerns itself with the manner in which responses occur in the presence of certain stimuli, and with the establishment of response patterns.

Behaviorism postulates that personality is developed through particular reinforced behavior patterns by means of associative learning. The behavior patterns that reduce the drive or tension evoking the response are stamped in, and thus learned. The resulting generalizations of stimuli and differentiations of responses include all the richness and variation of human behavior.

PSYCHOANALYSIS

In psychoanalysis, behavior is considered as functionally related to early frustration of instinctual strivings and their degree of fixation during the psychosexual stages of development. The energy, or force that activates the instinctual basic urges is, of course, the libido, which is, in its dualistic and dialectic forms, Eros, the life energy, and Thanatos, the destructive energy. The libidinal energy is structured and regulated by Freud's three dynamic agents, the id, ego, and superego.

The development and interaction of the id, ego, and superego, the way in which the libidinal energies are handled, as determined by psychosexual history, and the methods by which the psychological mechanisms of defense and adaptation dispose of these libidinal energies generally constitutes personality in psychoanalytic doctrine.

As a psychological frame of reference, psychoanalysis is concerned with subjective and central, rather than peripheral facts of emotional significance. Inferred and imagined feeling-states call for a conceptual approach rather than a positivist one. The scope of the psychoanalytic approach is molar rather than elementaristic. As such, it is inclined to doctrines of immanence and emergence. It attempts to know the inner nature of man, by both conscious, rational inference from items of observation and by an un-analyzable and non-measurable act of empathic intuition. In its inferential approach, it parallels behaviorism; in its intuitive approach, it is quite unlike behaviorism. In opposition to the sensationalists, who believe that personality reacts to outer stimulation only, the psychoanalysts are dynamicists who ascribe action to inner forces, drives, impulses, and urges.

EXISTENTIALISM

The new frame of reference, existentialism, is not a specific school, but an increasingly pervasive expression. It is not yet a theory, but a depth attitude. Historically, the existentialists began with what was considered a humanly justifiable protest against the abrogation of personal freedom and responsibility contained in the doctrines of the absolute sovereignty of God, predestination, and the total depravity of man in Calvinistic Protestantism.

In the philosophical writings of Kierkegaard and Nietzsche, this protest developed into a subjective humanism, a view later called existentialism, which succeeded where nineteenth century theological philosophies failed. In the character of Zarathustra, Nietzsche's proclamation that "God is dead" forcefully and somewhat formally established the anthropocentric over the theocentric viewpoint. But it also, however, contributed to man an intense anguish related to his being free and connected to himself, as against the psychological security that he had from being confined and connected with a given, guardian theology.

Currently, existentialism's attack is leveled at the pan-determinism and its attendant moral irresponsibility of behaviorism, psychoanalysis, and historical inevitability. In a broad psychosocial sense, existentialism refers to the undercurrent of protest against fractional individualism, depersonalizing collectivism, and the endemic psychological decompensation of Western man. In an ideological sense, it remonstrates against positivism, theological imposture, unconscionable scientism, and assertive materialism. On the positive side, existentialism expresses radical concern for moral values, human commitment, and a sense of community, central to which is an experience-anchored, present-oriented, authentic selfhood.

Unlike the classical philosophies, existentialism refuses to construct human experience out of stated propositions and abstract ideas. As a European philosophy of being, it increasingly concerns itself with the actual, immediate, and existent. It refuses to think and intellectualize being; instead, it attests and accepts being. The existentialists differ from classical philosophers, also, in that they deal with the separation of man from himself. If there is a need in our lives for rationalism and positivism, the existentialists say, it does not justify denuding the human being of his unique, fully conscious capacity of experiencing himself, as the rationalists and positivists seem to have done. But, although man is socially conditioned to rationalize away his feeling and constantly surrenders his identity and subjectivity to the material objects he produces, there is a deeper unconscious dimension in man which forces him to despair in the conscious experience of his dehumanization.

Man experiences this despair because he is nowhere able to experience a meaningful relationship to himself or to his world. His materialism and technology have blunted his self awareness and almost regulate him. He experiences himself as a technical network of reactions to competing ideologies, contesting dogmas, and manipulated *Weltanschauung*, to which he has been conditioned to respond automatically. He experiences himself as outside himself, a captive of external forces which obscure the way back to the security of himself. Whatever happens to him has little reality and little inner, personal, and private meaning to him. The reality we begin with, the existentialists say, must be the reality we feel.

The existentialist philosophers deal also with the separation of man from the world, suggesting that man has no logical space or essence before his existence. As Abraham Kaplan (5) points out, "First, a man IS; and what he IS is settled in the course of his existence and is not predetermined, not an antecedent condition of his existence." Man does not belong to the order of things on earth which have no choice. Unlike all other things whose essence precedes their existence, man has no predetermined place on earth.

An earlier view of the universe, Plato's metacognitive effort, was an idealistic vision of an intelligible, progressive cosmic order, a rational harmony repeated in man. In comparison, the existentialist's metacognitive effort is an unsettling vision of man's relationship to a fortuitous and indifferent world. But he does not, however, lapse into disillusionment or nihilism, or depressive resignation. Instead, in attesting and accepting his separation from the world, man is thrown back upon himself—alone, free, frightened, responsible, finite, choosing.

Blackham (2) states: "If the speculative fantasies of the classical rationalist philosophers were true in principle, and individuals could be assigned an appointed place in a system, man, as man, would cease to exist. ... [To the existentialists] man's separation is a malaise, it is not a nostalgia for the Platonist's great chain of being." But as a malaise—and this is the crucial point—"man's separation is also what founds and refounds the human order of possibilities."

Man is hard to define because he has no given essence or place, but only painful separation. He makes his essence, which means that his definition of himself depends on what he does with his freedom to choose and become. And it is in this predicament, existentialism claims, that the existing individual has no refuge from unceasing responsibility. Man is responsible for his own definition; it is not given. Frightened, he once refused to define himself. Instead, he defined a god, a resolute, powerful, authoritative figure (however external and non-experienced) who offered him a purposeful relationship to the world and central place in the universe. With heavy stipulations about his behavior, this authoritative god promised man a heavenly, infinite life, which assured his essence. Man thus gave up choice, freedom, and becoming in order to protect himself from decision, finitude, full consciousness, and estrangement.

Existentialism, then, deals with separation, not by trying to justify or deny it, but by constantly focusing on the breadth, depth, and meaning of the separation itself, a separation which can be experienced as loss or liberation, helplessness or responsibility, apathy or urgency, a separation which constitutes the personal experience of existing. Thus, as Blackham (2) has said, existentialism focuses on the actions of individuals "whose being is ambiguous, both bound and free, joined and separated, in a total existence which is ambiguous, both finite and infinite . . . a plenitude and nothing." The total existence is also meaningful and meaningless. Almost all existentialists emphasize that the latter aspects of the antinomies of freedom, separation, and finitude are opposed to philosophies that emphasize the former, in being bound, joined, infinite. In doing so, the existentialists focus on those aspects that make man central, and the natural world peripheral. They side with man, not against him, and thus they appeal.

In contrast to other philosophies, existentialism does not deny the ambiguity arising out of man's discontinuity or separation from a world in which he has no essential participation. The separation is existential and has to be lived; it is not a problem solved by thought. The separation means the loss of a vast system of values and beliefs, dogmas and ideologies which once gave man structured meaning and security. To the existentialist, there is no *a priori* meaning to life. Its only meaning is what man gives it.

To some existentialists, freedom is man's essence, in his capacity to choose, become, and change. As the most fundamental metaphysical category, existence is perhaps also the most fundamental metapsychological experience point for his becoming, a becoming which is considerably less determined by compelling physical laws than the becomings of plants, animals, and minerals—things that already have essence. "The human existence is at least partly a conscious and free becoming," Van Kaam has written. "We 'become' consciously and we 'become' in freedom."

But what of the hopelessness and heavy despair of existentialism? We have already said that man is free and responsible for his life, that while matter remains what it is, man can transcend himself by choosing. The existential conclusion is that man largely determines his essence; his capacity for free choice is his most human quality and makes his existence real. But this very experience of being free, the unbearable fact of his responsibility, is described as man's illness. Freedom to be, and responsibility, may be for man far more than he can accept, more than he is emotionally equipped to handle, more than he asked for in a world he had nothing to do with creating. Existential anguish is his response. He is filled with despair, boredom, and the crippling pain of too much consciousness. On the positive side, however, the central concept of freedom which is given back to man balances the losses of the culturally prescribed securities, the determinism of his psychology and history, the unalterable predestination of his Protestantism.

In his anguished aloneness, he finds himself and is forced back on his own capacities and resources, made more accessible by his freedom. In literary and technical expositions of existentialism, we first find the quality of hopelessness and despair, and in our own despairing, sometimes do not go beyond it. Only upon later reflection and understanding do we realize the monumental quality of the freedom inherent in the existentialism.

FUNDAMENTAL, COMPARABLE ASPECTS OF THE THREE FRAMES OF REFERENCE

Behaviorism seeks to establish, usually in quantitative language, functional relationships between the cue values of stimuli and the magnitude of their associated responses. Psychoanalysis focuses on analyzing and understanding the unconscious, and subsequent changes of behavior by means of the interpretations of the unconscious. But existentialism stresses undiluted experience of what it means to be free, human, and individual.

Whereas the behaviorists tend to emphasize habits of response, and speak very little about motives except in terms of physiological drives or learned secondary motivations, the psychoanalyst under-estimates the response aspects of behavior, seeing them only as clues to what ego functions or mechanisms produce them. To the existentialist, response is almost identical with the clear acceptance of the responsibility for the response. Man is forced to be self-conscious about the consequences of his responses, to be intentional in his acts. Temporally, heavy emphasis is put on responding in the lived-now to the choices in the lived-now.

The infantile experiences and biological drives, as the major facts in Freudian personality development, tend to minimize the signifi-cance of the current situation. The existentialists, on the other hand, vaguely relate consciousness of one's existence and being-in-the-current-world to stimuli. Specifically, the accepted moral framework and commitment to moral participation as well as the constant awareness of choice stimulate both moral and choosing behaviors.

In behaviorism, man is defined only in terms of behavior patterns that can be described, predicted and explained. In psychoanalysis, man is determined by, and is rooted in, his history. He is defined by his past or by his past reactivated in the present. He is made anxious by the reenactment of the past, and is sometimes lost to the unrecoverable past. In existentialism, man is seen as present to himself, rooted in the ahistoric here and now, defined and described by his responses, acts, and commitments. He cannot hide, as he might in Freudian theory, in the vertical, deterministic past, about which he can plead ignorance and claim no responsibility. Braced by the exhilaration of his freedom, existential man must face the anxiety of the choices he makes, the pain of his awareness, the responsibility to himself and others in the broad, horizontal, selectively determined present.

Regarding their practical epistemologies, behaviorists acquire knowledge by means of empiricism and rationality, using empirical correlations and mathematical statements of measured and manipu-lated cues, stimuli, deprivation and the resulting response magni-tudes, generalization, and differentiation. They objectively observe what known and controlled antecedent conditions produce. The psychoanalyst, on the other hand, acquires knowledge by means of intuition and rationality, empathy and inference, with the aid of both his personal analysis and a guiding monolithic theory.

The existentialist acquires knowledge phenomenologically. He rejects dogmatic and explanatory, exploitative, and masterful approaches to the world in favor of a conscious *lived participation* in it. Theoretically, existentialism differs from modern philosophies which isolate and give critiques of ultimate abstractions and meanings. For the existentialist, being, having, becoming, and doing are more important than reflex mechanisms, philosophical categories, impulse, historicity, and psychological defenses. The rationale for the phenomenological approach is acceptance of and respect for things as they are experienced. Reductive analysis and theoretic synthesis are rejected. The epistemological concern of existentialism then, is not to question, measure, infer or rationalize existence, but to drive home the dimension of existence until it engages the whole man, and is experienced as personal, urgent, crucial and referential to himself.

The behaviorist's explanation of causality is implicit in the concept of the association of stimulus and response, an explanation no less explicit than the psychoanalyst's to explain causality. In contrast to these, the existentialists' main explanatory concept of behavioral causality is conation; it however, does not embrace or even approximate voluntarism. Although exaggerated at times to the point of total conation, its intent is to rescue for man the dignity of his accountability and the feeling of purposeful, self-intentionality.

Motivation is explained by the behaviorists as derived from basic psychological drives such as hunger, thirst, pain, fear, or conditioned anxiety. To the psychoanalysts, motivation is based on frustrated or unresolved unconscious drives which press for expression and satisfaction in the form of character types, symptoms, dreams, thoughts. In existentialism, motivation is seen as the result of the energy liberated by the conscious experience of freedom from which man may derive realistic commitment and responsibility to himself and mankind. Responsibility is crucial in existentialism, whereas in behaviorism it is non-existent and in psychoanalysis, it is vaguely and peripherally treated, if at all.

Out of man's freedom, a wholly necessary precondition, comes total and continuous responsibility, the existentialists say. Man has no escape. In freedom, man knows that he alone carries the responsibility for his fate. But he also returns his freedom, which is a requisite condition for success in individual responsibility. This is a point which the depressive and pessimistic quality of European existentialism rarely suggests. This life-stimulating freedom and its painful conscious response, responsibility, can be treated as a platitude or may be held as the fundamental truth about the individual. Man is intensely anguished about the implications of this total, freedom-based responsibility. It constantly forces him to rely on himself and to be aware of the implications of his acts. And the existentialists conclude, man is only authentically man insofar as he lives and acts in the full consciousness of his freedom and awesome responsibility.

Though behaviorism has no use for the concept of the unconscious, it is the very touchstone of psychoanalysis. To the existentialists the unconscious is not a specific object for analysis. The full awareness of the present and all its possible choices are their concern. The confrontation of the knowable reality of the present, rather than the unconscious, is their point of concentration.

Psychic determinism is a fundamental concept in psychoanalysis. The past influences the present, and can be behaviorally reenacted in the present. By the behaviorists, determinism is no less highly regarded than by the psychoanalysts. The behaviorists' obvious disregard of subjective, conative phenomena occurring between stimuli and responses seems to be largely a result of the rules of their positivistic game. Their disregard of the subjective aspects of man forces them to a mechanistic view of determinism.

To the existentialists, man has been weighed down by the habit of deterministic explanation present in positivism, behaviorism, and psychoanalysis. Existentialism attempts implicitly to help man work his way out from under all the heavy deterministic ideologies to a position of freedom, a preconditioned *Weltanschauung*, a consciousness of being. Specifically, the existentialists believe that the past does not fully determine the present or future. Rather, as Rollo May (9, p. 88) clearly suggests, man's choice about his present and future determines how he is to use his past. Psychological determinism is thus relegated to the background, and, at the same time, the causal role of free, existential choice is increased. In a practical sense, if man can free himself from or at least appreciably decrease the power of the dogmas, symbols, and myopic ideologies to which he has been unconsciously conditioned to respond, he can then relatively increase the strength and freedom of conation and conscious choice. No longer can man point to the determinism of past conditioning or to the predestination of his future to reduce his accountability for his present life, the existentialists imply.

The different ways in which behaviorism, psychoanalysis, and existentialism explain anxiety clearly differentiate the three. To the behaviorist, anxiety is a conditioned form of fear; a need expressed by a behavior is paired with a painful stimulus. To the psychoanalyst, anxiety is equated with the giving away of counter-cathexis energies and the concomitant forcing of the unmet needs of the unconscious into an unprepared consciousness. Its everyday utility is usually that of a danger signal to which covering-up defenses or useful adaptations are instituted.

Opposed to these is the existentialists' acceptance of anxiety as a dimension of man's being, resulting from awareness of his stance in a contingent world and his separation from it. Unlike the psychoanalysts, who generally regard most anxieties as signs of neurosis, the existentialists regard many anxieties as signs of being conscious of one's ambiguous relationship to the world. Not to sense tension and anxiety is, today, to be very much lost.

Therapeutically, the behaviorists tend to positively reinforce and support selected response patterns. They teach both discrimination of stimuli and differentiation of responsibility, and attempt to extinguish non-discriminative, generalized, and maladaptive behaviors. The psychoanalysts attempt to rearrange the unconscious forces, reducing the therapeutically intense transference neurosis to allow the id more expression, the ego more mastery, and the superego less control.

Therapeutically, the existentialists insist that the patient face himself as the referent in a phenomenological context by experiencing what is called "existential anguish" or "anxiety," that is, the horrendous encounter with one's self during face-to-face confrontation with the limits of one's existence, and the tremendous impact of its painful, resultant implications of finitude, estrangement, and freedom.

Although existential therapists seem to omit mention of the realistic limitations of self-determined choice, and the unalterable reality of fixed, alternative choices in any physical circumstance or psychological situation, they seem to do so while underscoring their major focus for the patient, the choice-freeing, ontic dimension of his life. At this point, it appears that the existential therapists are more concerned with having the patient know that he can be free, rather than how free, with the qualitative experience of freedom which the therapist presumes must precede knowledge of the breadth of choices.

In existential psychotherapy, as in existential philosophy, little attention seems to be paid to psychological determinism, neurotic or non-neurotic, as a limitation upon choice. Instead, the existentialists seem constantly, if implicitly, to emphasize that the patient's compulsive, repetitive choosing is never final, and that the energies hidden from him by chronic ego defenses can become liberated and used to overcome his conditioned, repetitive behaviors. They suggest also that the psychic energies made available to the self through the existential experience enable the self to restructure itself to the point of being able to accept and live with the existential implications of life.

The existential therapist would never, at least theoretically, reinforce or focus upon the limiting, unfree, deterministic, static image which the patient very likely has of himself, which is, in part, quite true. Instead, he tries to change that image so as to include the awareness of ontic boundaries, existential meanings, moral commitments, and choice-directed becoming.

In sum, the existentialist therapist attempts to create a process, rather than a static definition of being, a process centered in the self in the present, with obvious choices and intense, ontic consciousness, rather than in the interplay between emergent unconscious patterns of the past and the reality of the present.

In general, existential therapists attack the learned referential confusion that underlies man's self-alienation. They point to man as his own referent, not to his institutions; the self, not the abstracts and idols which the self is taught to libidinize, as the referent of experience. Their time referent is the present. Implicit in this is their attempt to reduce man's emphasis on though not his ability in defining and experiencing himself by reconstructing his past. As a time referent, the present serves to increase the vitality and freedom which results from referring to the lived-now for meaning about one's life and self, as well as to the experience that life is still happening to one's self. The existentialists' therapeutic goal is the development of the self, the motivation for which stems from the tension created by the experienced discrepancy between what man is and what he feels he has the potential, the freedom, and the responsibility to become, through his existential encounter.

The fundamental, comparable aspects of the three frames of reference are listed below.

In sum, existentialism may be both too naive and overwhelmingly out of reach for those of us steeped in rationalism and logical positivism, who demand high levels of empiricism. Because of this, we may be quick to view existentialism as a tricky pulpit philosophy, or a literary, apocalyptic psychology already implied by such beat writers as Kerouac. We may regard it also as a romantic pessimism that our literary colleagues are promoting because it sells, or our "soft-headed" psychological colleagues are embracing because they never could accept "hard-headed" behaviorism. More than that, it may be seen as a depressive, literary psychopathology that could

Behaviorism	Psychoanalysis	Existentialism
Nomothetic	Idiographic	Idiographic
Historic	Historic	Ahistoric (some handling of future)
Rational	Rational	Phenomenological
Inferential	Inferential	Experiential
Conceptual	Conceptual	Non-conceptual
Molecular	Molar	Molar
Mechanical model	Biological-mechanical model	Social-anthropological model
Reductive	Reductive	Non-reductive (phenomenological)
Materialistic concept of personality	Bio-materialistic concept of personality	Non-materialistic concept of personality (deals with unfolding capacities possible to man)
Theoretical	Theoretical	Atheoretical
Empirical orientation	Intuitive-analytic orientation	(attempts to be) Being orientation
Object-scientist relationship	Physician-patient relationship	Person-person relationship (encounter)

have no effect on psychology save that of immobilizing it with despair. To consider it as one or more of the above is to miss the point entirely. Although it excels in poignant protest, iconoclasm, and challenge, existentialism is essentially a work of salvaging the self, linked closely to the dissatisfaction with exalted reason, advertized happiness, and "looming nihilism." It is most fundamentally concerned with the salvation and freedom of man's psychic life before man's errant cognitions and ideologies totally obscure the rich humanism which is already cloaked by decreasing self-awareness.

The existentialists are not presenting a new, academically-conceived philosophy, but a new consciousness of man who lives in a painfully amorphous state, embedded in the violent, anti-humanistic and ambiguous situation of his time. They are concerned with man creating the spirit of the Second Coming, by making the fact of his own being immediate to consciousness instead of unrealistically and broodingly waiting for Godot. As the expositors of a ground-swelling undercurrent of despair, a despair related to outdated ideologies, cognitions, and institutions, crumbling icons and symbols which have lost their soothing authority and anxiety-binding properties, the existentialists seem profoundly in touch with the human condition, deeply concerned about man's maintaining himself as the referent for his own experience, and deeply fearful that man may lose his humanistic control to rational, materialistic, and collective forces. For us to be totally unaffected by the existentialists and to have no regard for them whatsoever, is for us to have perhaps unknowingly suffered inroads on our own humanism.

REFERENCES

1. Barrett, W., *Irrational Man: A Study in Existential Philosophy*. (New York: Doubleday, 1958).

2. Blackham, H.J., *Six Existentialist Thinkers*. (New York: Harper, 1959.)

3. Frankl, V.E., "Dynamics, Existence, and Values," *J. Existential Psychiatry*, 1961, 2, 5-13.

4. Kahler, E., *The Tower and the Abyss: an Inquiry into the Transformation of the Individual* (New York: Braziller, 1957).

5. Kaplan, A., *New World of Philosophy* (New York: Random House, 1961).

6. Koestenbaum, P., "Existential Psychiatry, Logical Positivism, and Phenomenology," *J. Existential Psychiatry*, 1961, 1, 399-425.

7. Kors, P.C., "The Existential Moment in Psychotherapy," *Psychiat: J. for Stud. Interpersonal Processes*, 1961, 24, 153-162.

8. Maslow, A.H., *Remarks on Existentialism and Psychology*. Greenville, Delaware: Psychosynthesis Research Foundation.

9. May, R., ed., *Existential Psychology* (New York: Random House, 1961).

10. May, R., E. Angel, & H.R. Ellenberger, eds., *Existence: a New Dimension in Psychiatry and Psychology* (New York: Basic Books, 1958).

11. Menninger, K., *Theory of Psychoanalytic Technique* (New York: Basic Books, 1958).

12. Mullan, H., Iris Sangiuliano, "The Subjective Phenomenon in Existential Psychotherapy," *J. Existential Psychiatry*, 1962, 2, 17-33.

13. Tillich, P., *The Courage To Be* (New Haven: Yale University Press, 1959).

14. Van Kaam, Adrian, *The Third Force in European Psychology*. Greenville, Delaware: Psychosynthesis Research Foundation.

Psychology:
A Prescriptive Science
Robert I. Watson

In the following article Watson states that the critical feature distinguishing psychology from the older, more mature, sciences is psychology's lack of a paradigm. The term *paradigm* was proposed by Thomas S. Kuhn, a philosopher of science, in his book *The Structure of Scientific Revolutions* (1962, 2nd ed. with postscript 1970) and defined as a principle that unifies, directs, and guides sciences for some time. Examples are the Ptolemaic, Copernican, and Newtonian paradigms. Psychology has not had such paradigms. According to Watson it was and is guided for extended periods of time simply by trends or themes, which he calls *prescriptions* because of the function they have performed in the development of psychology. In his definition, prescriptions are the "prevailing inclinations or tendencies to behave in a definable way in a particular science, in a particular country at a particular time." He identifies 18 contrasting pairs of prescriptions and shows how they manifested themselves in the history of psychology. However, they do not account for all of the history; thus a historian of psychology has to consider other factors, such as the prevailing contentual problems (that is, problems that originated in philosophy), the use of methods, personality characteristics of psychologists, and social circumstances.

The article is the address that Watson, as first president of the newly created Division of the History of Psychology (of the American Psychological Association) delivered at its charter meeting in 1966.

In a recent analysis of the dynamics of the history of the older, more mature sciences Kuhn (1962, 1963) holds that each of them has reached the level of guidance by a paradigm. In one of its meanings a paradigm is a contentual model, universally accepted by practitioners of a science at a particular temporal period in its development. With this agreement among its practitioners, the paradigm defines the science in which it operates. In a science where a paradigm prevails, one recognizes that a particular paradigm concerns chemistry, astronomy, physics, or the biological science. Illustrative in astronomy is the Ptolemaic paradigm which gave way

Robert I. Watson, Psychology: A prescriptive science, *American Psychologist,* 1967, **22**, 435-443. Reprinted by permission of the author and the American Psychological Association.

to the Copernican paradigm, and in physics is the Aristotelian paradigm which gave way to the Newtonian dynamic paradigm, which, in the relatively recent past, was superseded by the paradigm provided by Einstein and Bohr. The great events of science which occur when a new paradigm emerges Kuhn calls a revolution.

The historical sequence Kuhn holds to be as follows: As scientists go about the tasks of normal science, eventually an anomaly, i.e., a research finding, which does not fit the prevailing paradigm, is obtained. A normal science problem that ought to be solvable by the prevailing procedures refuses to fit into the paradigm or a piece of equipment designed for normal research fails to perform in the anticipated manner. Failures in science to find the results predicted in most instances are the result of lack of skill of the scientist. They do not call into question the rules of the game, i.e., the paradigm, that the scientist is following. Reiterated efforts generally bear out this commitment to the accepted paradigm that Kuhn calls a dogmatism. Only repeated failure by increasing numbers of scientists results in questioning the paradigm which, in turn, results in a "crisis" (Kuhn, 1963). The state of Ptolemaic astronomy was a recognized scandal before Copernicus proposed a basic change, Galileo's contribution arose from recognized difficulties with medieval views, Lavoisier's new chemistry was the product of anomalies created both by the proliferation of new gases found and the first quantitative studies of weight relations. When the revealed anomaly no longer can be ignored, there begin the extraordinary investigations that lead to a scientific revolution. After sufficient acceptance of this anomaly is achieved from the other workers in the field, a new paradigm takes the place of the one overthrown and a period of normal science begins. Since a paradigm is sufficiently open-ended it provides a host of problems still unsolved. In this period of normal science the task of the scientist is to fill out the details of the paradigm to determine what facts, perhaps already known, that may be related to the theory, to determine what facts are significant for it, to extend to other situations, and in general to articulate the paradigm. In short, it would appear that the activities of normal science are a form of "working through" in a manner somewhat akin to that task which occupies so much time in psychoanalytic psychotherapy.

When a new anomaly appears and is given support, the cycle then repeats.

The bulk of Kuhn's monograph is taken up with a historical account of the events leading up to scientific revolutions, the nature of these revolutions, and the paradigmatic developments thereafter, with many familiar facts of the history of astronomy, physics, and chemistry cast in this particular perspective. It is here that the persuasiveness of his point of view is to be found. The test of the correctness of Kuhn's views rests upon the fit of his data with the available historical materials. Kuhn uses the key concept of paradigm in several degrees of breadth other than contentually defining and it is difficult to know precisely what differentiates each of the usages. Fortunately, I can leave to the specialist in the history of the physical sciences the evaluation of the correctness of his reading the details of their history and the various meanings of paradigm, for I am more concerned with what can be drawn from what he has to say about other sciences that he contends lack a contentually defining paradigm.

In all of its meanings, a paradigm has a guidance function. It functions as an intellectual framework, it tells them what sort of entities with which their scientific universe is populated and how these entities behave, and informs its followers what questions may legitimately be asked about nature.

What are the consequences in those sciences that lack a defining paradigm? Foremost is a noticeable lack of unity within a science, indications of which Kuhn acknowledges as one of the sources for his paradigmatic concept, which arose in part from his being puzzled about "the number and extent of the overt disagreement between social scientists about the nature of legitimate scientific methods and problems [1962, p. X]" as compared to the relative lack of such disagreement among natural scientists.

That psychology lacks this universal agreement about the nature of our contentual model that is a paradigm, in my opinion, is all too readily documented.[1] In psychology there is still debate over

---

[1] Others have expressed themselves about the lack of unity in psychology. If one were asked what is the most comprehensive treatment of psychology since Titchener's *Manual* the answer must be the multivolumed *Psychology: A Study of a Science*, edited by Sigmund Koch (1959). Its general introduction makes considerable capital of the diversity of tongues with which psychologists speak and the preface comments that psychology proceeds along "several quite unsure directions, [p. V]." To turn to but one other source, Chaplin and Krawiec (1960) close their recent book on systems and theories with the prophecy that the task of the future is "to integrate all points of view into one. . . ."; to provide "a comprehensive theoretical structure with the integrating force of atomic theory . . . . [pp. 454-455]."

fundamentals. In research, findings stir little argument but the overall framework is still very much contested. There is still disagreement about what is included in the science of psychology. In part, at least, it is because we lack a paradigm that one psychologist can attack others who do not agree with him as being "nonscientific" or "not a psychologist," or both. Schools of psychology still have their adherents, despite wishful thinking. And an even more telling illustration, because it is less controversial, is the presence of national differences in psychology to such an extent that in the United States there is an all too common dismissal of work in psychology in other countries as quaint, odd, or irrelevant. National differences, negligible in the paradigmatic sciences such as physics and chemistry, assume great importance in psychology. A provincialism in psychology in the United States is the consequence, provincialism on a giant scale, to be sure, but still a provincialism which would and could not be present if a paradigm prevailed.

Before its first paradigm had served to unify it and while still in "the preparadigmatic stage" each physical science was guided by "something resembling a paradigm," says Kuhn. Since it was outside his scope, Kuhn said hardly more than this about the matter.

Psychology has not experienced anything comparable to what atomic theory has done for chemistry, what the principle of organic evolution has done for biology, what laws of motion have done for physics. Either psychology's first paradigm has not been discovered or it has not yet been recognized for what it is. Although the presence of an unrecognized paradigm is not ruled out completely, it would seem plausible to proceed on the assumption that psychology has not yet had its initial paradigmatic revolution. The present task is to answer the question—if psychology lacks a paradigm, what serves to take its place?

It would seem that it follows from Kuhn's position that whatever provides the guidance could not have the all-embracing unifying effect of defining the field in question since if it did so, a paradigm would exist. What seems to be required is some form of trends or themes, numerous enough to deal with the complexity of psychology and yet not so numerous as to render each of them only narrowly meaningful. Those which I have isolated follow.

THE PRESCRIPTIONS OF PSYCHOLOGY ARRANGED IN CONTRASTING PAIRS

Conscious mentalism-Unconscious mentalism (emphasis on awareness of mental structure or activity—unawareness)

Contentual objectivism—Contentual subjectivism (psychological data viewed as behavior of individual—as mental structure or activity of individual)

Determinism—Indeterminism (human events completely explicable in terms of antecedents—not completely so explicable)

Empiricism—Rationalism (major, if not exclusive source of knowledge is experience—is reason)

Functionalism—Structuralism (psychological categories are activities—are contents)

Inductivism—Deductivism (investigations begun with facts or observations—with assumed established truths)

Mechanism—Vitalism (activities of living beings completely explicable by physico-chemical constituents—not so explicable)

Methodological objectivism—Methodological subjectivism (use of methods open to verification by another competent observer—not so open)

Molecularism—Molarism (psychological data most aptly described in terms of relatively small units—relatively large units)

Monism—Dualism (fundamental principle or entity in universe is of one kind—is of two kinds, mind and matter)

Naturalism—Supernaturalism (nature requires for its operation and explanation only principles found within it—requires transcendent guidance as well)

Nomotheticism—Idiographicism (emphasis upon discovering general laws—upon explaining particular events or individuals)

Peripheralism—Centralism (stress upon psychological events taking place at periphery of body—within the body)

Purism—Utilitarianism (seeking of knowledge for its own sake—for its usefulness in other activities)

Quantitativism—Qualitativism (stress upon knowledge which is countable or measurable—upon that which is different in kind or essence)

Rationalism—Irrationalism (emphasis upon data supposed to follow dictates of good sense and intellect—intrusion or domination of emotive and conative factors upon intellectual processes)

Staticism—Developmentalism (emphasis upon cross-sectional view—upon changes with time)

Staticism—Dynamicism (emphasis upon enduring aspects—upon change and factors making for change)

The overall function of these themes is orientative or attitudinal; they tell us how the psychologist-scientist must or should behave. In short, they have a directive function. They help to direct the psychologist-scientist in the way he selects a problem, formulates it, and the way in which he carries it out.

The other essential characteristic is that of being capable of being traced historically over some appreciable period of time. On both counts, the term *prescription* seems to have these connotations.[2] It is defined in the dictionaries as the act of prescribing, directing, or dictating with an additional overtone of implying long usage, of being hallowed by custom, extending over time.[3]

[2]A fortunate historical precedent for using prescriptions in this way is to be found in a quotation from Leibniz in his *New Essays Concerning Human Understanding* (1949). It may help to make clear what is meant. "The discussions between Nicole and others on the *argument from the great number* in a matter of faith may be consulted, in which sometimes one defers to it too much and another does not consider it enough. There are other similar *prejudgments* by which men would very easily exempt themselves from discussion. These are what Tertullian, in a special treatise, calls *Prescriptiones* . . . availing himself of a term which the ancient jurisconsults (whose language was not unknown to him) intended for many kinds of exceptions or foreign and predisposing allegations, but which now means merely the temporal prescription when it is intended to repel the demand of another because not made within the time fixed by law. Thus there was reason for making known the *legitimate prejudgments* both on the side of the Roman Church and on that of the Protestants [Book IV, Ch. 15, pp. 530-531]."

[3]Something akin to the prescriptive approach has been suggested in the past. In the early part of the last century Victor Cousin (1829) followed by J.D. Morell (1862) developed a synthetical system of the history of philosophy based upon a division into the four aspects of sensationalism, idealism, scepticism, and mysticism.

In the '30s, Kurt Lewin (1935) was groping toward something similar in his discussion of the conflict between the Aristotelian and Galilean modes of thought. Lewin's shift of modes of thought from the Aristotelian to Galilean, although admitting of partial overlap, impress me as too saltatory, too abrupt in movement from qualitative appearance to quantitative reality, from search for phenotypes to search for genotypes, from surface to depth, from disjointed descriptions to nomothetic search for laws. They are, in my opinion, not so much a matter of qualitative leaps as they are gradual changes with the older views still very much operative. Lewin's conceptualizing in relation to the historic facts seems similar in spirit to Piaget's brilliant strokes on the process of development. I suspect that if we were to take Lewin as seriously, as did the American investigators who followed the leads of Piaget into painstaking detailed research, we would find that there was much blurring and overlap of these Lewinian shifts, as there seems to be at the Piagetian levels.

In applying the shift in modes of classification from the Aristotelian to Galilean syndrome, Brunswik (1956) placed psychology as showing the shift between Titchener in 1901 and Lewin in 1935. It is unfortunate that an arbitrary impression of finality emerges. Prescriptions, at any rate, are not conceived as emerging with such definitiveness; they appear gradually and tentatively to disappear and then to reappear.

Brunswik (1955, 1956) also casually used the term, "Thema" in somewhat the same broad sense that I use prescription, but without working out its meaning or scope. He also used the same term to apply to the seeking of analogical similarity to the content of another science (1955) and even to psychological content, as such (1956).

In his *Historical Introduction to Modern Psychology* through the 1932 revision but not his 1949 revision, Murphy (1932) in his summing up of the decades of 1910 and 1920 utilized quantification as the integrating theme to unify psychology but gave previous consideration to problem trends over the time expressed such as from structural to functional, from part to whole, from qualitative to quantitative and experimental to genetic-statistical. It is important to reiterate that these were used as guiding themes only for a summary of 2 decades, and not for the earlier history of psychology. When Murphy faced the task of summarizing from the vantage point of the late '40s, he abandoned this form of summarization.

It is for the reason of persisting over relatively long periods of time that prescriptions can be of historical moment. In fact, in choosing the particular prescriptions with which I deal the presence of historical continuity over at least most of the modern period was a major decisive factor. If an instance of some conception serving a directive function was of relatively short temporal dimension, it was not considered a prescription. It is for this reason that some prominent trends in psychology today do not appear as prescriptions. Physicalism and operationalism are very much part of the current *Zeitgeist* in psychology but because they are relatively new upon the psychological scene, they are not considered prescriptions. Instead, they serve as challenges to utilize the prescriptions for their explanation. It is characteristic of prescriptions that modern, more specifically formulated versions of the more general historically rooted ones may appear. Empiricism-rationalism have modern descendants in environmentalism-nativism.

To arrive at a reasonably complete and appropriate categorization of the prescriptions, I carried out two separable, although actually intertwined steps. I considered the present scene, for example, in a paper on national trends in psychology in the United States (1965), in order to ascertain what seemed to characterize psychology today, and then turned to the very beginning of the modern period in the history of psychology in the seventeenth century to see if these

---

Bruner and Allport (1940) analyzed the contents of psychological periodicals for the 50-year period, 1888-1938, in terms of individual "author's problem, his presupposition procedure, explanatory concepts and outlook in psychological science [p. 757]." The material provided the basis for Allport's 1939 Presidential Address to the American Psychological Association. In his summarization, Allport (1940) indicated that his survey showed an agreement with an earlier one by Bills and not only stated that is psychology "increasingly empirical, mechanistic, quantitative, nomothetic, analytic and operational," but also pleaded that should not psychology be permitted to be "rational, teleological, qualitative, idiographic, synoptic, and even nonoperational [p. 26]?" Thus, Allport and I show substantial agreement since five out of six "presuppositions" as he calls them, are among those in my schema of prescriptions. The reason that one exception, operational-nonoperational presuppositions, is not included in my schema is that I consider it, as explained before, historically rooted in other older prescriptions.

Allport and Bruner's work cries out for follow-up and I hope to have someone working on it in the near future. Allport did, however, use something akin to his schema in a comparison of American and European theories of personality published in 1957.

A more recent related publication is that of Henry Murray, who in the course of an overview of historical trends in personality research, made a plea for "a comprehensive and fitting classification of elementary trends" (1961, pp. 15-16), which he then classified as regional, populational, theoretical, technique, data ordering, intentional (pure or applied), and basic philosophical assumptional trends. This last, the basic philosophical assumption, was not in any way spelled out so there is no way of knowing what he had in mind.

themes were then discernible in recognizable form. In the 300-page manuscript that I have so far prepared, I can say that I find encouraging indications of the historical roots of these prescriptions somewhere in the contributions of Bacon, Descartes, Hobbes, Spinoza, Leibniz, Locke, and Newton, and in those of the lesser figures of the seventeenth century.

Turning to its directive-orientative function, it will be remembered that this theory of prescriptions is more than a classificatory system, more than a convenient means for a particular historian to order his account. These prescriptions were and are part of the intellectual equipment of psychologists. Psychologists are always facing problems, novel and otherwise. They do so with habits of thought, methodological and contentual, which they have taken from the past. This applies today with just as much force as it ever did in the past. In short, they are dynamic because psychologists accept, reject and combine prescriptions, thus thinking in certain ways and not in others.

In the above list, prescriptions have been presented in one of the ways they function—as contrasting or opposing trends.[4] At some point in their history most of these prescription pairings have been considered as opposed, even irreconcilable for example, naturalism as opposed to supernaturalism, and empiricism as opposed to rationalism.

A summarization, such as the list gives, inevitably distorts its subject matter. Especially pertinent here is the false impression of

----

[4] There is a precedent for considering the trends studies in terms of antithetical pairs. In his critical study, *Biological Principles,* J.H. Woodger (1929) considered the problems of biological knowledge to center on six antitheses: vitalism and mechanism, structure and function, organism and environment, preformation and epigenesis, teleology and causation, and mind and body. His emphasis was upon examining the current views circa 1929. Although he showed a lively appreciation of their historical roots, his task was not essentially historical.

W.T. Jones (1961) also has developed a means of evaluation of so-called "axes of bias" of order-disorder, static-dynamic, continuity-discreteness, inner-outer, sharp focus-soft focus, this world-other world, and spontaneity-process. Content high on the order axis shows a strong preference for system, clarity and conceptual analysis while that for disorder shows a strong preference for fluidity, muddle, and chaos. Illustrative applications to samples of poetry, painting, and documents in the social and physical sciences were made. Syndromes for the medieval, the Renaissance, the enlightenment, and the romantic periods were developed. The last, receiving the most attention, was characterized as showing soft-focus, inner-disorder, dynamic, continuity, and other-world biases. The results so far reported show it to be a promising technique.

Brunswik (1956) also speaks of the survival of dichotomizing doctrines, such as the four temperaments as illustrative of a prescientific syndrome in psychology.

tidiness this arrangement of antithetical isolated pairs gives. Consider the dichotomy, mechanism-vitalism. Does this oppositional way of presenting them exhaust the matter? By no means, mechanism bears relation to molecularism, and molecularism may come in conflict with supernaturalism, which in turn, relates to certain forms of dualism.

Prescriptions are by no means simple, dominant, isolated themes moving monolithically through history. In a recent analysis of the history of mathematical concepts in psychology, George Miller (1964) warns expressly against this kind of oversimplification. His treatment of what he calls the "varieties of mathematical psychology" (p. 1), that I consider to bear considerable relation to the quantivistic prescription, is further subdivided into several categories and subcategories. As he indicates, a more extensive treatment would require still others.

Their oppositional character does lead to explication of another characteristic of prescriptions. At a time, past or present, when both of the opposed prescriptions had or have supporters, it is possible to make some sort of an estimate of their relative strength; in other words, we may speak of dominant and counterdominant prescriptions. Rationalism dominated in seventeenth-century England; Locke was nearly alone in advocating empiricism. Nomotheticism dominates today in the United States; an idiographic prescription is sufficiently viable to make itself heard in protest against the prevailing state of affairs. Hence, idiography is counterdominant.

The presence of dominant and counterdominant prescriptions helps us to see how competitions and conflict may result. Whether purism or utilitarianism dominates in American psychology today, I would be hard put to say, but we can be sure of one thing—both prescriptions have sufficient protagonists to make for a prominent conflict. Dominance may shift with time; at one time supernaturalism dominated decisively, there followed centuries of conflict and today naturalism dominates almost completely.

Although important, their oppositional nature is not always present. Empiricism-rationalism has been presented as a contrasting pair, yet at least to the satisfaction of some psychologists and philosophers of science, they have been reconciled today at a higher level of synthesis. Induction and deduction were also considered antithetical once. In actual practice today, the scientist often sees them as aspects of an integrated method which permits him to weave them together. Sometimes prescriptions, rather than being contradictory, are contrary; there may be gradations, or relationships of degree as seems to be the case with methodological subjectivity-objectivity.

Reinforcing its directive character is the fact that prescriptions sometimes are "prejudgments," presuppositions or preconceptions that are acted upon without examination, that are taken for granted.[5] Some prescriptions are characterized by their being tacit presuppositions taken as a matter of course and even operating without explicit verbalization. What psychologist today says to himself that the problem he is considering is one that I must decide whether I should or should not quantify; instead he immediately starts to cast the problem in quantitative terms without further ado. Similarly, most psychologists are monists. That many psychologists would react to being called monists with a sense of incredulity and even resentment nicely illustrates my point. We think monistically without using the term. Similarly we are apt to follow empiricistic and naturalistic prescriptions without much thought to the fact that we do so. But there was a time when the issues of quantitativeness-qualitativeness, of monism-dualism, of empiricism-rationalism, and of naturalism-supernaturalism were very much explicit issues, occupying the center of the psychological stage. Often their implicit character seems to have come about when one became so dominant that the other no longer stirred argument. Sometimes no clear-cut agreed-on solution was verbalized, instead they were allowed to slide into implicitness. A shift of interest, rather than resolution with a clear-cut superiority of one over the other seems characteristic. Old prescriptions never die, they just fade away. Naturally, at some times and to some extent a prescription became less relevant to psychology, but these are matters of degree.

Much of psychology's early history is, of course, a part of philosophy. Many of these prescriptions had their roots in

---

[5] Of course, implicitness of historical trends is not a novel idea. Whitehead (1925) remarked that when one is attempting to examine the philosophy of a period, and by implication to examine a science as well, one should not chiefly direct attention to those particular positions adherents find it necessary to defend explicitly but to the assumptions which remain *unstated*. These unverbalized presuppositions appear so obvious to their adherents that it may even be that no way to state them has occurred to them. In similar vein, Lovejoy (1936) has observed that implicit or incompletely explicit assumptions operate in the thinking of individuals and ages.

philosophical issues, and are even still stated in what is current philosophical terminology as in monism-dualism and empiricism-rationalism to mention the two most obvious. I do not hesitate to use philosophical terminology because psychology cannot be completely divorced from philosophy either in its history or in its present functioning. This state of affairs is cause for neither congratulation nor commiseration. Psychology is not the more scientific by trying to brush this sometimes embarrassing fact under the rug as do some of our colleagues by teaching and preaching psychology as if it had no philosophically based commitments. They are psychology's Monsieur Jourdaines who deny they talk philosophical prose. Denying there is need to consider philosophical questions does not solve the problem. The very denial is one form of philosophical solution.

Since they were originally philosophical issues, it will be convenient to refer to some prescriptions as "contentual" problems. To bring home this point, the areas of philosophy in which certain of the prescriptions fall might be identified. Rationalism and empiricism have their origins in epistemology, monism and dualism in ontology (nature of reality), and molarism and molecularism in cosmology (structure of reality).

A major task in the history of psychology is to trace how the field individuated from the philosophical matrix. In this process, the prescriptions that served as major guidelines in the emergence of psychology as a separate discipline originally had a philosophical character, which took on a general scientific character with the emergence of the physical sciences in general, and psychological science in particular. It is in this sense that they can be referred to as philosophically contentual in character. Moreover, consideration by psychologists and others in the sciences transformed them sometimes in ways that only by tracing their history can one see the relation to their parentage.

Often the traditional terminology used herewith, for example, its dualistic and mentalistic locus has had to give way to objectivistic and monistic terminology. Confused and confusing though these terms might be, they still referred to something relevant to psychology. As they are formulated, psychologists may be repelled by "old-fashioned" air of the statement of many of the prescriptions. Justification is found in the fact that these are the terms in psychology's long history until a short 50 years ago.

Lacking a paradigm has meant that psychology looked to other scientific fields for guidance. It is characteristic of prescriptions that borrowing from other fields has taken place. Psychology's heritage from philosophy could be viewed in this manner. But there are other forms of borrowing which have entered into prescription formation. There has been noteworthy borrowing from biology, physiology in particular, signalized by Wundt's calling his work "physiological psychology" in deference to the methodological inspiration it was to him. But physics, highest in the hierarchy of the sciences, has just as often served as the model science. Psychology has had its dream of being a changeling prince. The rejected child of drab philosophy and low-born physiology, it has sometimes persuaded itself that actually it was the child of high-born physics. It identified with the aspiration of the physical sciences, and, consequently, acquired an idealized version of the parental image as a superego, especially concerning scientific morality, i.e., the "right" way for a scientist to behave.

Psychologists looked to these other sciences for methodological guidance.[6] This methodological cast is particularly evident in the prescriptions concerned with nomothetic law, inductivism-deductivism, quantitativism-qualitativism, methodological objectivism and subjectivism, and determinism-indeterminism. It follows that these prescriptions apply to varying degrees to other sciences. So, too, does the puristic-utilitarian prescription, and working through the naturalistic-supernaturalistic problem.

Some of the contentual prescriptions have counterparts in other sciences. Salient to all biological sciences are developmentalism-statisticism, functionalism-structuralism, mechanism in its various guises, and molecularism-molarism. It is also at least possible that many of these prescriptions would be found to have counterparts in other non-scientific areas of knowledge, such as literature, religion, and politics. After all, man's reflective life, as the "Great Ideas" of Adler and Hutchins and their cohorts show, has much more interpenetration into the various compartmentalization of knowledge than is customarily recognized. But to explore this further would be to extend discussion beyond the scope of the paper.

In the preparadigmatic stage of a science, a scientist may also become an adherent to a school, that is to say, he may accept a set of

---

[6] It should be noted that this looking to other sciences and finding evidences for prescriptions implies that paradigmatic sciences are not denied the presence of prescriptions. Exploration is, however, outside of the scope of this paper.

interlocking prescriptions espoused by a group of scientists generally with an acknowledged leader. Functionalism, behaviorism, Gestalt psychology, and psychoanalysis are representative.

The orientative character of prescriptions is also present in a school. As Marx and Hillix (1963) recognize, each school seems to follow a directive—you should be primarily concerned with the study of the functions of behavior in adapting to the environment and the formulation of mathematical functions relating behavior to antecedent variables: *functionalism*—you ought to study the stimulus-response connections through strict methodological objectivism; *behaviorism*—you can arrive at useful formulations of psychological principles through consideration of molar units of both stimulus and response, i.e., configurations or fields; *Gestalt*—you should be concerned with the interplay and conflict of the environment and native constituents of the disturbed personality with special attention to its unconscious aspect, *psychoanalysis.*

Salience or nonsalience of particular prescriptions characterize schools. Behaviorism is both contentually objectivistic and environmentalistic (empirical). However, the former is salient; the latter is nonsalient. Contentual objectivism is central and indispensable, environmentalism is not crucial to its central thesis. Behaviorism would still be behaviorism even if all behaviorists were nativistic in orientation.

In broad strokes based on salient prescriptions, functionalism is functionalistic, empiricistic, quantitativistic and molecularistic. Behaviorism has as salient orientative prescriptions, contentual objectivism, and molecularism. Gestalt psychology may be said to make salient molarism, subjectivism, and nativism. The salient directive prescriptions of psychoanalysis seem to be dynamicism, irrationalism, unconscious mentalism, and developmentalism.

The differing patterns of salient prescriptions of the schools serves also to make more intelligible their differing research emphases upon particular contentual problems—the functionalists with their empiricistic salience upon learning; the behaviorists with their peripheralism upon motor activity (including learning); Gestalt psychology with its molarism and nativism upon perception; and psychoanalysis with its dynamicism and irrationalism upon motivation.

There is an even broader level of prescriptions, that of national trends exemplified by the Symposium on National Trends at the

XVIIth International Congress to which reference already has been made (Watson, 1965). Here greater diversity than that of the schools is expected. Instead of patterns, it is most meaningful to couch their discussion in terms of dominance and counterdominance.

Immersion in the current scene as a participant-observer, adds immeasurably to the already complicated task of the historian who is apt therefore to approach the present with a great deal of trepidation. What will be hazarded is inclusive broad, therefore, crude overall characterization of the current scene of psychology in the United States. It will serve as another exercise in the application of the prescriptive approach. Although couched in terms of a somewhat different array of prescriptions than now is being used, for reasons explained earlier, I will quote from the concluding summary of my paper on this Symposium:

> It has been seen that national trends in modern American psychology follow certain dominant prescriptions. Determinism, naturalism, physicalism and monism, although very much operative, are judged to incite relatively little opposition. Functionalism, operationalism, quantification, hypothetico-deductivism, environmentalism, and nomotheticism are likewise dominant, but there are counterprescriptions which tend to oppose them. As for the schools of psychology, psychoanalysis, very obviously, and Gestalt psychology, less firmly, still stand apart. Serving as counterprescriptions to those dominant in psychology are those calling for increased complexity in theorizing, for an increased attention to philosophical matters, for general acceptance of phenomenology, for increased attention to existential psychology and in a somewhat amorphous way almost all of the areas of personality theory calls for counterprescriptions of one sort or another [p. 137].

It is important to note that most national prescriptive trends have been stated in terms of dominance and counterdominance, which reflects diverseness, not integration. Indeed, the highest level of integration in psychology is still that of the schools, not that of the nation. Different patterns of dominance and counterdominance are present in different countries. For the sake of brevity, but at the risk of oversimplification, methodological and contentual objectivity, particularly in the form of operationalism prevails in the United States, while methodological and contentual subjectivity, especially in the form of phenomenalism, does so in large segments of Continental Europe.

It follows that patterns of dominant prescriptions characterize a given temporal period and geographical area. When we wish to emphasize the then current intertwined pattern of dominant prescriptions as having a massive cumulative effect, we refer to the *Zeitgeist*. The *Zeitgeist* in itself is empty of content until we describe that which we assign to a particular *Zeitgeist*. The strands that enter into the *Zeitgeist* include the dominant prescriptions of that time. So the *Zeitgeist* and prescriptive concepts are considered complementary. One of the puzzling facets of the *Zeitgeist* theory is just how to account for differential reaction to the same climate of opinion. The prescriptive approach may be helpful in this connection. Plato and Aristotle, Hobbes and Spinoza, Hume and Rousseau, each experienced the same *Zeitgeist* but also had idiosyncratic, non-dominant prescriptive allegiances.

What I have said about prescriptions by no means exhausts this complexity. Prescriptive trends fall and rise again, combine, separate, and recombine, carry a broader or narrower scope of meaning, and enter into different alliances with other prescriptions, change from implicitness to explicitness and back again, and concern with different psychological content and its related theories. Beyond this, I hesitate to go, except to say I am confident there are probably other as yet unrecognized ramifications. Prescriptions endure while the psychological facts, theories, and areas which influenced their acceptance are ephemeral and ever changing.

If I have stressed the directing and guiding phase of the effect of prescriptions on a scientist's thinking, it is not because of blindness to the other side of the coin, the originality of the scientist. A scientist not only is guided by but also exploits both paradigms and prescriptions. He does so in terms of his originality, and other factors that make for individuality.

My enthusiasm for prescriptions may have left you wondering whether this is all that I can see in the history of psychology. Let me reassure you at this point. The usual contentual topics of psychology, most broadly summarized as sensation, learning, motivation, and personality and the hypotheses, laws, and theories to which their investigations give rise are still considered very much a part of its history. As differentiated from philosophically oriented contentual prescriptions, it is these and related contentual topics which show that a concern for psychology is the subject matter of historical investigation. These contentual topics are the vehicles with which all historians of psychology must work. Even here there is another point about prescriptions that I might mention. There seems to be some historical evidence of an affinity between certain prescriptions and certain contentual topics, e.g., dynamicism with motivation, developmentalism with child and comparative psychology, personalism, idiographicism, and irrationalism with personality, and empiricism with learning. Individual psychologists who have been strongly influenced by particular prescriptions are apt to reflect them in their work. Although the evidence has not yet been sought, it is quite plausible to believe that, reciprocally, choice of problem area may influence allegiance to certain prescriptions. In similar vein, I suspect that prescriptions tend to cluster in non-random fashion. Off hand, acceptance of supernaturalism seems to have an affinity for teleology, indeterminism, and qualitativism; naturalism with mechanism, determinism, and quantitativism; nomothesis with determinism; rationalism with deduction; empiricism with induction.

To return to extraprescriptive aspects of psychology, the methods of psychologists—observation and experiment—cannot be neglected in a historical account. Psychologists' use of these methods are an integral part of that history. However, certain prescriptions, particularly those identified earlier as methodological in nature, allow casting considerable historical material in the way that has been sketched.

Any adequate history of psychology must reconsider the personality characteristics of individual psychologists and the extra-psychological influences, such as social circumstance, which have been brought to bear upon each psychologist. Can one imagine that Hobbes' psychological views were independent of his detestation of organized religion, adoration of a strong central government, and fear of the consequence of political disorders?

I would like to summarize briefly some of the functions that I consider prescriptions to serve. They provide classification and summarization through a conceptual framework which can be applied historically. Prescriptions provide principles of systematization which are related to, and yet to some extent are independent of, the particular contentual or methodological problem of the individual psychologist. They are also mnemonic devices which make it possible to summarize and convey a maximum of meaning with a minimum of words. Going beyond anything even hinted at in the paper, prescriptive theory might also help to make history a tool for investigation of the psychology of discovery, and also serve as a framework for studies using content analysis applied to historical documents.

Prescriptions are characterized by an oppositional character manifested in dominance and counterdominance, an implicit as well as explicit nature, a philosophically based contentual character, a methodological character borrowed from the other sciences, a presence in other fields, an interlocking in schools of psychology with some salient and others nonsalient, a clash of prescriptions at the national level and a participation of prescriptions at the national level, and a participation of prescriptions in the *Zeitgeist*. Since psychology seems to lack a unifying paradigm, it would seem that as a science it functions at the level of guidance by prescriptions.

REFERENCES

Allport, G.W. The psychologist's frame of reference. *Psychological Bulletin*, 1940, 37, 1-28.

Allport, G.W. European and American theories of personality. In H.P. David & H. von Bracken (Eds.), *Perspectives in personality theory*. New York: Basic Books, 1957. Pp. 3-24.

Bruner, J.S., & Allport, G. W. Fifty years of change in American Psychology. *Psychological Bulletin*, 1940, 37, 757-776.

Brunswik, E. The conceptual framework of psychology. In O. Neurath et al. (Eds.), *International encyclopedia of unified science*. Chicago: University of Chicago Press, 1955. Pp. 655-760.

Brunswik, E. Historical and thematic relations of psychology to other sciences. *Scientific Monthly,* 1956, 83, 151-161.

Chaplin, J.P., & Krawiec, T.S. *Systems and theories of psychology*. New York: Holt, Rinehart & Winston, 1960.

Cousin, V. *Cours de l'histoire de la philosophie*. 2 vols. Paris: Pichon & Didier, 1829.

Jones, W.T. *The romantic syndrome: Toward a new method in cultural anthropology and history of ideas*. The Hague: Nijhoff, 1961.

Koch, S. (Ed.) *Psychology: A study of a science*. Study 1. *Conceptual and systematic*. New York: McGraw-Hill, 1959.

Kuhn, T.S. *The structure of scientific revolutions*. Chicago: University of Chicago Press, 1962.

Kuhn, T.S. The function of dogma in scientific research. In A.C. Crombie (Ed.), *Scientific change*. New York: Basic Books, 1963. Pp. 347-369.

Leibniz, G.W. *New essays concerning human understanding*. (Trans. by A.G. Langley) La Salle, Ill.: Open Court, 1949.

Lewin, K. The conflict between Aristotelian and Galilean modes of thought in contemporary psychology. In, *A dynamic theory of personality*. New York: McGraw-Hill, 1935. Pp. 1-42.

Lovejoy, A.O. *The great chain of being.* Cambridge: Harvard University Press, 1936.

Marx, M.H., & Hillix, W.A. *Systems and theories in psychology.* New York: McGraw-Hill, 1963.

Miller, G.A. (Ed.) *Mathematics and psychology.* New York: Wiley, 1964.

Morell, J.D. *An historical and critical view of the speculative philosophy in Europe in the nineteenth century.* New York: Carter, 1862.

Murphy, G. *An historical introduction to modern psychology.* (2nd rev. ed.) New York: Harcourt Brace, 1932.

Murray, H.A. Historical trends in personality research. In H.P. David & J.C. Brengelmann (Eds.), *Perspective in personality research.* New York: Springer, 1961. Pp. 3-39.

Watson, R.I. The historical background for national trends in psychology: United States. *Journal of the History of the Behavioral Sciences,* 1965, 1, 130-138.

Whitehead, A.N. *Science and the modern world.* New York: Mentor, 1925.

Woodger, J.H. *Biological principles: A critical study.* New York: Harcourt, Brace, 1929.

Psychological Science versus the Science-Humanism Antinomy: Intimations of a Significant Science of Man
Sigmund Koch

Sigmund Koch, associated with Duke University from 1942 to 1964 and now Stiles Professor of Comparative Studies at the University of Texas, is known to American psychologists for his role in editing and publishing the multivolume *Psychology: A Study of a Science*, on which more than 80 scientists participated. He studied at New York University, the University of Iowa, and Duke, where he received his Ph.D. in 1942. His chief interests are motivation, learning, and, particularly, theoretical psychology. For 30 years Koch has been examining every aspect of contemporary psychology and its scientific status. In an article published in 1969 he concluded that psychology as a science or a coherent discipline has been misconceived and has failed to fulfill the expectations that its program raised. In the following article he discusses the relationship of psychology to the humanities and explores psychology's possible role in bridging together mankind's two great strivings, the scientific and the humanistic. The reading of this article may not be easy, but it should prove rewarding and thought provoking for those who make the effort.

I am going to engage a problem for which I have feeble intellectual tools. It relates to an issue that if not yet a *cause célèbre* seems on the way to becoming so—that concerning the relations between science and the humanities. If my tools for this task are feeble, I claim some extenuation merely from the fact that I am a psychologist. Little that my field has done during its brief history as an independent science could equip me for work on the present question. Moreover, the climate of my field has not been such as to develop any sensibility in humanistic domains. Indeed, if there ever was such sensitivity, its suppression, starvation, and eventual atrophy seems to have been a necessary condition for Guild membership.

The reason I speak on this theme is that sooner or later someone from my field *must*. The situation is becoming embarrassing.

Sigmund Koch, Psychological science versus the science-humanism antinomy: Intimations of a significant science of man. *American Psychologist*, 1961, **16**, 629-639. Reprinted by permission of the author and the American Psychological Association.

Physicist-philosophers have addressed the theme. Physicist-literary critics have not been silent. Physicist-novelists have joined the issue. Physicist-administrators have not gone unheard. Sociologists have spoken. From the other side of the fence, historians, literary critics, and philosophers have been vocal. And more and more stridently there have of course been the educators, politicians, and last, but not least, military men. Psychologists have been strangely silent. That in itself is a fact worth pondering.

Against a silence so charged, anything one says must sound explosive. One might thus just as well speak with utter abandon from the start. I will state my main thesis boldly right now.

In any consideration of the science-humanities antinomy, the position of psychology must be given special, if not central, attention. In any assessment of the actual relations—similarities, differences, interpenetrations—of the work of science and of the humanities, psychological questions and modes of analysis must almost as a matter of definition be paramount. In any creative redefinition of the relations between science and the humanities, in any readjustment of the images, lay or technical, of these two great areas of the human cognitive adventure, which might more justly and precisely convey the essential unity of knowledge, psychological questions are again paramount. If psychology is to live up to the purview of its very definition, then it *must* be that science whose problems lie closest to those of the humanities; indeed, it must be that area in which the problems of the sciences, as traditionally conceived, and the humanities intersect. Relative to the present divisive situation in the world of knowledge, psychology, then, might be seen as a third force. It *could* be seen as a third force whose ranks, when they arrive in no man's land in sufficient numbers, would fill up the gap separating the contenders and reveal all three forces for what they really are: detachments from the same army which had forgotten that there was a common enemy.

Note the shift from the descriptive to the normative in the last paragraph. As I have already hinted, far from having been a "third force," psychology (and the social sciences—my remarks will concentrate on psychology, but hold as well for the social sciences) in the twentieth century has perhaps done more to solidify, sharpen, perpetuate, thus obfuscate, the division between science and the humanities than any other "force" in the culture. It has sold to man an image of life as being nastier and more brutish, if longer, than any that Hobbes could have entertained—an image which could leave to the humanist only the role of the idle *voyeur* peering tenderly into a sewer.

Among the brute facts that must be faced are these: Ever since its stipulation into existence as an independent science, psychology has been far more concerned with being a science than with courageous and self-determining confrontation of its historically constituted subject matter. Its history has been largely a matter of emulating the methods, forms, symbols of the established sciences, especially physics. In so doing, there has been an inevitable tendency to retreat from broad and intensely significant ranges of its subject matter, and to form rationales for so doing which could only invite further retreat. There has thus been, at least until very recently, an ever widening estrangement between the scientific makers of human science and the humanistic explorers of the content of man. Indeed, in its search for scientific respectability, psychology has erected a widely shared epistemology, and a conceptual language which render virtually impossible the exploration of the content of man in a differentiated way. So deeply engrained are these latter in the sensibilities of inquirers that even those who seek to study subtle or complex human phenomena are badly handicapped.

When phenomena of the sort that might concern the humanist *are* approached, a drab and sodden "middlebrowism" prevails. Humanists who stumble upon the results of such efforts are likely to feel revulsion. Perhaps fortunately they are unlikely so to stumble, in that scientific or academic psychology (exclusive of the psychiatric disciplines) has had only slight *direct* effect upon the culture at large. This fact of minimal direct representation in the culture is in itself significant. On the other hand, the indirect effects on the culture are I think profound.

With only a few exceptions, major twentieth century psychologists have had limited background in the humanities and, what is worse, limited sensibilities at esthetic levels and even as savorers of experience. The psychology of esthetics has practically not existed in the twentieth century. Psychology seems not even to have had its due share of individuals who have made significant independent contributions in humanistic areas. I can think of only one living psychologist who has, but of several living *physicists*.

Having observed that psychology must be a third force and then that throughout its history it has done little other than create the need for one, it is now only fair that I consider a number of matters which might reduce the stress between these observations. I begin by itemizing—to save time, summarily and dogmatically—some signs that something that could become a third force may be shaping up in psychology. Then, more positively, I (a) address a specific, though general, problem of a sort which psychology must engage in preparing to approach questions of joint import to the humanities and itself, and finally, (b) consider certain aspects of psychology's role in any effective redefinition of the relations between science and the humanities, and certain consequences thereof for problems of education in general and in psychology.

Of the factors predisposing psychology to confront problems of humanistic import, the first is indigenous; the second, though compelling, is indirect.

1. Psychology, after a long interval of imaging its ends and means on the model of physics, as interpreted and mediated by logical positivism, operationism, neopragmatism, and related movements, seems ready, perhaps for the first time in its history, to rise to its problems in free and *sui generis* ways. Simplistic theories of correct scientific conduct no longer occasion monolithic conformity. Behaviorist epistemology is under stress; neobehaviorism on the defensive; while neo-neobehaviorism enfolds itself in a womb of its own manufacture. There is a strongly increased interest in perception and central process, even on the part of S-R theorists: in fact a tendency for the central area of psychological interest to shift from learning to perception. There is a marked, if as yet unfocused, disposition on the part of *even* fundamental psychologists to readdress human phenomena and to readmit questions having experiential reference. Along with such changes, there is a marked devaluation of hypothetico-deductive formalization as an end in itself, and a shift of emphasis from the *form* of theoretical formulations to their meaning, empirical adequacy, and even illumination value. These and many cognate changes are conspicuous in the general literature and emerge with special force from the pages of *Psychology: A Study of a Science*. I have summarized the complex of changes to which I here allude in the "Epilogue" to Study I (Koch, 1959) of that enterprise,

and happily offer that reference in exchange for the extensive development of the present assertions that might here be desirable.

Such changes *could* liberate psychology for the engagement of problems of direct humanistic concern. Though not tantamount to actual progress on such problems, the change of atmosphere is so marked as to betoken deep dissatisfaction with recent and traditional constrictions upon the range of research, even on the part of those fundamental psychologists whose purity is as the driven snow. The unrest has in fact led to a broadening of the range of problems investigated within more or less conventional terms and a diversification of the systematic and conceptual options that have been asserted.

2. Coincident and interrelated with these signs are others. An important set is provided by the changing image of the nature of science projected by the philosophy of science and by certain elements in the scientific community at large. These trends, uneven and disorderly, but pointing up and condoning a thoroughgoing pluralism of ends and means in science, are sure to influence the future direction of psychology. The picture I have in mind here is an enormously complex movement within recent scholarly culture—indeed one which has done much to prepare the grounds for the present general interest in exploring, and perhaps recentering, the relations between science and the humanities. I refer to such diverse matters as the weakening grip of logical positivism and related analytic philosophies; the relegitimation of metaphysics; the recognition of substantial areas of mootness in many problems of scientific method (e.g., the nature of definition, of "interpretation," of mathematics itself) which had been considered solved. Moreover, men like Bronowski, Polanyi, and others have at least begun to show that science, especially at theoretical levels, involves creative processes which no formalism can reduce to rule, processes in fact not dissimilar to those mediating the activity of poets, artists, historians, and other residents on the other side of the barricades. Such developments have been remarkably slow to register on psychology. For instance, the philosophy of science still talked in psychological literature is approximately 20 years out of date. But such developments are *beginning* to influence psychology.

I have said that psychology (and social science) has constructed a language which renders virtually impossible a differentiated exploration of the content of man. Such a constraint upon the very possibility of a sensitive analysis of experience is precisely what has kept psychology away from questions that could be of concern to the humanist. The humanist, I fear, has no particular reason for regretting this loss. Psychology, however, *must*, in that if the awesome range of its subject matter be the functioning of organisms, there is no sound basis for it to defect at precisely that point at which such functioning becomes most interesting and, by the judgment of civilization, valued. As an illustration of the type of constraint that must be loosened if psychology is to effect contact with phenomena of import to the humanities (and thus itself), I should like to consider some issues pertaining to the analysis of motivation.

This illustration will demonstrate, I think, that major psychological problems cannot be embraced except in terms of levels of experiential sensitivity commonly cultivated, in the past, only in the humanities. It shows, further, that when such embracement *does* occur, psychology can begin to say things which are relevant to the humanities and indeed can reveal itself to the humanist as an ally. Again, I think that this illustration will make clear that we need a new kind of psychologist who fuses a scientific temperament with a humanistic sensibility, and perhaps a subspecies of humanist with a similar admixture of traits.

A few years ago, I suggested some ideas concerning what I consider an essential rephrasing of certain motivational phenomena. There is no reason why they should have been especially difficult. Yet they have proven so slippery to psychologists, and even to myself at times, that there seems no alternative but to refer this to the immense power of those schematisms which at some rock-bottom level regulate psychological thought.

My point of departure was something like the following. In the common sense epistemology of the West, there has long been a tendency to phrase all behavior and sequences thereof in goal directed terms: to refer behavior in all instances to ends, or end-states, which are believed to restore some lack, deficiency, or deprivation in the organism. I have called this deeply embedded presumption a kind of rough-and-ready "instrumentalism" which forever and always places action into an "in order to" context. In this common sense theory, behavior is uniformly assumed predictable and intelligible when the form "X does Y in order to . . ." is completed. In many instances in practical life it is possible to fill in this form in a predictively useful way. Often, however, a readily identifiable referent for the end-term is not available. In such cases we assume that the form must hold, and so we hypothesize or invent an end-term which may or may not turn out to be predictively trivial and empty. For instance, X does Y in order to be happy, punish himself, be peaceful, potent, respected, titillated, excited, playful, or wise.

Precisely this common sense framework—syntax if you will—has been carried over into the *technical* theories of motivation of the modern period, of which there have been bewilderingly many. In the technical theories, the central assumption is that action is always initiated, directed, or sustained by an inferred internal state called variously a motive, drive, need, tension system, whatnot, and terminated by attainment of a situation which removes, diminishes, "satisfies," or in any other fashion alleviates that state. The model is essentially one of disequilibrium-equilibrium restoral and each of the many "theories of motivation" proposes a different imagery for thinking and talking about the model and the criterial circumstances or end-state under which such disequilibria are reduced or removed. Matters are rendered pat and tidy in the various theories by the assumption that all action can be apportioned to (*a*) a limited number of biologically given, end determining systems (considered denumerable, but rarely specified past the point of a few "e.g.'s" like hunger and sex), and (*b*) learned modifications and derivatives of these systems variously called second-order or acquired motives, drives, etc.

My proposal, I think, is a quite simple one. In essence, it points up the limitations of referring *all* action to extrinsic, end determining systems, as just specified; it challenges the fidelity to fact and the fruitfulness of so doing. At the most primitive level it says: if you look about you, even in the most superficial way, you will see that all behavior is *not* goal directed, does not fall into an "in order to" context. In this connection, I have presented (Koch, 1956) a fairly detailed descriptive phenomenology of a characteristic sequence of "creative" behavior, which shows that if this state of high productive motivation be seen by the person as related to an extrinsic end (e.g., approval, material reward, etc.), the state becomes disrupted to an extent corresponding to the activity of so seeing. If, on the other hand, some blanket motive of the sort that certain theories reserve for such circumstances, like anxiety, is hypothesized, one can only say that the presence of anxiety in any reportable sense seems only to disrupt this creative state, and in precise proportion to the degree of anxiety.

If such states seem rare and tenuous, suppose we think of a single daily round and ask ourselves whether *everything* that we do falls into some clear-cut "in order to" context. Will we not discover a rather surprising fraction of the day to be spent in such ways as "doodling," tapping out rhythms, being the owners of perseverating melodies, nonsense rhymes, "irrelevant" memory episodes; noting the attractiveness of a woman, the fetching quality of a small child, the charm of a shadow pattern on the wall, the loveliness of a familiar object in a particular distribution of light; looking at the picture over our desk, or out of the window; feeling disturbed at someone's tie, repelled by a face, entranced by a voice; telling jokes, idly conversing, reading a novel, playing the piano, adjusting the wrong position of a picture or a vase, gardening. Yet *goal directedness* is presumably the *fact* on which virtually all of modern motivational theory is based.

The answer of the motivational theorist is immediate. He has of course himself noticed certain facts of the same order. Indeed, much of motivational theory is given to the elaboration of detailed hypothetical rationales for such facts, and these the theorists will have neatly prepackaged for immediate delivery. I will not detain the discussion by unwrapping these packages, but merely guess at a few of the contents. There will be some containing the principle of "irrelevant drive"; others, "displacement" and other substitutional relations. An extraordinarily large package will contain freely postulated motives with corresponding postulated end-states, as, e.g., "exploratory drive" and its satiation, "curiosity drive" and its satisfaction, perceptual drives, esthetic drives, play drives, not to mention that vast new complement of needs for achievement, self-realization, growth, and even "pleasurable tension." Another parcel will contain the principle of secondary reinforcement or some variant thereof like subgoal learning, secondary cathexis, etc. Another will provide a convenient set of learning principles which can be unwrapped whenever one wishes to make plausible the possibility that some acquired drive (e.g., anxiety, social approval) which one arbitrarily assigns to a bit of seemingly unmotivated behavior, *could* have been learned. Another contains the principle of functional autonomy. There are indeed a sufficient number of packages to make possible the handling of any presumed negative instance in *several* ways. Why skimp?

The answer to all this is certainly obvious. The very multiplication of these packages as more and more facts of the "in and for itself" variety are acknowledged, makes the original analysis, which was prized for its economy and generality, increasingly cumbersome. But more importantly, it begins to get clear that the *search* for generality consisted in slicing behavior to a very arbitrary scheme—the result was a mock generality which started with inadequate categories and then sought rectification through more and more ad hoc specifications. In the end, even the apparent economy is lost and so largely is sense. Worst of all, much of the research which continues to get done in terms of the standard model, the problems that are raised, the phenomenal analysis that takes place, become senseless. To take but one conspicuous example, it should never have taken the amount of research that it has to establish (and *still* not to the satisfaction of all) that the drive reduction hypothesis is inadequate.

The positive part of my proposal would commence with an analysis of what seems involved in behavior which is phenomenally of an "in and for itself" variety as opposed to clear-cut instances of the "in order to" sort of thing. Take "play" to start with. I would resent being told that at any time I had a generalized need for *play* per se. I do not like to think of myself as that diffuse. I never liked cards. Nor even chess. And indeed my present girth is fairly solid testimony to the fact that I never had an insistent urge for the idle agitation of my musculature. My play "needs," or activity "needs," etc. have been such that if described with any precision at all, we soon find ourselves outside the *idiom* of "needs." I have been *drawn towards* certain specific activities which—because they fall into no obvious context of gainful employ, biological necessity, or jockeying for social reward, etc.—could be *called* play. But I have been drawn to these activities, and not others, because (among other reasons) they "contain," "afford," "generate" specific properties or relations in my experience towards which I am adient. *I like these particular activities because they are the particular kinds of activities they are*—not because they reduce my "play drive," or are conducive towards my well-being (often they are not), or my status (some of them make me look quite ludicrous), or my virility pride (some are quite girlish).

Do I like them, then, by virtue of nothing? *On the contrary*, I like them by virtue of something far more *definite*, "real," if you will, than anything that could be phrased in the extrinsic mode. Each one I like because of *specific* properties or relations immanent, intrinsic within the given action. Or better, the properties and relations *are* the "liking" (that, too, is a terribly promiscuous word). Such properties and relations in any ongoing activity are no doubt dated instances of aspects of neural process which occur each over a family of conditions. Similar properties or relations would be produced (other factors constant) the next time I engage in the given activity. And no doubt there are families of activities which share similar properties and relations of the sort I am trying to describe. Thus there may be a certain consonance (by no means an absolute one) about the *kinds* of "play" activities that I like. But more importantly, properties or relations of the same or similar sorts may be generated within activity contexts that would be classified in ways quite other than play: eating, esthetic experience, sexual activities, problem solving, etc.

I call such properties or relations "value properties," and the (hypothetical) aspects of neural process which generate them, "value determining properties." Value or value determining properties to which an organism is adient, I call "positive"; those to which the organism is abient, "negative." Adience and abience of organisms are controlled by value determining properties (or by extension, value properties) of the different signs.

It can be instructive to consider from the point of view just adumbrated any of the types of "in and for itself" activity to which it is common gratuitously to impute extrinsic, end determining systems with their corresponding end-states. Thus for instance, one can only wince at the current tendency to talk about such things as "curiosity drives," "exploratory drives," "sensory drives," "perceptual drives," etc. as if the "activities" which are held to "satisfy" each of these "drives" (if indeed they are distinct) were just so much undifferentiated neutral pap that came by the yard. I am inclined to think that even the experimental monkeys who learn discrimination problems for the sole reward of being allowed visual access to their environments from their otherwise enclosed quarters, are being maligned when it is suggested that what their "drive" leads them to

seek is "visual stimulation." Could it not be that even for the
monkeys there are sights they might prefer not to see? Be this as it
may, when explanations of this order are extended, say, to visually
mediated esthetic activities in man, the reduction to a pap-like basis
of particulate experiences to which many human beings attribute
intense (and differentiated) values, can only be held grotesque.

To make such points graphic and further to clarify the notion of
"value properties," it may be well to take the hypothetical instance
of a person looking at a painting. I will quote a passage (Koch, 1956)
in which I once introduced the notion through such an example.

> X looks at a painting for five minutes, and we ask, "Why?" The
> grammar of extrinsic determination will generate a lush supply of
> answers. X looks in order to satisfy a need for aesthetic experience. X
> looks in order to derive pleasure. X looks because the picture happens
> to contain Napoleon and because he has a strong drive to dominate. X
> looks because "paintings" are learned reducers of anxiety. . . . Answers
> of this order have only two common properties: they all refer the
> behavior to an extrinsic, end-determining system, *and* they contain very
> little, if *any* information. . . .
>
> A psychologically naive person who *can* respond to paintings would
> say that an important part of the story—the essential part—has been
> omitted. . . . Such a person would say that *if* the conditions of our
> example presuppose that X is really looking at the painting *as* a
> painting, the painting will produce a differentiated process in X which
> is correlated with the act of viewing. That fact that X continues to view
> the painting or shows "adience" towards it in other ways is equivalent
> to the fact that this process occurs. X may report on this process only
> in very general terms ("interesting," "lovely," "pleasurable"), or he
> *may* be able to specify certain qualities of the experience by virtue of
> which he is "held" by the painting.
>
> . . . Suppose we assume that there are certain immanent qualities
> and relations within the process which are specifically responsible for
> any evidence of "adience" which X displays. Call these "value-
> determining properties." We can then, with full tautological sanction,
> say that X looks at the painting for five minutes because it produces a
> process characterized by certain value-determining properties. This
> statement, of course, is an empty form—but note immediately that it is
> not necessarily more empty than calling behavior, say, "drive-
> reducing." It now becomes an empirical question as to *what* such
> value-determining properties, intrinsic to the viewing of paintings, may
> be, either for X or for populations of viewers.

> Though it is extraordinarily difficult to answer such questions, it is
> by no means impossible. The degree of agreement in aesthetic
> responsiveness and valuation among individuals of . . . varied environ-
> mental background but of comparable sensitivity and intelligence is
> very remarkable indeed (pp. 73-74).

It becomes important now to note that even in cases where the equilibrium model seems distinctly to fit, it may still yield an extraordinarily crass specification of the activities involved and either overlook their subtle, and often more consequential, aspects, or phrase them in a highly misleading way. Thus, for instance—though I do not have time for the analysis of the large class of activities imputed to so extensively studied a drive as hunger—I know of no account which gives adequate attention to the facts that in civilized cultures cooking is an art form, and that the discriminating ingestion of food is a form of connoisseurship. There is no reason in principle why value properties (or classes thereof) of the sort intrinsic to eating processes may not yield to increasingly accurate identification. Further, though we should not prejudge such matters, it is possible that certain of the value properties intrinsic to eating processes may be of the same order as, or in some way analogous to, value properties involved, say, in visual art-produced processes.

Because these ideas are often found difficult, let us take the case of another activity-class which can be acceptably, but only very loosely, phrased in a language of extrinsic determination: sexual activity. On this topic, the twentieth century has been a vast liberation of curiosity, scientific and otherwise. Yet the textbook picture of sex, human sex, as a tension relievable by orgasm—a kind of tickle mounting to a pain which is then cataclysmically alleviated—is hardly ever questioned at theoretical levels (at least in academic psychology). When it is, it is likely to be in some such way as to consider the remarkable possibility that some forms of "excitement" (e.g., mounting preclimactic "tension") may them- selves be pleasurable, and this may be cited, say, as a difficulty for the drive reduction theory, but not for some other drive theory, say some form of neohedonism like "affective arousal," which recognizes that the transition from some pleasure to more pleasure may be reinforcing. But our view would stress that sexual activity is a complex sequence with a rich potential for value properties; for ordered, creatively discoverable combinations, patterns, structures of value properties, which are immanent in the detailed quiddities of sexual action. Sexual experience, like certain other experiential contexts, offers a potential for art and artifice not unnoticed in the history of literature, fictional and confessional, but rarely even distantly mirrored in the technical *conceptualizations*. (The technical *data language* is another matter, but even here the "fineness" of the units of analysis involved in much empirical work is aptly symbolized by Kinsey's chief dependent variable, namely the "outlet" and frequencies thereof.) The vast involvement with this theme at private, literary, and technical levels, has produced little towards a precise specification of experiential value properties, certainly none particularly useful at scientific levels.

Sex, eating behavior, activities written off to curiosity, play, perceptual drives, creative behavior, etc., are contexts each with a vast potential for the "discovery" and creative reassemblage of *symphonies* of value properties. Doubtless each such context offers a potential for differential ranges of value properties, but it is highly likely that there is marked overlap among such ranges. Indeed, formal or relational similarities in experiences that "belong" to quite different contexts of this sort suggest that Nature sets a fairly modest limitation on the number of "fundamental" value properties implicated in activity. There is much reason to believe, from the protocols of experientially sensitive and articulate people, as well as from the observation of behavior, that certain of the value properties intrinsic to such varied contexts of events as the "perception" of (and directed behavior towards) a picture, a poem, of a "problem," whether scientific, mathematical, or personal, of a "puzzle" in and for itself, are of an analogous order and in some sense overlap. And as we have just tried to show, it is reasonable to believe that the so-called consummatory aspects of hunger or of sex "contain" relational qualities not dissimilar to some of the value properties immanent in "complex" activities like those listed in the last sentence.

Once the detailed phenomena of directed behavior are rephrased in terms of intrinsic value properties, it becomes possible to reinspect the extrinsic language of drives and the like, and determine what utility it might actually contain. For *some* behaviors clearly are brought to an end or are otherwise altered by consummations, and organisms clearly show both restless *and* directed activities in the absence of the relevant consummatory objects. Questions about the relations between what one might call extrinsic and intrinsic grammar for the optimal phrasing of motivational phenomena are among the most important for the future of motivational theory.

Whatever is viable in the drive language is, of course, based in the first instance on "organizations" of activity sequences which converge on a common end-state. Each such organization, if veridical, would permit differential (but overlapping) ranges of value properties to "come into play." No doubt *primary* organizations of this sort, when veridical, are related to deviations of internal physiological states, the readjustments of which play a role in the adaptive economy. When such deviations are present, it is probable that certain value properties, or ranges thereof, are given especial salience and effectiveness with respect to the detailed moment-to-moment control of directed behavior. That all activities, however, must be contingent on such deviation-states, on the face of it seems absurd. Behavior will often be directed by value properties which have nothing to do with gross organizations of this sort, and which may in fact conflict with the adjustment of the concurrent deviation. Much of what is called "learned motivation" will consist not in "modifications of primary drives"—whatever that can mean—but rather in the building up of expectations and expectation-chains which terminate in anticipated processes with value properties. Whatever might be meant by the learned drives would be built up as systems of anticipation of value property constellations and sequences.

This, however, is not the place to develop whatever exists of the more detailed aspects of the formulation. The purpose was to suggest a line of thought which might bring psychology into contact with phenomena of fundamental concern both to itself and to the humanities. If I have established the barest possibility of such a development, that is all I could have wished.

You will now wish from me concrete illustrations of the "value properties" which I have talked about with such indirection. Your wish is unfair. Much as I would like to oblige, I cannot accomplish, in passing, what several thousand years of human, humanistic, and scientific analysis has failed to do. In the case of visual art-produced experience, the typical kinds of things that the estheticians, articulate artists, and art critics have been able to come up with in millennia of analysis, have been such global discriminations as harmony, symmetry, order, "significant form," "dynamic tension," "unity in variety," the "ratio of order to complexity," etc. By "value properties" I have in mind far more specific relational attributes of experience. They could, to borrow a cue from Gibson, be contingent upon subtle relational invariants in arrays of stimulation, as distributed over space and cumulated over time. They are almost certainly related to what Gibson would call "high order variables of stimulation" and are themselves high order relational variables within experience. The isolation of such value properties will not be accomplished within any specifiable time limit, will require learning to use language in new ways, and will require most of all the efforts of many individuals of exceptional and specialized sensitivity in significant areas of experience.

What, in effect, I am doing is merely drawing attention to certain particulate phenomena which all of us "know" are there. We have never *directly* set ourselves the problem of isolating and precisely delineating such phenomena. There are many reasons for this, some implicit in our common-sense conceptual categories and even the structure of our language, and others related to the fleeting character and extraordinary embeddedness of these "phenomena" in the flux of our experience. As I have just said, to approach these matters, we will have to learn to attach language to experience with a new kind of specificity. We will have to arrive at a highly differentiated set of metaphors, each of which is isomorphic with a significant relational aspect of experiential process, and learn to use these *intersub-jectively*—i.e., so as to achieve reliability of communication among groups having relevant sensitivity, but not necessarily esoteric levels thereof.

Such a system of metaphors must thus be *teachable*, and to achieve this as well as their initial "isolation," we must depend on all available knowledge, method, and technical lore of *perception psychology*. Experimental technique deriving from psychophysical method in the broadest sense must be tapped, as must knowledge and method concerning sensory mechanisms, neurophysiology of perception, perceptual learning, etc.

The great advances within psychology to date—and these must not be underestimated by humanists or anyone else—have been in the domain of discovering the pitfalls involved in any attempt to isolate functionally significant units or variables determining organismic action and experience, and in methods for coping with, compensating for, circumventing these pitfalls. If the humanist complains that many of the variables thus far isolated and studied by psychology seem to him insignificant, that is nothing to the point. Some substantial core of the experimental analysis, statistical compensation, environmental "input" control, and control or measurement of background variables within the organism emerging from this work has quite general significance for the analysis of organismic systems, whatever the "units" of analysis, problems, or hypotheses that are entertained. That is the real contribution of psychology to modern culture—of which laymen and humanists alike have never been apprized.

Recently the British physicist-novelist, C.P. Snow, has stirred much discussion by virtue of a distinction that he makes between "two cultures"—the "scientific" and the "traditional" or "literary-intellectual"—which he sees as almost completely insulated one from the other and at cross purposes.[1] He finds this a blight on the world intellectually, but he is more concerned with practical consequences that may in fact threaten the future of the world, in that he feels that the ruling establishment, which (in England at least) receives a purely humanistic education, must become increasingly incapable of wise decisions without an understanding of science. His proposed solution for this—not an unradical one for England, where the undeniable charm of its archaic educational forms can instill vast defensive passions—is that the curriculum be diversified, that science be gotten into humanities programs, and vice versa. Snow, of course, is dealing with a pressing practical problem and, in light of the educational traditionalism in England, he is not to be criticized for posing so limited a solution. But it seems to me to be indeed so limited as to be almost beside the point.

No fertile integration or even interplay between science and the humanities can come about—either in individual minds or in the scholarly community as a whole—merely by juxtaposing scientific and humanistic subject matters in the same curriculum. Snow, for instance, complains that at a literary gathering he attended, not a single individual proved to have knowledge of the second law of thermodynamics. Had they been taught this information at Cambridge, I doubt that they would have found it particularly titillating.

---

[1] In his provocative anatomy of the two cultures (Snow, 1959), it is clear that by the "traditional" he has broadly in mind the humanistic culture, while by the "scientific" he means specifically the physicist-engineer culture. He leaves psychology and social science out of the picture and thereby, I think, effects a serious distortion. For, one of the unique features of psychology is precisely that this is an area at which the two cultures must be in contact.

What is needed is not merely more joint education in these two great divisions of subject matter, but a *new and more significant mode* of education which will present them in such a way as to reveal their relatedness and represent human knowledge for the organic thing that it is.

But such a proposal must remain largely empty until we know *what kind* of "organic thing" knowledge is, know this precisely and in detail. Only then can the ideologies and images of science and the humanities be adjusted in such a way as to reduce the arbitrary gap that still exists; only then could such ideologies and images find their place within a single more inclusive organization. *Such* changes would of course automatically be reflected in education and *only then* could we expect to see once more in the world a type of individual who has not been with us since the nineteenth century: the scientist-humanist (or, of course, humanist-scientist). He will not of course be the same such individual as that of the nineteenth century, just as the nineteenth century version was not the same as that of the Enlightenment or the Renaissance. He will be highly specialized (the present differentiation of knowledge demands this of its scholars), but whether his work falls into an area allocated to science or a humanity, he will have deeply within him a sense of its relations to whatever areas are actually *relata*, however they be named. He will also have a sense of the relatedness of all inquiry and be not ignorant of, or uninterested in, at least a few of the things that exist across the gulf that so effectively separated his recent forebears.

But all this is contingent on the prior exploration of relations between science and the humanities, no easy task when assayed for its dimension away from the conference table. Returning to our major theme, it is psychology which, as third force, must take the lead. This is not to be seen as altruism, still less as imperialism. Its subject matter leaves it no choice. It can only blame itself for having elected to be the empirical science of the functioning of intact organisms, including intact human ones, in all of its forms. It is trapped. Even if, say, it defensively held that esthetic experience were illusory, it would still have to prove this, thus study and account for esthetic experience.

My discussion of value properties was but one illustration of a context in which rapprochement with matters of humanistic concern (and with humanists) could not only augment knowledge in valuable ways, but lead to a surer understanding of its organization. There are many other connections in which psychology must play an important, if not central, part in getting the nature of man's knowledge, and thus its texture, into better focus. This of course is tantamount to saying that psychology may have a central responsibility in helping put the ideology and image of science into finer correspondence with its actual content. I should like to mention in passing one especially vital context in which psychology could contribute to such an end.

I have in mind the need for effective psychological analysis of the nature of language, especially certain of the relevant problems like those of definition, meaningfulness, and meaning, which have too long been left in the hands of philosophers of science and, to some extent, linguists (which latter group to the best of my knowledge seems to have pretty much side-stepped them). The philosopher of science regards these as problems in epistemology and treats them mainly in terms of that tradition. It is, incidentally, my growing conviction that many problems still allocated to epistemology will receive little further clarification until they are recognized for the psychological problems they are.

The relevance of questions of definition and meaning to the present issue is this: most dichotomies advanced as between science and the humanities depend fundamentally on the assumption that they use "concepts" and "terms" of disparate type, that they seek differing "explanations" (or modes thereof), and that they generate different modes of meaning. If this is so, then an adequate analysis of language should have something to say about whether and to what extent such differences exist. If one begins with the premise (which everyone admits) that scientific language develops as a specialization of the natural language, and recognizes further that the natural language is what humanists use when they use language, then a psychological analysis of the functioning of natural language could well be instructive.

I have recently become interested in such matters and am amazed at what a bit of preliminary thinking seems to reveal. If we look at the problem of definition, for instance, psychologically, we immediately see that a definition, if apprehended by a recipient, must result in a process of perceptual learning and that what is learned is the discrimination of the properties, relations, or system thereof, which the definer wishes to designate by the term. This clearly means that definition, at bottom, is a *perceptual training process* and that everything that we know about the *conditions* of perceptual training and learning must apply to the analysis of definition. Adding to this a few obvious circumstances concerning the genesis and status of words in the natural language—circumstances that can be inferred from a study of something no more esoteric than dictionaries—quite a few matters take on a new light. It emerges, for instance, that contrary to what we were once told by logical positivists and others, no natural language and no scientific one of any richness can be regarded as organized into logical levels such that all terms are reducible to, or definable upon, a common (and usually, as the story goes, extremely restricted) definition base. On the contrary, if we want to pinpoint with a term any reasonably subtle, embedded, or delicately "contoured" relation or property, we must often, if using verbal means of definition, build up our defining expression from words that are *just as*, or even more, "rarified" (remote from the presumptive definition base) as the one at issue. Moreover, for defining abstract or subtle concepts, or ones based on "new" discriminations, we will have to go outside of language and relate the term to a carefully controlled "perceptual display" (as it were) far more often than any logical positivist, especially of an older day, would care to admit.

Such findings, if they are that, are related to others at considerable variance with our lore and strictures concerning our *own* definitions in psychological discourse. Thus one thing that eventuates is the utter irrationality of expecting that all terms will be understood and used with equal nicety by all people in a scientific field (even with a "competent investigator" clause thrown in), depending only on the adequacy of the "operational" definitions. More generally, it becomes clear that in science, as in the humanities, communication (and in the first instance, observation) must depend on the ability to make certain specialized discriminations, which in turn depends on the individual's learned "backlog" of discriminations, *and* on special perceptual sensitivities. Universality of communication (relative to given language communities) therefore is achievable *neither* in science nor the humanities, and unless we want to disenfranchise the "advance fringe" ideas of the best minds in science—at the phase when communication can be accomplished only among a scattering of individuals—we will have to accept it that science cannot in principle be differentiated from the humanities on that basis.

Considerations of the order just adduced suggest that in each field of science and, of course, the humanities, there will necessarily be a plurality of language communities consisting in each case of individuals owning differential stocks of learned discriminations and differentially specialized discriminative capacities. Typically there will be also a vertical stratification of sublanguage communities within the same area of a given science, each corresponding to groups of individuals who have learned to make, or are capable of making, discriminations of different degrees of fineness. Suppose we call a certain criterial overlap of learned discriminations and special discriminative capacities, as among a number of individuals, a discrimination pool. We can then say that a language community (or subcommunity) of whatever size is characterized by a specified discrimination pool. Since in psychology *problems concerning any range of human endeavor or experience can be the object of study*, a unique feature of psychology is that it must premise its research on discrimination pools each of which overlaps to some definite extent with the discrimination pools in all of those widely ranged human areas. Thus a special demand upon psychology is that it contain a more widely diversified, and probably larger, collection of language communities than any other department of knowledge currently institutionalized. Among these must be groups of individuals whose specialized perceptual sensitivities overlap with humanists' in each of the areas in which humanistic endeavors are pursued. That is a large requirement. Where it is not met, no humanistic work of any import can be done. It is grotesque to suppose that someone totally devoid of the special discriminations and sensitivities of the artist could do meaningful psychological work in that field; similarly that an illiterate could contribute to the psychology of language or of literature.

Our brief comments on language have thus pointed up the difficulties that must be overcome if psychology is to move into its responsibility as "third force." It is clear that psychology needs many individuals having sensitivities overlapping with those of the humanist. Yet the same individuals must, in the first instance, have the special aptitudes and sensitivities—whatever they be—which equip them for *scientific* modes of analysis! For reasons foreshadowed in our remarks concerning education, it cannot expect them in even remotely adequate numbers. The absolute number of such individuals turned out by the culture at large is in itself pathetically small.

Such individuals in general are not attracted to psychology, in that the very sensitivities at issue are what preclude their interest.

The emergence of a third force can at best be expected to be painfully slow and contingent on considerable skill with the bootstrap. So-called "recruitment" philosophies which currently see the ideal candidate as a kind of *Übermensch* in theoretical physics and carpentry at once, will of course have to be redefined, but not *derigorized.* If anything, the requirement will be more stringent, not less. That such a requirement will be met by few is no fatal objection. As with all requirements, compromise will continue to be the general rule. Of greater importance is that psychology be so imaged as to convey the need, the possibility, and the importance of work in areas of humanistic import. This may bring to us some of the individuals having the requisite combination of aptitudes, who now bypass us because of their uncongeniality towards the current image. Most important, we must work towards those more general educational changes at all levels which might increase the absolute number of such individuals in the culture at large.

Feeble and gradual as such a "program" may seem, the stakes are very high. For what has hardly been in the picture except by innuendo so far, has been the world outside the cloisters. Despite the "creativity" fad, and despite the recent spate of social criticism which has made organization men, lonely crowds, affluent societies, ex-urbanites, and their ilk seminar topics at every shopping center, the gentle process of dehumanization which twentieth century man has so cosily accepted continues unabated. Indeed, the truly frightening fact is that so much of the social criticism itself reproduces, at second remove, the qualities of the object criticized. Take the "beatnik" whose devastating critique of an inarticulate society is to form a cult of absolute inarticulateness.

The reduction of man to his present dimension need not be temporary. When the ability to differentiate among experiences is lost, experience is lost. When the perception of differential values as they inhere in the quiddities of experience and action is lost, then value is lost. Nothing says that these things need return. In this homogenization of experience, the recent images of science and of the humanities have played a profound part. The newer outgrowths of science—psychology and the social sciences—which, had they pursued their appropriate subject matter, could have helped resolve knowledge into its proper spectrum, turned away from that subject matter. Rejecting the first force from which all knowledge had germinated, they became camp followers of that second force called "science," or at least their image of that force. Have they the courage to become the third force that could some day cause the end of armies?

REFERENCES

Koch, S. Behavior as "intrinsically" regulated: Work notes towards a pre-theory of phenomena called "motivational." In M.R. Jones (Ed.), *Current theory and research in motivation.* Vol. 4. Lincoln: Univer. Nebraska Press, 1956. Pp. 42-86.

Koch, S. Epilogue to study I. In S. Koch (Ed.), *Psychology: A study of a science.* Vol. 3. New York: McGraw-Hill, 1959. Pp. 729-788.

Snow, C.P. *The two cultures and the scientific revolution.* New York: Cambridge Univer. Press, 1959.

Pebble Picking vs. Boulder Building
Joseph R. Royce

Joseph R. Royce, director of the Center for Advanced Study in Theoretical Psychology and professor of psychology at the University of Alberta in Canada, studied at the University of Chicago and received his Ph.D. with Thurstone in 1951. His main interest is theoretical psychology; he has also pursued factor analysis and behavior genetics. He is the author of *The Encapsulated Man* (1964) and editor of *Psychology and the Symbol* (1965) and *Toward Unification in Psychology* (1970). He is also an associate editor of the journals *Multivariate Behavioral Research* and *Psychological Record*. In this article Royce expresses the opinion that psychology has suffered from "an empirical overload" and from the lack of an integrating theory. Moreover, he finds psychology sufficiently mature now "to readmit . . . the deliberation of philosophical issues as well as attempts to evolve theoretical structures."

As you know, this symposium,[1] while primarily a celebration of the first 50 years in the life of a leading university, also marks the first official function of the American Psychological Association's Division of Philosophical Psychology. As a spokesman for the Steering Committee, consisting of Joseph Lyons, James Royce, Edward Scott, E.J. Shoben, and myself, and as a representative of the new division, I have been asked to offer a few remarks celebrating the official remarriage of psychology and philosophy after almost 100 years of legal separation. The point of my remarks will be that psychology and philosophy were divorced in name only, for the good of the children, that it was, in fact, good for the children, but that it will no longer be necessary to live in sin.

The close relationship which existed between psychology and philosophy at the end of the 19th century is well known. Perhaps

Joseph R. Royce, Pebble picking vs. boulder building. *Psychological Reports*, 1965, **16**, 447-450. Reprinted by permission of the author and Southern Universities Press.

[1] The Banquet Address presented at the Rice University Symposium on Behaviorism and Phenomenology: Contrasting Bases for Modern Psychology, March 20-22, 1963. The major addresses by S. Koch, R. MacLeod, N. Malcolm, C. Rogers, M. Scriven, and B.F. Skinner appear in Wann (1964).

not as well known is the fact that 5 of the first 13 presidents of the American Psychological Association were philosophers—William James, John Dewey, Josiah Royce, and J.M. Baldwin. William James was president twice, in 1894 and 1904. (The only other two-timer was G. Stanley Hall.) Two of these philosopher-psychologists, James and Dewey, were certainly listened to by psychologists as well as philosophers. But the cumulative effect of laboratory demonstrations on how to experiment on the mind had a tremendous and, in my opinion, a desirable, impact on the development of modern psychology around the turn of the century, and the pendulum properly swung away from the arm-chair.

While it was necessary for the scientific psychology of Wundt's time to cast aside the arm-chair in order to effect a clear cut separation from the onus of speculative philosophy, it is no longer necessary or even desirable for us to allow the pendulum to continue swinging in the direction of super-empiricism. A solid observational base is absolutely essential for the growth and development of a young science. But, if it stakes too much of its future on naive empiricism, it runs the same risk of extinction which befell the dinosaur, which could not survive because of an overload of bodily bulk. Contemporary psychology is suffering from a comparable overload, namely, that of empiricism. While it will always be true that we can stand more precise observations, and while we shall always require empirical data, we are currently in the condition of not knowing what to do with the masses of data already accumulated. The mere accumulation of facts does not necessarily lead to the development of a unified science. I have labeled this rather naive approach as "pebble picking." And, while I will be one of the first to defend the necessity for pebble pickers, since the scientific enterprise is simply impossible without such observations at its base, I want to develop the thesis that it is necessary for us to proceed more consciously in the direction of boulder building.

Ivan Petrovitch Pavlov (1941) put it rather nicely in his intellectual last will and testament, at the age of 87, when he said:

> Facts are the air of the scientist. Without them you can never fly. Without them your "theories" are useless efforts. Yet while studying, experimenting, and observing try not to stay on the surface of the facts. Do not become the archivists of facts. Try to penetrate to the secret of their occurrence, persistently search for the laws which govern them (p. 189).

Unfortunately, the psychological Zeitgeist for the past 25 or 30 years, due primarily to the previously mentioned concern for being identified as "scientific," has been essentially anti-rational. This anti-thought or pro-data bias of contemporary psychology is particularly true of American psychology. This is not to say that psychological theories have been verboten; nor does it follow that such outstanding theorists as Tolman, Hull, and Thurstone have not had a big impact. What I do want to say is that we have armies of empirical pebble pickers, and a mere handful of rational boulder builders. And, since the bulk of graduate training is under the control of the army of empiricists, they tend to perpetuate the present empirical-rational imbalance.

Unfortunately, the concern for the practical and the observable, and the corresponding lack of concern for the theoretical and the philosophical, pervade our entire American culture, and to a considerable extent, the culture of Western civilization. It is generally agreed that scientific theorists have come out of European rather than American institutions of higher learning. The revolutionary thinkers, such as Einstein, Darwin, and Freud, are outstanding examples of this point. American science, on the other hand, has been strong in the applied fields, in the technology of motor cars, military hardware, and clinical and industrial psychology. I have no objection to America's strength in applied science; I am simply deploring our lack of similar concern for basic science, and, in particular, within the framework of pure science, our lack of support for the theoretically and philosophically oriented scientist.

One type of evidence as to what a nation values can be ascertained by an analysis of how it spends its money. We all know that the U.S.A. does not have much faith in the egghead by virtue of how little it spends, proportionately, on intellectual matters. The proportion of the national income which is spent on education and research is something like 6 or 7%. And, as you know, 95% of research funds are devoted to the physical sciences, with the bulk of that money being spent on such humanistic items as atomic and hydrogen bombs and rockets. Most of the remaining 5% is distributed among the biological and medical sciences. A tiny fraction of the 5% is available for the behavioral and social sciences. Most of this research money is devoted to efforts which show a fairly immediate practical payoff, and, of course, the assumption is that results will only pay off if we somehow gather data, even if much of the data gathering is being done within a framework of inadequate methodology and theory and questionable philosophic assumptions. Putting all this another way, how many granting agencies can you point to for support of purely theoretical research? Omitting the obvious, although limited contributions on the part of academic institutions (How many professors of theoretical psychology are there?), the only foundation support which allows the behavioral scientist time to think has come from the Ford Foundation—and the "think tank" at Stanford is only good for one year!

In spite of the fact that we know we cannot have applied science unless we have basic science, we do little to support basic science. In spite of the fact that basic science requires integrating theory in order to "fly" in the manner suggested by Pavlov, we do little to support basic theory. In spite of our very real awareness that, in the long run, there is actually nothing more practical than good theory and sound philosophy, we do little to support their development. We promote empirical concern at the expense of theoretical concern in many ways. We do it by glorifying the gathering of data. We do it by not permitting theoretical doctoral dissertations in our graduate schools. We do it by publishing personal diatribes and opinions under the banner of theory instead of requiring as rigorous training and performance in this facet of science as we do in the empirical facet. And why do we do all this? Because mid-20th century psychology has been dominated by a powerful myth which says that theoretical efforts are not scientific. Such stuff smacks too much of the arm-chair we are told. The error which is committed in this view is the usual straw man error—no serious theoretical scientist is concerned about concepts, principles, and laws unless they will eventually mesh with the observed facts. He recognizes the attendant risks in theorizing, but he also realizes that without theory there is no science. In this connection, Boring (1953), says that:

> Psychology *is* theory, just as science is theory—descriptive theory sometimes, and explanatory theory at other times, yet theory, because it is concerned with constructs that are things and their relations. Psychology and science are theory, empirically based. You check constantly against phenomenal particulars but you are after the generalities that the particulars yield (p. 182).

Cornelius Lanczos (1959), a European theoretical physicist, in a recent article on Einstein and the role of rationalism in contemporary physics, shows that science is not only theory, but that it is inextricably intermeshed with philosophy. Take these two quotations, for example: "What Einstein did was not a formal accomplishment. He did not approach the problem from the standpoint of finding some mathematical equation which will describe a certain group of phenomena. Something much more fundamental was at stake, namely, *the critical evaluation of the entire foundation of theoretical physics.* Certain things which were always taken for granted were put under scrutiny and their falseness proved. This was no longer mere physics and mathematics" (p. 47) and "Here started that dogged uphill fight of Einstein which lasted for 10 years and which is perhaps unparalleled in the entire history of the human mind: a fight which did not arise from any experimental puzzle but from a purely philosophical puzzle of the mind" (p. 48). This metaphysical foundation which underlies the assumptions of any scientist is insightfully expounded in such efforts as the physicist-philosopher Margenau's (1950) book, *The Nature of Physical Reality.* He elaborates, for example, the following six metaphysical requirements for good theory in science: (1) Constructs must possess logical fertility. (2) Constructs must have multiple connections. (3) Theory must have permanence and stability. (4) Extensibility of constructs is required. (5) The requirement of causality and (6) the requirement of simplicity and elegance may be pointed to. His answer to the question, Where do metaphysical guiding principles come from? is: "They first emerge in the stream of experience as tentative expedients, grow into implicit beliefs with increasing application, and finally, strengthened by repeated success, pervade the entire texture of our theories about the world" (p. 81).

Well, if Boring, Lanczos, and Margenau are right when they say that science is theory and that philosophy is unavoidable, hadn't we better stop killing the goose that lays the golden egg? We not only must stop the anti-think Zeitgeist, we'd better promote a Zeitgeist of philosophic awareness and sophisticated theory building if we wish to develop a healthy basic and applied psychology. It is at least as important to the growth of psychology that we develop and support rational boulder builders as to continue to turn out empirical pebble pickers![2]

[2]Those who share this opinion will possibly be pleased to learn of a local development which is designed to do something about the shortage of creative thought in contemporary psychology. The University of Alberta, under the aegis of the Department of Psychology, has proposed a Center for Advanced Study in Theoretical Psychology. (The Center is now under review by the University Board of Governors.) The major idea behind the Center is to

REFERENCES

Boring, E.G. The role of theory in experimental psychology. *Amer.. J. Psychol.*, 1953, **66**, 169-184.

Lanczos, C. Albert Einstein and the role of theory in contemporary physics. *American Scientist*, 1959,47, 41-59.

Margenau, H. *The nature of physical reality.* New York: McGraw-Hill, 1950.

Pavlov, I.P. *Conditioned reflexes and psychiatry.* New York: International Publishers, 1941.

Wann, T.W. (Ed.) *Behaviorism and phenomenology.* Chicago: Univer. of Chicago Press, 1964.

bring theoretical psychology into clearer focus so as to meet an urgent need within the discipline—a need to advance our understanding of behavior by conceptual integration—and to train a small handful of potential young theoreticians (at the doctoral and post-doctoral levels) to continue such efforts. The present staff of the Center is as follows: L. von Bertalanffy, J. R. Royce, W. Rozeboom, H. Tennessen (Dept. of Philosophy), and T. Weckowicz (Depts. of Psychology and Psychiatry). The Center will sponsor its first Conference on Theoretical Psychology at the university's mountain campus in Banff, Alberta, in April, 1965, under the theme *Toward the Unification of Psychology.* The major participants include invited guests S. H. Bartley, R. B. Cattell, L. K. Frank, E. Galanter, W. Koehler, D. Krech, R. MacLeod, O. H. Mowrer, plus the Center staff. It is anticipated that papers and discussion will be published.

Dimensions of Psychological Theory
Richard W. Coan

Historians of psychology usually identify and describe theoretical trends on "an armchair basis." For this reason they often differ in their analyses. How could these trends be analyzed not in a speculative but in a more objective and scientific way? In this article Richard W. Coan proposes an objective method of analyzing "basic trends in psychological theory both over time and at any given point in time" and shows how this method can be effectively implemented in determining the strength, duration, and interaction of various theoretical dimensions. Such a method can be a powerful tool in the historical study of theoretical psychology.

Richard W. Coan, who received his Ph.D. at the University of Southern California in 1955, is professor of psychology at the University of Arizona. His publications and interests are in personality theory and measurement and in theory construction.

One form of human behavior that has always interested psychologists is the construction of psychological theory. Possibly because of our personal involvement in this behavior, however, there has been little effort to subject it to systematic scientific investigation. The main concern of the present paper is the basic trends evident in psychological theory both over time and at any given point in time. This seems an appropriate site for multivariate research. Yet with few exceptions, all the relevant analyses to date have been conducted on an armchair basis—sometimes, fortunately, with rather penetrating insight.

Every reader is already familiar with some of these speculative analyses. Gordon Allport (1955) has distinguished between a Lockean tradition and a Leibnitzean tradition in psychological theory. The first has predominated in Anglo-American psychology. Its stress on a reactive organism may be traced through associationism to such modern manifestations as environmentalism,

Richard W. Coan, Dimensions of psychological theory. *American Psychologist,* 1968, **23**, 715-722. Reprinted by permission of the author and the American Psychological Association.

behaviorism, stimulus-response psychology, positivism and operationism, and a stress on the peripheral and molecular. The Leibnitzean tradition assumes an active or self-propelled organism, and its influence is best seen today on the European continent in such movements as phenomenology and Gestalt psychology.

In a similar vein, Rogers (1961) spoke of two basic trends in present-day American psychology, which he called objective and existential. The first is characterized by rigorous hard-headedness, reductionist theory, operational definitions, objective methods, and an emphasis on the concrete and specific. The existential trend, on the other hand, is concerned with the experiencing person and with the whole spectrum of human behavior.

Ansbacher (1961) employed a comparable dichotomy in a paper on holism. He recognized two basic viewpoints in psychology—the elementaristic and the holistic. Elementarism is said to be generally associated with determinism, mechanism, reductionism, and the espousal of a "spectator" theory of knowledge, while holism and organicism are accompanied by an emphasis on becoming, creativity, growth, and self-actualization and by a conception of the learner as a concerned participant in the learning process.

The dichotomous classifications we have thus far considered are all reminiscent of one proposed by Murray (1938) in the 1930s. Murray claimed that there were two basic types of psychologists—the peripheralists and the centralists. The peripheralists tend at the same time to be positivists, mechanists, elementarists, sensationists, and objectivists, while the centralists tend to be conceptualists, totalists, intuitionists, dynamicists, and subjectivists. A still earlier and obvious parallel is the distinction which James (1907) made between tender-minded and tough-minded philosophers.

The above schemes constitute a meager sampling of pertinent speculation, but they represent a common pattern that could easily be illustrated more extensively. The classification is unidimensional, and there is surprising agreement regarding the grouping of component variables—I say surprising because it is so easy to think of individual theorists and movements that combine these variables into nonconforming patterns. There is much casual evidence to suggest that some of these variables actually constitute mutually independent, or at least semiindependent, dimensions.

In a somewhat more sophisticated treatment of this problem, Brunswik (1952) insisted on what amounts to a two-dimensional system. He distinguished two basic issues in psychological theory. The first is concerned with the rigor of fact finding, inference, and communication, or with what we might call the quest for certainty. There are essentially two ways of handling this issue. One is subjectivistic, mentalistic, and "introspectionistic"; the other is objectivistic. The first is associated with the rationalistic and idealistic outlook prevalent on the European continent since the time of Descartes. The second is associated with the empiricism and positivism of England and the United States. The second issue is the level of complexity of theory. Here, of course, theory ranges from the holistic to the elementaristic, or, in Tolman-Brunswik terms, from the molar to the molecular.

According to Brunswik, there is a continuous historical progression from subjectivism to objectivism as well as from molecular to molar approaches. Within a sample of theorists well distributed over time, we might thus expect the two dimensions to be correlated, so that they might be less distinguishable empirically than they are logically. In the light of Brunswik's more detailed analysis of historical trends, a total collapsing of the two dimensions into a single factor seems unlikely, but we should expect a positive association between objectivism and molarity. This expectation runs counter to the other speculation we have noted. It may well be that the trends that are seen are governed by the theoretical biases of the viewer—they depend, for example, on whether he favors a molar objectivism, as Brunswik does, or a molar subjectivism, as do most of the other psychologists mentioned.

PROCEDURE

It was hoped that an analysis of rated variables applied to a substantial number of psychological theorists would reveal both historical trends and covariational trends independent of time. The first task was to select an appropriate sample of theorists, and this was done on the basis of the rated importance of their contributions to psychological theory.[1] In the course of an investigation reported earlier (Coan & Zagona, 1962), ratings were obtained for 142 theorists both with respect to overall importance and with respect to the significance of their contributions during specific decades in

[1] The author is grateful for the collaborative efforts of Salvatore V. Zagona in the early stages of this research.

which they were active, from the 1880s to the 1950s. In subsequent work, attention has been confined to those theorists who emerged among the top 50 in overall ratings or among the top 10 in the ratings for any decade. By virtue of the overlapping of these lists, this constitutes a total of 54 different theorists.

The construction of a list of variables posed a different kind of problem. It was essential that the variables provide a comprehensive coverage of all basically important aspects of psychological theory. At the same time, the list could not be too long if cooperation of raters was to be ensured. Furthermore, it was necessary that each variable be applicable to all theorists and that it be fairly clearly ratable. Words like "empirical" or "objective" that were unnecessarily vague or ambiguous had to be avoided. In general, it seemed best to avoid any assumptions regarding inherent relationships among variables. For this reason, for example, "holistic" and elementaristic" were treated as separate variables potentially applicable to different aspects of the same body of theory. The ultimate list comprised 34 variables gleaned from an earlier compilation of about twice this length. It is convenient to think of these as falling roughly into four categories, depending on whether they are concerned with content emphasis, methodological emphasis, basic assumptions, or mode of conceptualization. They include the following:

Content Emphasis

1. Learning
2. Sensation and perception
3. Motivation
4. Conscious processes, conscious experience
5. Observable behavior, action, performance
6. Unconscious processes
7. Emotion
8. Self-concept, self-perception
9. Biological determinants of behavior
10. Social determinants of behavior
11. Heredity, constitution
12. Influence of past experience on behavior
13. Immediate external determinants of behavior
14. Total organization of behavior
15. Uniqueness of individual personality
16. Persisting traits of individuals

Methodological Emphasis

    17. Introspective reports of experience
    18. Rigidly controlled experimentation
    19. Statistical analysis
    20. "Armchair" speculation
    21. Naturalistic observation

Basic Assumptions

    22. Voluntarism
    23. Determinism
    24. Finalism, teleology
    25. Mechanism

Mode of Conceptualization

    26. Operational definition of concepts
    27. Elementarism, atomism, description or analysis of events in terms of relatively small units
    28. Holism, totalism, treatment of phenomena in relatively global terms
    29. Nomothetic approach, formulation of general principles
    30. Normative generalization, statistical generalizations about groups of people
    31. Quantitative formulation of principles and relationships
    32. Quantitative description of individuals and behavior
    33. Conceptualization in terms of hypothetical entities
    34. Use of analogies based on physical systems

The next step, of course, was to relate the variables to the theorists. Perhaps the ideal method would involve an exhaustive content analysis of the published work of each theorist. For the sake of securing a comprehensive picture in a relatively brief period, it was decided instead that ratings would be solicited from presumably qualified experts. For this purpose, a list of 232 correspondents was compiled. This contained an initial core of psychologists widely dispersed throughout the United States who were known either to have taught a course in the history of psychology or to have interests in the realm of history and systems. The core was supplemented by many additional names of psychologists known through personal contact or through correspondence with others to have appropriate interest and background. The theorists were divided into three equal subgroups, and each correspondent was asked initially to rate only 18 theorists, approximately one third of the correspondents receiving each list of 18. In a follow-up mailing, each correspondent was given an opportunity to rate the 36 remaining theorists. In both instances, the rater was permitted to confine his ratings to those theorists with whom he felt sufficiently familiar, but he was requested to furnish a complete set of ratings for each theorist that he selected. The number of complete sets of ratings returned for any theorist varied from six (for Charcot) to 38 (for Freud), the average being about 20 sets per theorist. All rating was done on a 5-point scale on which +2 represented marked positive emphasis on the given variable, +1 represented slight positive emphasis, 0 represented no particular emphasis either way, −1 represented slight rejection of the given variable, and −2 represented marked rejection.

The present method of data collection is certainly defensible as a convenient means of gathering a large sample of reasonably valid ratings, but it is well to acknowledge certain inevitable kinds of bias in our data. Some theorists tend to be known primarily through secondary sources. To the extent that raters depend on these, they may be using a common fund of misinformation or slanted interpretation. Permitting a free choice of theorists minimizes this source of bias but does not eliminate it. The theoretical predilections of the rater constitute another source of bias, one whose effects are most subtle and systematic when a pervasive contemporary outlook is involved. Because of these and certain more trivial influences, some distortion is to be expected in mean values derived from the present data. Fortunately, the correlation coefficients used in this study and the values derived from them are less likely to be affected systematically by the sorts of bias we have just noted.

DIMENSIONS OF THEORY

For each theorist the ratings from different correspondents were averaged, and a basic score matrix of order 54×34 was thus obtained. The intervariable correlations yielded by this matrix were subjected to centroid extraction, and six factors were obtained. After an initial Varimax rotation, the factors were rotated blindly to the best approximation to simple structure. Both factor-pattern and factor-structure matrices—matrices of loadings by and correlations with the factors, or primary axes—were derived.[2] Finally, a set of factor scores was obtained for every theorist by multiple-regression procedures.

We can most readily gain an impression of each factor by noting the most salient variables to which it contributes and by considering the theorists who stand near the extremes of the continuum that it represents. In the following lists two numerical values are reported for each variable; the first is a factor loading, and the second is the factor-variable correlation. Each list of theorists starts with the individual whose factor score is most extreme, whether positive or negative.

Factor 1

  4. Conscious processes, 1.07, .92
17. Introspective reports, .96, .96
22. Voluntarism, .81, .92
24. Finalism, .76, .86
20. "Armchair" speculation, .70, .87
  2. Sensation and perception, .55, .31
  6. Unconscious processes, .54, .66
  8. Self-concept, .55, .76
33. Hypothetical entities, .54, .26
  5. Observable behavior, −.95, −.84
23. Determinism, −.60, −.82
25. Mechanism, −.57, −.87
26. Operational definition, −.57, −.85
  9. Biological determinants, −.43, −.37
  1. Learning, −.39, −.67
13. Immediate external determinants, −.35, −.59

    Positive theorists: McDougall, Jung, Brentano, Adler, Piaget, Fechner, Janet, Hall.

    Negative theorists: Estes, Watson, Pavlov, Spence, Skinner, Miller, Hull, Guthrie, Harlow.

At the positive pole, Factor 1 displays a pattern that might be described as subjectivistic, mentalistic, phenomenological, or

[2] For score matrix and the most important matrices derived from it, order NAPS Document NAPS-00004 from ASIS National Auxiliary Publications Service, c/o CCM Information Sciences, Inc., 22 West 34th Street, New York, New York 10001; remitting $1.00 for microfiche or $3.00 for photocopies.

psychological. The negative pole might be described as objectivistic, physicalistic, positivistic, materialistic, or behavioral. Perhaps the best label for the factor as a whole would be Subjectivistic versus Objectivistic.

Factor 2

14. Total organization, .96, .91
28. Holism, .95, .94
15. Uniqueness of individual, .65, .75
21. Naturalistic observation, .55, .68
 5. Observable behavior, .54, −.25
10. Social determinants, .42, .43
24. Finalism, .36, .80
27. Elementarism, −.95, −.94
12. Influence of past experience, −.65, −.26
23. Determinism, −.51, −.66
25. Mechanism, −.46, −.76
29. Nomothetic, −.28, −.36

Positive theorists: Goldstein, Köhler, Koffka, McDougall, Allport, Wertheimer, Lewin, Rogers.

Negative theorists: Spence, Titchener, Estes, Ebbinghaus, Hull, Wundt, Pavlov, Skinner.

In Factor 2 we find a pattern that might be called holistic, totalistic, or molar, opposed by a pattern that might be called elementaristic, atomistic, or molecular. This factor may best be labeled Holistic versus Elementaristic.

The independent status of the first two factors is consistent with Brunswik's formulations. There is some vindication for Allport and other unidimensionalists in the fact that there is a substantial positive correlation between subjectivism and holism. On the basis of Brunswik's work, we might have expected the opposite, although it does not strictly follow from his analysis. It is to Brunswik's credit that these two factors emerge as the factors of greatest variance, but it is clear at the same time that we need several additional factors to account adequately for the structure of psychological theory.

Factor 3

29. Nomothetic, .89, .69
34. Physical analogies, .87, .76

13. Immediate external determinants, .69, .83
2. Sensation and perception, .62, .43
33. Hypothetical entities, .60, .01
18. Rigidly controlled experimentation, .50, .75
1. Learning, .31, .36
16. Persisting traits, −.66, −.84
15. Uniqueness of individual, −.57, −.76
30. Normative generalization, −.40, −.19
10. Social determinants, −.29, −.44
7. Emotion, −.26, −.50
6. Unconscious processes, −.21, −.65

Positive theorists: Koffka, Köhler, Hull, Estes, Wertheimer, Skinner, Lashley, Titchener, Müller.

Negative theorists: Rorschach, Binet, Adler, Jung, Terman, Janet, Allport, Charcot, Hall.

Factor 3 makes good sense psychologically, but it is difficult to label satisfactorily. It could be called experimental versus clinical, but these terms overemphasize the methodological expression of the factor. At the positive pole we see a pattern that is consistently nomothetic, in the sense that it stresses the process or the structure of behavior or experience rather than the behaving or experiencing individual or characteristics of the individual. The negative pole emphasizes characteristics of the individual, but not necessarily in the sense of an idiographic approach. The essence of the former tendency is a certain mode of abstraction, but it is not abstraction per se, since the latter orientation would admit the sort of abstraction found in personality theory. For the present, this factor will be labeled Transpersonal versus Personal.

Factor 4

19. Statistical analysis, 1.05, .95
32. Quantitative description, .88, .97
31. Quantitative formulation, .79, .93
30. Normative generalization, .76, .75
18. Rigidly controlled experimentation, .48, .75
26. Operational definition, .47, .71
5. Observable behavior, .44, .55
11. Heredity, .41, .16
29. Nomothetic, .26, .35
7. Emotion, −.48, −.54
6. Unconscious processes, −.29, −.60

20. "Armchair" speculation, −.28, −.73
12. Influence of past experience, −.23, −.01
23. Determinism, −.23, .38
17. Introspective reports, −.18, −.54

Positive theorists: Estes, Thurstone, Spearman, Terman, Spence, Binet, Ebbinghaus, Miller.

Negative theorists: Freud, Janet, Goldstein, Charcot, Jung, Wertheimer, Sullivan, Köhler, Koffka.

This is the one factor that draws together the four variables that might be called quantitative. These are accompanied by variables suggesting an emphasis on methodological precision and on content that lends itself to quantitative treatment. At the negative pole we find a suggestion of procedures and content that do not readily permit quantitative treatment. This factor will be called Quantitative versus Qualitative. The label, like the factor itself, is somewhat more sharply definable at the positive pole.

Factor 5

3. Motivation, .98, .94
12. Influence of past experience, .80, .67
33. Hypothetical entities, .73, .47
1. Learning, .57, .42
10. Social determinants, .55, .73
7. Emotion, .49, .67
29. Nomothetic, .38, −.14
6. Unconscious processes, .38, .45
8. Self-concept, .39, .51
24. Finalism, .32, .34
16. Persisting traits, .22, .52
2. Sensation and perception, −.32, −.59
17. Introspective reports, −.14, −.22
32. Quantitative description, −.16, −.38
30. Normative generalization, −.15, −.23

Positive theorists: McDougall, Jung, Adler, Mowrer, Sullivan, Freud, James.

Negative theorists: Titchener, Wundt, Mach, Fechner, Wertheimer, Ebbinghaus, Spearman, Külpe.

The variables associated with the positive end of Factor 5 show a concern with ongoing processes or with things that tend to produce processes or change. The negative pole is less well defined, but suggests more emphasis on features that might be considered static or on methods that might be used to isolate such features. A fairly accurate label would be Dynamic versus Static, though these terms have become a bit too value laden to be entirely satisfactory.

Factor 6

9. Biological determinants, .80, .59
11. Heredity, .78, .75
34. Physical analogies, .40, .10
21. Naturalistic observation, .38, .56
10. Social determinants, −.39, −.14
1. Learning, −.21, −.35
8. Self-concept, −.16, .19
26. Operational definition, −.17, −.42
13. Immediate external determinants, −.16, −.40

Positive theorists: Galton, Freud, Jung, Hall, McDougall, Cannon.
Negative theorists: Skinner, Titchener, Ebbinghaus, Angell, Hull, Rogers, Watson.

Here we find a biological emphasis at the positive end, with such contrasting concerns as social influences and the learning process at the negative end. A constitutional emphasis apparently tends to go with the former and an environmental emphasis with the latter, but the nature-nurture dichotomy evidently does not represent the central focus of the factor. Rather, the essential distinction seems to be between the contrasting orientations—toward the internal sources of behavior and toward the external sources—that find occasional expression in the nature-nurture controversy. A label that might capture the basic outlooks is Endogenist versus Exogenist.

These six factors are intercorrelated, of course, and an analysis of their correlations yields two factors at a second stratum. When rotated to a position of simplest structure, the second-order factors yield the following loadings on the first-order factors: Factor A: .82, .75, .00, −.88, −.14, .14; Factor B: −.10, .13, −.72, .00, .64, .36.

Factor A displays a subjectivistic, holistic, and qualitative trend opposed to an objectivistic, elementaristic, and quantitative trend. This dimension clearly coincides with Allport's Leibnitzean-Lockean dichotomy, and it brings together the basic constellation which Ansbacher attributed to holism. A possible general label would be Synthetic versus Analytic.

Factor B contrasts a dynamic personal approach with a static transpersonal approach, with an emphasis on internal or biological sources of behavior tending to accompany the former. The factor is somewhat reminiscent of the clash between James and the experimentalists of his day. It might be broadly characterized as Functional versus Structural.

If the labels suggested for the second-order factors appear to lack precision, it must be remembered that we are dealing with influences whose effects tend to be dilute to the extent that they are general. This rule holds as we move up one more stratum. It so happens that the two second-order factors have a correlation of .55. To this extent, we may think of them as sharing a still more general, but weak, dimension that might be designated fluid versus restrictive. The former pole suggests a basic predisposition to experience people and life in all their complexity in a rather relaxed fashion, while the latter suggests a tendency to deal with reality in a more controlling and compartmental fashion, through restriction of attention and through isolation of entities and events. It has long been obvious that theoretical orientation is at least partly a function of temperament. Perhaps the broad factor we see here points to one important personal source of intellectual outlook. Of course, the personality variables associated with the first-order factors would offer a basis for more specific understanding and prediction. We must note that relatively few psychologists display either extreme on the broad general dimension in a consistent way. In the present sample, James, McDougall, and Jung are fairly clear examples of a fluid orientation, while the restrictive pole is best represented by Skinner, Ebbinghaus, and Estes.

Figure 1 provides a convenient overview of the entire system of variables and factors with which we are dealing. They are shown in a double hierarchy in which the converging lines represent the major links between a given set of trends and those on a higher level of generality. The two sides of the diagram represent opposite trends. In this scheme, of course, information is sacrificed for the sake of simplicity. The crisscrossing of lines is minimized because connecting links are shown for only the highest combinations of loadings and variable-factor correlations. Furthermore, the interrelationships among the elements of a given stratum cannot be properly depicted in a two-dimensional diagram. This is particularly true at the level of the original variables. In all, the hierarchy provides a convenient way

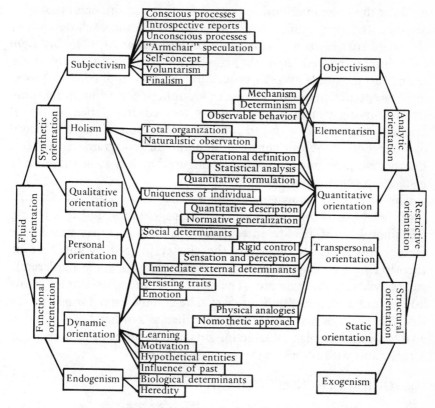

Figure 1. A Bipolar Hierarchy of Theoretical Variables. (The variables shown in the middle are relatively specific, while those on the left and right sides represent more general and mutually opposing trends.)

of conceptualizing certain prototype theoretical perspectives. For a variety of less common patterns of orientation, it is somewhat less useful.

TYPES OF THEORISTS

Since all the theorists employed in this study are widely known, it seemed worthwhile to examine their interrelationships more directly by some kind of Q-technique analysis. Factor analysis, however, is an inappropriate tool for this purpose. It yields more obscure results in Q technique than it does in R technique, since persons are more complex than variables. A clustering technique is preferable, and Ward's hierarchical grouping procedure (Ward, 1963) was chosen for the purpose.

Since the score distributions varied somewhat from one variable to another, the first step was to convert the values in each column of the score matrix to a normalized standard form. All theorists were then intercorrelated, and the correlation coefficients were transformed to d^2 values. Ward's procedure was then applied. This procedure essentially performs successive groupings, according to the similarities among elements and clusters formed from them, until all original elements are grouped into a single cluster. From the record of the process, one can construct a hierarchical diagram that reflects the relative proximities in a test configuration (or, as in the present instance, a person configuration).

The results are shown in Figure 2. The clustering does not conform neatly to recognized "schools" of psychology, but it is clearly meaningful. It is readily interpretable in terms of patterns in the factors discussed above. Thus, the cluster formed by the first six theorists in the diagram is personal and qualitative and moderately subjectivistic and dynamic. The next five theorists display more holism and a bit more subjectivism. The grand cluster formed by the first 22 theorists may be broadly described as synthetic. This kind of analysis could furnish valuable insights into patterns of influence and interactions within various theoretical traditions.

HISTORICAL TRENDS IN THEORY

In our earlier study, theorists were rated by decades in order that an examination of temporal changes might later be made. For this purpose, we focused on the scores for the 10 theorists whose contributions within each decade were deemed most important. Such a group is obviously not fully representative of the great mass of conflicting activities occurring in any one segment of time, but it tends to embody those tendencies which attract greatest attention in each period and which have the greatest influence on subsequent developments.

If the factor scores for each set of 10 theorists are averaged, we obtain the results shown in Table 1. The clearest trend by far is for Factor 1, which shows a progressive increase in objectivism. This agrees with Brunswik's hypotheses. An "objective" approach to methodology, of course, is better represented by Factor 4, for which the progression is basically ∪ shaped. The marked upsurge in quantitative orientation in recent decades is consistent with Brunswik's views.

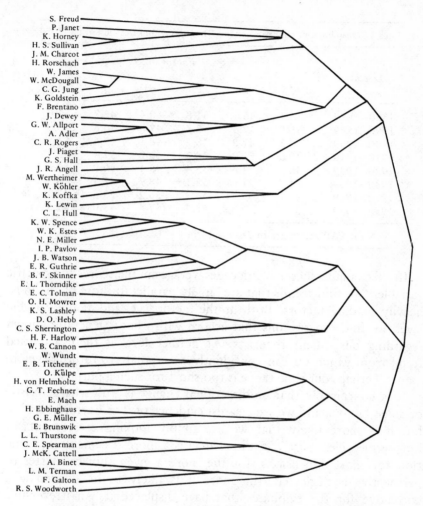

Figure 2. The Hierarchical Grouping of Theorists. (The relative positions of points of juncture are a function of the degree of similarity of theorists and clusters of theorists—the farther to the left the point is, the greater the similarity.)

From Brunswik's formulations, we might also expect an upward trend in Factor 2. Instead, we find an inverted ∪-shaped progression, with a peak for holism in the 1920s. The remaining three factors display more irregularity. Factor 3 shows an initial ∪ trend settling in a plateau on the transpersonal side. In Factor 5 there is a nearly monotonic progression from the static to the dynamic. Initial fluctuation in Factor 6 culminates in an endogenist peak between 1910 and 1919, followed by a monotonic trend toward the opposite pole.

Table 1. Mean Factor Scores for Leading Theorists within Decades: 1880–1959

Decade	Factor no.					
	1	2	3	4	5	6
1880–1889	56.1	46.1	51.8	50.4	42.7	51.0
1890–1899	55.5	47.4	47.2	47.8	46.8	53.0
1900–1909	50.5	47.8	48.7	48.1	47.6	51.5
1910–1919	49.6	53.0	48.3	46.2	52.4	55.1
1920–1929	46.2	54.8	55.4	45.4	49.9	52.6
1930–1939	43.9	51.9	55.1	48.7	53.4	48.5
1940–1949	42.1	49.4	56.3	56.2	53.8	43.7
1950–1959	39.4	46.6	55.5	57.4	55.0	42.3

Note.—All values are in T-score form.

If we examine successive decade averages in the scores for specific variables, we find trends that are largely parallel to those of the most heavily loading factors. Both at the factor level and at the variable level, we find progressions that accord with what is generally known regarding our salient theorists. At neither level is there a unified trend from which we can confidently extrapolate to future developments. Perhaps our time range is too short for such a purpose.

It is conceivable that unidirectional change is truly characteristic of some factors, and we see clearest evidence of it in Factors 1 and 5, but it is more likely that we are simply looking at segments of long-term cycles. Surely cyclic change is a more reasonable expectation for most dimensions, for the more a given subject matter or perspective is neglected, the more it is likely to be needed as a corrective for the emphases that have displaced it. An irreversible trend toward objectivism in psychology would surely lead to substantive sterility within this science. The desirability of cyclic change is clear in most of the factors. There are certain things to be gained, for example, both from concern with totalities and from attention to particulars. A temporary shift along the endogenist-exogenist continuum may become fruitful by virtue of a fresh innovation in physiological thought or a new method of studying organism-environment interaction.

There are some forms of change for which our present methods are not suitable. There is little doubt that some historical developments can be viewed in terms of a succession of triads, wherein the reconciliation of a given polarity is followed by a new division of viewpoints. On this basis, we might expect a succession or a concurrent interaction of the two polar constellations of a factor to be followed by a drastic realignment of variables, so that new patterns of covariation emerge and a new factor replaces the old one. This is only one of several ways in which we might envision the transmutation of factors over time.

Perhaps a more important complication to consider in any temporal analysis is that opposing movements do tend to operate concurrently, not merely in succession. For this reason, the mean value on a variable or factor for a given decade may be somewhat misleading. A measure of variance applied to a larger sample of representatives for each period might better indicate the salience of a particular issue or dimension at any point in time. There is much that remains to be illuminated by the appropriate application of multivariate methods to problems in the history of psychological theory.

REFERENCES

Allport, G. W. *Becoming: Basic considerations for a psychology of personality.* New Haven: Yale University Press, 1955.

Ansbacher, H. L. On the origin of holism. *Journal of Individual Psychology,* 1961, **17**, 142-148.

Brunswik, E. The conceptual framework of psychology. In, *International encyclopedia of unified science.* Vol. 1, No. 10. Chicago: University of Chicago Press, 1952.

Coan, R. W., & Zagona, S. V. Contemporary ratings of psychological theorists. *Psychological Record,* 1962, **12**, 315-322.

James, W. *Pragmatism.* London: Longmans, Green, 1907.

Murray, H. A. *Explorations in personality.* New York: Oxford University Press, 1938.

Rogers, C. R. Two divergent trends. In R. May (Ed.), *Existential psychology.* New York: Random House, 1961.

Ward, J. H. Hierarchical grouping to optimize an objective function. *Journal of the American Statistical Association,* 1963, **58**, 236-244.

IV

American
Psychology

William James, the father of American psychology, began interpreting German psychology for Americans in the early 1870s. During the 1880s and 1890s many Americans went abroad to study scientific psychology. Although they borrowed German methods and concepts, most of these American students, after their return from Leipzig, fashioned a new kind of psychology that was functional in spirit and approach. In the past many historians of psychology attributed the character of early American psychology almost exclusively to a scientific and functional *Zeitgeist*. In the first selection in Part IV, historian Dorothy Ross argues that religion has been overlooked as a potent force in molding this psychology. Highly critical of the *Zeitgeist* interpretation, she has further suggested that the promotion of scientific psychology by the American pioneers, including James and Hall, might well have stemmed from a conflict between two allegiances—science and religion.

After 1890, as functional psychology became deeply rooted and as the practical applications of psychology were expanded in the United States, only the British-born and Leipzig-trained E. B. Titchener remained faithful to Wundt. Titchener became the protagonist of what he termed structural psychology, in contrast to functional psychology. He defended Wundt against American critics, notable

247

among whom was William James, who vigorously objected to Wundt's elementism and just as vigorously insisted that functional psychology was the only real psychology. In 1909 James wrote, "The 'function' of Titchener's 'scientific' psychology (which 'structurally' considered is pure will-of-the-wisp) is to keep the laboratory instruments going, and to provide platforms for certain professors." In the second selection, Walter B. Pillsbury discusses Titchener's attitude toward James and suggests that Titchener's alleged lack of esteem for James derived chiefly from the fact that James was not an experimentalist and had little regard for the Wundtian tradition.

After James' death in 1910, a more powerful force, behaviorism, emerged and ultimately annihilated structuralism. Titchener, the structuralist, and John B. Watson, the founder of behaviorism, have traditionally been presented by historians of psychology as opponents with highly divergent theoretical views. The third selection, based principally on an analysis of the correspondence of Titchener and Watson by Cedric Larson and John J. Sullivan, presents evidence that these two psychologists enjoyed a cordial and friendly relationship despite their opposing viewpoints. In 1923, Titchener described their relationship as follows: "I think that our trust in each other is pretty well established whatever may be our difference of intellectual outlook. I always rejoice to confound the current notion that difference of opinion must necessarily lead to personal enmity."

The controversies among the schools of psychology from 1910 to the mid-1930s stimulated much experimental research and advanced psychology as a science. After 1940 professional psychology, which had progressed slowly in the early 20th century, developed so rapidly that by the 1960s the majority of American psychologists were engaged in practice. The author of the fourth selection, Robert I. Watson, who has scrutinized the trends in this phenomenal development of psychology in the United States, has characterized modern American psychology as predominantly deterministic, naturalistic, physicalistic, and monistic. He has also identified dominant tendencies toward functionalism, operationalism, quantification, hypothetico-deductivism, environmentalism, and nomotheticism. However, according to Watson, there are counteracting forces that demand increased attention to theory, insist on more concern for philosophical issues, and focus on various facets of personality theory.

The final selection in Part IV assesses the American contribution to contemporary psychology and speculates about American influence on the psychology of the future. In discussing the relationship of American and European psychology, Daniel E. Berlyne, a psychologist of international repute, declares that during the last quarter century psychologists around the world have looked to American psychologists for inspiration and leadership, have read American textbooks and journals, and have studied at American universities and visited American laboratories and clinics. However, he admonishes that the tremendous influence that the United States has exerted will not persist. Berlyne predicts that foreign psychologists can be expected to make significant and substantial contributions to psychology as science and as profession in the near future.

The "Zeitgeist" and American Psychology
Dorothy Ross

Here Dorothy Ross, a historian with a special interest in American psychology, assesses the validity of the *Zeitgeist* concept, which, as we noted in an earlier selection, was employed as a principle of historical explanation by E. G. Boring, the eminent historian of psychology. Ross stresses the idealist origins of the *Zeitgeist* concept and affirms that it is too confused, simplistic, and inadequate to be a principle of historical explanation. Its limitations as a causal concept are illustrated with specific reference to the development of early American psychology and particularly to G. Stanley Hall's role.

The problem of the *Zeitgeist* in Boring's writings has also been critically examined by Saul Rosenzweig in "E. G. Boring and the Zeitgeist: eruditione gesta beavit," published in the *Journal of Psychology*, 1970, **75**, 59-71.

American psychologists who have tried to understand the origins and development of their discipline have frequently turned for their historical explanations to the rise of certain ideas and attitudes under the aegis of the "Zeitgeist." In the work of Edwin G. Boring and the many psychological historians he has influenced, the concept of the "Zeitgeist" is frequently used as a causal explanation of historical change; that is, as an answer to the question "What is the chief cause, the chief determining factor, of this or that development in the history of psychology?"[1]

Professor Boring often goes on to discuss the problem of determinism in history and, more specifically, the problem of

Dorothy Ross, The "Zeitgeist" and American psychology. *Journal of the History of the Behavioral Sciences*, 1969, **5**, 256-262. Reprinted by permission of the author and the Psychology Press.

[1]Professor Boring has used the concept in all his historical work. See particularly, Boring, *A History of Experimental Psychology* (New York: Appleton-Century-Crofts, Inc., 1950), Second Edition; and the collection of articles in Boring, *Psychologist at Large* (New York: Basic Books, 1961), 295-337, and in Boring, *History, Psychology and Science: Selected Papers* (New York: John Wiley and Sons, 1963), Robert I. Watson and Donald T. Campbell (eds.).

individual creativity in the history of science. It is possible that his great attachment to the "Zeitgeist" concept is due to the deterministic position it allows him to hold in regard to these problems.[2] The concern with these more special matters, however, can obscure the fact that the "Zeitgeist" is not an adequate principle of historical explanation. It does not do justice to the complexity of history. Indeed, it does not do justice to the careful and illuminating scholarship of Professor Boring himself, nor of other psychologists who have adopted the term.

The term "Zeitgeist" apparently came into use among German historians and men-of-letters in the late eighteenth and early nineteenth centuries, to express what was then a new insight into the relativity of history, a recognition of the fact that each period and each culture is organized in a way unique to its time and place, and must be understood and judged in its own terms. The "Zeitgeist" was understood to mean the prevailing opinions and tastes of the period. Goethe, to whom Boring traced the word, at one point defined it as the strain of opinion which dominates the current moment of history and which unconsciously shapes the thought of those who live within its sway.[3]

---

[2]Professor Boring deals with these problems intermittently in all his historical work, and most fully in "Eponym as Placebo," *Selected Papers*, 5-25. For an analysis of Professor Boring's commitment to the deterministic position, see Robert A. Friedman, "Edwin G. Boring's 'Mature' View of the Science of Science in Relation to a Deterministic Personal and Intellectual Motif," *Journal of the History of the Behavioral Sciences*, III (January, 1967), 17-26. Professor Boring's treatment of the problem of determinism in history deserves an independent critique. I will only point out here that the "Zeitgeist" in this context suffers from infirmities similar to those it carries as a general explanatory principle. Stating the problem of determinism in terms of two independent and monolithic elements, the individual and the "Zeitgeist," presents it in its most elementary form. In fact, the individual and the culture are constantly intertwined and the more difficult and important issues concern how they influence and limit each other: How has the culture shaped the mind of the individual in question? To what extent can individual psychological factors or social factors account for his behavior or ideas? To what extent are these psychological or social factors idiosyncratic or shared by others in the culture? To what extent did his institutional and disciplinary roles limit or deepen his ideas? How much flexibility and range did these roles allow him as an individual, compared to similar roles in other contemporary or historical situations? The psychologist is obliged to face such issues if he is to write meaningful history; he is also uniquely equipped to advance our understanding of them. For a similar criticism of Professor Boring's use of the "Zeitgeist" as a factor in historical determinism, see the paper presented by Dr. David Shakow, September 2, 1967, at the APA meetings in Washington, D.C., "Schools of Psychology: Psychoanalysis."

[3]Jacob and Wilhelm Grimm, *Deutsches Wörterbuch* (Leipzig: S. Hirzel, 1956), XV, 558-59; Ernst Cassirer, *The Philosophy of the Enlightenment* (Boston: Beacon Press, 1955), chapter 5; Johann Wolfgang von Goethe, "Homer noch Einmal," in *Goethes Sämtliche Werke* (Stuttgart and Berlin: J. G. Cotta, 1902-1907), XXXVIII, 77-78.

With Hegel and his students, the term took a more formal place in the idealist philosophy of history. Hegel posited a "Weltgeist" which progressively realizes itself in history. "Der Geist einer Zeit" and "der Geist eines Volkes" give a unique stamp to each period and people, a common character pervading their state, laws, art, religion, philosophy, etc. German historians of the nineteenth century influenced by Hegel were led by this concept to seek the ruling spirit or unifying rationale underlying the development of the historical period or subject matter they were studying. Hegel's concept was also, according to Karl Mannheim, the origin of the idea of "Weltanschauung," the total world-view common to a period or culture, and thence, of Marx's and his own idea of "ideology." Hegel's concept could also be taken as an expression of the modern idea of culture, for it stated that a unity underlay the institutional forms, as well as the thought, of a society.[4]

This brief sketch of the history of the "Zeitgeist" concept suggests some of the difficulties it holds for the empirical historian of today. Most glaringly, its deep roots in idealist philosophy encourage the historian to reify the term. In practice, the "Zeitgeist" tends to become an entity entirely disconnected from the individuals who in fact constitute it. It has been stated, for example, that neither James, Dewey, Hall, Thorndike, Cattell, Galton, nor Darwin were necessary to the rapid development of educational psychology in America, for that was the trend of the "Zeitgeist."[5] But certainly, we only know what the "Zeitgeist" in fact *was* by the way in which James, Hall, Cattell, Darwin, and others behaved. If they had not thought and acted the way they did, neither would the "Zeitgeist" they are said to embody. To suggest otherwise is to suggest a "Something," beyond the actual historical phenomena, whose nature explains the phenomena, a strategy psychologists have long since learned to avoid.[6] The idealistic origin of the term, which still surreptitiously

---

[4] Georg Wilhelm Friedrich Hegel, *Einleitung in die Geschichte der Philosophie* (Hamburg: Felix Meiner, 1940), Johannes Hoffmeister (ed.), 148-149, 284; Hegel, *Reason in History: A General Introduction to the Philosophy of History* (New York: The Liberal Arts Press, 1953), Robert S. Hartman (tr.), 66-67; Karl Mannheim, *Ideology and Utopia* (London: Kegan Paul, Trench, Trubner & Co., 1936), 49-62; Carl J. Friedrich (ed.), *The Philosophy of Hegel* (New York: Random House, 1953), xxx-xxxi.

[5] Boring, *History*, 570.

[6] The classic presentation of this argument for American psychology was William James' discussion of the concept of soul in his *Principles of Psychology* (New York: Henry Holt, 1890), I, 342-50; and of the concept of substance in the third lecture of *Pragmatism* (New York: Longmans, Green, 1907).

clings to it, makes one forget that the "Zeitgeist" is only a shorthand name for specific ideas and attitudes, held by specific people, and that it has no meaning apart from the facts it represents.[7]

Just what facts the term represents, however, is by no means clear. Its Hegelian roots make it subject to a number of different meanings and hence to great confusion. The concept of "Zeitgeist" which developed from Hegel implies a fundamental unity in the thought and opinion of a given culture, a rationally explicable configuration of beliefs at its base. If and at what level of culture such unity exists, however, was and still is a matter of debate. One could mean by the "Zeitgeist" a principle which accounts for the interconnectedness of the entire culture, institutional as well as intellectual. Or, narrowing the term solely to the body of thought and opinion characteristic of the culture in a given era, one could mean a systematic body of assumptions and beliefs which are determined by the system of social relations—an "ideology." Historians of psychology do not specify any such unified system of ideas or cultural principles when they talk about the "Zeitgeist" that influenced their discipline, yet something of these meanings persist when they speak of the "Zeitgeist" as "the current of credence," a phrase which implies a single, homogeneous stream of history.[8]

Professor Boring's definition of the "Zeitgeist" simply as "the total body of knowledge and opinion available at any time to a person living within a given culture," in effect tries to free the concept of these earlier connotations.[9] Historians of psychology do seem most often to think of the "Zeitgeist" as a collection of intellectual trends, at various levels of generality, developing unevenly in time and space and not necessarily tied together in a rationally coherent way. Thus, for example, late nineteenth-century American thought can be understood to include naturalistic, mechanistic, organic, evolutionary, and religious trends of thought which hold sway over particular problems, people, and

---

[7]Professor Boring has stated very clearly, in his essay, "Dual Role of the 'Zeitgeist' in Scientific Creativity" (1955), *Psychologist*, 327-28: "Today the 'Zeitgeist' is certainly *not* a superorganic soul, an immortal consciousness undergoing maturation with the centuries, an unextended substance interpenetrating the social structure. The 'Zeitgeist' must be regarded simply as the sum total of social interaction as it is common to a particular period and a particular locale.... This interaction *is* the 'Zeitgeist'...." Yet in *History*, 550, he remarks, "The 'Zeitgeist' becomes comprehensible when it is analyzed into the interactions of persons, one with another."

[8]Boring, "Eponym," *Selected Papers*, 9.

[9]Boring, "Dual Role," *Psychologist*, 336.

circumstances, which interact and change and lead in many different, often contradictory, directions. Once the "Zeitgeist" is redefined in this way, however, its use as an explanatory tool becomes dubious.

The "Zeitgeist" in this sense offers only the most elementary kind of causal insight. To attribute the cause of an intellectual event to "the total body of knowledge and opinion" in the culture is a truism of historical explanation. Every intellectual event generated by the culture can be referred to the same cause. If the concept does not help to sort and analyze this complex body of knowledge and opinion, if it does not clarify and focus the historian's attention, it can be of little use to the modern student of history.

There are some large contexts of historical analysis where it can be useful to deal with the thought of a culture as a whole. In the comparative study of cultures or periods, or when setting off the individual from the whole cultural climate around him, it may be useful to refer to the main lines which characterize a cultural epoch and give this sketch a single name.[10] These contexts generally compose, however, only a small portion of the historian's work, and in view of the ambiguities inherent in the term "Zeitgeist," one would be well advised when working in these contexts to use a different term. "Climate of opinion," "cultural epoch," etc., are neither elegant nor totally clear terms—it is always best to refer directly to the particular intellectual tendencies one has in mind—but as general, shorthand terms, they would lead to less confusion than "Zeitgeist."[11]

When one must analyze the cultural climate into its components and interactions with particular people, however, the term "Zeitgeist" becomes a positive obstacle to understanding.[12] When

[10]See, e.g., Boring, *History*, 507-8. It is not clear to what extent the body of verified scientific fact and theory is or ought to be considered a part of the "Zeitgeist." Professor Boring tends to include current scientific discoveries as part of the "Zeitgeist," yet in large measure these scientific products transcend any one culture and its special viewpoint. Professor Boring does not really examine the problem of cultural relativity; his views on historical determinism lead him to attribute anything outside the individual to "the culture" or the "Zeitgeist" seen as a single entity. I am grateful to an unknown auditor for pointing this out to me when an earlier version of this paper was presented September 4, 1967, at the APA meetings in Washington, D. C.

[11]To my knowledge, professional historians today rarely use the term, in this context or any other.

[12]In "Dual Role," *Psychologist*, 325, Professor Boring recognized that in changing the definition of the "Zeitgeist" from that configuration of the culture which only unconsciously influenced the individual, as Goethe at one point defined it (See note 3, *supra*), to the total body of culture, he was changing the context of the term from "the way in which

historians of psychology try to trace a new idea or development in psychology to its causes in the "Zeitgeist," they do not describe the "Zeitgeist" in all its complexity, but rather pick out one particular strain of the culture which appears relevant to their problem. In practice, the "Zeitgeist" becomes that tendency in the culture which fostered the event in question, a process of reading back from the historical result to its prior analogues, rather than of independent historical analysis.[13]

In this way, too, the definition of the "Zeitgeist" of a period shifts each time one considers a different event of the period. When analyzing a complex intellectual situation, one can be forced to include in the "Zeitgeist" both the rising, but still minority, view among psychologists and the contrary opinion which still prevails in the profession;[14] both the "common sense" of the populace and the scientific opinion moving away from it;[15] both the broad scientific tendencies in a particular direction and the religious and philosophical tendencies which limit its advance.[16] By attaching the same name to these disparate tendencies, one gives the appearance of always talking about the same thing and of using a concept with wide explanatory power. In fact, one is always talking about different things and the single name given to them confuses, rather than clarifies, the pattern of causation.

The practice of looking at a cultural epoch to find this partial "Zeitgeist," this tendency which fostered the event we are trying to explain, has another serious defect. It encourages one to overlook the complex way in which different strains within the culture interact and the effects which the whole cultural

---

the climate of opinion affects thinking at a given time to the way in which the climate and its effects keep continuously changing." In the historical work using the "Zeitgeist" concept, however, this distinction has not been maintained and both definitions and contexts appear without notice of change. See, e.g., Boring, *History,* 242-43, 507, 642.

[13] The case of the unexpected event which is ignored or opposed in its own time is the exception proving the rule. The "Zeitgeist," in that case, becomes the cultural tendency opposing the event in question.

[14] See, e. g., Professor Boring's treatment of Helmholtz's measurement of the speed of the neural impulse as shaped by both the rising naturalistic "Zeitgeist" and the dominant skeptical "Zeitgeist" of the profession, in *History,* 41-45; *Selected Papers,* 90, 157.

[15] See, e. g., Professor Boring's treatment of both the conventional, personalistic theory of mind and the contrary view of scientific naturalism as the nineteenth century "Zeitgeist," in "Great Men and Scientific Progress," *Selected Papers,* 32, 39.

[16] See, e. g., Professor Boring's analysis of the rise of measurement and the limitations on its use in "Measurement in Psychology," *Selected Papers,* 142, 157-58.

configuration has on any one strain within it.[17] The role of religion in shaping American psychology, for example, has been largely ignored, I think, in part because of this limitation in the "Zeitgeist" concept.[18] The search for the scientific or functional "Zeitgeist" in American culture does not easily lead one to consider American Protestantism. Yet I suspect that the way American psychologists responded to the scientific and functional tendencies of their age was significantly affected by their religious experience.

For example, a thoughtful individual growing up in a culture in which both science and religion made claims on his allegiance, as often happened in nineteenth century America, would inevitably find his attitudes toward one influenced by the other. Certainly this was the case with Stanley Hall. During the 1880's and early 1890's Hall was the leading and most outspoken advocate of a strictly scientific psychology, free of all religious and philosophical ties, and this attitude was reflected in his influential founding of psychological laboratories and the *American Journal of Psychology*. At the same time, Hall assured popular audiences and university administrators that science would eventually prove the essential truths of religion and that scientific psychology could safely replace religion as the moral guide for such functions as child-rearing and education. On close examination, it becomes clear that both Hall's aggressive scientism within psychology and his popular attempts to clothe science in religious garb were products of the conflict he felt between his allegiance to both religious and scientific norms.[19]

How profound a factor this was in the scientific attitudes of others of the early American psychologists I cannot say with as much certainty, but the role of science as a substitute or foil for religion, its new position in a culture deeply imbued with religious norms, may well account for some of the force and character of American psychology's scientific ideal: its messianism, its intense desire to

17Professor Boring himself, and others who use the "Zeitgeist" concept, such as David Shakow and David Rapaport in "The Influence of Freud on American Psychology," *Psychological Issues*, IV, No. 1 (1964), have a lively sense of the complexity of history which survives the use of this block concept. My point is only that the concept itself hinders, rather than helps, the historian in finding and analyzing the full range of historical interaction.

18Other reasons for this oversight probably include the natural tendency of psychologists to concentrate on areas closer to their field of competence and to ignore an area their tradition largely regards as alien and hostile.

19Dorothy Ross, "G. Stanley Hall, 1844-1895: Aspects of Science and Culture in the Nineteenth Century," Doctoral Dissertation (Columbia University, 1965), chapters 1, 8, 10.

uproot from psychology any semblance of the religious tradition and its enthusiastic desire to subject traditional moral problems to exact, or allegedly exact, methods.[20]

The position of psychology in late nineteenth century America as a scientific replacement for religion may help to explain, as well, the extremely rapid growth of scientific psychology in America. In this country religious conceptions still maintained their influence over those raised in their sway and yet were fast losing cast to the rising power and prestige of natural science. Scientific psychology offered a young intellectual many ways to resolve the tensions created by these two diverging norms. In the framework of a scientific psychology, one could both escape and satisfy religious impulses, while engaging in science. This conflict between two diverging sets of ideals and status valuations clearly directed Stanley Hall's and William James' choice of scientific psychology as a career. It might also account for the relatively large numbers of others who quickly followed them into this new field.[21]

Religion may also have contributed to the early functional tendency of American psychology, a tendency generally attributed to that strong functional "Zeitgeist" which made Americans adopt evolutionary ideas more quickly and pervasively than others.[22] Christianity and evolutionary science, during the second half of the nineteenth century, were not as opposed as the popular conflict between Darwinians and Christian spokesmen would lead one to believe. In England and America, those versed in science tended from the start to see evolution as a semi-religious compromise with positivism, as a way of softening the more austere implications of modern science by incorporating into it notions of morality and liberalized Christian doctrine. Hall, for example, was well aware of the religious dimension of evolutionary theory, having learned it in

[20]Cf. Frank M. Albrecht, "The New Psychology in America: 1880-1895," Doctoral Dissertation (Johns Hopkins University, 1960). An exchange between E. B. Titchener and William James also suggests the way in which the religious climate of the culture at large goaded psychologists into being as rigorously and exclusively scientific as possible: James to Titchener, May 6, May 21 and May 31, 1899, Titchener Papers, John M. Olin Research Library, Cornell University; Titchener to James, May 28, 1899, James Papers, Houghton Library, Harvard University.

[21]Ross, "G. Stanley Hall," chapter 5; Joseph Ben-David and Randall Collins, "Social Factors in the Origins of a New Science: The Case of Psychology," *American Sociological Review*, XXXI (August, 1966), 451 ff; Dorothy Ross, "On the Origins of Psychology," *Ibid.*, XXXII (June, 1967), 468-69.

[22]Boring, "The Influence of Darwin on American Psychology," *Selected Papers*, 159-84.

this country from Spencer and in Germany from Haeckel. The ability of evolution to confirm Hall's belief in dynamic pantheism and in the inevitability of moral progress greatly encouraged him to explore the implications of evolutionary ideas for psychology and to construct a psychology on a functional, evolutionary model, rather than on the traditional Wundtian one.[23] Here again, we miss much of the way in which history works if we look only for a particular, partial "Zeitgeist."

Finally, the "Zeitgeist" is limited in still another way as a causal concept. It refers only to ideas and attitudes and hence ignores the psychological, institutional, social, economic, and political factors which also affect developments in the profession.

Let us return to the case of educational psychology in America. It is true that certain functional trends within psychology led into work in education, and the psychological historian who has adopted the "Zeitgeist" concept may be tempted to stop his analysis there. However, a great many other people were turning to the problems of education and child-rearing at this time, as well; educators themselves were becoming self-conscious and professionalized; and compulsory school attendance laws were being passed in state after state. This broad pattern of educational reform, educational psychology included, can be traced to changes in the economy, the size and attitudes of the middle class, the composition of the teaching force, and political pressures on the educational system.[24]

So, too, institutional factors more closely connected with psychology were involved. The novelty and relative insecurity of the university in American society, and of psychology within the university, made psychologists particularly sensitive to these larger currents.[25] Personal psychological factors also made a number of

[23] John H. Randall, Jr., "The Changing Impact of Darwin on Philosophy," *Journal of the History of Ideas*, XXII (October, 1961), 435-62; Ross, "G. Stanley Hall," chapters 6, 8, 12. The moral and religious implications of Darwinism were also important in William James' development of a functional psychology: see Ralph Barton Perry, *The Thought and Character of William James* (Boston: Little Brown and Co., 1935), I, 490.

[24] See Lawrence A. Cremin, *The Transformation of the School* (New York: Alfred A. Knopf, 1961), Part I.

[25] Hugh Hawkins, *Pioneer: A History of the Johns Hopkins University, 1874-1889* (Ithaca: Cornell University Press, 1960), 63-78, 202; E. L. Thorndike, "Edward Lee Thorndike," in Carl Murchison (ed.) *A History of Psychology in Autobiography* (New York: Russell and Russell, 1961), III, 266; John A. Magni to G. S. Hall, January 30, 1911, and O. Scoop to G. S. Hall, February 8, 1911, Clark University Papers, Clark University.

psychologists seek the practical relevance or popular approval they could not find in traditional laboratory work.[26]

In the case of Stanley Hall, such social, institutional, and psychological factors were decisive in causing him to develop an educational psychology. For a decade Hall resisted the logic of his evolutionary views and refused to integrate his work in pedagogy into his psychology. It was the pressure of these other factors, which came heavily to bear on Hall in the early 1890's, which finally forced him to do so.[27] Without examining the total historical scene, there is no reason to assume *a priori* that certain intellectual tendencies are the chief causal factor in any event or series of events in the history of psychology.

These arguments may seem to place an impossible burden on historians of psychology, an impression I do not want to leave. Psychologists and historians are each equipped by training and preference to examine certain parts of the historical fabric better than other parts and an amiable division of labor is certainly possible. No one, moreover, can do more than approach the total analysis an historical event ideally requires. Whichever aspect of history we choose to work at, however, we should be aware of the existence of the total scene; we should use concepts which are appropriate to the questions we are asking, which allow as much precision as possible, and which mirror as closely as possible the full complexity of history. The notion of a "Zeitgeist" is too confused and simplistic to meet these standards.

At an earlier stage of the history of psychology, the term may have served to call attention to the fact that there was a surrounding intellectual milieu from which psychology developed and in which its roots must be traced. Psychologists surely need no longer to be reminded of that fact. If they now bring to their historical studies as much sophistication, critical analysis, and methodological expertise as they have already brought to their purely psychological work, they will find more adequate historical tools.

---

[26]Jane M. Dewey (ed.), "Biography of John Dewey," in Paul A. Schilpp (ed.), *The Philosophy of John Dewey* (New York: Tudor Publishing Co., 1951), 27; Boring, "Lewis M. Terman: 1877-1956," in *Psychologist*, 272-76, 278.

[27]Ross, "G. Stanley Hall," 263-65, 359-60, 425-26.

Titchener and James
Walter B. Pillsbury

One of the first generation of psychologists trained in the United States, Walter B. Pillsbury (1872-1960) obtained his doctorate under Titchener at Cornell in 1896. Thereafter he spent his entire academic life at the University of Michigan until his retirement in 1942. Pillsbury's bibliography includes numerous journal articles as well as *The Essentials of Psychology*, *The Fundamentals of Psychology*, and *The History of Psychology*. In addition to holding various editorships, Pillsbury served as president of the American Psychological Association (1910) and as vice-president and chairman of the psychological section of the American Association for the Advancement of Science (1913). He was also elected to membership in the National Academy of Sciences (1925). As Karl Dallenbach observed in writing Pillsbury's obituary, "He was one of the pioneers ... who prepared the way for the generations of psychologists who followed him. He received, in recognition of his achievements, all the honors within the power of his confrères to bestow upon him."

The following selection was one of a commemorative series published on the 100th anniversary (1942) of William James' birth. Here Pillsbury discusses the relationship of his former professor, E. B. Titchener, with William James, the father of American psychology. James is perhaps best known to the psychology student for his theory of emotions, which maintained that the subjective experience of emotion is aroused by bodily changes. Pillsbury asserts that Titchener's alleged lack of esteem of James was based on personal student impression and probably stemmed from the fact that James was "outside the true experimental group" and "not sympathetic with the Leipzig tradition."

The reaction of Titchener to James and his work was a phenomenon of some interest to the early Cornell students and may be worth a note. They were two of the more prominent American psychologists in the 1890's. James was at his zenith in the early years of the decade and Titchener increased in recognition during that and the following decennium. To several of us in the early nineties it seemed that Titchener esteemed James rather less than was his due. This impression was based upon casual references rather than upon

Walter B. Pillsbury, Titchener and James. *Psychological Review*, 1943, **50**, 71-73. Reprinted by permission of the American Psychological Association.

specific statements. One special bit of evidence was the choice of Sully's *Human mind* rather than of James' *Principles* as a text for the year's course in general psychology, 1893-94.

The occasion for the general coolness toward James may well have been his rather contemptuous references to Fechner and the psychophysical literature, and also to Wundt's system. Titchener was extremely loyal to his friends and to the tradition in which he had been reared.

I have sought for specific instances of Titchener's criticism of James, but find few signs of hostile reaction except to the theory of emotion. This first showed itself in Irons' articles on emotion in the *Philosophical Review*.[1] Irons was a student of philosophy, but was very close to Titchener and undoubtedly mirrored his opinion. Irons discussed emotion from the standpoint of classification and insisted that bodily responses were only incidental to emotions, not their real core. James' theory was treated with due respect and many of the criticisms made against it were similar to those made by Cannon much later, but of course without the experimental contribution that Cannon had at his command.

Titchener himself wrote more definitely on the James theory in 1914, after James' death. This article was not so much a criticism of the theory itself as of the credit that James gave to his predecessors.[2] In substance it quotes the initial statement of James in his 1884 article in *Mind* that he had derived his theory "from fragmentary introspective observations." Titchener then proceeded to enumerate, with quotations, eighteen authors before James who had mentioned bodily accompaniments as important to the emotions. The article apparently was written to intimate that James received more help than he credited from earlier writers, although it states only that James' wide reading must have acquainted him with the views of these men. Titchener said: "Even when he quotes Henle with the remark: 'Note how justly this expresses our theory'—even then he fails to quote Henle's definition of emotion, occurring on the very same page, as 'a presentation accompanied by sympathetically excited sensations, muscular movements, and secretions.' " Titchener explained the lack of acknowledgments as due to the fact that after

---

[1] David Irons, The nature of emotion, *Phil. Rev.*, 1897, 7, 476-486.

[2] E. B. Titchener, An historical note on the James-Lange theory of emotion, *Amer. J. Psychol.*, 1914, 25, 427-447.

all of his reading, "as the theory shot to a focus in James' thought, it carried with it a blaze of illumination; here, at long last, was something other than the classical descriptions and the endless classifications. . . . All in all, James' acceptance of the complete novelty of his theory must, I believe, be left to stand as something of a curiosity in the history of psychology." This conclusion he reached after mentioning that James gave complete recognition of Lange's independence in developing practically the same theory. Thus Titchener implied that James was less original than he and most psychologists had thought.

This criticism seems on the whole to have been rather captious. True, since Plato, references had been made to bodily accompaniments of emotion, but only with James do responses become the core of the emotion and not merely an accompaniment. This change was partly due to James' vividness of expression, but more to the increased emphasis that he put upon the bodily response. Whatever the reason, the scientific world attributes the theory to James and has given emotion a very different place ever since James wrote.

Aside from these references to the emotion, there is no indication in Titchener's published work that would belittle James. James is quoted more frequently by Titchener in his textbooks, aside from the Laboratory Manuals, than any other author but Wundt. Any indication of lack of esteem must depend upon personal student impression. So far as it existed it probably rested upon the feeling that James was outside the true experimental group and was not sympathetic with the Leipzig tradition.

Watson's Relation to Titchener
Cedric Larson
John J. Sullivan

Cedric Larson is a school psychologist from Long Island, New York, as well as an instructor in psychology at Rutgers University in Newark, N. J. His special interests are the psychology of leadership, public opinion, and the history of psychology. His co-author, John J. Sullivan, teaches psychology at the New York University School of Education and is much concerned with philosophical and historical aspects of psychology. Under Sullivan's leadership, the International Society for the History of the Behavioral and Social Sciences, the Cheiron Society, was organized in 1968. The two men have made several contributions to recent literature on the history of psychology. The following article sheds new light on the relationship of two pivotal figures in early-20th-century American psychology—Titchener and Watson. Known to most psychologists principally as the protagonists of the two rival schools of psychology, Titchener the structuralist and Watson the behaviorist are here presented not as avowed opponents but as friends who had a high personal regard and professional respect for each other.

Apart from describing the personal relationship of these two prominent psychologists, this selection portrays the status of early American psychology. It provides deep insight into the struggles of the schools of psychology and the issues inciting the rivalry between the schools. Larson and Sullivan have done more than offer a case study of the Titchener-Watson friendship; they have described an important era in American psychology.

Of some historical interest to us today are the personal and professional relationships between John Broadus Watson and Edward Bradford Titchener. It is well known that these two men were poles apart in their theoretical views about psychology. What is not so well known is that these men seem to have been on fairly good terms during a period of roughly two decades. They came closer together from 1920 until the death of Titchener in 1927. The earlier date marked Watson's exit from the academic world.

When we consider the very strong—we might even say dominating—personalities of these two early leader-figures in American

Cedric Larson and John J. Sullivan, Watson's relation to Titchener. *Journal of the History of the Behavioral Sciences,* 1965, 1, 338-354. Reprinted by permission of the authors and the Psychology Press.

psychology (neither of whom could brook contradiction easily) an interesting question arises: Could this association be called a friendship in the ordinary sense of the word, or a protracted cordial professional relationship that was essentially casual, or perhaps merely a coincidence? As psychologists start building archives of the letters and manuscripts of their "greats" questions such as the foregoing can now be examined with more precision than was heretofore possible.

Titchener seemed basically to have an affable disposition. As Dr. Boring stated in a recent letter to the writers: "Titchener's grace and charm, his warm hospitality, were his notable traits. It wasn't until someone offended him that the cold side appeared."

To begin with, Titchener had come, via Wundt in Germany, to America from England. In this connection, Dr. Boring writes in his obituary of him: "A foreigner settling in a new country is not always welcomed, particularly when necessities of life like laboratories are scarce. Especially may this be true of a dominating personality. Yet Titchener seemed always ready to respond to friendship."[1] In discussing his relation with Sanford, Boring wrote that "there remained a warm cordiality between these two men" until Sanford's death. On the other hand, it was hard for Titchener to establish interpersonal relationships: "He was probably not constituted for team-work."[2]

Boring's obituary cited above was reprinted in *Psychologist at Large,* published in 1961, but minus the original footnotes. The

---

In the preparation of this paper, the writers wish to acknowledge the valued assistance of Mr. John Buchanan, former Assistant Archivist of the Collection of Regional History and University Archives, John M. Olin Research Library, Cornell University; the manuscript collections of the Yale Medical Library; and comments and suggestions of sources of material for the study from Dr. Edwin G. Boring of Harvard University, who also perused the first two drafts of this paper and offered many trenchant observations on them which were useful guides to the completion of the final version. The two authors read an earlier version of this paper at the American Psychological Association convention, Los Angeles, Sept. 7, 1964. The senior author's attendance at this convention was supported by the Board of Cooperative Educational Services, Second Supervisory District of Suffolk County, Long Island, New York.

The many letters quoted from in this article may be found in the Boring collection, Harvard University Library; Yerkes Collection, Yale University Medical Library; and the Titchener collection, Collection of Regional History and University Archives, John M. Olin Research Library, Cornell University. The authors are greatly indebted to Dr. Boring for guidance and comments in this selection of materials and references.

[1] Edwin G. Boring, "Edward Bradford Titchener, 1867-1927," in *The American Journal of Psychology*, Vol. XXXVIII, No. 4, (October, 1927), pp. 489-506. (p. 495)

[2] Boring, *loc. cit.* In this connection, Boring made the following observation in a communication to the authors about Titchener: "He secluded himself from his colleagues at Cornell so much (1910 onward and perhaps earlier) that many of the Cornell faculty thought of him as a German and did not know what a staunch Briton he was."

reprinted article, however, had four new prefatory paragraphs, viewing Titchener in perhaps more balanced retrospect. Boring, who took his Ph.D. under Titchener at Cornell in 1914 and thus had the opportunity of knowing him intimately, speaks here of ". . . the brilliant, erudite, magnetic, charming Titchener . . . but demanding loyalty, deference, and adherence to the advice so freely offered." He goes on to tell us: "In the last twenty years of his life Titchener had few contemporary friends and remained surrounded by younger disciples." A few sentences further he is termed "the erudite egotist."[3]

In a recent communication to the writers, Dr. Boring, recalling the Titchener of the 1910-27 period, remembers him as a man whose closest relationships were to his graduate students toward whom he "took a paternal yet autocratic relationship." He recalls Titchener as a "person who was paternal to anyone who agreed with him or who would express loyalty to him . . . But the pattern for Titchener is never one of equal status in a personal relation . . ."[4]

The picture that we get of Titchener then, emerges something as a man of contrasts and paradoxes, yet withal a commanding figure, a capsule definition, possibly, of any genius of sorts. Changeable in his personal relationships, he seemed to counter-balance it, in a peculiar way, by his unswerving devotion to the pursuit of scientific truth, as he saw it, in the laboratory. Such, then, in bold strokes, are the dimensions of the older of the two men we are dealing with.

The first inkling we have of the Watson-Titchener relationship is a letter Watson wrote the Ithaca psychologist on Dec. 19, 1908, when Watson had just come to Johns Hopkins University, and four years before he announced his distinctive break with classical psychology in what has been called by Woodworth the "behaviorist manifesto" in 1913. Watson wrote Titchener in part:

> . . . I think I wrote you once about my regard for you. Angell and Donaldson have been like parents to me and I am sure that they will live in my memory as long as I live. My first debt is to them. It is an intellectual, social and moral debt. After these two men I have always

[3] Boring, "Edward Bradford Titchener: 1867-1927," in *Psychologist at Large* (New York, Basic Books, 1961), 246-265. (p. 246)

[4] On this point, Boring explains further in a letter to the authors: "The covert pattern was never of equal status, but the overt pattern was. This was one bit of Titchener's magic. He regarded himself as a genius and always used the first person plural in talking with a colleague or graduate student. So the student felt exalted. But let the student begin to stand out against Titchener, and then the pattern changed."

placed your work and what I know of you personally. I am not so sure that I do not owe you as much as I owe them. I think if I had to say where the stimulus for hard persistent research came from I should have to point to you. I did not know a great deal of experimental psychology until your *Instructor's Manual* fell into my hands. I went to work on that and then I began to see the amount of work you must have done in order to have written that. This made me work up on my German and then the German field opened up to me in a way that had been lacking before. Of course Angell's training made it possible for me to get hold of your work.

Münsterberg, Jastrow and Cattell might never have lived so far as influencing my work. I sadly fear that there are many students in the same catalog. Somehow in looking over their work one does not feel impressed either with their sincerity or their accomplishments. I defy anyone to follow your work and not be stimulated to go likewise and do a hard piece of work.

In his short autobiographical sketch, Watson[5] says: "For two years at Hopkins I taught a modified James type of general psychology, using Titchener's experimental manuals in my experimental courses." The manuals of Titchener in this area were probably the most widely used in America during the first three decades of this century.[6] Boring says that "Külpe is said to have called them [the manuals] the most erudite psychological work in the English language . . ." And shortly after this Boring's own estimate: "Even now, half a century later, it is hard to name a more erudite set of volumes or single book in English, in psychology, by a single author."[7]

At this point an interesting question emerges: When did Watson and Titchener first meet? While we cannot be positive on this point, we do have a letter which Titchener wrote to Yerkes on May 22, 1909 in which he says: "I didn't see as much of Watson at Princeton

[5] Carl Murchison, ed., *A History of Psychology in Autobiography*, Vol. III (Worcester, Mass., Clark Univ. Press, 1936), "John Broadus Watson," p. 276-7.

[6] Titchener, Edward Bradford, Experimental Psychology: A Manual of Laboratory Practice (New York, Macmillan, 1901), Vol. I, *Qualitative Experiments; Pt. 1 Students' Manual, Pt. 2 Instructors' Manual.* In 1905 appeared Vol. II, *Quantitative Experiments; Pt. 1 Students' Manual, Pt. 2 Instructors' Manual.* Of these manuals, Boring wrote the authors: "It was Vol. I, Pt. 1, 1901, that was used so generally because it fitted the standard undergraduate elementary laboratory course. It was Vol. II, Pt. 2 that began to show the erudition, but the peak of erudition (and of accuracy) came in Vol. II, Pts. 1 and 2, especially in Vol. II, Pt. 2." One might say that the *Qualitative Manuals* were probably the most widely used, but from the standpoint of erudition, the *Quantitative Manuals* excelled.

[7] Boring, Edwin G., *A History of Experimental Psychology, Second Edition* (New York, Appleton-Century-Crofts, 1950), 413.

as I should have liked; but it was pleasant to see what I did of him. I think that he has a big career, and I like him very much personally." This last sentence is of particular interest since Titchener was scarcely a man given to unstinted praise or the use of superlatives. We wonder then if perhaps he saw in the young Watson of 1909 the exuberant and brash ego that he must have had or wished for in some measure himself when as a young man he was educated under the restraints of Oxford and Leipzig. This expressed almost immediate liking of Watson by Titchener turned out to be an enduring attitude. Here was young Watson, bright and brash, and yet deferential to Titchener. And Titchener was himself, so to say, something of a maverick in terms of his career development in America (but not a maverick, of course, to the Wundtian tradition). The Cornell psychologist did not simply fit into the American scheme of things— as Boring so aptly says: "Titchener never became a part of American psychology."[8] Similarly in the American scene Watson was another maverick. There must have been some kind of mutual but unspoken recognition of the fact by the two. Conjectural? Yes, but in an area where no assertion could really be made, but it would help to explain their professional affinity.

Watson's "behaviorist manifesto" in 1913 provoked private cries of anguish from conservatives and adherents of classical psychology alike. Titchener was of course the expected leader of the opposition, and in this role could hardly ignore this cry of revolt from the young Johns Hopkins University professor. But paradoxically, he proved to be a rather silent leader in this instance. Titchener limited his counterarguments to a very few published articles or comments, the principal one of which was a paper that he read before the American Philosophical Society in Philadelphia on April 3, 1914, and which bore the title: "On 'Psychology as the Behaviorist Views It'." In it he said, in part:

> It is . . . a misunderstanding that has prompted the polemical para-graphs of Watson's recent articles on what, I suppose, we must be content to call Behaviorism.
>
> This doctrine, as set forth by Watson, has two sides, positive and negative. On the positive side, psychology is required to exchange its individualistic standpoint for the universalistic; it is to be "a purely objective experimental branch of natural science" in the sense in which

[8]*Ibid.,* 413.

physics and chemistry are natural sciences. . . . The erection of this special science is both justified and made possible by the practical goal of behaviorism, which is the working out of general and special methods for the control of behavior, the regulation and control of evolution as a whole.

On the negative side, again, psychology is enjoined by the behaviorist to ignore, even if it does not deny, those modes of human experience with which ordinary psychology is concerned, and in particular to reject the psychological method of introspection. [9]

Titchener examined Watson's charges against traditional psychology in some detail, and then remarked:

... I should like to record two general impressions that the reading of his [Watson's] articles has made upon me. The first impression is that of their unhistorical character; and the second is that of their logical irrelevance to psychology as ordinarily understood. [10]

Throughout the course of his article of seventeen pages and 36 footnotes, Titchener commented on behaviorism point by point. "Watson is asking us, in effect, to exchange a science for a technology," Titchener complained. He added that ". . . behaviorism can never replace psychology because the scientific standpoints of the two disciplines are different; we now see that Watson's behaviorism can never replace psychology because the one is technological, the other scientific."[11]

Doubtlessly these opinions expressed the views of many psychologists of the day. But Watson had a great following and the next year, possibly because he gave voice and aspiration for many psychologists of his time, he was elected president of the American Psychological Association.

In a letter to Yerkes, dated April 2, 1914, which dealt with the foregoing paper, Titchener wrote:

I have just sent to the Philos. Soc. at Phila. a paper on Watson's two Behaviour articles. It is severe, but I hope courteous. They promise to publish in May, and I shall be glad to have your opinion of my criticisms. Watson is the kind of man, I think, who should never trust himself to write on general questions, but should stick to his concrete work. He has no historical knowledge, and no power of continuous

---

[9] E. B. Titchener, "On 'Psychology as the Behaviorist Views it," in *Proceedings of the American Philosophical Society*, Vol. LIII, No. 213 (Jan.-May, 1914), p. 2-3.

[10] *Ibid.*, p. 4.

[11] Titchener, *loc. cit.*, p. 14.

thinking in the realm of concepts. Strong language!—but I hope you will agree that my paper substantiates the remarks.

. . . There is now a flurry in favor of behaviourism; but that is largely because the thing is so far all positive, and no criticism worth mentioning has appeared. No doubt the point of view will permanently appeal to certain temperaments (as it has appealed in the past; it is no more new than pragmatism was!). But the present hullabaloo will quiet down after a few critical papers have made their appearance; and then we shall get our perspective again. I do not belittle behaviourism by hoping that it may soon be set in its right place! but I get a trifle tired of unhistorical enthusiasms.

While Titchener characterizes his own article as "severe," some psychologists felt that Titchener had been too soft on Watson! For example, we may use a letter that Watson's former teacher and associate, James R. Angell, wrote to Titchener in 1915:

. . . You have let Watson down more amiably than most persons will think he deserved. My own disposition would have been to poke a little fun on the historical side of the case. Indeed, I think if Watson had ever had my historical courses, which were developed after he graduated, he could hardly have fallen into some of the pits which have entrapped him. My own position has been rendered rather difficult by virtue of my personal attachment. Of course I am wholly impatient of his position on this issue which seems to me scientifically unsound and philosophically essentially illiterate. Meantime for much of his actual work I have very high regard, as I have for him personally. I shall therefore be glad to see him properly spanked, even tho I cannot publicly join in the censuring.

Whatever their theoretical differences, however, Titchener and Watson both had strong underlying commitments to make psychology "scientific"—a science, but each in a different way. Grace Adams, one of Titchener's Ph.D. students who obtained her degree under him in 1923 summarized her mentor's aspirations in this direction some years later: "Titchener had foreseen the day when all the data of psychology could be expressed in terms as mathematical as those of a physical equation."[12] This was also the aim of Watson. Titchener and Watson had gotten to know each other through two avenues. Starting about 1909 and 1910 there was a movement afoot

[12]Grace Adams, *Psychology: Science or Superstition?* (New York, Covici-Friede, 1930), p. 211.

to bring the next meeting of the International Congress of Psychology to the United States. It was assumed that William James would be the president of this Congress. A partial slate of officers was set up, and Watson was named secretary. He wrote numerous psychologists, including Titchener, about the projected Congress. However, William James died on August 26, 1910. While the details are missing, it is supposed that there were three candidates for successor to James: Cattell, Titchener, and Münsterberg. Apparently no agreement could be reached as to who would replace James. Feeling was so strong that it was felt that whoever was chosen, the other two and their followers would boycott the Congress. Apparently Titchener felt that he had the backing of Watson, if we may believe a letter that he wrote to Yerkes, dated March 19, 1910, on the subject of the Congress: "I had to mind Cattell, as James minded him. But I have had the vote and goodwill of James, Baldwin and Watson,—and I am very proud of that. I have now proposed that we have a referendum-vote on the whole slate: vice-presidents and president both. I do not know if the other men will agree. You are very good to take my side in the matter. I did not want to be president at all; but I was willing to shoulder the duty and responsibility if they fell to me. I do want the Congress, for the sake of our standing in the world. . . ." While this letter was written some five months prior to James's passing, his failing health had probably made clear to colleagues that he would be unequal to the presidency. Here again it is interesting to note Titchener felt "very proud" of Watson's support. However, in the stalemate that developed about the holding of the Congress in America, the months slipped by, efforts languished, and the project died. The first meeting of the Congress in America was not held until 1929, at Yale.[13]

Their other avenue of contact was through the Society of Experimental Psychologists, which was founded by Titchener and some others at Cornell in April, 1904. This Society was one of Titchener's fondest projects. Membership was by invitation only, and members were selected with much care. Watson was admitted into this select circle in 1909 or 1910. In his short sketch of the history of the Society Boring wrote:

[13]There is very little in print about the movement to have the International Congress of Psychology have its world meeting in America in the period prior to the outbreak of World War I. The first I. C. P. after the war (WWI) was in 1923 at Oxford, and, according to Dr. Boring, Claparede, when the question of taking the Congress to America was discussed, warned: "But I hope you are not going to let us down the way you did last time."

J. B. Watson was host at Hopkins in 1910. There was no printed report of the meeting. He recalls the presence of Titchener, Holt, Yerkes, Baird, H. S. Langfeld and H. M. Johnson. It was the first meeting for Langfeld and Johnson, as well as for Watson. Holt and Yerkes called each other by their first names, and Titchener was distressed by such unBritish conduct.[14]

Since we have seen in a letter quoted previously that Titchener had seen Watson in 1909 at the Princeton meeting, Boring's statement that this was the first meeting for Watson seems to be in error. At any rate, at the tenth meeting of the Society in 1913 in Wesleyan, Boring noted that "there was a more lively discussion of Watson's new school of behaviorism and a seemingly unanimous dissent from his views; but Watson was not there."[15]

Holt wrote a short letter to Yerkes on March 13, 1917, apparently about the meeting of this group that spring. (He addressed Yerkes as "Dear Rob"):

> Warren's list of persons invited last year, as revised by Titchener for this year is—Goddard, Franz, Yerkes, Doll, Rogers, Miles, H.M. Johnson, N.J. Melville, W.F. Dearborn, J.P. Porter, Frost, S.P. Hayes, J.W. Hayes, Boswell, Watson, Angier, Dodge, Sanford, Woodworth, Baird, McComas. Watson is asking Dunlap and Lashley.

Mentioned above by Boring was Titchener's marked preference for calling persons by their last names, something of a British tradition. It is interesting to note in reading a large number of letters that Watson wrote to psychologists, physicians, scientists, associates and friends, Watson employed the Titchenerian custom: *e.g.* "Dear Smith," or "Dear Jones," usually omitting the "Mr." and hardly ever addressing even a close friend by his first name. Titchener had a

[14] E. G. Boring, "The Society of Experimental Psychologists, 1904-1938," in *The American Journal of Psychology*, Vol. LI, (April, 1938), pp. 410-421. (413) According to a recent communication from Dr. Boring there was no generally continuing "membership" for Titchener's experimentalists. The title "Society of Experimental Psychologists" was not devised until after Titchener's death. In one of his letters, Titchener remarks that he once proposed to call it "the Fechner Society," but the proposal was not accepted. Boring explains: "Attendance (membership in one particular year) was by invitation, in the sense that the host, who had been specified the year before, invited whom he wished with that person's graduate students, but was expected to submit his list of invitations to Titchener for approval or additions in advance." Watson infrequently attended it appears. While Titchener attended faithfully he apparently needed urging to do so in at least one year, since Robert Yerkes wrote him a three-page letter on March 31, 1914, and the entire first page was a plea to Titchener to come: "I wish we might persuade you to look upon it as a duty to help us keep the group alive. It is your group, and if you drop out, it will disintegrate . . . ."

[15] *Ibid.*, p. 414.

"rigid specificity" (to use Boring's phrase) for such details, and it is not hard to surmise that Watson picked up this habit there.[16]

Robert M. Yerkes was a good friend to both Watson and Titchener. In a letter to Titchener from Cambridge, Mass., dated Nov. 12, 1909, Yerkes wrote:

> . . . God knows there are few enough really scientific psychologists. . . . Watson and I are just on the point of becoming psychologists or of turning from it into physical science forever. Your responsibility, so far as I am concerned, has been fully and generously met, but as to Watson I feel that you and Angell are the men who can do most to keep him in psychology. I want you to give him the sort of start in the subject that you gave me and I wish to goodness that I could discover some way of bringing just that about. . . . I want him to discover that there is something different from Angell's psychology.

We learn in a letter of April 22, 1910, from Watson to Titchener, that the Cornell professor had been a houseguest of Watson's at the Baltimore meeting of the Experimentalists: "I can't begin to tell you how glad I am that you could come to us. . . . I shall always look back upon the week with great pleasure. I hope occasion may again offer us a similar visit. My wife and youngsters join me in kindest regards."[17]

Titchener was highly respected by all psychologists of whatever theoretical conviction, even the ones with whom he disagreed. A quotation from a letter of E. B. Holt to Titchener of November 16, 1918, sheds some light on this seeming paradox: "Your friendship for me and my affection for you exist, to some extent now and will in the future probably to a more obvious degree, behind two public, shall I say, masques, which are very different from each other, and to some extent show glances of hostility." Holt might very well have been speaking for Watson in this case. The point here of course is

---

[16]Dr. Boring recalls a letter from Watson in which he complained about the American psychologists' habits of calling each other by their last names, and suggested that this was due to Titchener's influence because it was British. Even if Watson did not like the custom he apparently felt that he had to conform.

[17]Dr. Boring advises that "every host at a meeting of the Experimentalists wanted Titchener as his house guest" and "it was natural for the host at the meeting to have Titchener as his guest."

that though many disagreed markedly with Titchener in formal approaches or theory of psychology, they were privately close to him.[18]

While many letters may not have survived, there is evidence that Watson and Titchener kept in touch by correspondence. For example, in a letter to Yerkes dated October 12, 1912, Titchener specifically says: ". . . and then I have also been writing to Watson and Holt on technical things . . ." Again, two years later, in another letter to Yerkes dated October 17, 1914, Titchener says: "I haven't time for a letter; but I send a line to thank you for yours, and for the enclosures; and especially to thank you for the hint about Watson. He very friendlily wrote to me himself. Of course I sent him the paper [undoubtedly a reprint of Titchener's paper before the American Philosophical Society]; as a matter of fact, I sent him the very first copy that I mailed at all. I expect he was away in Canada—I must have sent to him, I think, early in July . . ." It might be added that Watson had a summer home in Ontario, Canada, and up until 1917 used to spend his summers up there.[19]

The War years (WWI) were of course a time of disruption for nearly all psychologists. Titchener remained a British subject, but the empire never called him to the colors, although he wrote to Boring that he had volunteered his services to Britain at the outbreak. Titchener wrote to Yerkes on Sept. 6, 1914 in this regard, winding up with a sly jab at Münsterberg (a German): "I have put Jack [his son] and myself at the disposal of the British Empire; but I hope that we sha'n't be wanted. I was an artilleryman in my callow youth, but have forgotten everything I knew; and at 47 one is not young. Possibly a duel with Münsterberg might be the right thing!" Watson served in the Army and rose to the rank of major, although, if we may believe his autobiography, he apparently was quite disillusioned over his experience in the war.

[18]Pursuant to this paragraph, Dr. Boring recalls: "Holt and Dodge lit into Titchener on introspection in the 1911 meeting of the Experimentalists, and Titchener delegated me to see Holt to the trolley after the meeting. Holt explained to me his affection for Titchener. He admired him for his scholarship and for his grace. Titchener's devotion to good manners told off, except when someone else offended against them and had to be put in his place."

[19]While at Johns Hopkins, Baltimore, Maryland (1908-1920) it was Watson's custom (except after America entered WWI) to take his family summers to Canada to their summer home. While it is conjectural, when going by rail, he could have stopped off at Ithaca either going or coming.

In our day there is much talk about one's self-image. How did Titchener see himself at about this time? In a letter to Yerkes dated March 4, 1916, Titchener affords us an interesting insight into how he sized himself up at the time: "Now I have the reputation of being a purist and a fanatic, and among the malevolent of being self-sufficient and unsocial; still I have a reputation of sorts, and it is strongest perhaps on the outside,—among the influential men who are not directly connected with psychology." A sentence or two later he refers to "my natural touch of crankiness" and shortly thereafter as "a man of my general aloofness . . ." The point here is that from the evidence the relation between Watson and Titchener seemed to become closer after Watson's exit from the academic world in 1920. Watson then was, in Titchener's words, "on the outside" and "not directly connected with psychology" so much any more, and hence it would be natural for him to draw closer to Watson, who now was no longer, so to speak, a competitor.

We need not go into the details which led Watson out of Academia, except to say that on account of his divorce he left Johns Hopkins University in 1920 and entered the world of advertising in New York City. There was quite a change in Watson's friendships at this time, according to his autobiography, but his warm feeling toward Titchener seemed to grow. When Watson's fortunes were at their lowest ebb in 1920, he turned to Titchener for personal references. Titchener did not fail him. Watson was deeply appreciative of this help, which materially aided him in getting a fresh start. About fourteen months later he wrote to Titchener, March 4, 1922, and said in part: "So forgive me if I seemed unappreciative of the interest you have shown in me. I am not. At heart I know I am more grateful to you than to any other psychologist. You have done more for me than all the rest of my colleagues put together."

Titchener apparently took Watson's dismissal from Johns Hopkins very much at heart—the way anyone would naturally feel toward a person who had suffered mishap or reverse of fortune to whom he entertained feelings of regard and friendship. Thus we find the following comment on the exit of Watson from university life by Titchener in a letter to Yerkes dated November 25, 1920:

> I am terribly sorry for the Watson children, just as I am sorry for W.
> [Watson] himself; he will have to disappear for 5 or 10 years, I am

afraid, if he ever wants indeed to return to psychology. It is perversely unfortunate that the Baldwin affair should have happened to a psychologist at the same university so recently. But what makes me indignant is that A. Meyer [Dr. Adolf Meyer, the renowned psychiatrist of the day at Johns Hopkins] and the Clinic in general couldn't have used their arts to keep W. [Watson] straight. They are so blamed keen on theory—in which they are after all only logical infants—that they forget that the business of the psychiatrist is to prevent and to cure. A little decent advice (for W. [Watson] is intrinsically a very decent and eminently likeable person) would have prevented the family tragedy. And it is the children who suffer most.

To explain the setting for some of the foregoing remarks we must note that Watson before he left Johns Hopkins had been associated with Dr. Meyer in important research work in the Phipps Clinic of the Medical School.

In a letter to Raymond Dodge of the National Research Council, dated April 19, 1923, Titchener was discussing a review that Watson had written, one that had caused some criticism. The Cornell professor noted that Dodge had said that he had been predisposed toward William McDougall "by Watson's invective." "For my own part," wrote Titchener, "I had a good deal rather be Watson than McDougall."[20]

For many years, Watson had been a prominent figure in experimental psychology. He had served as an editor of the *Journal of Experimental Psychology* for many years.[21] Apparently around 1923 there was some dissatisfaction with the quality of this publication. Professor H. C. Warren of Princeton wrote to Titchener about his views on the matter, and also about his feeling of Watson's connection with it. In a candid letter on the subject, dated October 23, 1923, Titchener wrote to Warren, in part:

> ... I have no doubt that the Experimental Journal is generally looked upon as not having fulfilled its original promise. I have heard a

[20]Dr. Boring notes in this connection that Titchener had no great admiration for McDougall. Titchener "disliked what he thought was the superficiality of his [McDougall's] experimental work in England and at his beloved Oxford. Of the British psychologists he believed in Myers."

[21]Dr. Boring has supplied the following information relative to Watson's connection with the *Journal of Experimental Psychology*: Vols. 1-8, 1916-1925, five editors listed, but Watson's name is first. He surely acted as editor-in-chief; Vol. 9, 1926, Bentley's name put first, but Watson's included in list below; Vol. 10, 1927, *et seq.*, Watson's name dropped.

good deal of casual comment on it from experimentally minded colleagues, and I am fairly sure that I am not mistaken in summing up their opinions in this way. I had never set myself to work out the reasons in detail. I can see now that Watson is under a double disadvantage as editor: first, he has no interest in experimental psychology, and therefore in all probability does not command the confidence of experimentalists; and secondly, there is still, in certain quarters, a very strong and bitter feeling against him on personal grounds. I am sometimes astonished and disheartened to find how bitter and persistent this feeling is.

On the other hand, Watson's name is very much to the front in newspapers and magazines, and your board might consider that his advertisement of the Journal offsets his technical lack of competence and lack of universal respect. I think that if I were myself a member of the board I should hesitate somewhat before accepting his resignation.

I am, however, quite clear about the status in general opinion of the Journal itself; and if you think that Watson, even if he is spurred up, will not be able to raise its scientific character pretty considerably, I think you would do well both scientifically and financially to secure another editor whose interests are more closely in line with the avowed purposes of the Journal.

Best congratulations on the start of the laboratory! . . .

Titchener served as associate editor of *The American Journal of Psychology* from 1895 to 1920, and as editor from 1921-25. He was quite jealous of its reputation. On October 1, 1924, he wrote to Watson thanking him for an offprint of a paper Watson had written for the *Psychological Review.* In this letter he said: "I wish that some day or other you would give us something for the *Journal.*"

Apparently one of the paradoxes of Titchener's life was that he had more influence abroad actually than in America in his professional field, if indeed we may believe the word of Grace K. Adams, Titchener's Ph.D. of 1923. She wrote[22] on this matter four years after her mentor's death (1931) as follows:

No psychologist who has ever lived in America has had such an enviable international reputation as Titchener—and few who have

[22]Adams, *op. cit.,* p. 100-101. Dr. Boring feels this may be somewhat dubious because of William James: "To validate her statement Adams should have compared the criteria for these two men, for James' influence was enormous, and the *Principles* well known. I think it was Külpe, though, who said that Titchener's *Experimental Psychology* (the books that caught Watson) was the most erudite psychological work in English, and a good case could be made for the volumes' being more erudite than James', even though James' must have had more influence." (E. G. B.)

written so much as a textbook have had so little influence on the thought of the country. Titchener's works have been translated into more foreign languages than those of any other psychologist. His text-book is the only official psychological text of France—the only one the French have ever had. It was on his recommendation and according to his requirements that an independent school of experimental psychology was built in Moscow.

So it should not surprise us that Titchener carried on correspondence with a Russian psychologist. In a two-page letter to Professor G. Tschelpanow of Moscow, dated October 25, 1924, he set forth some of his views on the behavioristic movement:

> . . . You are to be heartily congratulated on having been able to keep scientific psychology alive during these years of storm and stress. . . .
>
> Behaviorism has spread over the country in a great wave, more or less as Freudianism did a few years ago. The actual experimental work that the behaviorists turn out is good enough; but the general logic of their position is ridiculously crude. Unfortunately, a large number of the younger men who enter the academic career in psychology have had no training whatsoever in general logic, and therefore have a certain contempt for it as well as for the general historical background of psychology. I don't think that the movement will continue very long; the newest fad that is appearing over the horizon is that of the Gestalt-psychologie; and I think that that may presently have its period of fashion, and that behaviorism may correspondingly dwindle. There is really no remedy for all these eccentric movements except time and the general logic involved in the progress of the science all around.[23]

In the same year, 1924, Titchener voiced his belief in important contributions that Watson was still making to academic psychology. In a letter to Philip W. Hausmann, dated November 11, 1924, he said: ". . . I think the most important papers of the year, published in America, are those of Watson in the *Psychological Review* and of Nafe in the *American Journal.*"[24]

In a letter to Watson dated November 12, 1924, Titchener talks of many things dealing with their respective children which only a warm relationship would indicate. One of Titchener's married children was

[23]Dr. Boring recalls that Tschelpanow had attended a meeting of the Experimentalists at Cornell. Occasionally distinguished visitors came to see Titchener at Cornell.

[24]Watson's papers were: "The Unverbalized in Human Behavior," *Psychological Review,* 1924, 31, 273-280; and "The Place of Kinaesthetic, Visceral and Laryngeal Organization in Thinking," *ibid.,* 339-347.

then living in New York, and he gave Watson their address, adding: "It will be delightful if you and Mrs. Watson could really find time and opportunity to drop in upon them." In the last paragraph he says: "I am very much interested to know of the marriage of your own daughter." This refers to his first child by his first marriage, Mary (nicknamed Polly) who was then nineteen and was being married. To this Titchener devoted a friendly paragraph. Now changing the subject he wrote in part: "It is quite true that the logic of the behaviorists is muddled; both Roback and I myself have pointed this out in print. The strength of the movement lies not in its fundamental logic but in its laboratory performance." In a letter to the authors, Dr. Boring commented on this letter: "Titchener was always interested in the families of his correspondents. This was the personal and charming side of him."

John B. Watson was included in Who's Who in America when he was only 29 years old. As far as the profession of psychologist is concerned, this is a record unequalled for youthfulness before or since. (The average age for initial inclusion in this biographical dictionary is about fifty). Watson was born January 9, 1878, and his sketch first appeared in *Who's Who in America* in Vol. V, 1908-09. The sketch was 14 lines in length. As his accomplishments increased, the sketch grew longer with each biennial edition. Watson's sketch was included in Vol. XI, 1920-21. When he dropped out of the academic world, his name was shown in Vol. XII, 1922-1923, and Vol. XIII, 1924-25, but his sketch is omitted and the reader is referred to Vol. XI. The editors of *Who's Who* stated at that time that they always omitted a sketch unless they got a reply from the author (biographee) to their periodic mailings that indicated that he was still active and living. For a year or two, they would print his name and refer to the volume in which the sketch had appeared. The implication was that they would revive the sketch if they heard from the biographee, but of course after a year or two they would stop trying to contact him.

In a letter to Watson dated April 23, 1923, E. G. Boring said: "I discovered that your sketch in *Who's Who in America* had been omitted from the last volume, and I mentioned it to Warren when I saw him a few weeks ago. We suspected some sinister reason, and Warren said he would write them about it." While the Marquis editors said Watson's sketch had been dropped because letters addressed to him in Baltimore had been returned, it is believed that they were not forwarded to Watson from the Maryland city. Through the good offices of Professor Boring, Warren, Titchener, McDougall and Thorndike all wrote to the Marquis editors in Chicago asking that Watson be reinstated. In a letter to Dr. Boring on the subject, Titchener wrote:

> In this Volume 12, (1922-23), as I have it, Watson's name is given, as that of a psychologist, and the reader is referred back for a sketch to Volume 11, 1920-21. I should have assumed, if I had come across the name casually, that the sketch had been omitted simply because Watson had given up his academic relationships; and scholarly people are very rarely included in *Who's Who* unless by reason of their connection with a university.

In a letter dated December 15, 1924, from Boring to Watson, he wrote: "After Warren, Titchener, McDougall, and Thorndike wrote to *Who's Who*, distributed by me over intervals of time in hopes of summation, McDougall finally got a letter regretting the mistake and assuring him that the sketch would be included in the next volume. There is nothing more to do then." Watson wrote back on December 18, 1924 to Boring: "Would you be good enough to extend my thanks to Warren, Titchener, McDougall and Thorndike, and take some for yourself for your assistance in straightening out *Who's Who*? I appreciate this more than I can tell you."

There is a happy ending to the story, for Watson's sketch was restored to the pages of *Who's Who in America*, when Vol. 14, 1926-27, made its appearance, and it was twice as long as before— 29 lines. By way of comparison in this same volume, Boring's sketch was 22 lines, and Titchener's 33 lines. Three Americans in every ten thousand are selected for inclusion in the pages of *Who's Who*. It has been called "America's biographic Hall of Fame."

Another instance of the warm relationship of Titchener and Watson is reflected in the case of Grace Adams, Titchener's Ph.D. student and protege. After getting her degree at Cornell, she was an instructor for a time at Goucher, but presently left the job. She apparently yearned for a career as a writer, and in 1924 Titchener wrote to Watson asking him to help her locate suitable work. He wrote Titchener on October 3, 1924: "I have had a great deal of fun meeting your little pet, Miss Adams. Without taking responsibility as to what she should do, I tried to locate something for her in New

York. I finally wrote to Boni & Liveright [New York publishing firm] and I think they have become interested in her."

Titchener replied to Watson on October 6, 1924 in part: "I am grateful to you for having put Grace Adams in the way of getting something to do. She is a girl of definite psychological ability. . . ." Watson replied October 10th: *"In re* our little friend—I am going to get my wife [Rosalie Rayner Watson] to lunch with her in a day or two and then we shall have her come out home and see us once in a while. In this way I can keep track of her and find out just what she plans to do. But I hope you will assure her mother that we shall have her in mind and will look after her a bit." Later that month Grace Adams appears to have landed a job (the firm not indicated) and on October 21st, 1924, Titchener wrote Watson a letter and thanked him for his efforts on her behalf: ". . . it is first rate of you to be looking after her and first rate for her to know that somebody of responsibility is keeping an eye on her." With this letter Grace Adams disappears from the Titchener–Watson correspondence.

However, Grace Adams went on to become something of a stormy petrel for the psychologists. She wrote a great many articles for the *American Mercury* about psychology from various aspects in the best Menckenian tradition. One of these bore the title "Titchener at Cornell," and appeared in the *Mercury* for December, 1931, and the article was featured on the cover. She also wrote for the *Atlantic Monthly*, and other magazines, and between 1931 and 1941 wrote four popular books. Miss Adams married another *American Mercury* writer and free-lancer named Edward Hutter. To complete this lady's career, a letter from John Buchanan, Assistant Archivist at the John M. Olin Research Library at Cornell dated December 6, 1963, reveals that she died in Spain in 1958 at Palma De Mallorca.

To return to Titchener and Watson: In a letter of Titchener's dated April 3, 1923, to Watson, we find feelings revealed of a close and cordial nature: "It was beautifully friendly of you to send me your review, and it would probably surprise McDougall if he knew that we were leagued against him. . . ." And at the close of this letter he says to Watson: "I think that our trust in each other is pretty well established, whatever may be our differences of intellectual outlook, I always rejoice to confound the current notion that difference of opinion must necessarily lead to personal enmity."

From the tone of these letters it would seem that the relation between Watson and Titchener in the last four or five years of Titchener's life did not lessen. This might have been due partly to the

Titchener's life did not lessen. This might have been due partly to the fact that Titchener unconsciously felt in the years following Watson's exit from academia that he was no longer even a potential professional threat to the Titchenerian system of psychology. And to Watson, Titchener undoubtedly remained a symbol of the academic life that he doubtlessly left with much regret. Hence an association that had been perhaps in the beginning an amicable and casual one, gradually ripened into a mature and abiding friendship from 1920 onward.

Titchener evidently was pleased at Watson's rapid rise in the world of advertising, yet a little apprehensive that he might neglect his first love—psychology. In a letter to Watson dated January 17, 1925, Titchener says:

> I expect that, from the material side, you are to be congratulated upon your advancement to a vice-presidency; I suppose that the position carries some sort of fabulous salary. I am naturally a little sorry, all the same, to get the news, since I fear it means that you will be more than ever tied up with commercial matters and will have less time than before to devote to what you are pleased to think is psychology. Here's hoping, at any rate, that you have energy for both these things.

In the first edition of *A History of Experimental Psychology,* Boring devotes over ten pages to Titchener, and gives this view of him:

> Titchener was very important in the history of American psychology because he represented this older conservative tradition against overwhelming numbers. West of the Atlantic in psychology there was "America" and there was Titchener. Names often stand out in history because their owners have opposed something older; movements of thought are always movements away from other thought. However, in Titchener's case the situation was reversed. He has stood in bold relief because every one near him moved away from him. Action and reaction were equal.[25]

The above book was published in 1929. In the second edition, published in 1950, twenty-one years later, the space devoted to Titchener is about the same, but the wording of the first sentence in the above paragraph was changed: "very important" was changed to "important" which might indicate a slight drop in how the author rated him. These changes in estimates about figures in any field of

[25] Edwin G. Boring, *A History of Experimental Psychology* (First Ed.) (New York, The Century Co., 1929), p. 412.

course are naturally bound to change with the passage of time, but the author added another new and final paragraph to the section on Titchener. Here was noted the decline in the work of the Ithaca psychologist in his last few years instead of a promised *magnum opus* and concludes:

> Somehow Titchenerism in America had been sustained by his magnificent personality. With his death it suddenly collapsed, dwindling rapidly from the status of a vital faith in the importance of consciousness to the equally essential but wholly inglorious state of having been an unavoidable phase of historical development.[26]

In 1928 Pillsbury wrote an estimate of Titchener in which he tells of the difficulty faced in assessment of the value of a person's life-work:

> It is an interesting if difficult task to evaluate or even summarize the work of an outstanding figure in the science, who has been a leader for a full generation. It is not easy to avoid the too favorable estimate that follows upon accepting the ideals and standards that the man himself held, on the one hand, or to avoid the opposite extreme of taking the standards of an opposing school. One must decide also whether to judge from the standpoint of the science at the beginning of the epoch or from the position it has attained at the end of his work. This is a particularly difficult problem in psychology. No other science has undergone quite so many changes in viewpoint, or has indulged in quite so bitter quarrels between exponents of fundamentally opposed theories.
> More than most Titchener was affected by this evolution.[27]

Just a year earlier, Boring had characterized the passing of his mentor in a sketch of his life as follows:

> The death of no other psychologist could so alter the psychological picture in America. Not only was he unique among American psychologists as a personality and in his scientific attitude, but he was a cardinal point in the national systematic orientation. The clearcut opposition between behaviorism and its allies, on the one hand, and something else, on the other, remains clear only when the opposition is between behaviorism and Titchener, mental tests and Titchener, or

[26] Edwin G. Boring, *A History of Experimental Psychology* (2nd ed.) (New York, Appleton-Century-Crofts, Inc. 1950), pp. 419, 420.

[27] W. B. Pillsbury, "The Psychology of Edward Bradford Titchener," in *The Philosophical Review*, XXXVII, No. 2 (March 1928), 95-108. (p. 96)

applied psychology and Titchener. His death, thus, in a sense, creates a classificatory chaos in American systematic psychology.[28]

At the close of this life sketch, Boring remarks:

> Certainly Titchener was a remarkable personality and a great psychologist. That his influence has been so effective in spite of his personal isolation from psychologists and his intellectual isolation from the national trend is, I take it, a test of greatness. A century hence it will be possible to say just where his psychology belongs in the history of science.[29]

The relationship between Titchener and Watson is difficult to reconstruct precisely even with the information we have now in terms of letters that were not known before, but it is an intriguing and challenging project. It seems to the writers to be an instance of two men, both strong-minded, and each, if not exactly a rebel, at least in isolation from their backgrounds. Watson was from Greenville, South Carolina, Titchener from Chichester, England. Each came from a small town and went to a major university and then in the case of Titchener he settled in a foreign country, while in the case of Watson, he finally ended up in a foreign (*e.g.*, advertising) field. Even in 1916, eleven years before his death, for example, after living in America so long, Titchener still saw himself as "different." Writing to Yerkes on March 4, 1916, he said at one point: "... you are an American and I am a European."

Likewise, both Watson and Titchener had the "grand manner." In Watson's later life he did things in great style and loved to show a display of power. Titchener was also an autocratic personality, which is to be distinguished from the aggressive personality. The "Titchenerian personality" is managerial, socially formal, and polite. With this type of person the right to manage the affairs of others is considered to be a privilege won by past achievement and work, and is a duty to be exercised over students. Titchener could be paternal and demanding and when this manner was threatened could be quite autocratic in putting the threat down and responding to the threat. The Cornell psychologist had a social code and a scientific code, both of which were held with vigor and rigor. Attacks on either one were

[28]Edwin G. Boring, "Edward Bradford Titchener, 1867-1927" in *The American Journal of Psychology*, XXXVIII, 4 (Oct., 1927), p. 489.
[29]*Ibid.*, p. 506.

met by resistance or perhaps a counterblast. Deviations from the social code and the scientific code were both treated the same way and not allowed to pass unchallenged or unpunished.

There is ample evidence to believe that there was a similar authoritarian manner in Watson. He was the brash young American version rather than the English type with touches of German over-lay. His instant respect for Titchener and Titchener's quick response to Watson is undoubtedly more than an intellectual appreciation of each other. One of the key sentences in their correspondence already referred to, was: "I think that our trust in each other is pretty well established, whatever may be our differences of intellectual outlook . . ." (1923) "Trust!"—the most important thing to each of these men. Their autocratic nature was accompanied by a very sensitive one which could easily be hurt and could certainly exhibit that well-known association of ego-grandiosity with feelings of not being appreciated or even misperceived. It is one of the features of persons of this type that although they have few real friends, where the trust itself is given, the loyalty is lifelong. If trust is committed, lifetime loyalty usually ensues. Individuals of this type also show an admiration for courage, energy and the ability to withstand isolation. Titchener was isolated from England and Germany, and he willingly endured it. Watson was isolated from South Carolina and later from the academic world of psychology, and was able to adjust to Madison Avenue.

Titchener's ascendancy over his students was so great that they tended to over-estimate his power and contributions early in their careers, and then tended to react to their earlier estimate later in their careers. It is the opinion of at least some, Gustav Bergmann among them, that Titchener was *the* psychologist in America to have a clear grasp of the fundamental issues of the philosophy of psychology, and that Watson during the 1910-20 period was the first to recognize clearly the specific implications of psychology constructed with a physicalistic language system. To clarify the point, which is important, we quote Bergmann:

> Titchener, the one first-rate mind among the Wundtians, gave Wuerzburg a consistent reply. Somewhat quixotically he insisted that whenever those critical "contents," awareness and meanings, occur, they can be introspectively decomposed into more orthodox ones. But he added that in many cases they do not occur at all. Take meaning, on

which he was more explicit, and consider again a person who both hears and understands (the meaning of) the word bell. Titchener then says three things. (1) More often than not such a person has on such occasions no other "contents" than, say, auditory ones. (2) These events, namely, the occurrences of the auditory "content," are among the causes of other events, among which are, as a rule, (the occurrences of) other *orthodox* "contents" of the person in question. (3) This latter fact, 2, is what a psychologist means, or ought to mean, by "meaning." Titchener's formula was: The meaning of a content is not another content but its *context*. Since I believe that there are (to speak with Wuerzburg) unanalyzable awarenesses (though not meanings!), I object to the qualification, orthodox, which I italicized. Otherwise Titchener's is the correct analysis of *one* of the commonsensical (and scientific) meanings of "meaning."[30]

Titchener's context theory of meaning today forms the framework of the theory of meaning to which most psychologists hold. It is an answer to the Würzburg school's claim that meaning comes from sets and impalpable acts. It appears to be one of Titchener's enduring and important contributions. Watson's contribution is similar but refers to behavior—not mind, but the meaning of behavior is to be described in contextual terms: namely, antecedent histories of the organism.

In 1956 Bergmann paid Watson the following compliment on the pages of the *Psychological Review*: "Second only to Freud, though at a rather great distance, John B. Watson, is, in my judgment, the most important figure in the history of psychological thought during the first half of the century. Nor is his impact limited to the science of psychology."[31] So in the lives of these two men, Watson and Titchener, strangely enough, intellectually the machinery was at work in both behavioristic and introspective research, to account for meanings by context.

Today, almost forty years after his death, we do not believe that Titchener's influence could be said in one sense to be only of historic interest. Titchener's influence is particularly impressive in its development of Boring (historian of experimental psychology) and Guilford (Titchener's psychology of the thought processes developed

[30]Gustav Bergmann, *Meaning and Existence*, (Madison, Wisconsin, The University of Wisconsin Press, 1960), p. 15.

[31]Gustav Bergmann, "The Contribution of John B. Watson," in *Psychological Review*, LXIII, No. 4 (1956), pp. 265-276. (p. 265)

and psychometricized). But there is more to Titchener than historicism and concern with mental processes. His concern with philosophical psychology seems to us to be the core of his thought, and the concern with consciousness which appears in the form of psychoanalysis is now challenging behavioristic psychology strongly. The earlier eclipse of Titchener paradoxically was due to Watson's emphasis on behavior, but with the rise of clinical psychology and problems again of mental process and the nature of consciousness, Titchener's long shadow falls over us again.

The Historical Background for National Trends in Psychology: United States
Robert I. Watson

The following article was Watson's address at a symposium entitled "The Historical Background for National Trends in Psychology," which he organized for the Seventeenth International Congress of Psychology in Washington, D.C., in 1963. Assuming the position that psychology is still in a preparadigmatic stage, he discusses American psychology in terms of prescriptions. He recapitulates the development of psychology as science and as profession in the United States and identifies certain dominant prescriptions and counterprescriptions, or opposing forces, in American psychology. Watson offers the reader a useful panoramic view and summary of American psychology.

In the early nineteenth century before the impress of the new psychology, Scottish faculty psychology of the philosophy of common sense prevailed in the universities, while outside their walls phrenology excited considerable influence, especially in medical circles (Watson, 1963). It is perhaps significant of a somewhat shamefaced attitude toward this pre-experimental period of our history that it is one about which we are uninformed. Parenthetically, I am not at all sure this attitude is justified, and an investigation is under way (Cardno and Watson).

Before the last twenty years of the nineteenth century, graduate education was in a sorry state. So superior was its European counterpart that in 1880 there were about as many Americans studying abroad as in all of our graduate schools (Albrecht). It was between 1880 and 1895 that many features of the German university system were introduced.

In the reform of university education, psychology spearheaded the attack upon what by then was regarded as the "oldfashioned" doctrine of faculties. Consequently, it was in a strategically favorable

Robert I. Watson, The historical background for national trends in psychology: United States. *Journal of the History of the Behavioral Sciences*, 1965, 1 130-138. Reprinted by permission of the author and the Psychology Press.

position; psychology not only was "new," it was "progressive." When introduced into the curriculum with the other new subjects, such as economics and political science, new departments were created for psychology in contrast to the European practice of a continued tie with philosophy.

In the general expansion and modernization of education, psychology profited mightily (Watson, 1963). In 1880 only two rather casually treated rooms at Harvard, first used five years before, could be called a laboratory; by 1895 there were 26 psychology laboratories. In 1880 no one could be called a full-time psychologist; by 1895 a flourishing American Psychological Association had been in existence for three years. As late as 1886 there was no psychological journal; by 1895 there were five. In fifteen short years psychology had emerged as a discipline.

Two individual architects of these changes were William James and G. Stanley Hall. James is the American psychologist most deserving of the name of genius in that he united within his person many diverse strands from the intellectual currents of his time to give forth something new, important, and exciting, which made psychology a subject to be respected. His *Principles of Psychology* serves as a refreshing stimulant for all succeeding generations. But he was neither an organizer nor an administrator, and not even an experimentalist.

G. Stanley Hall shared with James the ability to stimulate enthusiasm in others, but otherwise was of quite a different stamp. He was an organizer and administrator, and an enthusiastic spokesman for experimental research, but not a theorist. He founded the first journal, *The American Journal of Psychology*, and then still other journals; he organized the American Psychological Association; he founded laboratories at Johns Hopkins and Clark Universities; and he trained a considerable number of the second generation of American psychologists.

Other leaders emerged shortly after. One was James McKeen Cattell, who, while taking his degree with Wundt, had brought to Leipzig his own alien problems of individual differences in reaction time. It is also significant of his attitude that he said of Francis Galton that he was the greatest man he had ever known. In later years Cattell did much to emphasize the study of individual differences; through serving as our psychological statesman, brought psychology to the attention of other sciences; and helped to make applied psychology a characteristic enterprise.

Another leader was that Britisher with an unshakable allegiance to Wilhelm Wundt, Edward Bradford Titchener. His attempt to introduce and to refine the content of Wundtian psychology in this foreign clime was a magnificent failure. It could not be grafted upon an already flourishing tree indigenous to our particular climate. At any rate, quite apart from content, his lessons of exactitude and respect for the dignity of science did somehow hearten other psychologists and we have been the better for his presence.

The years of the schools of psychology—Functionalistic, Behavioristic, Gestalt and Psychoanalytic—extend from about 1910 through the early 1930s. Suffice it to say at this point, that, today, American psychology has moved away from schools, each as a demarcated system with a body of theories unique unto itself, a claim of universal applicability of a particular set of tenets and ego involvement in that point of view. A distinguished exception is psychoanalysis, and to some extent Gestalt psychology.

It is not enough, however, to leave the period through the thirties as that of the schools alone. Far removed from their clamor was the careful quantitative work of L. M. Terman on intelligence tests, L. L. Thurstone on factor analysis, E. L. Thorndike on human and animal learning, K. S. Lashley on brain physiology and the first appearance of the definitive *History of Experimental Psychology* by E. G. Boring.

Today the American Psychological Association has 20,000 members. With the second edition of the *International Directory* expecting to record 10,000 entries for psychologists outside the United States, it appears that two out of three psychologists live and work in the United States.

Historical developments in psychology when they met certain social forces gave us the contemporary scene in psychology. Industrialization, secularization and urbanization have left their mark upon modern psychology and serve as the background for the professionalism and increased social orientation of American psychology.

World War II helped considerably to bring about an increase in professional orientation and in sheer numbers. It created a situation in which many of the then younger psychologists transferred their skills to work quite foreign to their earlier training. Since the public proved enormously receptive to these efforts, many psychologists continued peacetime pursuits related to these experiences; others returned to the universities and developed training programs in line with these experiences.

The number of psychologists now engaged in professional practice is revealing. In 1962 a representative sampling of American psychologists (Lockman) showed that 39 per cent were employed in colleges or universities, and, that of the rest, 36 per cent were in federal and local governmental agencies, 10 per cent in private non-profit agencies, 10 per cent in industry and business, and 5 per cent were self-employed. Assuming that in each group an equivalent proportion belied the nature of their work by their locus, it is possible to conclude that 6 out of 10 psychologists are primarily concerned with the applications of psychology.

There are various current indications of professional practice—the American Board of Examiners in Professional Psychology which issues diplomas certifying competence in several specialities, and state legislative action in the form of licensing or certification. The American Psychological Association, although spending a major portion of its income for publications, also has increased its budget to meet professional demands. Since my European colleagues expect it of me, I should mention that in 1962 the Association had assets of over two million dollars and an annual budget of over one million dollars.

Closely related to professionalization is the increased social orientation of American psychology, taking place both at the university and on the larger social scene. In our universities, psychology has a dual image. In the so-called divisional faculty structure into which departments are grouped based on presumed commonality of interest, some psychology departments are placed in the natural sciences while others are in the social sciences. At a national level, the American Psychological Association has representation both on the National Research Council (for the natural sciences) and on the Social Science Research Council. This dual representation signalizes that academic psychology is considered to be both a social and a biological science. The socially oriented phases will receive attention later.

The universities are the stronghold of the biologically oriented psychologists. Confining myself to members of the National

Academy of Sciences, the universities have been the locus of the work of F. Beach on neural and hormonal behavior, C. H. Graham on sensory psychology, H. F. Harlow on primatology, D. Lindsley and C. Pfaffmann on psychophysiology, S. S. Stevens on the psychophysics of vision, and E. G. Wever on audition. Incidentally, hereafter I shall take the perhaps cowardly way out of referring by name to living psychologists only if they are members of this august body, roughly the equivalent of the Royal Society, or past presidents of the American Psychological Association—with three exceptions which I shall leave for you to detect.

If one uses as the criterion the social or biological *orientation* taken by an individual psychologist, and disregards self-consciousness about its locus, American psychology outside university walls is overwhelmingly social in orientation despite there being only a relatively small number who refer to themselves as "social" psychologists. The consent of the governed as a prerequisite to that governing requires that we secure considerable bodies of information from our citizens by psychological techniques. Moreover, almost all of the professional activities of psychologists are social in orientation. From prognostic and therapeutic work with patients, through management consultation to the selection of bomber crews, psychologists are involved with problems of social interaction.

Central to the organization of an important recent analysis by Kuhn (1962) of the history of the physical sciences is his use of paradigms, that is, those contentual models accepted at a given period of scientific development. A paradigm, Kuhn argues, defines to some extent the science in which it operates. One readily recognizes that a particular paradigm concerns chemistry, astronomy or physics.

Not too many years ago "convergent trends in psychology" was a theme in which we took comfort and pride. From today's perspective, I am not so sure that this is more than wishful thinking. The seven volumes, *Psychology: a study of a science*, edited by Koch are an obvious source to which to turn because the intellectual climate of American psychology set the limits to the scope of the study. The general introduction to the project begins by stressing the diversity of tongues with which psychologists speak. Similarly, the preface begins with a comment that psychology proceeds along "several quite unsure directions" (Koch, 1959, p. V).

Psychology is still in the pre-paradigmatic stage. Contentually defined and internationally accepted paradigms do not yet exist in psychology.

Some term is necessary which allows for recognition of national differences, for opposition and cross-currents within the science, and, paradoxically, for a reference wider than that of one science. To convey these characteristics the term, prescription, will serve. As I shall use it, prescriptions are those prevailing inclinations or tendencies to behave in a definable way in a particular science in a particular country at a particular time. These ways of behaving are often of such general nature as to be shared with other sciences and to some extent with scientists in other countries. Some prescriptions can be identified as dominant, others as counter-dominant. Some of the latter exist as direct alternatives to dominant prescriptions; others do not stand in specific opposition, they are more generally counter to prevailing dominant prescriptions.

Unlike a paradigm, a prescription does not have to define contentually the field in question. Certain prescriptions, such as determinism, monism, and naturalism, are shared with the other sciences; environmentalism applies with equal force in biology; operationalism was borrowed from physics and the philosophy of science as well as having roots in our own past.

Prescriptions are also alternatives in that selection may be made from among them. Often, this does not occur deliberately; a prescription is apt to be first accepted by the young psychologist as immutable truth, alternatives being discovered only later when the prescription has set so firmly as to be changed with difficulty.

A prescription, when deeply ingrained, tends to be unverbalized and utilized as a matter of course, unless circumstances force one to see its inapplicability. As he begins a piece of research how often does an American psychologist say to himself that it must be quantified? He behaves in a way that shows he makes this an implicit assumption.

No more than other scientists, do psychologists use these words often and fluently. Their significances are implicit in their activities as research workers but not part of their universe of discourse.

Some dominant prescriptions—determinism, naturalism, physicalism and monism—although characteristic of American psychology are mentioned only in passing. Freedom of the will, supernaturalism, spiritualism, and dualism are hardly serious counter-prescriptions. This is not the same as saying that these particular counter-prescriptions are not viable in disguised forms as a fuller exposition would give me an opportunity to bring out.

A functional spirit had been very evident in James in his Monday, Wednesday, Friday self. When this spirit became a school it was represented most vocally by Dewey, Angell and Carr at the University of Chicago, but the more eclectic Columbia University functionalists, led by Cattell and then by Woodworth, were also influential. As a school, it expired gracefully; as a prescription, it is very much a part of our present scene. It is expressed in the stress on "activities" as utilities, in the acceptance and advancement of the applications of psychology, and in the utilization of the contingent meaning of function in research planning and interpretation. Following in the footsteps of Monsieur Jourdain, most of us speak functional prose whether or not we are aware of doing so.

After its disappearance as a school, the behavioristic spirit, with its crudities and brash crusading evangelism refined away, continued to exert influence through stress on objectivity. A case could be made for referring to American psychology as objective, rather than subjective in its emphasis, but in the interest of precision, it is, perhaps, preferable to refer to more specific manifestations in operationalism, quantativism and hypothetico-deductivism.

In the thirties, quite apart from the influence of Behaviorism, American psychology was in a receptive state for operationalism since a pragmatic attitude prevailed. The then currently popular definition of intelligence as whatever intelligence tests measure suffices as an illustration.

Operationalism is intimately related to Comte's positivistic efforts (1853), to Mach's experiential positivism (1914), and to the logical positivism of the Vienna Circle. American psychologists, however, were introduced to operationalism through a work first published in 1927 by the physicist, P. W. Bridgman (1927).

In brief, concepts that are used must be tied to the conditions of observation. Instead of Machian experience, the ultimate primary data for most American psychologists turned out to be behavior, a belief to which most of them were already committed. Others, such as Boring, Gibson, Köhler and Rogers, in the spirit of Mach's experiential positivism would see variables having direct experiential reference as legitimate sources for systematic analysis. The operationalistic prescription serves as a credo, and as a means of evaluation, not as the slogan of a school. It is shared by psychologists of otherwise quite different theoretical orientations.

S. S. Stevens (1935a, b) and E. G. Boring (1933) were among the first to recognize operationalism's psychological implications and to bring it to the attention of psychologists. E. C. Tolman (1936) contributed the intervening variable as characteristic of what he called operational Behaviorism. C. L. Hull utilized "symbolic constructs, intervening variables, or hypothetical entities" (1943, p. 22) in his discussion of the principles of learning. After Tolman the intervening variable was soon elaborated by others. The meaning of operational validity was considerably clarified by the 1948 paper of K. MacCorquodale and P. E. Meehl (1948) concerned with the distinction between hypothetical constructs and intervening variables.

Desire to follow a quantitative prescription in research is very evident. The urge toward quantification that is, "the assignment of numerals to objects or events according to rules" (Stevens, 1946, p. 677) is drilled into all American psychologists. Speculation, no matter how brilliant, is apt to be considered worthwhile only if it be a prelude to a form in which it can be restated so as to be measured. Speculation leads to quantitative hypothesis formation formulation and is not an end in itself. S. S. Stevens' clarifying and classificatory papers on quantification have been influential (e.g., 1946, 1951).

There is little question that boldness and originality has characterized many of these quantifications. Consider the work of G. Murphy in psychometrics, of R. R. Sears in child development, of J. McV. Hunt, L. F. Shaffer, O. H. Mowrer, and E. L. Kelly in personality, of T. M. Newcomb in attitude study and L. J. Cronbach in test development. D. O. Hebb, a Canadian, also ranks among these men with his work on brain function and learning. The wide variety of fields in which they showed ingenuity in finding ways of quantifying without sacrificing complexity is noteworthy.

The present fervent attachment to the hypothetico-deductive prescription helps to account for American psychology following through from one research study to the next to the relative exclusion of the development of new theories. Deductive elaboration of already existing hypotheses is its metier. Hull's hypothetico-deductive theory of rote learning is a classic instance. With its powerful support, psychologists are more comfortable in dealing with systematic elaboration than in striking out in new directions. The "bandwagon effect" is characteristic of many psychological research areas. However, the hypothetico-deductive prescription is not without its challengers, among others, Skinner, Guthrie, and Tolman (Koch, 1959).

An environmentalistic prescription prevails. Although not derivable directly from Behavioristic tenets, Watson was the major voice in crusading for an uncompromising environmentalism. Potential adaptive variability at the expense of fixed innate propensities also owes something to functionalism. In a larger sense, the democratic, latitudinarian ideal in the United States contributed. In present day research, if heredity is considered at all, it is apt to be as a variable to hold constant as in matching groups in intelligence. Even when intelligence is studied directly, it is characteristic to try to show the effect of some form of environmental influence.

The environmentalistic research problem *par excellence* is that of learning. Hence, it is not surprising that it is the research area attracting the most attention in the United States. The work of C. L. Hull, E. R. Guthrie, and E. C. Tolman in the recent past and that of K. W. Spence, B. F. Skinner, W. K. Estes, E. R. Hilgard, N. E. Miller, and D. G. Marquis in the present, along with all of the work that they stimulated, stands witness to this fact. The wide scope given to learning is shown by a tendency to equate learning with behavior in the titles selected for books and theories in which learning is used more or less synonymously for behavior. Even the increased interest in perception that some see as a prominent recent development does not weaken the point. This increased interest (*e.g.*, Koch, 1959) turns out to be in perceptual *learning*.

The search for general laws, even if expressed within the modest limits of miniature theories, clearly marks American psychology as primarily nomothetic in character. There are, of course, staunch defenders of the idiographic, for example, in Gordon W. Allport and many clinical psychologists.

Certain counter-prescriptions deserve specific attention. While not having the greater specificity of the counter-prescriptions so, too, does psychoanalysis and Gestalt psychology. They are similar in that they run counter to dominant prescriptions.

In many respects, psychoanalysis still stands apart, unintegrated into the psychological body as a whole. To be sure, there are individual neo-Freudian psychologists who have come to terms with psychoanalysis, but they are islands unique unto themselves. H.A. Murray has been most outstanding in uniting psychoanalysis with diverse strands from psychology and other related fields in a point of view that is shared by others. Nevertheless, his integration has not received national acceptance.

If psychoanalysis is to achieve scientific status, the majority of psychologists would insist that it must be tested by either the appropriate adaptations of available research methods or by the derivation of more appropriate ones. The operative word here is "appropriate" with strong differences of opinion over its meaning.

When Gestalt psychology arrived on these shores in the persons of M. Wertheimer, W. Köhler, and K. Koffka, we were ready to receive them—as psychologists of perception. There is no question today that configurations, patterns, and equipotentialities in perception are accepted as commonplace. To this acceptance was later added their major contribution to what was to become contemporary field theory. Psychologists, generally, would say that the worthwhile facets of Gestalt psychology have now been assimilated. Gestalt psychologists, themselves, are not so sure about the integration and point to additive connectionism as a flagrant instance of the lack of integration. Just as there are articulated objects within a larger field, so, too, Gestalt psychology is distinguishable from the field of American psychology in general. In standing apart, it helps to maintain phenomenalism and to stave off contemporary molecular pressures.

Moving on to counter-prescriptions, there seems to be a somewhat amorphous objection to the dominant demand for rigor in theorizing. That which for its adherents is rigor, modesty or cautiousness becomes timidity, lack of imagination, lack of adequate complexity, or antitheoretical bias to its antagonists. Sometimes this position is taken, not because they object to the dominant prescriptions reflecting rigor as ideal, but because they consider psychology not far enough advanced to be ready for them (Royce, 1957). There are also those who appeal for more theory on humanist or other grounds.

There is also a counter-prescription calling for increased attention to philosophical matters (*e.g.*, Misiak, 1961). Historically, the independent organization of our departments of psychology and, with the exception of William James, the lack of first-rate philosophers among our pioneers makes an anti-philosophical attitude understandable. It is doubtful if more than a handful of American schools insist upon or even encourage work in philosophy on the part of its graduate students. An exception to this lack of interest in matters philosophical, must, however, be made of the philosophy of science where Meehl, Bergmann and others have made important contributions, and in phenomenology and in existential psychology.

It seems worth mentioning that philosophical interests and theoretical boldness both seem to be on the increase in the last few years, attributable in part to the influence of phenomenology, existentialism and personality theory.

Another counter-prescription is psychological phenomenology which calls for reconstructing the world of the other person so as to be able to understand it. This stands in contrast to a psychology interested only in the prediction and control of behavior (MacLeod, 1947). Words not welcome in a foreign country have a way of not being translated. Neither *Geisteswissenschaften* nor *Verstehen* have exact English equivalents. Existential psychology, also a counter-prescription, has recently stirred a relatively sharp increase in interest but again only among a small proportion of American psychologists (May, 1961).

Although strongly sharing in the social locus and environmentalistic prescription, the area of so-called personality theory otherwise is rife with counter-prescriptions, such as in self theory and those theories dependent upon unconscious motivation. Trends here defy brief summarization.

It has been seen that national trends in modern American psychology follow certain dominant prescriptions. Determinism, naturalism, physicalism and monism, although very much operative, are judged to incite relatively little opposition. Functionalism, operationalism, quantification, hypothetico-deductivism, environmentalism, and nomotheticism are likewise dominant, but there are counter-prescriptions which tend to oppose them. As for the schools of psychology, psychoanalysis, very obviously, and Gestalt psychology, less firmly, still stand apart. Serving as counter-prescriptions to those dominant in psychology are those calling for increased complexity in theorizing, for an increased attention to philosophical matters, for general acceptance of phenomenology, for increased attention to existential psychology and in a somewhat amorphous way almost all of the areas of personality theory call for counter-prescriptions of one sort or another.

REFERENCES

Albrecht, F. M. The new psychology in America: 1880-1895. Unpublished Ph.D. dissertation, Johns Hopkins, 1960.

Boring, E. G. *The physical dimensions of consciousness.* New York: Century, 1933.

Bridgman, P. W. *The logic of modern physics.* New York: Macmillan, 1927.

Cardno, J. A., and Watson, R. I. Affective and volitional concepts: 1797-1874. In progress.

Comte, A. *Positive philosophy.* (Trans. and condensed by Harriet Martineau) London: Chapman, 1853.

Hull, C. L. *Principles of behavior.* New York: Appleton-Century, 1943.

Koch, S. (ed.), *Psychology: a study of a science. I. Conceptual and systematic. Vol. 1: Sensory, perceptual and psychological formulations.* New York: McGraw-Hill, 1959.

Kuhn, T. S. *The structure of scientific revolutions.* Chicago: Univer. of Chicago Press, 1962.

Lockman, R. F. Characteristics of APA members in the 1962 National Scientific Register. *Amer. Psychologist,* 1962, *17,* 789-792.

MacCorquodale, K., and Meehl, P. E. On a distinction between hypothetical constructs and intervening variables. *Psychol. Rev.,* 1948, *55,* 95-107.

Mach, E. *The analysis of sensations.* (5th ed.) LaSalle, Ill.: Open Court, 1914.

MacLeod, R. B. The phenomenological approach to social psychology. *Psychol. Rev.,* 1947, *54,* 193-210.

May, R. (ed.), *Existential psychology.* New York: Random, 1961.

Misiak, H. *The philosophical roots of scientific psychology.* New York: Fordham Univer. Press, 1961.

Royce, J. R. Toward the advancement of theoretical psychology. *Psychol. Rep.,* 1957, *3,* 401-410.

Stevens, S. S. The operational basis of psychology *Amer. J. Psychol.,* 1935a, 47, 323-330.

Stevens, S. S. The operational definition of psychological concepts. *Psychol. Rev.,* 1935b, *42,* 517-527.

Stevens, S. S. On the theory of scales of measurement. *Science,* 1946, *103,* 677-680.

Stevens, S. S. Mathematics, measurement, and psychophysics. In S. S. Stevens (ed.), *Handbook of experimental psychology.* New York: Wiley, 1951, pp. 7-49.

Tolman, E. C. Operational behaviorism and current trends in psychology. *Proc. 25th Anniv. Celebr. Inaug. Grad. Stud.,* Los Angeles: Univer. Southern California Press, 1936.

Watson, R. I. *The great psychologists: from Aristotle to Freud.* Philadelphia, Pa.: Lippincott, 1963.

American and European Psychology
Daniel E. Berlyne

British-born Daniel E. Berlyne, currently professor of psychology at the University of Toronto, is a psychologist of international reputation. He holds a B.A. and M.A. from Cambridge University and a Ph.D. in psychology from Yale. He has taught psychology at various universities here and abroad. Among his research interests are behavior theory, motivation, and symbolic processes. His many publications include *Conflict, Arousal, and Curiosity* (1960) and *Structure and Direction in Thinking* (1965).

With his background of training, teaching, and research in America and Europe, Berlyne is eminently qualified to discuss the relationship of American and European psychology. In the following article, presented as an address to the American Psychological Association Convention in Washington, D.C., in 1967, he states that American psychology attained world leadership in psychological science as a result of its vigorous development during the previous 75 years. Berlyne examines various aspects of this American predominance and the factors that have contributed to it. The United States' role of "principal guardian of psychology" cannot be expected to persist, he observes. He already discerns "signs of a more even distribution of effort and influence in psychology." This selection alerts American psychologists to the necessity of paying increased attention to developments in psychology in other countries.

In a recent article Basalla (1967) analyzed a phenomenon that he calls "colonial science." The term is introduced to designate the kind of tutelage that the European scientist has exercised over the scientists of various non-European areas in turn. He hastened to point out that there is no necessary connection with political colonization. According to Basalla's description of the "colonial" state of affairs,

> a formally trained scientist will have received some or all of his scientific education in a European institution; if informally trained, he will have studied the works of European scientists and will have purchased his books, laboratory equipment, and scientific instruments

Daniel E. Berlyne, American and European psychology. *American Psychologist*, 1968, **23**, 447-452. Reprinted by permission of the author and the American Psychological Association.

from European suppliers. This training will direct the colonial scientist's interest to the scientific fields and problems delineated by European scientists. Colonial scientific education is inadequate or nonexistent; the same can be said for colonial scientific organizations and journals. Therefore, the colonial scientist seeks the membership and honors of European scientific societies and publishes his researches in European scientific journals [p. 611].[1]

As an account of the relations between American psychology and psychology in the rest of the world today, this would be a severe exaggeration. Several countries outside North America have thoroughly respectable training programs, journals, and psychological societies of their own. Nevertheless, at least some features of a colonial relationship are in evidence. It is difficult to know what proportion of the world's psychologists live in the United States at present, but the lowest estimate I have ever encountered is 50%, and I have heard suggestions that the proportion might be as high as 80%. Psychologists from all over the world, and particularly from Western Europe, flock to the United States in much the same way, and for essentially the same reasons, as painters flocked to Italy in the seventeenth century and to France in the early twentieth century. Some come for a limited time as part of their training. Others find working conditions in the United States that induce them to establish themselves there permanently. In fact, a Western European psychologist is not held to have completed his studies or to have won the right to speak authoritatively on psychological matters until he has spent some time in an American university. How advanced psychology is in a particular country depends more than anything else on how quickly that country's psychologists have been able to swallow their patriotic pride and settle down humbly and diligently to learn as much as possible of what American psychologists have to teach. Although national psychological societies and psychological journals are sprouting in one new country after another, the American Psychological Association and its publications exercise a special leadership that is by no means confined to North America. And many vigorous research programs going on all over the world in psychology and neighboring areas have owed their existence to United States Government agencies and private foundations, since

[1] Copyright by the American Association for the Advancement of Science, *Science*, May 5, 1967.

adequate financial support has so often been difficult or impossible to obtain locally.

In Eastern European countries, and particularly in the Soviet Union, the situation has of course been a little different. Russian psychology developed along its own isolated lines for a long time and independently produced some surprising parallels to what was going on in the United States during the same period. In recent years, there has been increasing interaction between the Eastern and Western traditions but, to judge by frequency of citation, Russian psychology still takes more notice of American psychology than vice versa.

I regret that I cannot speak from first-hand experience of the days when the importance of American psychology was beginning to impress itself on the rest of the world. But I can well remember the time, just after the Second World War, when a few adventurers had actually seen American psychological laboratories with their own eyes. When they returned, we clustered around them and bombarded them with questions of much the same kind as were directed 10 years later at the first Western psychologists to have visited Russia and will, no doubt, be directed 50 years from now at the first psychologists to return from Mars or Venus.

For the European psychology student in those days, America was an alluring but puzzling place. The great names that we first encountered in bibliographies were enveloped in a legendary aura. For American students, these names must have conjured up stodgy professors' faces like any of the others that one is apt to meet along the corridor. But they played the same part in our lives as names like Zeus and Apollo play in the life of the classical scholar. Some years later, I was fortunate enough to meet the possessors of some of these revered names during the more convivial moments of APA annual conventions. I must confess that, when I recalled Ovid's accounts of the revelries of the ancient gods, the Olympian analogy was not altogether dispelled! The high reputation of leading American universities was well known to us, and their achievements in psychology compelled our respect. But our only knowledge of American academic life came from films with titles like "College Rhythm." It was certainly hard to see how the personnel of the institutions depicted in these films could find the time to compose epoch-making contributions to psychological literature. We were also a little bewildered by textbooks in which a great deal of psycho-logical stress was stated to result from failure to gain admittance to a fraternity (whatever that was!). In Great Britain, nobody was ever invited to join a fraternity, but not a single case of neurotic breakdown seemed to occur in consequence.

It was only natural that some European psychologists, especially of the older generation, should view the hegemony that the Americans were assuming with some disgruntlement. "After all," they felt, "since scientific psychology began in Europe, these newcomers who entered the game so recently surely cannot be beating us at it! Surely the centuries of work that went into laying the foundations for modern psychology cannot count for so little! Surely our rich intellectual history must have endowed us with advantages that people in such remote parts of the world could hardly aspire to or even appreciate! It does not seem credible! It does not seem reasonable! Above all, it does not seem fair!" So there was often a strong inclination to believe that American psychology, though unsurpassed in the scale of resources on which it could draw, missed the essentials. American psychologists, we were often told, both in general and with reference to particular instances, are apt to concentrate on superficialities of technique, on pretentious theoretical constructions, on trivialities, on fancy apparatus. They are prone to excessive preoccupation with niggling details of methodology. They lack the deep understanding that leads one to investigate the truly fundamental issues. They are taken in by a succession of passing fads. Even if these accusations turned out to be based on shaky evidence, it seemed that American psychologists ought to possess these faults, if only out of elementary decency and respect for their elders!

These attitudes are, of course, ones that parents always have when, as so often happens in a changing society like our own, their offspring have a higher social status than they and are able to do things that they have never been able to do. It is a trying situation for any parent, especially when the successes enjoyed by the next generation owe much to his own hard work and sacrifices. But for European psychologists it was even worse. Parents generally receive some reflected glory when their children have come up in the world to compensate for the painful disdain that they have to suffer. But the veterans of European psychology received no comparable kudos from being told that virtually everything that they had done was wrong.

The curious thing is that American psychology did not always have the paramountcy that it now enjoys. When experimental psychology first began, the colonial relationship was in the opposite direction, and budding American psychologists looked to Europe, especially Germany, as the seat of authority. I do not know whether such a reversal of scientific colonialism is unprecedented. Something of the sort has, of course, characterized the relations between America and Europe in other branches of science and of non-scientific scholarship. But as far as I can tell, the reversal is nowhere as extreme as in the case of our own discipline. So it might be worthwhile to look for some factors that are likely to have contributed to the extraordinary predominance of the United States in psychology.

First, some widely recognized features of the American culture pattern and national character are of obvious relevance. A character in a recent novel (Gilbert, 1967) states that "America has one philosophy, change. Change itself is a very way of life." This is, of course, very much of an oversimplification. There are some departments of life in which Americans are more resistant to innovation than, say, Western Europeans. But in matters of applied science and technology, as well as in pure science and higher education generally, Americans are quicker than others to take up promising new ideas and techniques and less ready to believe that they must be inferior to the old and tried. In accordance with this attitude, psychology departments are commonly among the largest departments in American colleges and universities, and it is relatively difficult to go through an undergraduate curriculum in the United States without taking a course in psychology at some stage or other. The application of the latest psychological knowledge to clinical and industrial problems and, more recently, to educational problems has been commensurate with the growth of psychology as an academic discipline. And this state of affairs has existed for some time. In Western Europe, on the other hand, the acceptance of psychology, both as a subject matter for study at universities and as a profession, has been notably slower, although progress is accelerating. For example, in Great Britain (which is the leading psychological country in Western Europe to judge by the size of its national psychological organizations), one or two of the long established universities had no psychology departments at all until a few years ago. In recent years, several new universities have been founded without psychology departments, even though, curiously enough, some of them set out with an explicit emphasis on the social sciences.

In addition, the people of the United States are mobile and energetic. A high arousal level is deeply rooted in the American way of life, and the social structure is so designed that feverish activity is reinforced and lethargy is penalized. In Western Europe, particularly in universities, it is certainly easier to spend time on investigations that are off the beaten track and that have a good chance of not paying off for a long time or of not paying off at all. On the other hand, it is also easier to spend one's time doing very little or not even keeping abreast of what is going on in one's field. Both the rat race of the American campus and the tranquility of the European "grove of Academe" have their shortcomings. I have often thought that the universities of the lost continent of Atlantis, if it were ever to rise from beneath the ocean, might turn out to have arrived at the ideal happy medium. But faced with the choice between the two extremes, there is a great deal to be said for a high activity level. When people are busily scurrying around and cannot find the time to question the presuppositions of their scurrying, it may not always carry them far from their starting point. But sitting still carries one an even shorter distance! Evolution depends on mutations. The vast majority of mutations that occur in the animal and plant kingdoms are useless or even harmful, but they are necessary if the rare fruitful mutation is to have a chance of appearing. Without any mutations at all, we should still be embedded in primeval ooze—which is not a bad description of the state of psychology in many parts of the world!

One factor whose influence should not be underestimated is the sheer size of the United States and, in particular, the size of its system of higher education. There are a large number of institutions in the United States that offer BA degrees—well over 1,000 and, according to some estimates, nearer 2,000. And many American universities are extremely large. The number of professors (i.e., full professors) of psychology in some American departments exceeds the total number in some of the more advanced West European countries. The advancement of psychology depends on individuals who supply new lines of thought and new lines of research. In the late eighteenth and early nineteenth centuries, many important contributions to science were made by men who had no connections with universities, but those days have passed. There is now little chance that worthwhile work in any branch of science, including psychology, will be done by somebody whose only affiliation is with his own private garret. It is necessary to have a position in a university or some other organization with research facilities, to obtain a research grant, and so on. All over the world, there is competition for these advantages, and the outcome of the competition depends on many factors. Merit and competence are no doubt among them, but a great deal inevitably hinges on subjective reactions to the kinds of work to which somebody is committed, and these subjective reactions must necessarily be affected by transient fashions, prejudices, and habits of thought. In a country with a small system of higher education, to insist on struggling against a preponderant current can be fatal. In a system as vast as the American, the scales are still weighted in favor of those who swim with the tide. But there are many tides, and if prevailing attitudes work against one somewhere, there is a good chance that they will work in one's favor somewhere else.

The hugeness of the individual American university, which is currently alarming so many people, has also redounded to the advantage of psychology. It has, for one thing, greatly increased the autonomy of the psychology department and, as expansion proceeds further, the autonomy of specialized subdepartments would seem to come next. In European universities, which are generally much smaller, the faculty or group of departments makes many of the decisions for which individual departments in the United States are responsible. This means that the fate of psychology in European universities can be controlled by representatives of supposedly neighboring disciplines who are all too often suspicious of modern psychology. At best, they regard it as unimportant and, at worst, as the embodiment of all the corrupting forces of contemporary society. I well remember the bitter meetings at a small but ancient university where I once worked, where the professor of Greek would assert that no undergraduate should learn about the psychology of language until he had mastered Latin and Greek, and where the professor of moral philosophy claimed that the study of why human beings act as they do, and what motivates them, belonged not to experimental psychology but to his own discipline.

In addition, there is the size of the individual psychology department, with its relative plethora of people occupying the upper and middle echelons. In non-English speaking European countries, universities have traditionally had positions corresponding to those of American instructors and positions corresponding to those of American full professors, who are also departmental chairmen. But until recently, they generally had next to no positions between the two. So anybody who was too old for the one and not old enough or not fortunate enough to occupy the other was likely to find himself in a precarious limbo with full intellectual, social, and economic dependence on the goodwill of a patriarchal figure. If the patriarch was an outstanding luminary, this system squeezed the most out of his potentialities. But whether he was or not, the morale and capacity for creative innovation of his associates all too often suffered. This state of affairs is, however, now being remedied in the leading countries where it used to obtain.

It will be understood, I hope, that I am not intending to belittle the roles of native pioneers—the William Jameses, the Thorndikes, the Watsons, and their many successors—if I suggest that American psychology has been singularly fortunate in the immigrants that it has received and owes a great deal to them.

First, every undergraduate who has taken a course on the history of psychology knows how Titchener went to Leipzig to study under Wundt and then tried to install experimental psychology at Oxford, his alma mater. He met with no encouragement there and consequently settled at Cornell University, where he became a figure of great power and repute and did much to establish the dignity of psychology in the United States. An Institute of Experimental Psychology was finally founded at Oxford in 1936, but there was no professor of psychology until 1947. According to a rumor for whose veracity I am in no position to vouch, one celebrated Oxford philosopher said that there would not have been a chair of psychology at Oxford even in 1947 if he had not happened to be away on leave at the time.

However, the one European who contributed most to American psychology, although this must have been the least of his preoccupations, was Adolf Hitler.

Through the efforts of men like Hall and Brill, interest in psychoanalysis appeared quite early in the United States, but the advent of the Nazi regime in Germany and Austria led to an influx of prominent spokesmen for this school of thought. It is perhaps of some significance that Freud himself was not among them, but moved to England instead. Whatever the causes, it is noteworthy that the so-called British school of psychoanalysis has developed along lines carrying it further and further away from both experimental psychology and the mainstream of psychiatry. In the United States, on the other hand, there has been a continuing interaction and interpenetration between the Freudian and other approaches to psychology, and various blends of psychoanalytic and other themes have been tried out from time to time.

It was a fortunate by-product of a tragic situation that both the major figures of the Gestalt school and those they considered their principal opponents found themselves working in the same country at the same time. The disputes between the Gestalt psychologists and the associationists and behaviorists were modernized versions of the quarrels that had for centuries separated the rationalist-spiritualist current (which dominated continental Europe with a few inroads in Scotland) from the empiricist-associationist current (which dominated Great Britain and, later, the United States, with a few inroads in France). Because of this geographical distribution, the philosophical and psychological issues became inseparably bound up with political and even economic and military rivalries. Everybody felt it his patriotic duty to take up a position as irreconcilable as possible with that of the other side. To admit that there might be any validity whatever in the other side's assertions was to acknowledge the superiority of the foreigner. It was tantamount to accepting his suzerainty or, worse still, to being beaten by him in an international athletic contest. But with the advocates of diametrically opposed schools of thought living and working in close proximity to each other and both producing disciples of the same nationality, each could at least seek to understand what the other side was saying and why. It was possible, if only sporadically, to judge either side's propositions and arguments on their merits and to pick out acceptable and unacceptable elements. Since the 1930s all American psychologists, whether they realize it or not, have been nurtured on some compound of Gestalt psychology and behaviorism, among other ingredients. Some have leaned more towards to one side and some towards the other. The discussions between those with different leanings have all too often been irrational and unnecessarily acrimonious. But it has at least been possible to face the issues dividing the two sides in a way that would have been quite out of the question if they had continued to appeal to opposed national prides.

We must, however, not confine our attention to immigrant psychologists and overlook the no less essential contributions of immigrant philosophers. The political upheavals in Central Europe caused leaders of the logical-empiricist movement, particularly those identified with the Vienna circle, to seek refuge in English-speaking countries. But here again, the consequences on both sides of the Atlantic have been different. In Great Britain, the prevailing school of linguistic analysis, under the influence of Wittgenstein, Wisdom, and several well-known Oxford philosophers, has concentrated on examining everyday language in a way that has little contact with empirical linguistics or any other area of empirical science. This school has, on the whole, shown an indifference and, at times, hostility to experimental psychology for reasons that are not altogether clear. They have, on the other hand, been extremely interested in psychoanalysis. In fact, the recognition of purported analogies between psychoanalysis and current methods of philosophical inquiry led to the use of the term "therapeutic positivism." Cynics are divided between those who believe that these philosophers espoused psychoanalysis solely because British experimental psychologists at the time were preponderantly against it and those who believe the reverse. But these are, no doubt, unfair distortions.

In the United States, however, the logical empiricists of the 1930s and 1940s studied specialized languages that could fulfill the requirements of logic, mathematics, and science. The influence of immigrants like Carnap, Feigl, Bergmann, and Hempel (to mention individuals who have had particular influence on psychologists) blended easily with the native American pragmaticist-operationalist tradition, represented by Peirce, Mead, Morris, and Bridgman. The impact, direct and indirect, acknowledged and unacknowledged, that such men have had on American psychology has been immense. Thanks to their work, American and American-influenced psychologists, while they are far from infallible paragons in this regard, have been trained to watch their language carefully. They are prepared to be pounced on at any moment and challenged to state exactly what they are asserting about empirical phenomena, to wonder whether they are asserting anything at all, to state precisely what reasons there are for believing that they are right, or, if such reasons are lacking, how one could find out whether they are right or not.

Some would see another stroke of fortune for American psychology in the fact that leading representatives of another philosophical current did not come to the United States. Here I am referring to the phenomenologist-existentialist current, which has been strong on the European continent for some time. Philosophers belonging to it have written copiously on psychological topics. Phenomenology had some influence on the Gestalt movement, and there have been attempts to plant its seed within American psychology from time to time. It is, in some ways, a great pity that this point of view has not had more of a hearing in the United States, since the problems that it raises are important and worth pondering. But the kind of psychology that the phenomenologists and existentialists envisage seems to be so different in its aims from psychology conceived as the science of behavior that no fruitful merger of the two seems possible. The least one can say is that the strength of this kind of philosophy in continental European countries, where philosophers carry great weight in intellectual circles, has done little to speed up the development of scientific psychology in those countries.

So to sum up, the United States has been the principal guardian of psychology during a vital formative period. It took charge of this foreign born and frequently disparaged waif in its early childhood and has carried it solicitously and munificently into a thriving adolescence. But this custody cannot be expected to last forever, and it is no doubt a good thing that it cannot. There are dangers as well as advantages in such an uneven geographical distribution of scientific activity. There is a danger that particular lines of research, having once become rooted, will acquire a momentum that keeps them going to the exclusion of others that are equally worthy. Particular problems may be investigated because the necessary apparatus is available, the necessary skills have been acquired, the journals and the research-supporting agencies are accustomed to them. Ideas may be distrusted because they are unfamiliar, and they may thus be unable to compete with others that lack this impediment. We generally think of a hidebound tradition as one that has gone on for at least 50 or 100 years. But we are told that 80% of all the scientists who have ever lived are alive at this moment. The proportion must be at least as high for psychologists, and one result of this explosive crescendo is that a quantity of hidebinding that used to take 50 years can now be squeezed into 5.

There comes a time when parents finally obtain their revenge for the uppitiness of their children, and that is when they become grandparents. They can then observe with wry amusement how the second generation has the same troubles with the third generation as the first had with the second, and how it reacts in much the same way. Some of the attitudes encountered in the United States when European psychologists offer new ideas are oddly familiar to anybody who can recall the kind of reception that American innovations received among European psychologists even 15 or 20 years ago. European psychologists seem generally to be pathetically out of touch. They seem so often to have missed the point of current debates. They do not know the literature thoroughly enough. They do not even know how to frame their points in the proper language. Surely these deficiencies preclude them from making contributions of any significance! Surely the long grind we all suffered in graduate school and the long hours we spent poring over APA journals cannot be dispensable! It does not seem credible! It does not seem reasonable! Above all, it does not seem fair! But now, as then, nature must take its course. At the beginning of this century, American psychologists were able to learn what Europe had to offer in the way of theory and technique and then did their best to separate the essentials in what they had been taught from the accretions of ankylosing habit. Consequently, they were able to lay sounder foundations at many points and impart to psychology an unprecedented series of creative fillips. There are certainly no signs of an impending decline in the productivity of American psychology. But in some areas especially, psychologists of other countries, who have eagerly absorbed everything that American psychology has to teach them, may be in the best position to appraise what is going on and to contribute the kinds of creative impetus that can come from fresh points of view.

Over the last 75 years, American psychologists have earned the abundant gratitude of the rest of the world. But like all parents of ambitious children, or like those who program computers that might beat them at chess, they had better not expect much in the way of thanks. Most of the important advances in psychology of the next few decades will, it is safe to predict, grow out of American psychology. But many of these will take place outside the United States.

REFERENCES

Basalla, G. The spread of Western science. *Science*, 1967, **156**, 611-622.

Gilbert, E. *The beautiful life.* New York: Longmans, 1967.

V

Psychology in Other Countries

In the last article of Part IV, Berlyne admonished: "Most of the important advances in psychology of the next few decades will, it is safe to predict, grow out of American psychology. But many of these will take place outside the United States." If there is any truth to this prediction, American psychologists will increasingly need to overcome the provincialism for which they have frequently been criticized in the past. As Robert I. Watson has observed, "In the United States there is an all too common dismissal of work in psychology in other countries as quaint, odd, or irrelevant." Furthermore, since psychology lacks a defining paradigm and therefore unity within the science, "national differences, negligible in the paradigmatic sciences such as physics and chemistry, assume great importance in psychology." Finally, as psychology becomes more international in its dedication to the promotion of human welfare, familiarity with the progress and status of psychology abroad becomes essential.

The readings in Part V furnish a general background for understanding the development of psychology in France, Great Britain, Germany, the Soviet Union, and Asia. They do not recapitulate the entire history of the science in each country. Points of comparison and/or contrast with American psychology are made to help the

313

reader appreciate some of the intellectual, cultural, social, and political factors that have produced certain trends in the psychology of these countries.

The first three selections describe the background for the psychologies of France, Great Britain, and Germany. These articles, together with Watson's selection from Part IV, were originally presented as a symposium under the chairmanship of Ernest R. Hilgard of Stanford University and organized by Watson for the Seventeenth International Congress of Psychology in Washington, D.C., in 1963. This symposium, entitled "The Historical Background for National Trends in Psychology," also included an address on Soviet psychology delivered by A. Leontiev, a senior Soviet psychologist, but no text was available for reprint. In reviewing the five symposium addresses, the Honorary President of the Congress and discussant, E.G. Boring, observed: "The most notable national difference lies at present along the dimension that extends from free theorizing to rigorous observation, the dimension from *Verstehen* to physicalism, in the order Germany, Great Britain, France, U.S.A., and U.S.S.R." As spokesman for psychology in the Soviet Union in this volume we have selected a well-known authority on Soviet psychology and psychophysiology, Gregory Razran. In his article he indicates the parallel and divergent trends in Soviet and American psychology.

The final selection of Part V, by Gardner and Lois Murphy, concerns Asian psychology. In the past, Western psychologists have tended to be inattentive to psychology in Asia, largely because of the language barrier. In recent years, however, as communication between East and West has improved, Asian psychology has attracted increased attention. The Murphys discuss the philosophical and cultural foundations of Asian psychology and compare it with Western psychology.

The Historical Background for National Trends in Psychology: France
Maurice Reuchlin

Maurice Reuchlin, director of the École Pratique des Hautes Études in Paris, is a specialist in measurement theory, differential psychology, and educational psychology. The author of numerous articles on testing, factor analysis, and applied psychology, he has also written two books, *L'orientation pendant la période scolaire: idées et problèmes* (1964) and *Histoire de psychologie*, the latest revision of which was published in 1966.

In the following article Reuchlin traces the development of French psychology from the theoretical framework of Ribot (the founder of French psychology), with his emphasis on pathology, to the "more objective, more rigorous, more experimental psychophysiology" of Piéron. The theoretical foundations for French psychology came from British associationism. Other British influences, including Herbert Spencer and the neurologist John Hughlings-Jackson, had a profound effect on Ribot. Here Reuchlin calls attention to a fact often overlooked by historians—namely, that the work of the French physiologist Claude Bernard and his students paved the way for the introduction of the experimental method into French psychology. Thus, although early French psychology took some of its inspiration from England and Germany, it soon pursued a course that corresponded to its own views and interests. The predominant emphasis was on psychopathology, and only a modest emphasis was placed on laboratory psychology until World War II. However, contemporary French psychology is characterized by diversification in research and application.

There is a period of the development of the French psychology seeming to me similar to the opening act by which well constructed theatrical works begin: it is the period which extended from the entrance of Théodule Ribot into the Collège of France, in 1888, to the eve of the First World War, the year 1912, when Henri Piéron received the heritage of the work of Alfred Binet.

At the raising of the curtain, the hero of the action, T. Ribot, is at the peak of his career. In order to enter the Collège, he has to

Maurice Reuchlin, The historical background for national trends in psychology: France. *Journal of the History of the Behavioral Sciences*, 1965, **1**, 115-123. Reprinted by permission of the author and the Psychology Press.
Translated from the French by Mrs. James Anderson.

overcome, with the help of Hippolyte Taine and especially of Ernest Renan, strong resistances: the spiritualism of Victor Cousin, Kantianism reign at the Sorbonne, while Ribot tries in 1870, in *Contemporary English Psychology* to found a scientific psychology on the pure and simple study of acts, fully independent of philosophy. Moreover, these oppositions, conquered at the Collège, are conquered again a year later when we see, in 1889, the creation of the Laboratory of Physiological Psychology of the Sorbonne, in the setting of the (applied) School of Advanced Studies. It is also on this occasion that Ribot revealed to us a trait of his character which has not been without consequences in the development of the action in the drama being unfolded. Ribot considered that he was not an experimenter and left the direction of the laboratory to the physiologist, Henri Beaunis, who turned it over to Binet in 1894. We say nothing of other characters in this first act, such as Pierre Janet, and Georges Dumas, in order to sketch the influences which affected Ribot, and through him affected them.

It may seem paradoxical to look for a link between the founder of the French scientific psychology and a philosopher, who in France has denied that psychology can be a science, i.e., between Ribot and Auguste Comte. There is little doubt that the positivist thought had exercised an influence on the man about whom one is able to say at least that he had the ambition to make a change in psychology from the metaphysical to the scientific state. One can see traces of it in Ribot since 1870, particularly in his opposition to Cousin's spiritualism and in his plan "to study the psychological states outside, not inside, in the material actions which translate them, not in the consciousness which gives birth to them." But we must go back again to the fact that certain disciples of Ribot will adhere to these principles even more strictly than he, himself. I am thinking of Alfred Binet and especially of Henri Piéron.

Another national influence, which could not help but act upon Ribot and of which I am surprised that it is not more apparent, is that of Claude Bernard. *The Introduction to the Study of Experimental Medicine*, published in 1865, when Ribot was 26 years old, is a major event in the history of biological sciences which incontestably influenced the introduction of the experimental method in psychology. The work of Bernard opened the way to the introduction of the experimental method in psychology. It is also well known that the idea of continuity between the normal manifestations and the pathological manifestations of the functioning of the organism, which occupied so much importance in the thought of Ribot, is to be found in Bernard. But Ribot, a man of letters rather than of the laboratory, hardly looked at physiology, and it is the disciples of Bernard who will pass on his influence to the disciples of Ribot: François Franck will teach physiology to Dumas and Lahy. A. Dastre will teach it to Pierre Janet, to Paul Guillaume, and, above all, to Henri Piéron.

One can, without leaving the area of physiology, ask oneself about the influence in France at that time, of the German psycho-physiologists. Ribot wrote in 1879 a *Contemporary German Psychology* which did not lead him to become an experimenter. Two other Frenchmen followed the teaching of Wilhelm Wundt; Benjamin Bourdon in 1886-87, who at Rennes in 1891 inaugurated a course of experimental psychology, and in 1896, a laboratory; Victor Henri in 1894-5, under the influence of Binet, leaned toward an individual psychology founded on the differential study of the "higher processes," rather than toward a general psychology of "elementary processes." Even if we recall that the Belgian, Albert Michotte, who will be one of the teachers of Paul Fraisse, began in 1905 to visit German laboratories, we can still only accord relatively small importance to German influences.

On the contrary, English influences appear to have affected Ribot much more profoundly. Ribot admired Herbert Spencer whom he considered the greatest philosopher of his time. The evolutionary ideas served as a base to this introduction of the work on the *Contemporary English Psychology* that Ribot published in 1870 and in which he outlined a program of work which, in fact, marks a large part of the field that modern psychology is going to cultivate. When Ribot outlined this program, he was only 31 years old. This philosopher by training could have regretted neither being a linguist nor a historian in order to study the evolution of societies; or not having been a neurologist in order to attempt to explain the physiological mechanisms of the "morbid disturbances." He could have regretted not being a naturalist so as to have been able to examine his materials in zoological observation. But Ribot chose to emphasize his lack of training in still another area, and his choice oriented French psychology for several decades: he regretted not being a doctor—"Become doctors in order to observe the sick directly," is the advice that he gave Janet and Dumas about 1880, creating thus the tradition of the French psychologists philosophically and medically trained, to which Blondel, Wallon, Poyer, Lagache—among others, in spite of their diverse orientations, will later cling. In this pathological sector cut in the vast domain that evolutionary doctrine opened to psychology, Ribot chose another Englishman, the neurologist, John Hughlings-Jackson, as a guide, he being a disciple of Spencer. The Jacksonian "dissolution" offered Ribot the means of remaining strictly in the domain of observable acts, avoiding, in his psychology, having to go to a level of analysis which is too elementary.

The influence of Spencer and of Hughlings-Jackson on Ribot and on the direction of French psychology at that time seems hardly contestable. It is also necessary to give its place to a properly French psychopathological tradition to which Janet thought fit to link directly the idea of dissolution. I mean the work of the first French psychiatrists (médecins alienistes), notably Baillarger, one of the founders of the *Annales Médico-psychologiques* whose publication has continued since 1843. These works themselves can be traced to the hierarchical conception of the "faculties of the soul" owed to the philosopher Théodore Jouffroy, in 1828. There is no doubt that the idea according to which the observation of the demented was a means of knowing the normal functioning of the mind, is an idea antedating Ribot, and that it may have had an influence on the choice by Ribot of the "pathological method." But this idea took a much more precise neurological content with Hughlings-Jackson. It is linked, in Spencer's evolutionism, to a much more general system.

The pathological method recommended by Ribot leads the French psychologists to follow at that time the teachings of the neuropathologist, Jean-Martin Charcot, at the Salpétrière. Charcot produced, about 1885, two ideas destined to have great success in psychology. He emphasized the importance, in the disturbances of mental genesis, of the memory of former shocks retained by the patient, and the importance of former events of the sexual life. These ideas are going to be gathered together and developed in France by Janet who is to practice "psychological analysis" attempting to produce a "moral disinfection" by disassociating the psychological systems constituted by the conscious or unconscious memory of an event and by the disturbances which are associated with it. It may be that a certain French taste for clear and rational explanations originated some inhibitions, which halted Janet's thought in this direction. At any rate, it was another pupil of Charcot who discovered psychoanalysis.

Binet, director of the laboratory of the Sorbonne, died in 1911. Janet and Piéron are among the candidates to his succession. Piéron wins and his nomination is going to mark the beginning of a change in direction. Pathological psychology, which had represented in France the leading trend of the new psychology, is going to see in the course of the second act the vigorous development of a psychology which intends to be more objective, more rigorous, more experimental—psycho-physiology.

If Ribot has been the principal actor in the course of the first act, it is incontestably Piéron who plays this role in the second act—between the two World Wars. Certainly he is not the only one on the scene. The work of his elders, Janet and Dumas, extends into this period. Others develop some areas which he did not enter, such as social psychology or child psychology, or reflect some influences to which he did not open himself, like psychoanalysis. He is nevertheless the center of the development of psychology during this period, as much by his scientific work as by his activity as an organizer.

Henri Piéron, born in 1881, did not follow the precept of Ribot, recommending to future psychologists to first become doctors. He chose to write as an epigraph to a report on his works, these words of Johannes Müller, *"Nemo psychologus nisi physiologus."* The masters who seem to have had the greatest influence on him are the physiologist, A. Dastre, pupil of Claude Bernard, and the biologist, A. Giard, under the direction of whom he took the greatest interest in animal ethology.

Psycho-physiological studies are those which constitute the main interests of Piéron and, under his influence, it is in this realm that French psychology will progress most during this period. Piéron is mainly interested in the physiology of the senses and it is a chair of Physiology of the Senses which is created for him at the Collège of France in 1923. He does not limit psychology to this area, however, assigning to it the role of studying the complex play of the functions that physiology studies isolately, "the mechanism of their

utilization which permits the continuation and perpetuation of life."
But this mechanism itself depends on complex physiological conditions so that the study of the global activity of the organism,
"comportement" as he calls it in 1908, ought to rest on physiology.
It is surely in this area that the influence of Piéron was the greatest.
Besides his personal contribution to the area of psycho-physiology, it
has developed a certain objectivist attitude which will characterize in
a lasting way an important part of French psychology.

Outside the strictly physiological domain, Piéron has largely
contributed to the development in France of zoological psychology.
Here one can also cite the works of E. Rabaud, whose findings on
insects constitute a beautiful example of this ethology, the whole
merit of which perhaps should not be attributed to Lorenz and
Tinbergen; and those of P. Guillaume and I. Meyerson who developed in an original way the earlier findings of Wolfgang Köhler on
bright monkeys.

E. Toulouse, director of a laboratory of experimental psychology
of the Practical School of Advanced Studies (L'École pratique des
Hautes Études), had engaged Piéron in the study of laboratory
techniques and their work of 1904 entitled *Techniques of Experimental Psychology* had a great influence inside and outside of
France. This direction of work had some theoretical goals, such as
the study of genius by individual examination of men like Zola or
Poincaré. But it aimed also at applications, particularly a rational
vocational guidance and selection. These methods of individual
examination will, under the influence of Toulouse and Piéron, tend
to remain as analytical as possible, like a laboratory experiment
should be, and this tendency will, to a certain extent, oppose itself to
global individual characterizations which Binet proposed, whose
works during this period will be more widely diffused in the United
States than in France. It is evidently in the realm of applications that
the work of psychologists came under the influence of social
problems of their time. This epoch is marked in France by some
social conflicts and by a step toward the democratization of
education: the bringing under the Ministry of Public Instruction in
1926 of a technical education which gives a place to a general and
human culture. The idea which stimulated and gave impetus to
Toulouse and his co-workers is that social problems can be solved
rationally by a scientific, physiological and psychological study of

conditions and demands of work on one hand, and of individual aptitudes on the other. These ideas are formulated by Toulouse around 1905, and a little later by J.M. Lahy, a follower or Ribot, who developed particularly these general rationalist principles in a course that he gave at the Grand-Orient of France in 1912. Lahy laid the foundation of the industrial applications in psychology in France, especially through the works of the laboratory of applied psychology that he directed at the "École pratique des Hautes Études" (Practical School of Advanced Studies). This direction, like that of the review, *Le Travail Humain*, will pass on to R. Bonnardel. Piéron, in this area of applications, devoted himself especially to vocational guidance. But he also played an important role in this realm, as in those of research and teaching by the organization of institutions.

I can only emphasize here what appears to be the general and essential character of the organic development of French psychology up to the Second World War: this development took place mainly in institutional frameworks more flexible than that of the Faculties. There are, in French Higher Education, organizations carrying the general title of "Grands établissements." They were created at different times of our university history, in order to facilitate the development of certain currents of ideas which found their place with difficulty in the more traditional teaching of Faculties. It is essentially in the framework of these "Grands établissements" that the institutions of the new psychology have been created: the Collège of France, created in 1530 by Francis the First, which recruited its professors and listeners without any condition and prepared no examinations, opened its doors to Ribot, Janet, Piéron, Wallon; the Practical School of Advanced Studies, created in 1868 by Duruy and which also recruited its professors and students without any degree requirement, was a nursery of laboratories of psychology which were created, subdivided, fused, and constantly changed title to fit the needs and interests of available men. Furthermore, Piéron has used in the same spirit, a decree of 1920 permitting some institutes of the University to be created, by bringing together the teachings given by professors, belonging to different scientific institutions: he created in 1921, the Institute of Psychology at the University of Paris, which will play an important role in later developments. Piéron used another law of 1875, to develop in 1928 (with Fontégne and Laugier) still another type of school, called a "free school of advanced teaching," the National Institute of Vocational Guidance. This Institute which has published a *Bulletin* since its opening, will be joined in 1941 to another "Grand établissement" founded by the Convention on the 19 Vendémiaire, year III of the first Republic, the National Conservatory of Arts and Trades. The intricacies of the French university institution thus offered a refuge to the new psychology.

This psychology continued to develop under Piéron as well as other influences. Thus, in 1937 P. Guillaume published a book on Gestalt Psychology. It was, on the other hand, in 1926 that the Psychoanalytical Society of Paris was founded after the publication, in 1914, of a Treatise by Hesnard and Regis, and the practical teaching given by a student of Freud, Eugénie Sokolnicka. It seems that many of those who under diverse titles study and diffuse the Freudian method and doctrine, E. Pichon, H. Claude, R. Dalbiez, do it with care for objectivity and enlightenment, in which some see a very general tradition of French thought.

Psychology also developed in France, in the course of this period, in an area that Piéron did not cultivate, that of child psychology. Child psychology is going to develop, especially by the works of the Frenchman, Henri Wallon, and by those of a Swiss, Jean Piaget, whose links with France are so direct that I shall permit myself to annex him to French psychology.

Like his teachers Janet and Dumas, Henri Wallon is a philosopher coming from the advanced normal school, and a doctor specializing in the study of the child. Thus it is partly the influence of the pathological method which he received first and transmitted in his early works of the 20s, in his teaching, and in the researches that he conducted, particularly in the laboratory of Psycho-biology of the Child at the School of Advanced Studies created for him in 1927. He played an important social role in the Resistance during the war, and at the liberation. He does not separate this social activity from his psychological thought, and was led to find in dialectic materialism "the most rational explanation for psychology." It could be shown that the importance given to evolution, to development, by Ribot since 1870, under the influence of Spencer, could truly find an extension in the dialectical materialism of Marx and Engels. It is important in any case to note that the work of Wallon, whose principal books appear in the 40s, is one of the ways by which Marxist thought has brought its contribution to the evolution of French psychology.

It is in an entirely different setting that the influence of Jean Piaget is felt. He manifested very early some interests in biology and the philosophy of the sciences. A student both of Dumas and Janet, it was while working at the standardization of tests in the Laboratory of Physiological Psychology at the Sorbonne that he discovered that the elementary logical operations, whose logistical formulation he was studying at the same time, furnished him a model permitting him to understand the steps followed by the reasoning of the children he was examining. He began to draw out all the conclusions from this idea only in 1940. It is around this idea that his later works organize themselves. It is this idea which animates the Center of Genetic Epistemology of Geneva founded in 1955, in which psychologists, logicians, and mathematicians work together around Piaget to make abstract, logico-mathematical, or probabilistic models correspond to psychological facts. The works of Piaget have powerfully contributed to the development in France of a psychology that one can qualify as abstract if one means by that, a psychology in which observations and measures do not constitute an end in themselves, but are used to attempt to realize certain abstract models and by that, to proceed to test the adequacy of these models.

With Wallon, with Piaget, and with this "abstract psychology," we have already reached the examination of the third act of French psychology on which the curtain rises at the end of the Second World War.

In the course of this third act in which we are the spectators and the actors, the original currents of French psychology are not tarnished. One can only wonder, sometimes whether they have not all, or in part, followed some paths leading them to cultivate other areas.

We can understand how, for example, Jean Delay, directed toward psychiatry by Dumas, like Wallon a pupil of Nageotte, the biologist and also, among others, of Janet and of Piéron, receiving from Pichon a didactic analysis, learning from Henri Claude to take an interest in biological shock methods, came to consider a dynamic and not mechanist conception of pathogenesis; we also understand Jean Delay to have, as he puts it pleasantly, some difficulty to know where he stands, "treated as a physician by psychologists and as a psychiatrist by neurologists." But it is of little importance that the remote heritage of Ribot, and of French psychopathology should now perhaps be found more often in the International Congresses of Psychiatry than in the International Congresses of Psychology.

It is also but of little importance that certain developments of psychophysiology seem to belong more directly to physiology than to psychology and that Piéron's most direct student, A. Fessard, teaches at the Collège of France in a Chair of General Neurophysiology. It remains true, however, that the certificates of psychophysiology created by Piéron are a part of the license of psychology, and that psychophysiologists sit with the other psychologists in the French Society of Psychology and at the National Center of Scientific Research.

But the contemporary period is characterized, above all, by a considerable development of non-physiological researches, some of which constitute attempts to keep the methodological rigor with which Piéron marked French psychology, while applying it to higher processes, and to more global behaviors.

We cannot here, on account of time, do justice to those works of research which have developed and modified former currents: animal psychology, with Viaud, Grassé, Chauvin; experimental psychology with Fraisse; child psychology, with Zazzo and school psychologists, with the review *Enfance*, with Oléron.

The contemporary period is marked in particular by a considerable development of social psychology, taught at the Sorbonne since 1947 by D. Lagache, and then by J. Stoetzel. This teaching, the work of the Laboratory of Social Psychology which is associated with it since 1952, is largely receptive to the American experimental social psychology. Another social psychology is being developed also by the works of I. Meyerson which are more in line with this "ethology of people" dominated by the evolutionary idea, that Ribot suggested as long ago as 1870. Meyerson proceeds, in fact, to the study of psychological functions by the comparative analysis of human works: languages, myths, morals, religions, sciences.

But it is the importance of the psychoanalytical movement which constitutes undoubtedly the most apparent characteristic of the recent developments. At the Sorbonne, the chair of general psychology and that of pathological psychology are occupied by two psychoanalysts: Juliette Favez-Boutonnier and D. Lagache, both members of the French Society of Psychoanalysis. An Institute of Psycho-analysis was created in 1952 by the Psycho-analytical Society of Paris (S. Nacht, M. Benassy, etc.). For at least certain of these psychoanalysts, the pathological psychology of Ribot and Dumas rests on an illusion. The pathological method is not a substitute for the experimental method because psychological experimentation cannot be based on an atomistic analysis, into distinct mental functions. One sees the importance of this change of direction.

In the area of institutions, since the war we have witnessed a multiplication of the number of chairs, of laboratories, of degrees and also of groups of psychologists and even groups of students in psychology, such as the *Groupe d' Études de l'Université de Paris*, which, since 1947, has published a *Bulletin of Psychology.* This increase in number has brought a diversification, and a degree of specialization which leads one sometimes to question the unity of psychology, to say nothing of that of the unity of psychologists.

The same development, the same diversification, took place in the field of applications. At first rather narrowly identified with differential psychology, these applications have overrun their frontiers: industrial selection made a place for human engineering, training methods, and, in still another direction, for human relation; school psychology, school and vocational guidance became concerned not only with differences in aptitudes but also with adjustment processes; and educational psychology has made an appearance.

This evolution took place under the effect of very diverse influences: the development of social psychology; criticisms of tests, particularly the flow of marxist criticisms in the early 50s in connection with the cultural and genetic debates held in USSR in the late 40s; the great need of industry in skilled personnel; and the democratizing of teaching. This evolution has not accomplished the ambitions of French promoters of the application of physiological methods, a scientific means to solve these problems. On the contrary, the necessity appeared for the psychologist to distinguish clearly between his personal social aspirations and his professional activity, a necessity which expressed itself particularly in a Code of Deontology elaborated by the French Society of Psychology and published in 1962.

And I would like to leave, without conclusion and as unaccomplished, this lecture devoted to a French psychology whose diversity cannot be encompassed and fixed in a formula, to a psychology which itself is a witness to this incompleteness by which life manifests itself.

BIBLIOGRAPHY

Beuchet, J. Benjamin Bourdon, pionnier de la psychologie expérimentale, *Bulletin de Psychologie,* 1962-3, *16*, 162-175.

Binet, A. Le bilan de la psychologie en 1910, *Année Psychol.*, 1944, *17*, V-XI.

Centenaire de Th. Ribot, *jubilé de la Psychologie scientifique française*, Agen, Imprimerie moderne, 1939.

Charpentier, R. La naissance de la Société médico-psychologique, *Annales médico-psychologiques,* 1952, *110*, tome II, 41-48.

Delay, J. *Études de psychologie médicale*, Paris, Presses Universitaires de France, 1953.

Delay, J. *Aspects de la psychiatrie moderne*, Paris, Presses Universitaires de France, 1956.

Fessard, A. Henri Piéron, *Année Psychol.*, 1951, *50* (volume jubilaire), VII-XIII.

Fraisse, P. L'Institut de Psychologie de l'Université de Paris, *Bulletin de l'Association internationale de Psychologie appliquée, 1957, 6*, No. 1, 40-50.

Hesnard, A. *L'oeuvre de Freud et son importance pour le monde moderne*, Paris, Payot, 1960.

Lagache, D. Préface à: Moscovici (S), *La Psychanalyse, son image et son public*, Paris, Presses Universitaires de France, 1961.

Piaget, J. Esquisse d'auto-biographie intellectuelle. *Bulletin de Psychologie,* 1959-1960, *13*, 7-13.

Piéron, H. *Notice sur ses travaux scientifiques*, Paris, Imprimerie Davy, 1923, *Supplément*, 1936. *Notice supplémentaire*, 1942.

Piéron, H. *Cinquante ans de psychologie française, Année psychol.*, 1951, *51*, 552-563.

Piéron, H. XXV° anniversaire de l'Institut national d'étude du travail et d'orientation professionnelle. La place de l'Institut dans l'histoire de l'orientation professionnelle. *B.I.N.O.P.*, 1953, *9*, N° spécial, 7-28.

Piéron, H. Histoire succincte des Congrès internationaux de Psychologie, *Année Psychol.*, 1954, *54*, 397-405.

Piéron, H. Pierre Janet: quelques souvenirs. *Psychologie française*, 1960, 5, 82-92.

Piéron, H. *De l'Actinie à l'homme*, Paris, Presses Universitaires de France, tome I, 1958; tome II, 1959.

Piéron, H. Sur le chemin des applications sociales de la psychologie, *L'Evolution psychiatrique*, 1962, *27*, N° 1, 151-159.

Piéron, H. Chronique, publiée dans chacun des volumes de *l'Année psychologique*.

Reuchlin, M. L'étude scientifique du travail humain: aspects de l'évolution des idées et des méthodes. *Journal de Psychologie*, 1955, *52*, 136-155.

Viderman, S. Aperçu sur l'histoire de la littérature psychanalytique. *In:* Nacht (S.), *La psychanalyse d'aujoud'hui*, Paris, Presses Universitaires de France, 1956, tome II, 785-839.

The Historical Background for National Trends in Psychology: On the Non-Existence of English Associationism
James Drever

The son of a distinguished psychologist who bore the same name and held the same position, James Drever is professor of psychology at the University of Edinburgh and a past president of the International Union of Psychological Science. His interests and publications have focused on perception, psychological theory, and the history of psychology. Here Drever attempts to explain why psychology in "the country in which associationism first developed has never really been associationist since psychology became a separate discipline."

Psychology in Great Britain in the 20th century has not followed the empiricist-associationist tradition of Locke, Hartley, the Mills, and Bain. The major influences have been Ward and Stout, on the one hand, and Galton and evolutionary theory, on the other. These two influences produced two different orientations in British psychology. One was philosophical, theoretical, holistic, and qualitative. The other — more experimental-analytic, quantitative, and practical — was interested in individual differences and their measurement.

Drever attributes the strange paradox of British psychology's failure to pursue the associationist tradition to Ward, who strongly pursued the German Kantian tradition. This tradition was characterized by a predominantly rationalistic orientation and the denial of the possibility of an experimental psychology. In consequence, British experimental psychology progressed slowly in the early 20th century. It should be pointed out, however, that British interest in individual differences, under Galton's inspiration, constituted a counterbalance to Wundtian psychology and paved the way for applied and clinical psychology. From the outset British contributions to psychological statistics, psychometrics, and educational psychology have been outstanding. Since World War II British psychologists have contributed significantly to psychology as a profession as well as to psychology as a science.

The story of British psychology begins, as do so many other stories, with three characters: an Englishman, an Irishman, and a Scotsman; in this case Locke, Berkeley, and Hume. They gave us our empiricism, and a certain intellectual informality which sometimes calls itself common sense. But these conspicuous ancestors of our

James Drever, The historical background for national trends in psychology: On the non-existence of English associationism. *Journal of the History of the Behavioral Sciences*, 1965, 1, 123-130. Reprinted by permission of the author and the Psychology Press.

ways of thought had other descendants who emigrated during the 19th century. Associationism, in particular, has never really been at home in Britain since the time of the Mills. It is true that Herbert Spencer and Alexander Bain made some use of association as an explanatory principle after 1850, but the former was soon discredited on philosophical grounds, and the latter seems to have had more influence in the United States than in his native land. At least his textbooks were widely used there, and met with less opposition from the theologians. So we have the paradoxical situation that the country in which associationism first developed had never really been associationist since psychology became a separate discipline. This is the "non-existence" to which my title refers. It seemed to me that I might try to give some explanation for it rather than do what our Honorary President [Boring] has done so well already, and give a general account of the development of British psychology.

Even at the beginning there is a sort of uncertainty. John Locke is often regarded as the father of Associationism, and history can be used to justify this view, but he would have refused to recognize the child had it ever been presented to him. In the fourth edition of the *Essay on the Human Understanding* he inserted a chapter on the "Association of Ideas," but he did so simply in order to show that accidents of circumstance and motive can *sometimes* determine the ways in which our ideas are linked. "Some of our ideas have a natural correspondence and connexion one with another: it is the office and excellency of our reason to trace these, and hold them together in that union and correspondence which is founded in their peculiar beings. Besides this, there is another connexion of ideas wholly owing to chance or custom. Ideas that in themselves are not all of kin, come to be so united in some men's minds, and the one no sooner at any time comes into the understanding, but its associate appears with it; and if they are more than two which are thus united, the whole gang, always inseparable, show themselves together." In other words the association of ideas seems to have been for Locke an occasional weakness of our minds rather than the basic way in which they become organized. So in taking our start from Locke we do not have to return to the chapter on the association of ideas, nor to the view that he was the first associationist.

But before we follow the more obvious line of development let us as a first step glance at some of the important figures who might have influenced our thinking but who lay outside the philosophical succession from Locke through the so-called English Empiricists. (I say "so-called" because not only Hume but James Mill and some others were Scots.) The great physiologists come to mind at once, from Charles Bell to Sherrington. These have undoubtedly influenced psychology, but it would be hard to demonstrate that their work has done much to change any ideas that we may have had about learning. This is true also in the case of Darwin and the biologists, in spite of Herbert Spencer's force and ingenuity. Galton, to be sure, has a few paragraphs on association, and a very interesting paper on what he called "generic images," but his interests were mainly in other things, and his contributions to the study of individual differences were not matched by any systematic work in general psychology. No other possible sources come to mind, and it would appear that what we are looking for must lie within the philosophical tradition, not outside it.

Let us go back to Hume, whose elementarism and associationism once posed a problem to thinkers throughout Europe. He claimed to show that the assurance which men have in knowledge relating to matters of fact is grounded in familiarity and expectation, not logic. Using the term "knowledge" in a strict sense, he denied that empirical knowledge could exist. To him this was quite tolerable, for he could extract sufficient satisfaction from conviviality and the daily round to deprive his philosophical doubts of any real power to disturb him. But more serious, though often less able, philosophers could not share his equanimity. He was attacked, misrepresented, and, by two men of unequal quality but in some ways similar views, he was refuted. These two men were Immanuel Kant, and Thomas Reid.

Since this is a paper on British psychology, I do not propose to spend much time on the former and greater of these two philosophers. But I shall hope to show later that at one point German philosophical psychology exercised a crucial influence upon British developments, and so it is impossible to leave Kant out. In any case the relevance of Kant to some contemporary psychological problems is often underestimated. His fate illustrates rather an important principle in the history of science. During the investigation of complex problems we often find ourselves in a blind alley and are forced to retrace our steps. We know we have to make a fresh start, but the point to which we must return is seldom clearly indicated. So we may retreat too far or not far enough. But although nothing may be there to guide us at the time, it is sometimes possible, looking back from a later stage in our exploration of the maze with a fuller knowledge of what other routes may lead nowhere, to discern a choice point at which we might profitably have taken a different line. When Kant, in his great attempt to answer Hume, subjected knowledge to a critical analysis, using the term "critical" here as he used it, men thought that a way of escape had been opened up from the skeptical position, at least to a modest phenomenalism. But the Hegelian elaboration of certain metaphysical aspects of Kant's thinking, aspects which are not essential to it, brought us to a full stop, and both linguistic philosophy and empirical psychology placarded the *cul-de-sac* with warning notices. In their discouragement many trooped back past Kant to the neighborhood of Hume's position. Throughout most of the present century they have been trying to make sense of atomistic associationism. Their efforts have been stubborn, because perhaps they could not see what else they might do, but have not, on the whole, been successful.

It is this return to Hume that has been less complete in British psychology, or indeed on the Continent, than in the United States. Some at least realized that Kant was very much more than just a precursor of Hegel. His thesis that the mind and the perceived world stand to one another in a relationship of mutual implication permits a much more limited and psychologically relevant kind of theorizing than is to be found in the Hegelian Dialectic. In particular a number of very able and acute thinkers, for whom the term "armchair psychologists" is sometimes disparagingly used, made important contributions. Some were phenomenalists, some could even be described as pragmatists; not all were ignorant of physiology. They had affinities with American Functionalism, but none with Behaviorism. One has only to look at the study of thinking by the Würzburg school, or Binet, or Piaget for that matter, and to consider the part played by Gestalt psychology, to realize how important these men were on the Continent. For us in Britain they were important too, because, as we shall see later, during the latter half of the 19th century one after another of our leading philosopher-psychologists spent some time in Germany and came home to restate a native point of view in new and more persuasive ways.

The purely British succession is less easy to trace, but it exists and has given to our psychology features which differentiate it from its counterparts across the Channel. I said that Hume was refuted twice: by Kant and by Reid. The latter is in many ways a minor figure, but for us he is interesting in that he based his refutation upon psychological not epistemological grounds. In fact the position which he took up was one that already existed in the hospitable but untidy pages of John Locke.

On March 2nd 1693 the "learned and worthy" Mr. Molyneux, "a thinking gentleman from Dublin," wrote to Locke as follows: "Suppose a man born blind, and now adult, and taught by his touch to distinguish between a cube and a sphere of the same metal, and nighly of the same bigness, so as to tell when he felt one and the other, which is the cube and what the sphere. Suppose then the cube and the sphere placed on a table, and the blind man to be made to see; *quaere*, Whether by his sight, before he touched them, he could not distinguish and tell which is the globe, and which the cube? To which the acute and judicious proposer answers: 'Not.' For though he has obtained the experience of how a globe, how a cube, affects his touch; yet he has not yet attained the experience that what affects his touch so or so, must affect his sight so or so; or that a protuberant angle in the cube, that pressed his hand unequally, shall appear to his eye as it does in the cube." Locke quoted this letter in the second edition of the *Essay Concerning Human Understanding*, and agreed with Molyneux that the blind man, at first sight, "would not be able with certainty to say which was the globe, which the cube, *whilst he only saw them*." This last phrase is one which the Locke of "simple ideas of sensation" should not have used. The elementarism of his best known and most influential chapters ought to have made him say that in the beginning there could be no visual object perception at all, or figure ground organization as we now tend to say. But Locke took it for granted, what von Senden found, that there are visual objects as soon as there is vision.

It is interesting to note that Molyneux, who was a tutor at Trinity College, later had Berkeley as his pupil. The presence of some of his ideas in *An Essay toward a New Theory of Vision* is unmistakeable.

There may never have been any scientific theory that has crept in with such scanty empirical credentials as sensory elementarism. Locke was equivocal, and, when taken off guard, appeared to reject it. Though Berkeley talked about a "minimum visible" and a "minimum tangible," he did so only in relation to the magnitude of seen objects, and at no time suggested that the perceptual world was built up out of such minima. Hartley was an elementarist, and defended his position by means of a speculative physiology derived from Newton. "Proposition IV. External Objects Impressed upon the Senses Occasion Vibrations of the Small, and, as one may say, Infinitesimal, Medullary Particles." Hume was an elementarist, and spoke as if no other view was possible. It is not without significance that only in Hartley, who owed much to Locke as well as Newton, and in Hume does Associationism emerge as an all-embracing psychological theory. It is to Reid's credit that he detected in Hume's empirical position the weakness that it did not have a genuinely empirical starting point.

Perhaps I should say a little more about this obscure person, lest you convict me of undue local patriotism. Our Honorary President refers to him several times in both his *History of Experimental Psychology* and his *Sensation and Perception in the History of Experimental Psychology*, but clearly does not think him important. Brett gave him more space but spoke disparagingly of his philosophical gifts, as does Watson. Thomas Reid lived from 1710-1796. He taught philosophy at Glasgow from 1764-1786, and tried to show that Hume's position was untenable. His work was influential outside his native land, coming to England by way of the writings of Dugald Stewart, Thomas Brown, and Sir William Hamilton. James Mill, incidentally, studied under Stewart. In France Reid was used to provide an alternative to the prevalent system of Condillac. He had some good ideas, though most of them are to be found in Locke. In a way he can be thought of as a sort of plain man's Kant.

The Natural Realism, which was Reid's common-sense starting point, simply denied Hume's premises. We start, not with impressions and ideas, but in a real world of which we are aware. Awareness of sensation is thus not the original condition of the mind; it is rather, in Reid's words, a kind of "abstract contemplation," attainable only by those who "with some pain and practice, can analyse a natural and original judgment." "Perhaps a child in the womb, or for some short period of its existence, is a merely sentient being," but this is taken to be a historical fact with no epistemological implications. Mere sentience, in this account, may precede perceptual awareness of an external world, but the latter is not dependent upon the former. It stands firmly on its own base as the point from which an analysis of knowledge must start. In this way we found our philosophy upon an assertion of psychological fact. It may sound an obvious enough fact to us, and, as Locke showed in his dealings with the thinking gentleman from Dublin, it was obvious enough to him to be accepted without much thought for its implications. But it was not a fact, or ought not to have been, for the Associationists, whose strength came from a denial of innate ideas and an assertion of elementarism.

There is an air of rustic simplicity about Reid's position which makes it seem very different from the elaborate logical structure of the *Critique of Pure Reason*, but Kant too had an empirical starting point. In his cautious way he gave as few hostages to fortune as he could, and all he assumed was our awareness of change or succession. Given that we are aware of change, he asked, what conditions seem to be required to make such awareness possible? As you remember, the phenomenal world of things and events was the basic condition, a world structured by the categories and ordered in space and time. This is very different from the clustering of elementary sense impressions under the laws of association. Oddly enough Reid and Kant were empirical in that they started from a fact. Hume and the Associationists started from a theory.

Considerations like these were not overlooked in England during the first half of the 19th century, but they were seldom conspicuous. There is a very revealing passage in a letter written by John Stuart Mill in 1834, where he confessed, "I know not that anyone can analyse or explain succession and coexistence, when reduced to their simplest forms. The theory of association presupposes them both, and divides association into synchronous and successive. We must . . . think, rank them as ultimate laws of our minds, or (what is the same thing in other words) of the phenomena of nature." Considerations like these still haunt the genuinely empirical student of human learning. "Certainly," said Bruner in 1957, "Hebb is correct in asserting, like Immanuel Kant, that certain primitive unities and identities within perception must be innate or autochthonous and not learned." Perhaps the most important contribution of Reid and his followers to British psychology was to give Associationism a sense of its own limitations. It prepared the way for a later appreciation of the much more sophisticated analysis carried out on the Continent by some of Kant's successors.

Key figures in the transition to a post-Associationist phase in the development of British psychology were Alexander Bain and James Ward, who taught philosophy at Cambridge in the decades around 1900.

Bain is perhaps rightly neglected nowadays. He reads like an old-fashioned contemporary rather than a genuine antique. But in his day he was considerable, and when he was attacked by William James or Bradley it was often for qualities that many might now consider virtues. Ribot thought him a worthy member of the "Scotch school" in that "he has followed that sure method which led them to sound discoveries, and that he has continued the tradition of the school better than the meta-physicians, like Ferrier, or the Kantists, like Hamilton." The tradition in question was that the methods of the natural sciences should be applied in psychology. Bain knew a great deal of physiology at second-hand, and used it well. He had something of the "taste for small facts" which Ribot attributed to the "Scotch school," but he had a system too, a qualified associationism based on a speculative neurology. There are other, much later, systems which differ only in their technical vocabulary.

Ward, on the other hand, was a "Kantist" in Ribot's sense. He is important for several reasons. To begin with, in his work the British and German traditions come together. Like many others from Britain in those great decades of the German universities, Ward crossed the Rhine to complete his education. He spent some time at Berlin, and at Göttingen, where Lotze must have brought the work of Brentano to his notice. He also became interested in experimental work after a visit to Leipzig, and encouraged the development of experimental psychology at Cambridge, though he did not like it once he had it. Unhappy events since 1914 have possibly made us forget this period of German dominance in the emerging psychological field. Ward was followed by Sully and McDougall to Göttingen, Spearman, who had links with Leipzig and Würzburg, as well as Göttingen, became almost as German in some ways as Titchener. The Watt who worked in Würzburg with Messer, Ach, and Bühler, later headed the Department of Psychology at Glasgow. It is interesting to note here that the dominant German influences in Britain tended to come from outside Leipzig. In the United States Wundt, through the mediation of Titchener, was the person whose theories, either by acceptance or by rejection, were pervasive. Now oddly enough, Wundt borrowed his learning theory from the English Associationists, as well as from

Herbart. His elementarism required something of the sort. But at Göttingen and Würzburg there were other views, and it was these other views that British psychologists found congenial.

Returning now to James Ward, we can identify the beginning of the post-Associationist age in Britain with the publication of his article on *Psychology* in the Encyclopedia Britannica of 1886. This article, in Brett's words, "clearly challenged the Associationists to show cause why they should continue to exist." Ward never, of course, denied that learning by association frequently happens. What he did was to insist that a mind is not a container, that consciousness is always part of the activity of a knowing, discriminating organism, and finally that mental bits and pieces—sensations, images, feelings, and all the rest—exist only as abstractions from this activity, never as its constituents.

Alexander Bain accepted the challenge on behalf of an association-ism he had himself in some ways rejected, and published a review of Ward's article on *Mind*. Then in 1887 he published a paper "On 'Association' Controversies" in which he tried to re-establish some part at least of the older faith. Basically the issue can be reduced to one point, Do we start with simple elements of some kind and build up complex wholes, or do we start with a confused awareness and discriminate within it? Bain, in the line of Locke and the Mills, chose the former. Ward, with real originality, though he might echo Kant and Brentano, chose the latter. It is a fact that Ward prevailed, and it may also be a fact that Ward was right.

It would not be fair to omit at this stage any mention of William James. You will all remember his "blooming buzzing confusion," and indeed he, like Ward, was in the tradition of Kant and Brentano. Darwin influenced him too in his functionalism, and even his pragmatism. He wrote with unequaled clarity and grace, yet it would be hard to say that his influence has played much part in the American psychology of the last twenty or thirty years. The story is a complicated one. Wundt's elementarism held its own in the work of Titchener until it was submerged under the flood of behaviorism. Thorndike was an associationist and an elementarist, at least in his early days, though the Law of Effect added a functionalist component. Hull provides us with an interesting illustration of how much some American learning theory, for all its experimental basis, shares with an older philosophical view. Consider James Mill's three criteria for the strength of an associative bond. These were

   (a)   Permanence or durability

   (b)   Certainty or correctness of response

   (c)   Facility or speed of response

Compare with them three of Hull's criteria of habit strength.

   (a)   Resistance to experimental extinction

   (b)   *Per cent* of correct reaction evocation

   (c)   Reaction latency or speed of reaction

It is clear that we have not two theories but Mark I and Mark II of the same theory.

American psychology is no longer Hullian perhaps, but it would be too much to say that Associationism is dead in the United States. On the other hand the functionalism of James, though it lost the early battles, may be winning the campaign. Some pockets of resistance, however, have still to be mopped up.

Back in Britain there were no hostilities. Ward, at Cambridge, taught Stout, who succeeded Bain as our writer of textbooks, and was himself an acute, and original thinker. In my own student days Stout's Analytic Psychology was a prescribed text, and the 10th impression of the 3rd edition of his Manual of Psychology came out less than forty years ago.

Perhaps even more important in its effects on British psychology was the fact that Ward also taught Sir Frederic Bartlett, who is happily still with us. Bartlett admired Ward and accepted his general position, but the teutonic rigors of abstract analysis were uncongenial. Bartlett thinks according to the older British style, like Locke before Hume made him too consistent. But unlike any of the philosophical psychologists, he is primarily concerned with data. In fact he might not see himself as a descendant of Ward at all, but claim Darwin as parent. The physiologists, especially Rivers, were also very important. Above all Bartlett was an experimentalist, not the first, but experiment came late to British psychology, in spite of Galton, and Bartlett was one of the pioneers.

What has done most to establish Bartlett's informal but characteristic way of thinking in Britain is the extent to which he has produced other psychologists. On a rough count more than half of our professors of psychology have been his pupils ever since we have had enough of them to require more than our fingers to count them on. Not all are disciples. P. E. Vernon, for example, belongs much more to the school of Spearman and Burt. But not one of them is an associationist, with the possible exception of Berlyne, who was exposed to Hull before the critical period for imprinting had lapsed, and has, it seems to me, been making gallant attempts ever since to reconcile a conflict which is irreconcilable.

So that when we come to answer the question with which we started: Why has psychology never been associationist in the country of associationism? we find our answer seems to depend on one or two individuals. This may be the right answer or it may not. Without Bartlett or Ward would the chain have been broken? Without Reid's common sense would we have been so prepared to extract what was empirical from the Kantian philosophy? It is hard to say and unprofitable to speculate. One thing is clear. In 1886 when the Associationists were asked by Ward to justify their continued existence they failed to do so. They would have failed, I think, anywhere on the Continent of Europe on this side of the Russian frontier. Pavlov and Thorndike gave them a second lease of life. The simplicity and objectivity of animal experiment obscured for a time theoretical difficulties that had long ago become apparent at the human level. But in Britain and Western Europe Associationism as an all embracing theory, though not as a special one, was dead by 1900. There are signs that before the end of the present century it will have been allowed to lie down.

The Historical Background for National Trends in Psychology: German Psychology
Wolfgang Metzger

One of Germany's senior psychologists, Wolfgang Metzger is professor of psychology and director of the Psychological Institute at the University of Münster. In 1960 he served as president of the Sixteenth International Congress of Psychology at Bonn. He has also been editor of several German psychological journals and is known for his researches on visual perception, productive thinking, and educational psychology. In discussing the historical background for national trends in the psychology of the German-speaking countries, Metzger furnishes an excellent summary of the development of German psychology. He emphasizes the reaction in Germany against Wundtian atomism and associationism. He calls attention to the powerful and enduring influence of Diltheyanism, with its distrust of empiricism and objectivism, its utter disdain for experimentation, and its promotion of free theorizing and *Verstehen*, or understanding psychology. In addition, Metzger delineates the effects of political factors and Nazism on German psychology. He stresses that these influences hindered the progress of psychology in Germany. However, the interest of the younger psychologists in modern developments speaks well for the future of German psychology.

As German participant in this symposium, I consider it as my task to speak of the historical background especially of German trends in psychology.

But what means "German" in this context? In science—just as in poetry, fiction, and all kinds of literature—at all times every person has been called German if his native language was German. The part of the map of Europe in which people speak German, includes not only the two halves of Germany of today but also the whole confederation of Austria and the German-speaking parts of Switzerland. It fits into this definition that scientists move from an Austrian or Swiss university to a German one (in the political sense) just as freely as they move within Germany as understood politically, e.g.,

Wolfgang Metzger, The historical background for national trends in psychology: German psychology. *Journal of the History of the Behavioral Sciences*, 1965, 1, 109-115. Reprinted by permission of the author and the Psychology Press.

between Heidelberg and Göttingen. This tradition has been broken for the first time by the communist regime of eastern Germany, and I am afraid the obstacles built up by them in the middle of Germany will last longer and become more impervious than any of us can imagine. But for my present purpose I may leave this aspect of the German tragedy out of consideration.

My second preliminary question is: What is a national trend? And how can it be ascertained? There are different ways of getting hold of them. One could make statistics of the predominating topics over a longer period. This was not possible in the short time left for the preparation of this report. So I have to rely on the—perhaps misleading—general impression of four decades of reading contributions to psychology from various countries. A second way would be to search for common traits of the great impulses given to psychology by members of German speaking peoples, traits, by which they possibly at the same time differ from those of other origin. One could also ask which psychological theories or innovations were likely to be accepted internationally or only by the compatriots of their authors. I think that all these ways of getting hold of what is meant by national trend should be attempted.

A last preliminary remark is necessary with regard to the concept of historical background. This concept may assume a number of different meanings, narrower and wider ones. We have to distinguish between political, sociocultural, ideological, scientific, and institutional conditions of psychological experimenting and theorizing. In the following discussion I shall first deal with the more sociocultural and philosophical atmosphere out of which the great impulses of German psychology originated, and only at the end with political and institutional influences. This order of presentation seems to me to be justified by the fact that political intervention in scientific discussion is a new acquisition of modern times, as it seems, one of the unexpected and unwished for by-products of what we call human progress.

From my many years' occupation with psychological literature I got the impression that there is at least one outstanding characteristic of German psychological thinking, viz., the widespread inclination towards personality theory, which has brought forth a variety of contributions to typology, to be sure of considerably varying value, which in some extreme cases led to the opinion that personality theory could entirely replace general psychology. The historical background of this seems to me to be the glorification of personality in the classic German literature, the after-effects of which are even observable in the theory of primary school education.

Besides this, I may with some confidence, mention at least the four following common traits: First, an inclination to phenomenology, though this can also be observed in Italian or Belgian contributions. Second, a deep rooted distrust in purely empiristic views which, on the other hand, are strikingly favoured in U.S. and U.S.S.R. psychology. Third, a certain reserve against elementarist assumptions which also differs greatly from the American and Russian trends. And, finally, a considerable reserve against an excessive and, as we believe, in its extreme forms suicidal objectivism.

About the background of these I can only utter conjectures. But no doubt they converge in the tradition of Continental epistemology which had consciousness as a legitimate scientific subject. And we shall never be convinced by the ever repeated objections of objectivists that conscious phenomena are of no scientific value, if these are observed carefully, by an unbiased observer, and under well defined conditions.

Let us now see whether we can gain more information from the great impulses given to psychology by German-speaking authors. There are in German psychology—as far as I see it—at least six great impulses between 1862 and 1912, that is, within an interval of fifty years.

First: The foundation of psychophysics by the introduction of the three fundamental methods of psychological measurement by Gustav Theodor Fechner in 1862, which was, at the same time, the foundation of psychology as an exact science. As an immediate consequence of this the first psychological laboratory of the world was founded by Wilhelm Wundt at Leipzig in 1875.

Second: The initiation of act psychology or intentionalism by Franz Brentano in the seventies.

Third: The proclamation of "geisteswissenschaftliche Psychologie" by Wilhelm Dilthey in the eighties, with his early insistence on a kind of psychological holism and, at the same time, his deplorable verdict against psychological experimentation. (The term, "geisteswissenschaftlich" is hard to explain to a non-German. It means a psychology that restricts itself to those methods of interpretation and elucidation as are practiced in the scientific treatment of poetry and fiction.)

Fourth: The development of psychoanalysis, that means, the first comprehensive attempt at building up a dynamic psychology by Sigmund Freud since the nineties,—including the secessions of Carl Gustav Jung and Alfred Adler. These facts are generally known and need no comment.

Fifth: The pronunciamento of "Ausdruckslehre," or theory of expression, or more concretely and correctly, of a new psychology centered about expression, as required in an imperative tone by Ludwig Klages.

Sixth: The holistic revolution of developmental psychology by Hans Cornelius and Felix Krueger, by which the picture of psychological development was upset: Instead of a sequence of associative and integrative processes, beginning with the sum of psychological elements, evolution of consciousness should now be understood as a sequence of processes of differentiation and finer articulation, beginning with the state of an undivided stream, as it had been postulated already by William James.

Seventh: The foundation of the "Würzburg school" of "Denkpsychologie" by Oswald Külpe.

In the eighth place I mention Gestalt theory, as the third holistic attempt at a general psychology. The way for it was broken as early as 1890 by Christian von Ehrenfels, but it was finally built up not before 1912 by Max Wertheimer, Wolfgang Köhler, and Kurt Koffka.

For the origin of most of these innovations specific national circumstances can be made responsible.

1. Of Fechner's foundation of experimental psychophysics it is known that it grew out of the encounter in one mind of a sober training in experimental physics with an abstruse kind of natural philosophy that was cultivated in the romanticist period in Germany and had a great vogue among educated people at those times. Fechner's original aim was to prove scientifically some assumptions about the relations between body and soul that he had derived from that philosophy.

2. Dilthey's combat against experimentation in psychology originated in another inheritance of German romanticism that lasted through the whole nineteenth century and in some disciplines, e.g.,

in education, has not yet been abandoned in our time. The pivotal idea of this doctrine of historicism is the assumption that you know all about a person or a fact, or even of an art, if you know its history. (*E.g.*, German high school teachers are prepared for their educational duties by lectures and examinations in history of education.)

3. The background of Freudianism is much more complex. It has often been said that the soil in which it rooted was the bourgeoisie of old Vienna with all its prudery and hypocrisy. There may be some truth in that. But it can be shown that Freud's theory has its well defined place in the history of German philosophy, especially in a stage of decay of transcendentalism. In the beginning of this philosophy the rational ego had been described as a kind of almighty creator. But later on it had, step-by-step, lost its supposed power, until at the psychoanalytic finale we find it in the role of a ship-wrecked who is the sport of overwhelming irrational powers from above and from below.

4. The psychology of Klages again has grown out of a late stage of Romanticism: an esoteric circle of poets, artists, astrologers, alchemists, and a variety of enthusiasts for all kinds of mysticism who assembled at Munich at the beginning of this century.

5. The genetic holism in the psychology of Cornelius and Krueger, now represented mainly by Sander and Volkelt is to some degree influenced by William James. But its history can be traced back to the preclassical period of irrationalism, the so called "Sturm und Drang," as represented by Herder and for psychology particularly by Tetens.

6. The tradition of Gestalt theory, on the other hand, goes—at least in certain essential points—unmistakably back to Immanuel Kant. Kant can be claimed as its philosophical forerunner at least in his criticism of David Hume's empiricist epistemology. And Max Wertheimer's inquiry into the factors of grouping can with good reason be considered as an experimental continuation of Kant's chapter on transcendental analytics.

The various ways of German psychology are so different and even opposite that it is not easy to find more common traits in them than are already known to us. But there is still an indirect symptom for what is a typically national trend. We have simply to compare the range and intensity of resonance of the various schools all over the world, as well as within their own nation.

If we go through our list, we find an almost immediate and unlimited international resonance for Fechner's psychophysics and Freud's psychoanalysis. We find a limited, slow, and reserved international acceptance for genetic holism and Gestalt theory. We find an influence of Brentano in western Europe: France, Belgium, and the Netherlands. And we find the doctrines of Klages and Dilthey exactly limited to the German speaking part of the map, and with no noticeable international resonance. At the same time, within the German area, including Switzerland, no school of psychology has ever been so generally accepted, so highly estimated and so predominant among educated people in general and particularly among the members of the university staffs as the "geisteswissen-schaftliche Psychologie" of Wilhelm Dilthey. This public opinion has been so effective that even at present it is hard for the representatives of scientific psychology to carry through those measures as are necessary to keep up with the international development.

So this Diltheyanism proves to be a typically German phenomenon. And, as such, it has, as just mentioned, become an external, one might say, a political factor of considerable and disturbing power.

By this way, the discussion of this psychological school leads immediately to my last question: how far and in which manner the development of psychology in Germany has been influenced or controlled by political factors. This question splits up into two sub-questions that I shall treat separately.

First, how far has the development of psychology as such—without regard to its special assumptions—been promoted or obstructed by the authorities of the state.

Second, which was the specific influence on psychological theory by political circumstances, more concretely, how far certain psychological ideas or schools were backed or supported and propagated by the state, while others were opposed to or attacked and possibly suppressed and persecuted.

As to the first of the two sub-questions, it may be said that since psychology had established itself as a science in the middle of the nineteenth century, in the absolute monarchy of old Prussian kingdom as well as in the constitutional monarchy of the Reich of 1870 and in the Weimar democracy of 1918, psychology enjoyed the same independence and, at the same time, modest financial support as any other university discipline.

But this is no longer the case in modern autocratic systems, no matter whether these understand themselves as a realization of an ideology or are simply the result of an usurpation. It is characteristic of autocratic systems that they are, without exception, full of distrust and aversion against this science. This looks exactly like a symptom of bad conscience directed against those who are most likely to bring forth a competent and well founded criticism of autocratic methods. So, all over the world where such an usurpation succeeds, be it in Germany, in Venezuela, or in South Korea, one of the first measures of the new rulers is to restrict psychological activity, to close psychological laboratories, and to dismiss psychologists. In Russia, psychology was preserved through the troubles of the revolution only because the great Pavlov had declared it a kind of brain physiology in advance.

Sometimes, *e.g.*, in eastern Germany, generally accepted experimental methods, *e.g.*, of intelligence testing, have been prohibited, at least temporarily, and I do not know how much of these prohibitions are still in force. By the way, these measures were "justified" by the consideration of human dignity. Under the German Nazi system we had no such prohibitions, but it must be taken into consideration that even in 1945 we were only in the beginning of this system. And on the other hand, psychology was, without such restrictions, hit in its roots since 1933 by the persecution and expulsion of the Jews and many of their friends. That meant in psychology the loss of at least 40 per cent of its personal substance, among them quite a number of scholars of highest international reputation.

There was still another circumstance to impair scientific activity in our discipline. Among younger students a concept of science spread more and more, according to which scientific activity was another kind of writing newspaper lead stories. Under these circumstances serious scientific research was hardly possible even in those laboratories which were not seriously disturbed by direct intervention of representatives of the state or party.

The situation was aggravated by the ever growing difficulty of securing scientific literature from abroad, which ended with being cut off entirely from the scientific progress of the world, which had particularly grievous consequences for psychology in view of the rapidly growing international standard of experimental and statistical methods.

So far my report restricted itself to the general political conditions of psychological activity. But, as already mentioned, beyond this it has to be asked how far political authorities tried to gain influence upon or control of psychological doctrine.

To this point it can be said that no German government before 1933 attempted to exert any influence upon theoretical trends of psychology or of any other science. It is true, the publications of the great Kant bear the license of the royal censorship of old Prussia. This authority went on working up to the middle of the nineteenth century. As far as I know it did not exist in the Reich of 1870 and undoubtedly not in the Weimar Republic. But even the censors of the old absolute kingdom considered as their task only to ascertain that religion, or morals, or the person of the sovereign were not offended in the publication under examination. Beyond this they never attempted to gain influence on the content or trend of the scientific writings that were examined by them. This was left to the Bolshevist and NS governments. The former have insisted up to this time that every psychological assumption had to conform to the Pavlovian system and to avoid any "idealistic" trait. Of course there were some fluctuations in the directives coming from above. But just by these fluctuations the situation was illustrated in a most impressive manner. During the fifties, when it was still easier than now to visit the German east and discuss scientific problems with friends living there, it was characteristic of the atmosphere prevailing beyond the Iron Curtain that everybody asked anxiously which was the official reading at the moment of the discussion.

As to the Nazi authorities, they demanded no less insistently that psychologists should renounce general psychology and restrict themselves to typological problems. Moreover those psychological schools which had one or another Jew among their founders or former representatives, were likely to be rejected without closer inspection.

No wonder that at the end of the Second World War German psychology was in a desolate condition which even now is not yet entirely overcome. It cannot be denied that German psychology, which had a leading position during the Wundtian era in the nineties and once more in the twenties when the

Berlin school was at its culminating point, is recovering pretty slowly. This has some important reasons in the institutional aspect of the historical background, *viz.*, in the organization of German universities.

In Germany there are no independent departments of psychology. This has its consequences for the status of the psychological laboratories as well as of the chairs of psychology. Every psychological laboratory belongs to one of the large faculties, in most universities to the faculty of arts and humanities, in some of them to the faculty of science. Formerly science and humanities had been united in one single faculty, the so called "Philosophische Fakultät." But since 1900 these faculties grew into more and more impracticable dimensions. So, during the last decades one after another of these huge structures were split into two divisions or branches, one of science and one of humanities. And by that time these divisions or branches became independent faculties. But while psychology had its place in the center of the old faculty, after the separation—as we say in German—it fell down between the chairs. Nobody knows where it belongs. For it is incontestably a science, but it deals exclusively with human problems. Now psychology may join the sciences. Then it will be looked upon as something not sufficiently scientific by the representatives of the older and more established sciences. (Something like that, by the way, seems to me to be one of the reasons for the overrating of methodological viewpoints in psychology that can also be observed in English speaking countries.) On the other hand, psychology may also join the humanities. But then it is looked upon with distrust by the other members of the faculty because of its scientific methods and at the same time is said to be immoderate in its financial claims. The requirements of an experimental science are measured here by the standard requirements of a historical discipline which consist of a studio, a library, and a room for meetings. So, in both situations it is a hard job to get a staff and an experimental outfit as is required for the research program and the training of the students. Only recently the faculty of arts, at least at Münster university, made up its mind to tolerate—as we used to say—that cuckoo's egg of a laboratory in their philosophical and philological nest, and to support its demands at the university administration.

At present, the recommendations of the so called "Wissenschaftsrat"—council of sciences—which enjoy great notice by the public and the authorities, gave a supplementary impulse towards a better appreciation of the material needs of scientific psychology.

But there is another problem involved, *viz.*, the problem of appointments for psychological chairs. Fortunately, the insight is growing that psychology cannot to its whole extent—including the experimental and statistical training of the students—be taught by a single person. But as psychology, as a part of a large faculty, cannot settle its affairs independently, the planned appointments are debated in commissions, in which the psychologist finds himself amidst a majority of philosophers, historians, and philologists. And these very nearly unanimously venerate Dilthey and still believe in his verdict against experimental methods. So they have a predilection for a philosophizing type of a psychologist, in other words, their estimation grows inversely to his experimental and statistical training. This attitude is but slightly modified by the fact that recently they have taken a liking to Freud. The decisive fact for us is that only very hesitatingly have they come to recognize that the progress of our science is guaranteed only by empirical research. This is a great hindrance to our efforts to reach the international standard again which had been lagged behind more and more by German psychology since 1933.

Fortunately, there is some comfort in the observation that a majority of younger psychologists have a feeling of this situation and try to follow the modern development of methods with a zeal that is only comparable with that of the young Americans who once gathered at Leipzig in the newly founded laboratory of Wilhelm Wundt.

Russian Physiologists' Psychology and American Experimental Psychology: A Historical and a Systematic Collation and a Look into the Future
Gregory Razran

Well known for his research and numerous publications on semantic, autonomic, and attitudinal behavior and conditioning, Russian-born Gregory Razran, professor of psychology at Queens College of the City University of New York, has been one of the United States' principal interpreters of Soviet psychology, psychophysiology, and reflexology. In the present article Razran describes the experiments and views of Sechenov, Pavlov, and Bekhterev and delineates the parallel developments of Russian physiologists' psychology and American experimental psychology. He notes that Watson's behaviorism, an independent American development, interacted early with Russian experimental psychology. Citing specifically the influence on American psychology of Pavlov and of the translations of his two books on conditioned reflex, Razran examines the relationship of Pavlov with later learning theorists such as Hull, Spence, Estes, and Hebb. This article, a valuable source of information on Soviet psychology, is further enhanced by an excellent bibliography.

In summary, Razran describes the language barrier as "a unique factor in Russo-American experimental and theoretical parallels and divergencies." In his opinion, however, "significant Russo-American rapprochements on the basics of psychology seem imminent."

In 1904, a distinguished Russian physiologist, Ivan P. Pavlov, was awarded the Nobel prize for his research in the physiology of digestion begun in 1877. He was the first Russian to be so honored. Yet a few years earlier Pavlov had already turned from what he called pure physiology to what he firmly believed would become a new experimental psychology. "Experimental Psychology and Psychopathology in Animals" was the title of an address he delivered, in 1903, at the Fourteenth International Congress of Medicine, in Madrid, in which, on the basis of several cogent laboratory experiments and some cogent scientific reasoning, he began to

Gregory Razran, Russian physiologists' psychology and American experimental psychology: A historical and a systematic collation and a look into the future. *Psychological Bulletin*, 1965, **63**, 42-64. Reprinted by permission of the author and the American Psychological Association.

fashion his new discipline of conditioned—and unconditioned—reflexes. Later, Pavlov named the discipline "the physiology of higher nervous activity" or, more exactly, "the physiology and pathology (or pathophysiology) of higher nervous activity" (in lieu of "experimental psychology and psychopathology"). But its scope and content remained unaltered—a thorough empirical and logical analysis of the laws of formation and disruption of conditioned reflexes which Pavlov pursued most assiduously and perspicaciously to almost the very last day of his life: February 27, 1936.

Pavlov freely expressed indebtedness to Ivan M. Sechenov, usually called the father of Russian physiology, who in 1863 published a classic monograph entitled "Reflexes of the Brain." In addressing the Moscow Society of Scientists on March 24, 1913, Pavlov said about the monograph:

> It presented in clear, precise, and charming form the fundamental idea [of psychic life as reflex conditioning] which we have worked out at the present time [Pavlov, 1913, p. 197, 1928, p. 222].

And again in 1923, in the Preface to his first book on conditioning, he stated:

> The chief motive for my decision [to study psychic life as reflex conditioning] arose out of the impression made upon me during my youth by the monograph of I.M. Sechenov. . . . In this work, a brilliant attempt was made, altogether extraordinary for that time (of course only theoretically, as a schema) to present our subjective world in terms of pure physiology . . . ideas that certainly are those of a genius [Pavlov, 1923, p. 8, 1928, p. 39].

Sechenov's involvement in psychology was, strikingly, even wider than that of Pavlov; yet, unlike Pavlov, he was dedicated not to forming a new rival or substitute discipline but to reforming the old one. The titles of a number of his later outstanding essays were: "Elements of Thought" (1878), "The Doctrine of the Un-Freedom of the Will" (1881), "Impression and Reality" (1890), "Object-Thought and Reality" (1892), "Object-Thinking from a Physiological Standpoint" (1894), and especially, "By Whom and How Should Psychology be Studied" (1873) in which the answer to "By Whom" was by physiologists and to "How" objectively and reflexively. See also his later collected publications (Sechenov, 1867, 1873a, 1873b,

1884a, 1884b, 1935a, 1935b, 1943, 1947, 1952, 1953, 1952-56, 1956). And, as late as 1957, S.L. Rubinshteyn, the chief theoretician of current Soviet psychology (not higher nervous activity), declared that "an article devoted to the great Russian psychologist [Sechenov] is not an article about the past but about the present and future of our science of psychology [Rubinshteyn, 1957, p. 7]." In 1889, Sechenov, the physiologist, and Troitsky and Grot, the psychologists, headed an 18-member Russian delegation to the First International Congress of Psychology in Paris. The American delegates were William James and Joseph Jastrow.

Vladimir M. Bekhterev (1857-1927) was a contemporary of Pavlov and a neurologist and psychiatrist as well as a physiologist (*Bekhterev's band, Bekhterev's nucleus, Bekhterev's reflexes, Bekhterev's symptom, Bekhterev's disease, Bekhterev's test* will all be found in any standard English medical dictionary). Bekhterev founded a laboratory of experimental psychology at the University of Kazan in 1884 and a periodical *Obozreniye Psikhiatrii, Nevropatologii i Eksperimental'noy Psikhologii* (Review of Psychiatry, Neuropathology, and Experimental Psychology)—the first time "experimental psychology" appeared in the title of a periodical in any language—in 1896. His historical article "Objective Psychology and Its Subject-Matter" appeared in 1904—years before any serious indication of such coupling in American psychological writings—and his 1907-10 3-volume 660-page text *Objective Psychology* was translated into both German and French in 1913—into German as *Objective Psychologie oder Psychoreflexologie* but, for some reason, into French only as *La psychologie objective*. Bekhterev published *General Principles of Reflexology* in 1917, changed it to *General Principles of Human Reflexology* in 1923, and revised and enlarged the changed text in 1925 and 1928. *Collective Reflexology* came out in 1921 and was followed by a number of articles on "genetic," "individual," "industrial," "pathological," "zoo-" and other types of "reflexologies." As might be suspected, Bekhterev, like Pavlov, aimed at a new and better discipline, reflexology instead of psychology, and in the first Soviet decade he, indeed, almost succeeded in the coup d'etat. Later, however, his system lost ground and finally disappeared in favor of a Soviet division of what we call psychology into the physiologists' basic science of higher nervous activity and the psychologists' superstructure of a modernized (and "marxized") traditional psychology.

American and Western experimental psychology is surely not an outgrowth of Russian physiologists' psychology. Its originators and original mentors—Wundt, Külpe, Ebbinghaus, Titchener, Cattell, and others—either knew nothing or cared nothing about the "experimental psychologies" of Sechenov, Pavlov, and Bekhterev. Yet, surprisingly and paradoxically, a perusal of the two current official periodicals of American experimental psychologists—the *Journal of Experimental Psychology* and the *Journal of Comparative and Physiological Psychology*—reveals that the periodicals are considerably more concerned with what the aforementioned Russian physiologists were saying and doing than with the sayings and doings of the aforementioned Western and American experimental psychologists—even if we add to the latter the names of James, Dewey, Thorndike, Watson, and Wertheimer. A recent survey of members of the American Psychological Association placed Pavlov second only to Freud in the members' estimate of who influenced most contemporary psychology. And there is no doubt that Pavlov would have ranked first, had the survey been confined to experimental psychologists or to the question of who influenced most comtemporary experimental psychology. In a glossary of America's recent standard text on conditioning and learning (Kimble, 1961)—admittedly the leading and most studied area in current American experimental psychology—we note 36 terms attributed to Pavlov and 25 to all American and Western psychologists combined.

The present article will thus be designed to offer a summary and an analysis, both historical and contemporary, of the relation of Russian physiologists' psychology to American experimental psychology. It is obvious that the former came to influence the latter radically. Yet it is equally obvious that the influence did not make the American and the Russian disciplines wholly similar to each other but that very significant and varying divergencies ensued and continue to ensue. Moreover, a divisive language barrier as a rule materially delayed and at times even totally limited the Russian influence, so that some similarities between the two disciplines are outcomes of parallel, rather than of influenced, developments. And of course there have been also Russo-American interactions of divergencies and similarities of views and findings, differing in compass and caliber. Nor, finally, must we ignore completely the reverse influence, that of American experimental psychology upon the Russian enterprise.

SECHENOV

Sechenov's psychological views will be considered first, not just because of their historical precedence and far-reaching original and continuing influence, but because of their extreme indigenousness. For while in their native land these views have exercised overriding influence not only on psychology as such but on Russian thought in general, in the West and in America practically nothing but Sechenov's physiological experiments have ever been cognized. No Western or American history of psychology or textbook of experimental psychology contains the name of Sechenov, and Boring's *History of Experimental Psychology* mentions him only in the second 1950 edition. Yet there is no doubt that since 1863, throughout his life, Sechenov was the very center of Russia's basic psychological, philosophical, and—in characteristic Russian fashion—ideological debates and controversies. I.S. Turgenev attended his lectures (Sechenov, 1907, p. 139), F.M. Dostoyevsky (1938, p. 259) and most Russian philosophers and psychologists deplored his materialism (Budilova, 1960), Saltykov-Shchedrin (1900, p. 519) and most scientists and physicians approved it (Budilova, 1960), and Tolstoy referred to "Reflexes of the Brain" (Sechenov, 1863) in his novel *Anna Karenina* (1903, p. 7).[1] And today in the Soviet Union, Sechenov's prestige and authoritativeness is in all respects second only to that of Pavlov, and, as indicated earlier, his views are continually referred to and elaborated. Seven editions of the "Reflexes" were published before the Revolution and 12 after it; a French translation appeared in 1884 and an English translation in 1935 and 1952-56.

Briefly stated, Sechenov's complete psychological system rests on five leading interrelated theses: (*a*) a consistent psychophysiological or physical monism, (*b*) a synonymity of reflex action with both physiological and psychical reaction, (*c*) the reflex as the mechanism of association, (*d*) the psychic as associative in genesis and central-neural in mediation, and (*e*) a radical environmentalism.

The first thesis of psychophysiological monism expressed in such statements as:

---

[1] Translators of *Anna Karenina* (English, French, and German) miss the significance of the quotation marks around "Refleksy Golovnogo Mozga" ("Reflexes of the Brain") in the novel—that is, they miss the fact that Tolstoy refers to a book—and they translate the three words merely as "reflexes."

No conceivable demarcation will be found between obvious somatic, i.e., bodily, nervous acts and unmistakable psychic phenomena [Sechenov, 1873, p. 151-152, 1952-56, p. 185] [and] A child laughing at the sight of a toy, a young girl trembling at the first thought of love, Garibaldi smiling when he was driven from his country because his love for it was too great, Newton discovering and writing down the laws of the universe—everywhere, the final act is a muscular movement [Sechenov, 1863, p. 462, 1952-56, p. 33]

is of course a reformulation of earlier French and British views. Likewise, the last thesis of environmentalism disclosed in

999 parts of the character of psychic content are due to training, in the broadest sense of the word, and only one part is due to individuality [heredity] [1863, p. 512, 1952-56, p. 137] [and in] The basic character of man's mind and his sensory faculties have not changed in the course of his history and are independent of race, geographic location, and level of culture [1873, p. 146, 1952-56, p. 180]

may well be related to Locke's *tabula rasa*. Yet it is highly significant to note that (*a*) the two theses were staunchly defended and skillfully propagated by Sechenov at a time when their antitheses, psychophysical parallelism and subjectivism and hereditarianism, fully dominated Western psychology and Western thought in general and (*b*) that their defense was expressed in a form that is strikingly reminiscent of early American behaviorism, some 50 years later. Students of the history of ideas might take cognizance of the East-West differential and think of its possible causes.

Sechenov's second thesis, reflex ubiquity, was even more radical and more daring in breaking with tradition than his first and last thesis, and it was wholly his own. A significant hint of it already appeared in a sentence in Sechenov's 1860 doctoral dissertation that "all movements bearing in physiology the name of voluntary are in a strict sense reflexive [1907, p. 123]." That is to say, Sechenov was already thinking of conscious or psychical movements as reflex actions—which he fully developed in his 1863 treatise. But there he went much further to declare that:

If a conscious psychical act is not accompanied by any external manifestations, it still remains a reflex [1863, p. 502, 1952-56, p. 114] [and that] A thought is the first two-thirds of a psychical reflex . . . only the end of the reflex, i.e., movement, is apparently absent [1863, p. 503, 1952-56, p. 116].

Or, in other words, what Sechenov finally postulated was that not only all neuromotor or effector reactions are reflex in nature but also central-neural or noneffector (receptor-adjustor) reactions—a doctrine beyond that of Bekhterev and Watson and early Skinner but one fully embraced by present-day Soviet psychophysiology.

It could, of course, be argued that such a ubiquitous concept of the reflex dilutes significantly its heuristic value. Yet it could be strongly rebutted that the concept bolsters much-needed methodological monism and that modern research evidence demonstrates the psychophysiological likeness of the central-neural and the neuromotor: The basic properties of simple conditioning of brain waves do not, for instance, differ substantially from those of the conditioning of glandular and motor action. Moreover, the Russians hold out also the didactic import of the view that the reflex is that all pervading unit of all organismic action—it points unswervingly to causal determinism and neural mediation, which, too, is a matter of consideration. And, interestingly, it might be added, despite their 100% unqualified adherence to the Sechenov reflex, present-day Soviet higher nervous activity and psychology are in fact less reductionistic in explanatory principles than are most current American behaviorists. Even the important modern neuropsychic thesis of neural feedback is implicit in Sechenov's system—since made amply explicit by Anokhin (1957, 1961), the present head of the Sechenov Neurophysiological Institute and chief Soviet protagonist of "reafferentation."

The third and fourth thesis, particularly the third, disclose best Sechenov's systematic perspicacity with respect to evidence and thought that has accumulated since his time. Only three sentences, repeated in various forms in all his writings, need be quoted here:

> Association is effected through continuous series of reflexes in which the end of a preceding reflex coincides in time with the beginning of a subsequent [1863, p. 498, 1952-56, p. 105]. *From the standpoint of process, there is not the slightest difference between an actual impression with its sequels, and the memory of the impression.* They are the same psychical reflexes having the same psychical content—only evoked by different stimuli [1863, p. 499, 1952-56, p. 108]. *Through absolutely involuntary learning of consecutive reflexes in all sensory spheres, the child acquires a multitude of more or less complete ideas of objects, i.e. concrete elementary knowledge. The integrated reflex . . . corresponds to the activity of the central element [adjustor] of the reflex apparatus* [1863, p. 481, 1952-56, p. 83].

The first sentence clearly contains the core idea of Pavlov's discovery that Aristotle's psychic association can be physicalized and "embodied"—that what has, for more than 2,000 years, been merely imaged and meditated could be made to flow, so to speak, in capillary tubes and electric batteries and thus become subject to all the refinements and measurements and means of verifications of all of modern science and technology. The sentence is, indeed, also most modern in stressing that physicalistic association (conditioning, nowadays) is a matter of a succession rather than of a simultaneity of events and it is even post-Pavlovian in asserting that the association (or conditioning) is a linkage between two unconditioned reflexes, as recently proposed by Asratyan (1952), the head of the Institute of Higher Nervous Activity of the USSR Academy of Sciences. The second Sechenov sentence, obviously, physicalizes memory and brings forward the principle of "different" or "substitute" stimulus, a staple of modern experimental psychology to this day. Finally, there is the third and last sentence which plainly states that not only single simple associations but also their total integration is reflex or neural in nature and origin, and further maintains that association (or conditioning) is the precondition of "concrete elementary knowledge" (read: perception) and that its neural mediation is central-neural. The last two of the three parts of the sentence are most tenable in the light of most recent research, and the first is usually assumed in modern psychology.

Space prevents discussion of Sechenov's other—for our purpose, more ancillary—views such as his thesis that not only the neural basis of psychical acts but the psychical acts themselves are reflex in nature—what present-day Russian psychologists call "the reflex doctrine of the psyche"—and his poignant analysis of the relation of sensation to thought, of thought to language, of will to consciousness, of animal "sensory-automatic" thinking, human "concrete-object" thinking, and the specificities of symbolic and mathematical thinking. What has been said so far should suffice, however, to convey that, allowing for some for-his-period understandable fallacies of fact and judgment, Sechenov was in his psychology many decades, often a whole century, ahead of his time.

PAVLOV

According to some of his students, Pavlov was fond of saying that he was no more than Sechenov's "podmaster'ye"—submaster or apprentice—and, as we have seen, there is no doubt that Sechenov ideated for Pavlov a general sketch of a new system of psychology. Yet, it is clear that the system itself was not only built but wholly planned by Pavlov himself—long and painstakingly modeled and fitted in both part and pattern, brick by brick and wall to wall, so to speak. The system's ideas needed, of course, specific methods and experiments to be tested and verified and the findings of the experiments called for integration into general laws and hypotheses, which is exactly what Pavlov had always done and striven to do. If I may be permitted another metaphor: Sechenov saw that psychology's and association's "mind" needed a "body," while Pavlov actually created the body and breathed it into the mind, the Lord's work in reverse.

So much of Pavlov's writings has been translated into English—all formal publications excluding only the six volumes of informal Wednesday Seminars (Pavlov, 1949b, 1954-57)—and so much has been written about him in English that a summary evaluation, rather than an exposition, of his chief contributions will be offered here. And we might begin with a word about the systematic state of Western and American experimental psychology when Pavlov entered the field, in 1903 and thereabout, 40 years after Sechenov's "Reflexes." In general, the system was one of states-of-consciousness' subjectivism and introspectionism, dominated by Titchener in the United States and by Külpe and even more orthodox Wundtians in Germany (little, if any, experimental psychology elsewhere). William James, a most articulate yet conservative critic of the system, did at long last note that psychology was still in an "ante-scientific condition" but did nothing to recreate it as scientific. At any rate, James had at that time left the field for the wider domains of philosophy (Chair of Professor of Psychology at Harvard changed, in 1897, to Professor of Philosophy) as did another important and more radical critic, John Dewey. The just-hatched mental tests of Alfred Binet and of J. McKeen Cattell were objective in a practical sense but at best were only very peripheral and technological in relation to the systematic basics of the science—while the pioneer animal experiments of C. Lloyd Morgan, Leonard Hobhouse, and Edward Thorndike (which, incidentally, were unknown to Pavlov) were, first, much behind Pavlov in radicalism of method, interpretation, and swoop over all of psychology, and, second, had as yet little impact on the field as such. The first American textbook in animal psychology was Margaret Washburn's (1908) *Animal Mind*—all Titchenerian.

In short, the Pavlov 1903 and 1904 statements that:

> Vital phenomena that are termed psychic are distinguishable from pure physiological phenomena only in degree of complexity. Whether we call these phenomena psychical or complex-nervous is of little importance, as long as it is realized and recognized that the naturalist approaches them and studies them only objectively, leaving aside the question of their essence [1903, p, 14] [and that] the physiology of the higher nervous system of higher animals [read: psychology] can be successfully studied only if one completely renounces the indefinite formulations of psychology and stands wholly upon a pure objective ground [1904, p 135]

were surely ahead of their time and would no doubt have shocked Western and American experimental psychologists had they known or thought about them at that time. The psychologists were shocked by an almost identical declaration of Watson (1913), 10 years later.

Six paragraphs will suffice, it is hoped, to highlight the essence of what Pavlov had done and stimulated others to do in his wake.

1. To date, approximately 6,000 successful experiments involving the exact Pavlov paradigm of pairing unconditioned reflexes (or unlearned reactions) with to-be-conditioned stimuli have been reported. All kinds of organisms, from protozoa to men and from neonates (even fetuses) to most advanced seniles in both men and animals, and all kinds of reflexes (reactions) and stimuli have been used in the experiments. Moreover, the outcome of the Pavlov paradigm, conditioning, has been related experimentally to almost all known other organismic changes, either as the changes affect the conditioning or as conditioning affects the changes. To cite two of possible hundreds of examples: Data of eight experiments are available on the effects of "experimental clinical death" on conditioning, that is, on the fate of conditioned reflexes when an animal is experimentally put to death and then revived (Negovsky, 1954); and data of 82 experiments are at hand on the effect of ionizing radiation on conditioning (Piontkovsky, 1962). I found reports of conditioning experiments in 29 different languages, although the predominant majority is in Russian and English. (I am not familiar with Chinese

publications but learn from Russian sources that the Pavlov system is popular there; English reports of conditioning experiments in Japan are substantial in both number and quality.)

2. Early in his experimentation, Pavlov noted that conditioning is not just a fully quantitative but a highly parametric area of study. That is to say, the study was capable of yielding patterns of interrelated functional laws or generalizations and of suggesting related patterns of testable hypotheses for further laws or generalizations, on the basis of which a complete systematic discipline could be erected. And gradually Pavlov proceeded to formulate the generalizations and hypotheses, and erected the system. In the main Pavlov's formulations—although not necessarily his whole system— have been verified and accepted by students of the field all over the world. The 36 glossary terms attributed to Pavlov in the aforementioned recent standard American textbook on conditioning and learning represent, of course, such Pavlov formulations (more could be cited). No experiment or idea in psychology and related fields has ever been so fruitful as that launched by Pavlov in 1903. Most modern experimental psychology could simply not operate without Pavlov-discovered conditioning, extinction, generalization, differentiation, inhibition, disinhibition, spontaneous recovery, higher-order conditioning, sensory preconditioning, experimental neurosis, and the several varieties and subvarieties of each.

3. The high systematic fertility of conditioning data is, on the one hand, a function of the complete control of experimental variables—stimuli, reflexes, and their intensive and temporal relations—that the Pavlov paradigm permits and, on the other hand, is no doubt related to the most plausible assumption that the outcome of the paradigm, the conditioned reflex, is the simplest yet most basic unit, we might say, the lowest common denominator of all significant learning. As such, the paradigm has, in recent years, become the most serviceable means of attempting to unveil the true neural basis of learning through recently-discovered microelectrodic and biochemical techniques. The enterprise is surely one of the most challenging in our age and is also one in which contact between research in the East and West has been very close: Moscow 1958 Colloquium on Electroencephalography of Higher Nervous Activity (Jasper & Smirnov, 1960); 1958, 1959, and 1960 Macy Conferences on the Central Nervous System and Behavior (Brazier, 1958, 1959,

1960); 1959 Montevideo Conference on Brain Mechanism and Learning (Delafreshaye, 1961); 1961 New York Pavlovian Conference on Higher Nervous Activity (Kline, 1961); and the 1961 California Conference on Brain and Behavior (Brazier, 1961). Pavlov himself lived when the techniques of direct probing of brain action during conditioning were as yet unknown, but he had postulated a very special schema of such brain action. The schema had long been challenged for lack of direct evidence. Yet, modern direct research tends to demonstrate that, in the main, Pavlov guessed right (Brain, 1963).

4. While a system of psychology based wholly on conditioned reflexes would be expected, at least on the face of it, to be highly mechanistic and reductionistic and not draw basic distinction between animal and human learning, Pavlov had, in his later years, prevented his system from becoming so. In 1927, he wrote:

> Of course a word is for man as much a real conditioned stimulus as are other stimuli common to men and animals, yet at the same time it is so all-comprehending that it allows no quantitative or qualitative comparisons with conditioned stimuli in animals [1927a, p. 407, 1927b, p. 429]

which in 1932 and 1933 became:

> Speech, especially and, first of all, its kinesthetic stimuli going from the speech organs to the cortex are second signals, signals of signals, that are in essence abstractions of reality and means of generalization constituting our extra *uniquely human higher thought* [1932a, p. 1154]. In man there comes to be . . . another system of signalization, a signalization of the first system . . . a new principle of neural action is introduced [1933, p. 292].

This is the Pavlov "second-signal system" principle, setting off verbal conditioning or language acquisition in man from first-signal conditioning in men and animals, which, for reasons that need not be gone into here, had for years almost lain fallow in the Soviet Union but then spurted strikingly to give rise to hundreds of experiments on the distinctness of each of the systems and their interaction with each other. The principle is clearly broader than that of most American behaviorists for whom language either is a mediator operating essentially according to the laws of the reactions that it mediates or is merely a conditioned vocal reaction. Semantic conditioning—a conditioning-to-meaning type of verbal conditioning—which I first reported in 1939 (Razran, 1939, p. 89) has since been duplicated and extended by a number of experimenters in both the Soviet Union and this country (Razran, 1961).

5. As specified in his 1903 address, Pavlov was, to begin with, concerned with the relation of conditioning to psychopathology—an unusual concern and connection for that time. He continued his concern, and Shenger-Krestovnikova (1920) in his laboratory demonstrated empirically CR (conditioned reflex) produced experimental neurosis, a topic to which henceforward Pavlov devoted a large portion of his experimental research and thought, supplemented by frequent visits to mental clinics. (Of 6 published volumes of Pavlov's Wednesday Seminars, 3—1,716 pages— are reports of clinical demonstrations in which Pavlov participated.) He postulated the "clash" of excitation and inhibition as the general cause of psychological disturbances and "protective inhibition" as a corrective cure. And he assumed the existence of special psychopathological forms of neural action which, following N.E. Vvedensky (1852-1922), he termed "paradoxical," "ultra-paradoxical," "total-inhibitory," and "egalitarian," and which he investigated through behavioral unconditioned and conditioned manifestations. Bykov (1935, 1942, 1944, 1947, 1954) and Ayrapet'yants and Balakshina (1935) began in the early thirties a most stimulating series of experiments on interoceptive conditioning, which only now are beginning to be duplicated in American laboratories, and which by themselves exude most promising leads to a fully objective psychopathology and psychosomatics. Petrova (1925) was an early pioneer in drug and sleep therapy, while a number of Pavlov's other students have made both etiologic and therapeutic use of concepts based, respectively, on disturbances and corrections of interactions between the patients' first and second signal systems (Traugott, 1957, for a summary). Pavlovian psychology, indeed learning psychology in general, has become so replete with tempting interpretations of psychopathology that, unfortunately, a good deal of uncritical writing has come forward in the area, both in this country and in the Soviet Union. Yet there is no denying the worth and almost inevitable soundness of the approach, which in the Soviet Union is the only one in existence and in this country is gaining adherence in the face of competing

approaches—notably inveterate psychoanalysis (note also long-begun endeavors to synthesize Pavlov with the latter).

6. The many Pavlov-discovered empirical generalizations were found to hold, in the main, also for learning situations that differed from the exact Pavlov paradigm-notably the paradigms of Konorski and of Skinner—and to be, in general, of decisive merit as a basis of most American learned behavior or behavior-theory systems—a leading aspect of Pavlov's essence that will be discussed in some detail in a later section.

BEKHTEREV

A Pavlov-Sechenov system of higher nervous activity and psychology is, as may well be judged by now, a wholly complete enterprise. Yet we must also, to complete the account, mention Bekhterev. For one thing, Bekhterev, as a psychiatrist and experimental psychologist, expressed *some* objective views on psychiatry and psychology years before Pavlov entered the field, and as early as 1886 studied the effects of the ablation of a dog's motor cortex on what we call now operant conditioning: trained paw lifting. For another, Bekhterev added, in 1908, to Pavlov's paradigm of "appetitive" conditioning the technique of "aversive" conditioning through the use of electric shock as the unconditioned stimulus, a technique that, at least in this country, is the one most commonly used. Furthermore, Bekhterev summarized the field in a book 13 years before Pavlov did so. Finally, despite Bekhterev's neurology, his system was more behavioral and less neural than that of Pavlov; that is to say, his models were more of a stimulus-response than of a neural-mechanism type, and thus closer to those of American behaviorists. Space prevents further discussion.

EARLY, 1914-28, GENERAL INFLUENCES: BEKHTEREV-PAVLOV ON WATSON AND OTHERS

No Russian influence on American psychology, to speak of, may be discerned prior to 1914. Bekhterev's 610-page *Objective Psychology* was translated in 1913, and while both Bekhterev and Pavlov regularly published short reports of their work and views in German and French periodicals, these had not, presumably, reached

American psychologists. Indeed, even Pavlov's 1906 Thomas Huxley lecture published in English with its epitomic pronouncement that:

> the naturalist has no right to speak of higher animals' *psychic* processes without deserting the principles of natural science—which is the work of the human mind directed to nature through studies that derive their assumptions and interpretations from no other source than external nature itself [p. 911]

passed somehow unnoticed and unimpressing. Likewise, little impression apparently accrued to Yerkes and Morgulis' (1909) article which abstracted some of Pavlov's experiments but not his views. Thorndike's (1913) address as President of the American Psychological Association began with: "The theory of ideomotor action has been for a generation one of the stock 'laws' of orthodox psychology." Above all: Nothing Russian is mentioned in Watson's (1913) "Psychology as the Behaviorist Views It," the key and prime article of American behaviorism. Watson founded a system, unaware that one very much like it had existed in another country or culture for at least 10 years and for 50 years, if Sechenov is included.

Watson became, however, influenced—very much influenced—by the Russians in 1914, when, as he himself states, he read the 1913 translation of Bekhterev's book and seemingly also some of Pavlov's articles. Elected President of the American Psychological Association in 1915, the title of his presidential address was "The Place of the Conditioned Reflex in Psychology" and the address was surely one that must have filled Bekhterev and Pavlov with pride and a wish to adopt it as one of their own. The term "conditioned" was of course Pavlov's—Bekhterev used "association-reflex"—but the method of Watson's reported experiments was Bekhterev's shock technique—and Watson's main rationale of argumentation was also closer to Bekhterev than to Pavlov. As is known, Watson continued in his later writings to uphold the conditioned reflex as *the* ontological and methodological solution and the high pragmatic hope of all behavioristic psychology: the basic and ultimate unit of behaviorism's chief operational category, habit; the method destined to successfully replace all introspection; the means of training all phases of personality; and even the philosophy of a better and balanced society—indeed of all that is modifiable in men and animals. Nor was psychopathology overlooked. Watson's (1961a) article entitled

"Behavior and the Concept of Mental Disease" together with Wells' "Von Bechterew and Uebertragung" (Freud's "transference"), published in the same year in the same journal, and Watson's (1924) "The Unverbalized in Human Behavior," admittedly purported to supplant psychoanalysis. The much-publicized experiment on fear conditioning of 11-month-old Albert hardly needs mentioning, but it might be added that the kernel of Watson's famous doctrine of thinking as subvocal speech is fully evident in Sechenov's (1863) statement that:

> When a child thinks he invariably talks at the same time. Thought in five-year-olds is mediated through words or whispers, surely through movements of tongue and lips, which is also very frequently (perhaps always, but in different degrees) true of the thinking of adults [p. 498, also 1952, p. 104].

Concurrent with Watson, Burnham of Clark University in 1914 set Mateer, a doctoral student, to repeat the experiments of Krasnogorsky, a pupil of Pavlov, on food conditioning in school children. In 1916 Mateer (see 1918) was awarded the doctorate for her study which was published as a 239-page book. Burnham himself devoted his interest in the field to writing on the application of the conditioned reflex to mental hygiene which, after publication of several articles, culminated, in 1924, in a 702-page book, *The Normal Mind*. The book was one of five of the period—the other four being Watson's 1919 basic *Psychology from the Standpoint of a Behaviorist* and 1925 popular *Behaviorism*, Smith and Guthrie's 1921 *General Psychology in Terms of Behavior*, and Allport's 1924 *Social Psychology*—to highlight most comprehensively the use and value of the conditioned reflex as the all-explanatory behavioristic principle of almost all of psychology. And equally significant were, of course, the actual conditioned-reflex experiments—besides those of Watson and Mateer—of a number of American psychologists and some physiologists at the time. Hulsey Cason (1922, 1923, 1924) pioneered in the conditioning of the eyelid and pupillary reflexes and tellingly used Pavlovian principles in his criticisms of Thorndike's learning laws of "use" and "effect." Liddell (1926) established a first-rate conditioned reflex laboratory at Cornell and studied extensively the conditioning of sheep, goats, and pigs, duplicating, among other things, Pavlov-discovered experimental neurosis. Lang and Olmstead (1923) were the first Americans to study the neural pathways of conditioning, and Kleitman and Crisler (1927) demonstrated the conditioning of morphine-produced reactions. Mary Jones (1924) experimented with conditioned-reflex elimination of a conditioned fear in two 34-month-old boys, and her husband, H.E. Jones (1928) investigated the conditioning of galvanic skin reflexes in three 3-9 month old infants. Schlosberg (1928) was the first in this country to probe penetratingly the conditioning of the patellar reflex.

Two key statements come to mind in contemplating the American status of the Russians' conditioned reflex in the 1914-28 period. First, it is obvious that the status was high and influential; the idea was received with great enthusiasm, if not indeed with overenthusiasm. American psychology had by that time, presumably, worn thin its long-plied subjectivism and complexedness and was ready for simplicity and objectivity. Yet it continued to be swayed by its tradition of associationism. The conditioned reflex combined both objectivism and associationism—a rather effective blend of the new and the familiar in the dynamics of influence which, furthermore, reaped the benefit of such skillful advocates as Watson, Smith and Guthrie, Burnham, and Allport, and others. Second, however, there is the fact that the actual amount of American experimentation in the field was as yet very small—by 1928 not more than 6% of the Russian output—and it was in the main gross and corroborative and qualitative rather than critical and innovatory and quantitative. That is to say, American experimenters were occupied in the main with corroborating the mere possibility of conditioning and extinction and not with probing their exact quantitative parameters or criticizing or innovating Russian methods and views. Their interest centered, to put it somewhat differently, on the "law" of conditioning, and not on its "system-forming" pattern of interrelated laws—the Russians' preoccupation by that time. Presystem, the 1914-28 condition-reflex period in America, was, in truth, one of honeymoon credence and hope and essentially, unquestioning newly-attained contentment.

LATER, 1929-53, SYSTEMATIC PERIOD: PAVLOV'S INFLUENCE AND PAVLOV-AMERICAN DIVERGENCIES

Just as the 1913 translation of Bekhterev's (1913a, 1913b) book initiated the early American conditioned reflex period, so did the translations of Pavlov's (1927a, 1928) two books install the later period. The 1928 translation, by Gantt of Johns Hopkins University, was one of a collection of Pavlov's 1903-28 articles that, for the most part, had originally appeared in German or French, and some in English. The 1927 book was a systematic text of lectures delivered in 1924 and published in Russian and translated by Anrep of Oxford University into English in the same year. It should be made clear, however, at the outset that the systematic influence of Pavlov on American system makers of behavior in the later period came to pass not through their full acceptance but through their revision of his system. More exactly, each of the American systematists based his system on a core of findings reported in Pavlov's two books, and of course each core, and even more, each system differed from each other.

Eight Pavlov-influenced American systems of modifiable behavior—one or two not fully developed—may be said to exist. However, only three—those of Hull, Skinner, and Guthrie—are direct or primary Pavlov-influenced sytems, in the sense that they were rather fully put together a few years after the English translations of Pavlov's two books. The other five systems—those of Miller, Mowrer, Spence, Hebb, and Estes—emerged later and thus are in reality largely revisions of revisions of Pavlov—Miller, Mowrer, and Spence participating, indeed, originally in passing Pavlov through Hull's wringer. The revisions of revisions may arguably be truer than the revisions, yet the latter, the older three American systems, must obviously be the overriding concern here. The newer systems will, however, also be considered briefly, the system of Skinner being both old and new, dominated as it still is by his research and thought.

Hull

A Russian physiologist fully versed in the tenets of both old and new Pavlovianism would no doubt be strangely impressed perusing Hull's writings. Continually, the physiologist would encounter in the writings—almost all completely represented in the 1943 chief treatise, *Principles of Behavior*, and the 1952 somewhat modified and extended text, *A Behavior System*—familiar, although at times renamed, concepts and generalizations: extinction, internal inhibition (renamed reactive inhibition), conditioned inhibition, disinhibition, spontaneous recovery, irradiation (renamed generalization, in turn, not an unfamiliar term) of excitation and of inhibition, summation of conditioned reflexes (renamed summation of habit strengths), compounding of conditioned stimuli (renamed afferent stimulus interaction), higher- and particularly second-order conditioning, and others. He would also note that Hull's treatment and integration of the important intensive and temporal variables in conditioning are in essence no different from those of Pavlov (except for the allegation that the optimum interstimulus interval in conditioned-stimulus reception is invariably .45 second, with which no Russian and, by now, few Americans would agree). And the physiologist would be further pleased by Hull's frequent extollation of Pavlov's unique all-embracing contribution to the empirics and theory of behavior and his general consistent and Soviet-type physicalism as expressed, for instance, in his address as President of the American Psychological Association that:

> to recognize the existence of a phenomenon [consciousness] is not the same thing as insisting upon its basic, i.e., logical priority. Instead of furnishing a means for the solution of problems, consciousness appears to be itself a problem needing solution [Hull, 1937, p. 30].

Hull was not aware, of course, that this view of consciousness "as an existent but not as a prius" is official Soviet—not only Pavlov's but also Lenin's.

On the other hand, the Russian Pavlovian would—one may assume—be quite nonplused by a system that reduces, the way Hull does, all of psychology to an array of 17 postulates, 17 corollaries, and 132 theorems. How is it, he would question, that, of all organic sciences, psychology, the most complex and varied one, could through mere clever conceptualization become so fixed and geometrically deductive? More than that, he would be positively stunned by the system's host of mathematical equations and alleged new units of measurements—the wat, the hab, the mote, and the pav—which, incidentally, an American student of Hull called, respectively, "entirely programmatic [and] pseudo-mensurational [Koch, 1954, p. 54]." And the Pavlovian would surely disagree with Hull's general accordance of systematic priority to behavior over neurophysiology, and would take strong issue with his lumping together data and generalizations on rats and men, simple primordial reflexes and complex phyletically new verbal reactions. And, even more pointedly, he might argue against Hull's general philosophy of basing his system largely on Pavlov-discovered findings and generalizations, yet deducing the observable conditioned reflex from the inferred concept of "reinforcement"—an approach which, the Russian might say, places the cart of deduction before the horse of induction or makes the tail wag the dog; or that, following Hull fully, psychology forsakes introspectionism for another fruitless and, in essence, no less traditional pursuit: overwrought deductionistic rationalism.

Another way of framing the Pavlov-Hull differential would be to hinge it all on Hull's key postulate of primary reinforcement (1952, Postulate III in *A Behavior System*). That is to say, a Russian Pavlovian might well state that he objects in principle only to Hull's third postulate that association or conditioning cannot be effected without concomitant drive reduction which, according to Pavlov, is only an energizer (as is drive in general) but not a sine qua non to the CR. The verbal formulations of the remaining 16 postulates, all 17 corollaries, and 7 explanations of trial-and-error learning are, the Russian might continue, just clever rewrites or possible parallels or mere ancillary extensions—but not, in essence, at variance with what Pavlov found and said. Pavlovians are, to be sure, not the only ones who disagree with the third postulate. So do American behaviorists of systems other than that of Hull, and, in light of recent experimental evidence, a number of the postulate's original adherents have also given it up by now. Or simply, a Pavlovian might say: Let Hull drop his third postulate, forget his ambitious mathematics, remember that he has a nervous system, and he will be one of us.

Skinner

Our knowledgeable Pavlovian—that is, knowledgeable in Pavlov but not American lore—would, I believe, be first impressed by the abundance of what he would call "factual material," that is, empirical data, in Skinner's and his associates' (Ferster & Skinner, 1957; Skinner, 1938, 1959) studies. And he would fully approve the fact that Skinner, unlike Hull, culls his main data through one circumscribed technique and from one or two circumscribed bits of behavior, the Skinner box and its lever pressing and button pecking. Pavlov did so, too! Again, the Pavlovian would feel much more at home with Skinner's language (than with that of Hull), a data language that adheres closely to what it observes, induces rather than deduces—in vein of the aforementioned statement by Pavlov that naturalists must "derive their assumptions and interpretations from no other source than external nature itself." More than that, the Pavlovian would hold that Skinner-derived behavioral (or reflex) generalizations are—despite some differences in labels—Pavlov's or like Pavlov's, and he would welcome Skinner's own additional empirical generalizations in the area of schedules of reinforcement. In short, in the Russian's lore, Skinner would at first blush be viewed not as a "reviser" but an "expander" of Pavlov.

Further and closer perusal of Skinner's writings would, however, no doubt engender in the Pavlovian animadversions and even downright objections. He surely would thoroughly disagree with Skinner's detachment of the behavioral from the neural, the manifestations from the base, and would not be impressed by the thesis that the neural has no information significant to the analysis of behavior. He would say that it has and will have and, at any rate, must have. Science in general, he would posit, is not a parochial-segmental but a pyramidal-hierarchical enterprise involving "must" interrelations of underlying and overlying disciplines; and clearly, he would insist, neural action underlies behavioral action. Otherwise, he would continue, the result is at best transient technology rather than enduring basic-science search and solution. In like manner, the Pavlovian would be set against Skinner's special cloistering of what he calls operant reactions (or reflexes) and his seeming severance of them from their stimulus sources. This, too, he would argue, is convenient technology rather than complete science which by its very nature leaves no existents unturned. The Russians are not uninterested in some differentials among the conditioning of types of reactions—visceral, sensory, motor—but would eschew both Skinner's invariant finalistic dichotomy and the basis of the dichotomy—specificity of source of stimulation.

Moreover, Russians are likely to take issue with Skinner's bent to sunder operants' stimuli also on general philosophical grounds. A vacuum, they would philosophize or ideologize, is thereby created, drawing and domiciling ghostly nonphysicalistic—in their terms, idealistic—concepts and interpretations. Operant → spontaneous → voluntary, and there arises ideomotor action. Finally, Russians would animadvert on Skinner's neglect of the evolutionary and ecological factors in conditioning and his underemphasis of the internal organism's visceral conditioning, and would contend that even his system's claim of superiority in technological training and control of animal (and human) behavior is contraindicated by the high success of their Pavlov-guided circus training. (Some of their circus trainers such as M.E. Gerd are full-fledged research-minded professional psychologists.) In short, the Russians like what Skinner does but do not endorse a good deal of what he says. In the words of a Russian jingle: "I love you dearly pretty comet but do not care for your long tail."

Guthrie

From a Russian physiologist's standpoint, Guthrie's (1935, 1938) favorable role in American behaviorists' system making is that he in the main opposed what the Russians would have opposed—Hull's drive reduction, Skinner's respondent-operant dichotomy, and the West's and America's general propensity to view motivation as a fully segregated category high in psychology's totem pole of primary determinacy. Guthrie certainly had fought gallantly, and largely successfully, for his concept of contiguity which generally, although by no means specifically, is like Pavlov's. And in insisting that separate movements and not whole acts of an organism are the data of its modifiable behavior, he assumedly warded off the peril of the minions of teleologic infiltration. Still, the Russians are not likely to accord—indeed, do not accord—a high status to Guthrie and his system. Pavlov (1932) himself labeled Guthrie "insufficiently analytic" and "philosophical," and his pupils would no doubt now contend that he had overgeneralized from insufficient data, had used unquantified qualitative concepts, and paid only lip service to strict inductive experimentation.

Replacing the concept of "association of ideas" with "association of movements" does not in itself, contemporary Pavlovians would contend, build an empirical physicalistic science; the movements must obviously be specified and specifically observed and tested, if the concept is not to be merely one of ideas about movements. Indeed, they, like Pavlov, consider wholly untenable Guthrie's leading concept of movement-produced stimuli as the sine qua non of conditioning—a Russian position fully supported by recent American reports of Solomon and Turner (1962) on successful conditioning in curarized animals in which no such movements are produced. Likewise, the Russians would deny unique all-or-none import to Guthrie's concept of "recency," merely regarding it as one of a number of quantitative parameters, and would disclaim "one-trial learning" as an invariant empirical generalization.

Miller, Spence, and Mowrer

For almost 10 years Miller and his associates (Delgado, Roberts, & Miller, 1954) have been pioneering in probing the parameter value of intracranial stimulation in conditioned behavior, and they have for even a longer time, been more generally engaged in correlating physiological and behavioral variables in the area (Miller, 1957; Miller & Kessen, 1952), both of which are top desiderata in present-day Pavlovianism. To be sure, Miller has always strongly emphasized the role of motivation and drive reduction which in themselves are un-Pavlovian in tradition. Yet, inasmuch as since 1941 (Miller & Dollard, 1941), he has championed the conception of drive not as a state but as "any stimulus" that "is made strong enough" and has constantly sought the physiological—indeed even more specifically the Pavlov-sired visceral—base of motivation, his system is thus closer to Pavlov's than the system of his teacher Hull ever was (the Russians no doubt also welcome his conditioned-reflex inroad of psychoanalysis [Miller, 1948]). Indeed, since it may be further argued that while a good number of American theorists have gone overboard with their view of motivation which the Russians have hardly ever noticed, the Miller approach may become an advancing core of reverse influence, that is, of American experimental psychology influencing Pavlovian Russian physiology. And, interestingly, Miller's conceptualization of motivation is empirically and even theoretically strengthened by Russian studies of interoceptive stimulation.

To a lesser degree but still perceptibly, Spence's 1956 formal revision of Hull's system is, as he himself repeatedly declares, a considerable return to Pavlov, as is also his more recent (1963) acknowledgment of the role of cognitive parameters in conditioning which the Russians would subsume under the effects of the second-signal system. However, the logical-neurological differential between Spence and the Pavlovians is, I fear, a chasm that can hardly be crossed and is hardly bridgeable. On the other hand, Mowrer's two-factor system, which was 50% Pavlov in its original version, is in its recent revision (Mowrer, 1960) in a way 100% Pavlovian. Yet it is now couched in concepts, language, and depth psychology that, at least on the face of it, are at variance with present-day Russian philosophy or philosophy of science. Not unlikely, the Russians would term Mowrer a Spinoza-type or Santayana-type spiritualistic or romantic mechanist or naturalist.

Hebb and Estes

At least formally, the system of Hebb (1949) may be regarded as the most Pavlovian of all the American systems we have discussed. Like the system of Pavlov, its conceptualization is wholly in terms of neural action, its view of drive is that it is an "energizer" or "engine" rather than a "guide" or "steering gear," its concept of t superordination is easily derivable from studies of compound-stimulus conditioning, and, plainly, it is wholeheartedly contiguously associationistic. Indeed, inasmuch as the system came into being in 1949, in pre-Sputnik days, it may be said to have done a Pavlov-type job at a time when Russian and Pavlov prestige was at a low ebb, and the fact that the system has been rather successful in its brain-behavior stress would indicate that American experimental psychology was at the time ready for such a stress. Moreover, obvious differences between views of Hebb and Pavlov may be said to be more semantic than real, stemming from the Western-American difficult-to-correct assumption that the Russians' image of a reflex is, like theirs, one of a frog's-leg preparation and not of central organization. Yet Pavlov (1949b) was a steadfast votary of interdependent and even holistic interaction, often talked about and experimented with dynamic systems—for example, the dynamic stereotype—and once stated that

> of course behavior is not just a sum of reflexes [and a] system is of course not a sort of sack filled pell-mell with potatoes, apples, cucumbers, etc. [Volume 2, p. 564].

His present-day students, Anokhin, Asratyan, and Kogan, are surely not behind American and Western homologues in utilization of organizing principles. On the other hand, it is highly regrettable that Hebb has hardly made use of the rich empirical data and generalizations of Pavlovian experiments—much less than Hull and less than Skinner and even less than Guthrie—which leaves his system in the main in a qualitative state. By 1949, Pavlov's 1927 book must have lost its novelty and freshness to Hebb, while important post-Pavlovian developments were available only in Russian.

The crux of Estes' system (1950, 1959) is Guthrie's assumption of one-trial learning (or conditioning) and consequent view of repeated trials as samplings of stimulus units and response units. Pavlov noted one-trial learning in monkeys and even dogs more than once but certainly opposed one-trial learning as an invariant empirical generalization for conditioning in all organisms. Moreover, from a Pavlovian standpoint, conditioning is by no means a matter of sheer contiguity—a dynamic variety of temporal, intensive, and neural-state variables is always involved. Hence, Pavlovians would consider the Estes—and, for that matter, also the Bush and Mosteller—enterprise much oversimplified and limited. On the other hand, a 1962 Soviet conference on the Philosophical Problems of Higher Nervous Activity and of Psychology (Matyushkin & Sokhin, 1962) and in the same year a Conference on the Philosophical Problems of Cybernetics (Mayzel & Fatkin, 1962) came out strongly for utilization of cybernetics, information theory, and mathematical models in Pavlov's teachings. Some reports of neural modeling came to light even prior to the two conferences (Savinov, 1960; Skornyakov, 1960) and more models, neurobehavioral rather than just neural, may well be expected.

COMMON PAVLOV-AMERICAN DIVERGENCIES

What has been discussed so far pertained only to basic divergencies of individual American systems from the system of Pavlov but not to divergencies common to all American systems. Indeed, on the whole the indications were that individual American systems diverged more from each other than from Pavlov and surely that the mean inter-American system divergence was greater than the mean Pavlov-American divergence. True, Pavlov's invariant commitment to neural interpretations stood out as distinctive. But this same commitment equally marks the system of Hebb, and, as we have seen, Miller has become progressively involved in neurophysiological bases; and some neural modeling is affecting other Americans to some degree. Yet two Pavlovian areas of research and thought continue as almost exclusively Russian: one, almost wholly ignored by American experimentalists and theorists; the other, almost entirely unaccepted by Americans.

The ignored area—more strictly, several areas— is that of neurobehavioral induction (positive, negative, simultaneous, successive) and of protective inhibition and pathologic "paradoxical," "ultra-paradoxical," "equalizing," and "total-inhibitory" neurobehavioral states. Literally, hundreds of Russian experiments have been devoted to the study of each phase of this area and each phase has become an integral pillar of the total Pavlov theoretical structure. Yet I know of only one American student of conditioned behavior who has made significant and successful use of Pavlovian induction—David Williams, a former student of both Skinner at Harvard and Sheffield at Yale, who has been experimenting the last few years at the University of Pennsylvania in a self-established modern laboratory of salivary conditioning in dogs (Williams, 1963). And I know of no one utilizing importantly the other phases of the ignored area.

The unaccepted area is Pavlov's doctrine of types of nervous systems running counter to American experimentalists' and theorists' points of view. The doctrine is indeed all-embracing—a high and wide claim that individual differences in unconditioned and conditioned effector reactions (in recent years also electroencephalographic reactions) demonstrate that the nervous systems of men and animals fall into several genotypic types which come to be the most potent differentiating factors in all phases of living and behaving: from susceptibility to disease (and ionizing radiation) and life-span expectancies to work styles, motor deftness, modes of thinking, and, of course, temperament, personality, and emotional balance. It is rooted in Pavlov's pentapartite view of neural action—strength of excitation and strength of inhibition, mobility of each, and balance between each—which, too, needs confirmation. In the West, only Eysenck (1957) has used, full scale, Pavlov's cortical mechanisms in personality differentiation but he has by no means gone as far as Russian Pavlovians. The doctrine is surely far-flung, but originally so were a number of other views of Pavlov, since embraced and made fruitful. Besides, the particular doctrine is not integral to the main system—which is independent of its acceptance or rejection. Finally, it might also be mentioned that post-Pavlovian Russian experimental extensions of Pavlov's concept of the second-signal system are so far almost terra incognita in this country.

PARALLELS

Parallel simultaneous, or rather near-simultaneous, independent formulation of leading scientific ideas and principles by two or even more scientists in different countries or in the same country is of course not unknown in the history of science. What is, however, under consideration here is a special many-years-apart parallelism allied to a special language barrier that often characterizes American-Russian developmental relation in ideas, principles, and even total philosophies of psychology. It has, it is believed, been demonstrated here that the 1913 rise of Watson's School of Behaviorism—no doubt the most important event in the history of American scientific psychology—was independently developed yet closely paralleled by the 1903-04 emergence of the Russian school of Pavlov and Bekhterev. And a similar relation is evident in (a) Skinner's 1932 unorthodox—and un-Western and un-American—ubiquitous conceptualization of the reflex as any correlation between a stimulus and a response, which was preceded, unknown to him, in 1863 by Sechenov's even more ubiquitous doctrine; and (b) Watson's 1920 well-publicized view of thinking as subvocal speech which, too, as was noted earlier, was largely voiced by Sechenov in 1863.

Again, in 1950, Harlow began to develop the fruitful view that food and noxious stimulation are not the only unlearned bases of animal learning but that, at least in monkeys, curiosity and manipulation are equally potent drives or unconditioned agents. Yet Pavlov (1949b, Vol. 1, p. 77, Vol. 2, pp. 68, 166), according to his Wednesday Seminars, had already in 1933 strongly emphasized the prepotency of investigatory and manipulatory reflexes in primates, for example, "Rosa's most distinctly selfless and purest curiosity." Voytonis (1949) and N.N. Ladygina-Kohts (1959), to mention only two Russian names, used and elaborated the concept in a series of experiments in the late thirties and early middle forties. Pavlov's Wednesday Seminars are untranslated and appeared in printed form in Russian only in 1949. Voytonis' 270-page book, *Prehistory of Intellect,* was published in 1949; Ladygina-Kohts' 400-page book, *Constructive and Tool-Using Activity of Higher Apes,* came out in 1960. Neither has been translated. Space permits mentioning—bare mentioning—of only three other specific examples of such parallel evolvings: (a) In 1939, Brogden reported an experiment on what he called "sensory preconditioning" which since has been verified by himself and others and used importantly in general conditioned-reflex theory in this country. In the Soviet Union, Narbutovich and Podkopayev (1936) published a report of exactly the same type of experiment which they named "associative conditioning," and it, too, was replicated many times and utilized in CR theorizations (Pavlov, 1949b, Vol. 2, pp. 213-214, discussed fully the experiments and their implications in a January 31, 1934, Wednesday Seminar). But there is no evidence that the experimenters and theorists of the two countries know even now of each other's existence and indeed of the existence of two terms for the same phenomenon. (*b*) Recent American results on learning sets and habit reversals closely parallel Russian findings on compound-stimulus conditioning and "transwitching"—and, again, so far there is no inkling of any interpenetration of information. (*c*) The highly important modern technique of single-cell microelectrode recording in brain tissue was perfected in Gerard's laboratory in the University of Chicago (Gerard & Graham, 1942) wholly independently of its use by Kogan in the University of Roston-on-Don in a 1934 report (Kogan, 1949).

To be sure, since Sputnik, a strong attempt to reduce the language barrier has been made through Russian-English translations. Yet I note with regret that the cover-to-cover translations of the *Pavlov Journal of Higher Nervous Activity* and of the *Sechenov Physiological Journal of the USSR* were suspended last year.

CURRENT STATUS AND INTERACTION AND LOOK INTO THE FUTURE

I shall begin the last section of this article with a simple statement: Pavlov's influence on current, from 1954 on, American experimental psychology is substantially greater than it was in the 1929-53 period. The statement must immediately be qualified as "Pavlov's *direct* influence" and further specified as: Both Pavlov-type thinking and Pavlov-type experimenting are definitely on the increase in this country. "Pavlov-type thinking" has particular reference to waning "Pavlov-through-Hull type of thinking" and "Pavlov-type experimenting" denotes specific growth vis-à-vis "Skinner-type experimenting."

Put differently, I might say that there is unmistakable evidence that current American psychology is gradually moving away from both the radical logical-deductive "explanationism" of Hull and the radical no-neurophysiology "descriptionism" of Skinner, and is turning to the old-fashioned conservative "behavior-description-neurophysiology-explanation" of Pavlov. Several developments combined to shake loose, if not wholly stub, American psychology's one-time inveterate and lordly fort of Hullian logical deductionism. We might mention, first, its own Dinosauric weight as pointed out by Koch as early as 1954, and its apparent intrinsic contradiction as evidenced in the somewhat amusing mirror image or reverse view of the role of reinforcement in the two-factor systems of earlier Mowrer and Spence. Second, the fort was battered, rather continually and at times mercilessly, by findings and views of American experimentalists and theorists of systems other than Hull's and by those having no system or nonaligned systems. Third—which is of particular concern here—Hull's "logicalism" appears to have been corroding all along in contact with Pavlov's "empiricism," which assumed prestigious proportions in post-Sputnik time.

The etiology of the retrogradation of earlier antegrading no-brain descriptionism seems even more readily discernible. Plainly, it is rooted in the spectacular, relatively recent, discoveries of relatable-to-conditioning electroencephalographic, partly also neurochemical, techniques, which not only have stimulated the thoughts and research interests of a number of most active American experimental psychologists but also have drawn strongly to the field once-uninterested American neurophysiologists who—it might be added and as might be expected—have always better "understood" Pavlov than Hull and even Skinner. The fact is that brain-behavior conditioning has become—and is further becoming—an area of almost elite research in both experimental psychology and neurophysiology in this country—indeed one that seems to be bridging the gap between elites in the two disciplines.

As such, the current period may be designated as a time of considerable rapprochement and interaction between American experimental psychology and Russian physiology—or, more strictly, between American experimental psychology that is in the process of becoming largely an experimental physiological psychology and Russian physiology and pathophysiology of higher nervous activity. For brain-behavioral conditioning had always been Pavlov's unswerving motto. And even if, during Pavlov's life, the motto had been only a program and a conceptual system, it clearly became, with the first discovery of appropriate technique, a fully empirical discipline of actual probing and juxtaposition of two physicalistic universes, to which the Russians dedicated themselves before we did and which they uphold more than we do. No report of conditioning seems to attain full status in present-day Russia, if it is not accompanied by analysis of correlative neurophysiological changes. It is called "grubo"—coarse (incomplete), if the inquiry is only behavioral. And concurrently, another rapprochement and interaction came into being in the wake of the Pavlov-American one, a native rapprochement and interaction between American experimental psychologists and American neurophysiologists—which in his own country Pavlov succeeded in inducting at the very launching of his physiology-psychology career.

Several specific examples are needed to demonstrate more concretely the increasing Russo-American or Pavlov-American interaction in basic behavioral research and thought. C.M. Schuster and J.V. Brady (1964) have just completed a study in monkeys combining Bykov's and Ayrapet'yants interoceptive conditioning with Skinner's lever pressing. Their results are highly instructive in bringing to light experimentally the subtle yet potent effects of internal states as stimulus controls of operant behavior, and are likely to inaugurate a new field of study which followers of Skinner have heretofore missed or ignored. Killam and John (1959) replicated and extended Livanov and Polyakov's (1945) and Livanov, Korolkova, and Frenkel's (1951) pioneer finding of conditioning as an "assimilation of rhythm." And John (1962), familiarizing himself with Russian work and views, particularly with those of Rusinov, has elaborated a psychophysiology of mind in terms of Ukhtomsky's "dominance" (1925), which in relation to conditioning I argued as early as 1930. Grings (1960) and Miller (1961) have, each in his own way, used Anokhin's (1957, 1961) theory of "reverse afferentation" —sometimes called by him "acceptor-action system"—in the theoretical integration of their empirical data. Four most modern laboratories of salivary conditioning in animals have in recent years been founded in this country (after a delay of more than half a century; my own experiments were with human subjects): by Sheffield (original founder), Lauer, Williams, and Schapiro, at the Universities of Yale, Indiana, Pennsylvania, and Houston, respectively. The empirical data of these laboratories reported at a 1963 National Science Foundation sponsored Symposium on Classical Conditioning were most consistent from laboratory to laboratory, more consistent, indeed, than any conditioning data with which I am familiar.

On the other hand, Russian Pavlovians are certainly interested in the work and views of American experimental psychologists and neurophysiologists. I have already mentioned the conference on electroencephalography and higher nervous activity in Moscow in 1958, the honorary presidents of which were Beritashvili (Beritov) of Tbilisi and Jasper of Montreal. Recently Stevens' (1963) 1,436-page *Handbook of Experimental Psychology* was translated into Russian, as were also translated earlier, Woodworth's (1950) *Experimental Psychology*, Magoun's *The Waking Brain* (1961), and several other treatises (Brillouin, 1960; Eccles, 1959; Goldman, 1957) in the area. Again, as already indicated, the Russians are all set to follow American leads in the field of mathematical models, information theory, and cybernetics. The books of Wiener (1958), Shannon (1959), Ashby (1959, 1962), Woodward (1955)—in fact, almost all non-Russian publications—have been translated into Russian. A periodical "Problemy Kibernetiki" (Problems of Cybernetics), edited by A.A. Lyapunov and begun in 1958, and several Russian books in the area appeared: for example, *Theory of Transmission of Information* (Kolmogorov, 1956), *Probability and Information* (Yaglom & Yaglom, 1960), and *Information and Vision* (Glezer & Tsukerman, 1961). For reasons that need not be discussed here, Russian Pavlovians have in the past made little use of the probability mathematics and other mathematics in which their countrymen are so prominent. But they are doing so now, and some interesting developments may be expected in the near future—indeed some significant contributions are already at hand.

Perhaps the most cogent specific systematic example of Pavlov resurgence in current American experimental and theoretical psychology is the recent metamorphosis of this psychology's regnant concept of reinforcement. At one time, the concept enjoyed a truly unquestioned omnipresent and omnipotent status in the systems of both Hull and Skinner. To Hull, reinforcement was almost an Aristotelian first or formal cause, immanently explanatory, from which, as was already noted, he had formally deduced conditioning. To Skinner, reinforcement is in a way even more immanent since he equates the term wholly with "what reinforces" and wants no explanation. With apologies for a bit of word play, I am tempted to say that Skinner extends Sir William Hamilton's agnosticism in the "philosophy of the unconditioned" to an agnosticism in the "philosophy of the conditioned," and to allege further that Skinner's positivism—as all positivism—is so much like the Wisdom of Sirach who long ago (circa 200 B.C.) counseled "not to want to investigate what is beyond one's strength [as] one has no need for things that are hidden."

Yet, it is quite clear that present-day American investigators do want to seek what is hidden "beyond reinforcement," eschew its mere Aristotelian or agnostic formulation, and seemingly think that what Hull was quoted earlier to have said about consciousness holds for reinforcement—namely, that "Instead of furnishing a means for the solution of problems . . . it appears to be itself a problem needing solution." The search for a solution almost inevitably leads to a Pavlov-like view of contiguity—uncovering (a) the hidden but true nature of both the contiguously paired reinforcing and reinforced and the contiguously paired unconditioned and conditioned changes in respective operant-instrumental and classical learning situations, and (b) the hidden but true nature of the relation of the reinforcing to the reinforced, the unconditioned to the conditioned, the reinforcing to the unconditioned, and the reinforced to the conditioned changes. True, the results of the mission are still very far from conclusive, and the search is really just beginning. Yet the attempt at the new and the discontent with the old have already proven most stimulating and refreshing and, interestingly, related to current Russian efforts in the same direction. Sheffield and Roby (1950) and later Premak (1959, 1962) have thoughtfully put forward the synthesizing concept of "prepotent reactions," which in essence is similar to Ukhtomsky's (1925) "theory of dominance" that I, as already noted, connected years ago with conditioning and recently reformulated and linked with Beritov's (1932, 1960, 1961) hypothesis of differentials in two-way conditioned connections (Razran, 1964). And then in 1962 there appeared Galambos' comprehensive brain-behavior analysis of the area and his most intriguing finding of a neural differential in Type I and Type II conditioning (Konorski's term for classical and instrumental). As said, there are beginnings.

Final Statement

American experimental and theoretical psychology has witnessed in recent years a high rise of a movement—or school or system—that might be described as brain behaviorism,[2] challenging existing and

[2] Essentially non-Pavlovian, the significant influence of Lashley's brain-behavior orientation is, for lack of space, not considered in the present article. Nor, it will be noted, has mention been made here of the admixed Pavlovian and un-Pavlovian system of Tolman. Analysis of either vis-à-vis Pavlov is a chapter by itself.

extant neobehaviorism. Both brain behaviorism and neobehaviorism draw their main logical premises and empirical generalization from Pavlov-founded higher nervous activity. But brain behaviorism is closer to Pavlov—particularly to current Russian Pavlovians—in resting its developing school or system on correlations of behavioral and neurophysiological data and in its thesis that "no-brain" behaviorism is an incomplete science leading to illusory self-containment and self-contentment and would-be autochthony and exclusiveness unenjoyed by other sciences: mere linguistic lifting-by-one's bootstraps' solution of problems. Experimentally, brain behaviorism is continually bolstered by rapidly increasing evidence on brain-behavior relations (Chow, 1961; Deutsch, 1962; Galambos & Morgan, 1960; Glaser, 1963; John, 1961; Morrell, 1961; Rusinov & Rabinovich, 1958) made possible through continuous improvement and discovery of instrumental techniques of brain recordings. And as such, it is further more linked than is neobehaviorism to other exact sciences whose advancement, too, is largely a matter of instrumentation, and is more truly and more unswervingly physicalistic than is neobehaviorism.

Put differently, one might say that the system of brain behaviorism fully approves behaviorism's passing from an SR, stimulus-response, psychology to an S-O-R, stimulus-organism-response, one. But it insists that the matrix of the organism's parameters must to the widest extent possible be rooted in present-day knowledge of neural and visceral action and not just be—particularly, forever be—an independent realm of inferred logical constructs. Pavlov's earlier-quoted statement that the natural scientist must gather "his assumptions and interpretations of nature from no sources other than external nature itself" does not mean external to the organism, whose external and internal environments are coeval and inseparable. And, Sechenov, too, was right when, 100 years ago, he equated behaviorally the psychic and the central neural.

REFERENCES

Allport, F.H. *Social psychology*. Boston: Houghton Mifflin, 1924.

Anokhin, P.K. New data on characteristics of the afferent mechanisms in conditioned reflexes. In B.G. Anan'yev (Ed.), *Materials of conference on psychology*. Moscow: Akademiya Pedagogicheskikh Nauk, 1957.

Anokhin, P.K. New conceptions of the physiological architecture of the conditioned reflex. In J.F. Delafreshaye (Ed.), *Brain mechanisms and learning*. Springfield, Ill.: Charles C. Thomas, 1961.

Ashby, W.R. *Vvedeniye v. kibernetiku.* [Introduction to cybernetics.] Moscow: Foreign Literature, 1959.

Ashby, W.R. *Konstruktsiya mozga.* [Design for a brain.] Moscow: Foreign Literature, 1962.

Asratyan, E.A. The physiology of temporary connections. In K.M. Bykov, A.G. Ivanov-Smolensky, & E. Sh. Ayrapet'yants (Eds.), *Transactions of the 15th Conference on Problems of Higher Nervous Activity Dedicated to the 50th Anniversary of the Teachings of Academician I.P. Pavlov on Conditioned Reflexes.* Moscow-Leningrad: Akademiya Nauk SSSR, 1952.

Ayrapet'yants, E. Sh. *Higher nervous function and the receptors of internal organs.* Moscow: Akademiya Nauk SSSR, 1952.

Ayrapet'yants, E. Sh., & Balakshina, V.L. Interoceptive conditioned connections. *Trudy Leningradskogo Obshchestva Estestvoispytateley,* 1935, 64(3), 429-443.

Bekhterev, V.M. Objective psychology and its subject-matter. *Vestnik Psikhologii,* 1904, No. 9, 650-666, 721-737.

Bekhterev, V.M. *Objective psychology.* St. Petersburg: Soikin, 1907-10.

Bekhterev, V.M. *Objektive Psychologie oder Psychoreflexologie: Die Lehre von den Associations-Reflexen.* Leipzig-Berlin: Teubner, 1913. (a)

Bekhterev, V.M. *La psychologie objective.* Paris: Alcan, 1913. (b)

Bekhterev, V.M. *General principles of reflexology.* Moscow: GIZ, 1917.

Bekhterev, V.M. *Collective reflexology.* Moscow: GIZ, 1921.

Bekhterev, V.M. *General principles of human reflexology.* Moscow: GIZ, 1923.

Beritov, I.S. *Individually-acquired activity of the central nervous system.* Tbilisi: GIZ, 1932.

Beritov, I.S. Morphological and physiological bases of mechanisms of temporary connections. In I.S. Beritov (Ed.), *Third Gagry Colloquium: Mechanisms of development of temporary nervous connections.* Tbilisi: GSSR Akademiya Nauk, 1960. Pp. 43-81.

Beritov, I.S. *Neural mechanisms of the behavior of higher vertebrates.* Moscow: Akademiya Nauk SSSR, 1961.

Boring, E.G. *A history of experimental psychology.* (2nd ed.) New York: Appleton-Century-Crofts, 1950.

Brain, W.R. Some reflections on brain and mind. *Brain,* 1963, 86(3), 381-401.

Brazier, M.A.B. (Ed.) *Central nervous system and behavior.* New York: Josiah Macy, Jr. Foundation, 1958.

Brazier, M.A.B. (Ed.) *Central nervous system and behavior.* New York: Josiah Macy, Jr. Foundation, 1959.

Brazier, M.A.B. (Ed.) *Central nervous system and behavior.* New York: Josiah Macy, Jr. Foundation, 1960.

Brazier, M.A.B. *Brain and behavior.* Washington, D.C.: American Institute of Biology and Science, 1961.

Brillouin, L. *Nauka i teoriya informatsii.* [Science and information theory.] Moscow: Foreign Literature, 1960.

Brogden, W.J. Sensory pre-conditioning. *Journal of Experimental Psychology,* 1939, 25, 323-332.

Budilova, E.A. *Struggle of materialism and idealism in Russian science of psychology.* Moscow: Akademiya Nauk SSSR, 1960.

Burnham, W.H. *The normal mind.* New York: Appleton-Century-Crofts, 1924.

Bykov, K.M. The formation of temporary connections to interoceptive stimuli. In A.V. Leontovich (Ed.), *Problemy biologii i meditsiny.* Moscow: Biomedgiz, 1935. Pp. 73-77.

Bykov, K.M. *The cerebral cortex and the internal organs.* Moscow: VMMA, 1942; Medgiz, 1944, 1947, 1954.

Cason, H. The conditioned pupillary reaction. *Journal of Experimental Psychology,* 1922, 5, 108-146.

Cason, H. The conditioned eyelid reaction. *Journal of Experimental Psychology,* 1923, 5, 153-196.

Cason, H. Criticisms of the laws of exercise and effect. *Psychological Review,* 1924, 31, 397-418.

Chow, K.L. Brain functions. *Annual Review of Psychology,* 1961, 12, 281-310.

Delafreshaye, J.F. (Ed.) *Brain mechanisms and learning.* Springfield, Ill.: Charles C. Thomas, 1961.

Delgado, J.M.R., Roberts, W.W., & Miller, N.E. Learning motivated by electrical stimulation of the brain. *American Journal of Physiology,* 1954, 179, 587-593.

Deutsch, J.A. High nervous function: The physiological bases of memory. *Annual Review of Physiology,* 1962, 23, 259-271.

Dostoyevsky, F.M. *Letters.* Vol. 3. Moscow: GIZ, 1928.

Eccles, J.C. *Fiziologiya nervnykh kletok.* [The physiology of nerve cells.] Moscow: Foreign Literature, 1959.

Estes, W.K. Toward a statistical theory of learning. *Psychological Review,* 1950, 57, 94-107.

Estes, W.K. Component and pattern models with Markovian interpretations. In R.R. Bush & W.K. Estes (Eds.), *Studies in mathematical learning theory.* Stanford: Stanford Univer. Press, 1959. Pp. 9-52.

Eysenck, H.J. *Hysteria, an experimental application of modern learning theory to the dynamics of anxiety and psychiatry.* New York: Praeger, 1957.

Ferster, C.B., & Skinner, B.F. *Schedules of reinforcement.* New York: Appleton-Century-Crofts, 1957.

Galambos, R., & Morgan, C.T. The neural basis of learning. In J. Field (Ed.), *Handbook of physiology:* I. *Neurophysiology.* Vol. 3. Washington, D.C.: American Physiological Society, 1960. Pp. 1471-1499.

Galambos, R., & Sheatz, G.S. An electroencephalographic study of classical conditioning. *American Journal of Physiology,* 1962, 203, 173-184.

Gerard, R.W., & Graham, J.Excitation and membrane potentials of single muscle fibers. *Federation Proceedings,* 1942, 1, 29.

Glaser, G.H. (Ed.) *EEG and behavior.* New York: Basic Books, 1963.

Glezer, V.O., & Tsukerman, I.I. *Information and vision.* Moscow: Akademiya Nauk SSSR, 1961.

Goldman, S. *Teoriya informatsii.* [Information theory.] Moscow: Foreign Literature, 1957.

Grings, W.W. Preparatory set variables in the classical conditioning of autonomic variables. *Psychological Review,* 1960, 67, 242-252.

Guthrie, E.R. *Psychology of learning.* New York: Harper, 1935.

Guthrie, E.R. *The psychology of human conflict.* New York: Harper, 1938.

Harlow, H.F., Harlow, M.K., & Meyer, D.K. Learning motivated by a manipulation drive. *Journal of Experimental Psychology*, 1950, **40**, 228-234.

Hebb, D.O. *The organization of behavior: A neuropsychological theory*. New York: Wiley, 1949.

Hull, C.L. Mind, mechanism and adaptive behavior. *Psychological Review*, 1937, **44**, 1-32.

Hull, C.L. *Principles of behavior*. New York: Appleton-Century-Crofts, 1943.

Hull, C.L. *A behavior system*. New Haven: Yale Univer. Press, 1952.

Jasper, H.H., & Smirnov, G.D. The Moscow Colloquium on Electroencephalography of Higher Nervous Activity. *Electroencephalography and Clinical Neurophysiology Supplement*, 1960, No. 13.

John, E.R. High nervous function: Brain function and learning. *Annual Review of Physiology*, 1961, **23**, 451-484.

John, E.R. Psychophysiology of mind. In J.H. Scher (Ed.), *Theories of mind*. New York: Free Press of Glencoe, 1962. Pp. 80-121.

Jones, H.E. Conditioned psychogalvanic responses in children. *Psychological Bulletin*, 1928, **25**, 183.

Jones, Mary. The elimination of children's fears. *Journal of Experimental Psychology*, 1924, **7**, 382-390.

Killam, K.F., & John, E.R. Electrophysiological correlates of avoidance conditioning in the cat. *Journal of Pharmacology and Experimental Therapeutics*, 1959, **125**, 252-274.

Kimble, G. *Hilgard and Marquis' conditioning and learning*. New York: Appleton-Century-Crofts, 1961.

Kleitman, N., & Crisler, G. Quantitative study of salivary conditioned reflex. *American Journal of Physiology*, 1927, **79**, 571-614.

Kline, N. (Ed.) Pavlovian Conference on Higher Nervous Activity. *Annals of the New York Academy of Sciences*, 1961, **92**, 813-1198.

Koch, S. C.L. Hull. In W.K. Estes, S. Koch, K. MacCorquodale, P.E. Meehl, C.G. Mueller, W.N. Schoenfeld, & W.S. Verplanck, *Modern learning theory*. New York: Appleton-Century-Crofts, 1954. Pp. 1-176.

Kogan, A.B. 1934 Report to Rostov Section of Soviet Society of Physiologists and Biochemists. Cited in, *Electrophysiological investigation of the central mechanisms of some complex reflexes*. Moscow: Akademiya Meditsinskikh Nauk SSSR, 1949.

Kolmogorov, A.N. *Theory of transmission of information*. Moscow: Akademiya Nauk SSSR, 1956.

Konorski, J. *Conditioned reflexes and neuron organization*. New York: Cambridge Univer. Press, 1948.

Ladygina-Kohts, N.N. *Constructive and tool-using activities of higher apes (chimpanzee)*. Moscow: Akademiya Nauk SSSR, 1959.

Lang, J., & Olmstead, J.M.D. Conditioned reflexes and pathways in the spinal cord. *American Journal of Physiology*, 1923, **65**, 603-611.

Liddell, H.S. A laboratory for the study of conditioned motor reflexes. *American Journal of Psychology*, 1926, **37**, 418-419.

Livanov, M.N., Korolkova, I.A., & Frenkel, G.M. Electrophysiological studies of higher nervous activity. *Zhurnal Vysshey Nervnoy Deyatel'nosti imeni I.P. Pavlova*, 1951, 1, 521-538.

Livanov, M.N., & Polyakov, K.L. Electrical processes in the cerebral cortex of a rabbit during the formation of a conditioned defense reflex to a rhythmic stimulus. *Vestnik Akademiya Nauk SSSR, Seriya Biologicheskaya*, 1945, **3**, 286-307.

Magoun, H.W. *Bodrstvuyuschy mozg.* [The waking brain.] Moscow: Foreign Literature, 1961.

Mateer, Florence. *Child behavior, a critical and experimental study of young children by the method of conditioned reflexes.* Boston, Mass.: Badger, 1918.

Matyushkin, A.M., & Sokhin, F.A. All-Union Conference on Philosophical Problems of the Physiology of Higher Nervous Activity and of Psychology. *Voprosy Psikhologii*, 1962, No. 4, 117-182.

Mayzel', N.I., & Fatkin, L.V. The Conference on Philosophical Problems of Cybernetics. *Voprosy Psikhologii*, 1962, No. 5, 184-189.

Miller, N.E. Theory and experiment relating psychoanalytic displacement to stimulus-response generalization. *Journal of Abnormal and Social Psychology*, 1948, **43**, 155-178.

Miller, N.E. Experiments on motivation. *Science*, 1957, **126**, 1271-1278.

Miller, N.E. A study of the physiological mechanism of motivation. *Voprosy Psikhologii*, 1961, No. 4, 143-156.

Miller, N.E., & Dollard, J.C. *Social learning and imitation.* New Haven: Yale Univer. Press, 1941.

Miller, N.E., & Kessen, M.L. Reward effects of food via stomach fistula compared with those of food via mouth. *Journal of Comparative and Physiological Psychology*, 1952, **45**, 555-564.

Morrell, E. Electrophysiological contributions to the neural basis of learning. *Physiological Review*, 1961, **41**, 443-494.

Mowrer, O.H. *Learning theory and behavior.* New York: Wiley, 1960.

Narbutovich, I.O., & Podkopayev, N.A. The conditioned reflex as an association. *Trudy Fiziologicheskikh Laboratorii imeni I.P. Pavlova*, 1936, **6**(2), 5-25.

Negovsky, V.A. *Pathophysiology and therapy of agonia and clinical death.* Moscow: Medgiz, 1954.

Pavlov, I.P. Psychologie et psychopathologie animale expérimentale. *Compte Rendu du Congrès International de Médicin, Madrid*, 1903.

Pavlov, I.P. Sur la secretion psychique des glandes salivaire (phenomènes nerveux complexes dans le travail de glandes salivaires). *Archives Internationales de Physiologie*, 1904, **1**, 119-135.

Pavlov, I.P. Scientific study of so-called psychical processes of higher animals. *Lancet*, 1906, **84**(2), 911-915. (*Science*, 1906, **24**, 613-619.)

Pavlov, I.P. Objective study of higher nervous activity of animals. *Russkiye Vedomosti*, 1913, No. 71, 188-198.

Pavlov, I.P. *Twenty years of objective study of higher nervous activity (behavior) of animals.* Moscow: GIZ, 1923.

Pavlov, I.P. *Conditioned reflexes: An investigation of the physiological activity of the cerebral cortex.* (Trans. by G.V. Anrep) London: Oxford Univer. Press, 1927. (a)

Pavlov, I.P. *Lectures on work of large cerebral hemispheres.* Moscow-Leningrad: Akademiya Nauk SSSR, 1927. (b)

Pavlov, I.P. *Lectures on conditioned reflexes: Twenty-five years of objective study of higher nervous activity (behavior) of animals.* (Trans. by W.H. Gantt) New York: Liveright, 1928.

Pavlov, I.P. The physiology of higher nervous activity. *Priroda*, 1932, 1139-1154. (a)

Pavlov, I.P. The reply of a physiologist to psychologists. *Psychological Review*, 1932, **39**, 91-127. (b)

Pavlov, I.P. Essai d'une interpretation physiologique de l'hysterie. *Encéphale*, 1933, **28**, 285-295.

Pavlov, I.P. *Complete works.* Moscow-Leningrad: Akademiya Nauk SSSR, 1949. 5 vols. (a)

Pavlov, I.P. *Pavlov's Wednesdays.* Moscow: Akademiya Nauk SSSR, 1949. 3 vols. (b)

Pavlov, I.P. *Pavlov's clinical Wednesdays.* Moscow-Leningrad: Akademiya Nauk SSSR, 1954-57. 3 vols.

Petrova, M.K. Curing experimental neuroses in dogs. *Arkhiv Biologicheskikh Nauk*, 1925, **35**, 3-16.

Piontkovsky, E.A. (Ed.) Problems of neuroradiology. *Trudy Instituta Vysshey Nervnoy Deyatel'nosti, Seriya Patofiziologicheskaya*, 1962, **10**, 1-200.

Premak, D. Towards empirical behavior laws: I. Positive reinforcement. *Psychological Review*, 1959, **66**, 219-230.

Premak, D. Reversibility of the reinforcement relation. *Science*, 1962, **136**, 255-257.

Razran, G. Theory of conditioning and related phenomena. *Psychological Review*, 1930, **37**, 25-43.

Razran, G. A quantitative study of meaning by a conditioned salivary technique (semantic conditioning). *Science*, 1939, **90**, 89-90.

Razran, G. The observable unconscious and inferable conscious in current Soviet psychophysiology: Interoceptive conditioning, semantic conditioning, and the orienting reflex. *Psychological Review*, 1961, **68**, 81-147.

Razran, G. Evolutionary psychology: Learning—and perception and thinking. In E. Nagel & B. Wolman (Eds.), *Scientific psychology: Principles and approaches.* New York: Basic Books, 1964.

Rubinshteyn, S.L. The psychological views of I.M. Sechenov and Soviet psychological science. In, *I.M. Sechenov and materialistic psychology.* Moscow: Akademiya Nauk SSSR, 1957.

Rusinov, V. S., & Rabinovich, M. Y. Electroencephalographic researches in the laboratories and clinics of the Soviet Union. *Electroencephalography and Clinical Neurophysiology*, 1958, Suppl. No. 8(1, entire issue).

Saltykov-Shchedrin, M. E. *Unfinished conversations.* St. Petersburg: Marks, 1900.

Savinov, G. V. Electrical modeling of homeostatic systems. *Problemy Kibernetiki*, 1960, **4**, 37-44.

Schlosberg, H. A study of the conditioned patellar reflex. *Journal of Experimental Psychology*, 1928, **11**, 468-494.

Schuster, C. R., & Brady, J. V. The discriminative control of a food reinforced operant by interoceptive stimulation. *Zhurnal Vysshey Nervnoy Deyatel'nosti imeni I. P. Pavlova*, 1964, **14**, 448-458.

Sechenov, I.M. Reflexes of the brain. *Meditsinskiy Vestnik*, 1863, 3, 461-484, 493-512.

Sechenov, I.M. *The physiology of sense organs.* St. Petersburg: Glovachev Printing House, 1867.

Sechenov, I.M. *Psychological studies.* St. Petersburg: Sushchinksy Printing House, 1873. (a)

Sechenov, I.M. By whom and how should psychology be studied? In, *Psychological studies.* St. Petersburg: Sushchinksy Printing House, 1873. (b)

Sechenov, I.M. Elements of thought. *Vestnik Yevropy*, 1878, No. 2, 39-107, 457-533.

Sechenov, I.M. The doctrine of the un-freedom of the will. *Vestnik Yevropy*, 1881, No. 1, 78-95.

Sechenov, I.M. *Etudes psychologiques.* Paris: Alcan, 1884. (a)

Sechenov, I.M. *Physiological sketches.* St. Petersburg: Stasyulevich Printing House, 1884.(b)

Sechenov, I.M. Impression and reality. *Vestnik Yevropy*, 1890, No. 5, 156-172.

Sechenov, I.M. Object-thought and reality. In D. Anuchin (Ed.), *Pomoshch golodayushchim.* Moscow: Russkiye Vedomsti, 1892. Pp. 193-209.

Sechenov, I.M. Object-thinking from a physiological standpoint. *Russkaya Mysl'*, 1894, No. 1, 255-262.

Sechenov, I.M. *Autobiographic notes.* Moscow: Nauchnoye Slovo, 1907.

Sechenov, I.M. *Selected works.* Moscow: GIZ, 1935. (a)

Sechenov, I.M. *Selected works.* (In German & English) Moscow: Medgiz, 1935. (b)

Sechenov, I.M. *Elements of thought.* Moscow: GIZ, 1943.

Sechenov, I.M. *Selected philosophical and psychological works.* Moscow: GIZ, 1947.

Sechenov, I.M. *Selected works.* Vol. 1. *Physiology and psychology.* Moscow: Akademiya Nauk SSSR, 1952.

Sechenov, I.M. *Selected works.* Moscow: UchPed-Giz, 1953.

Sechenov, I.M. *Selected physiological and psychological works.* Moscow: Foreign Language Publishing House, 1952-56.

Sechenov, I.M. *Selected works.* Vol. 2: *Physiology of nervous system.* Moscow: Akademiya Nauk SSSR, 1956.

Shannon, C.E. *Teoriya informatsii i yeyo prilozheniye.* [Information theory and its application.] Moscow: Foreign Literature, 1959.

Shannon, C.E., & Weaver, W. *Matematicheskaya teoriya sviazey.* [Mathematical theory of communication.] Moscow: Foreign Literature, 1953.

Sheffield, F. D., & Roby, T. B. Reward value of a nonnutritive sweet taste. *Journal of Comparative and Physiological Psychology*, 1950, 43, 471-481.

Shenger-Krestovnikova, N. R. Contributions to the physiology of differentiation of visual stimuli and determination of limit of differentiation by the visual analyzer of the dog. *Byulleten Instituta Lesgafta*, 1920, 3, 1-43.

Skinner, B. F. On the rate of formation of a conditioned reflex. *Journal of General Psychology*, 1932, 7, 274-285.

Skinner, B. F. *The behavior of organisms: An experimental analysis.* New York: Appleton-Century, 1938.

Skinner, B. F. *Cummulative record.* New York: Appleton-Century-Crofts, 1959.

Skornyakov, L. A. On one class of automatic (nervous system). *Problemy Kibernetiki,* 1960, 4, 23-35.

Smith, S., & Guthrie, E. R. *General psychology in terms of behavior.* New York: Appleton-Century, 1921.

Solomon, R. L., & Turner, L. H. Discriminative classical conditioning in dogs paralyzed by curare can later control discriminative avoidance responses in the normal state. *Psychological Review,* 1962, 69, 202-219.

Spence, K. W. *Behavior theory and conditioning.* New Haven: Yale Univer. Press, 1956.

Spence, K. W. Cognitive factors in the extinction of the conditioned eyelid response in humans. *Science,* 1963, 140, 1224-1225.

Stevens, S. S. *Eksperimental'naya psikholgiya.* [Experimental psychology.] (Rev. ed.) Moscow: Foreign Literature, 1963.

Thorndike, E. L. Ideo-motor action. *Psychological Review,* 1913, 20, 91-106.

Tolstoy, L. N. *Anna Karenina.* Moscow: Kushner, 1903.

Traugott, N. N. *Disturbances of interactions of the signal systems.* Moscow-Leningrad: Akademiya Nauk SSSR, 1957.

Ukhtomsky, A. A. Principles of dominance. *Novoye Refleksologii i Fiziologii Nervnoy Sistemy,* 1925, 1, 60-66.

Voytonis, N. Yu. *Prehistory of intellect.* Moscow-Leningrad: Akademiya Nauk SSSR, 1949.

Washburn, Margaret F. *Animal mind.* New York: Macmillan, 1908.

Watson, J. B. Psychology as a behaviorist views it. *Psychological Review,* 1913, 20, 158-177.

Watson, J. B. Behavior and the concept of mental disease. *Journal of Philosophy, Psychology, and Scientific Methods,* 1916, 13, 589-597. (a)

Watson, J. B. The place of the conditioned reflex in psychology. *Psychological Review,* 1916, 23, 89-116. (b)

Watson, J. B. *Psychology from the standpoint of a behaviorist.* Philadelphia, Pa.: Lippincott, 1919.

Watson, J. B. Is thinking merely the action of language mechanisms? *British Journal of Psychology,* 1920, 11, 87-104.

Watson, J. B. The unverbalized in human behavior. *Psychological Review,* 1924, 31, 273-280.

Watson, J. B. *Behaviorism.* New York: Norton, 1925.

Watson, J. B., & Rayner, R. Conditioned emotional reactions. *Journal of Experimental Psychology,* 1920, 3, 1-14.

Wells, F. L. Von Bechterev and Uebertragung. *Journal of Philosophy, Psychology, and Scientific Methods,* 1916, 13, 354-356.

Wiener, N. *Kibernetika.* [Cybernetics.] Moscow: Sovetskoye Radio, 1958.

Williams, D. R. Classical conditioning and incentive variation. Paper read at Symposium on Classical Conditioning, State College, Pennsylvania, August 1963.

Woodward, P. M. *Teoriya veroyatnosti i teoriya informatsii.* [Probability and information theory.] Moscow: Sovetskoye Radio, 1955.

Woodworth, R.S. *Eksperimental'naya psikhologiya.* [Experimental psychology.] Moscow: Foreign Literature, 1950.

Yaglom, A. M., & Yaglom, I. M. *Probability and information.* Moscow: Fizmatgiz, 1960.

Yerkes, R. M., & Morgulis, S. The method of Pavlov in animal psychology. *Psychological Bulletin,* 1909, *6,* 257-273.

Asian Psychology:
A Backward Glance
Gardner Murphy
Lois B. Murphy

Gardner and Lois B. Murphy, husband and wife, both received their Ph.D.s in psychology from Columbia University. After teaching for many years at Columbia and at City College in New York City, Gardner assumed the Henry March Pfeiffer Research Teaching Chair in Psychiatry at The Menninger Foundation. A past president of the Society for the Psychological Study of Social Issues (1938), the Eastern Psychological Association (1942), and the American Psychological Association (1944), he is currently affiliated with George Washington University. His many publications include *Personality: A Biosocial Approach to Origins and Structure* (1947), *Historical Introduction to Psychology* (Rev. ed. 1949), and *Human Potentialities* (1958). Lois has served as professor of psychology at Sarah Lawrence College, research psychologist at The Menninger Foundation, and senior research consultant on infant research study at Children's Hospital, Washington, D.C. Among her many contributions to psychological literature is *The Widening World of Children: Paths toward Maturity* (1962). In addition to *Asian Psychology*, the Murphys have also jointly edited *Western Psychology* (1969).

In *Asian Psychology* the Murphys do not present the history of psychology in the various Asian countries, as one might suspect. This history, long neglected by Western psychologists largely because of the language barrier, has been made available in several recent textbooks. *Asian Psychology* focuses on philosophy, not psychology. It presents the Eastern views of man's psyche as revealed in both ancient and modern philosophical writings of India, China, and Japan. In this selection, which is the final chapter of their book, the Murphys speculate about the relationship between Asian cultures and Asian psychologies. After examining aspects of difference between Oriental and Occidental psychologies, they conclude that "the two are coming together very fast indeed."

In introducing this volume, we made a good deal of the geographical setting within which Asian cultures have developed and the broad cultural matrix within which philosophies and psychologies arose. Now that our brief survey is over, and the reader has some glimmering of the kinds of psychological teachings which the great Asian philosophies developed, we shall offer a few more tentative

From Gardner Murphy and Lois B. Murphy (Eds.), *Asian psychology.* New York: Basic Books, 1968. Pp. 223-231. ©1968 by Basic Books, Inc., Publishers, New York. Reprinted by permission of the authors and the publisher.

guesses about the relation between Asian cultures and Asian psychologies.

If a speculative note be allowed to prevail, one may ask first about the *family system* and interpersonal relations in general as a fact predisposing to one type or another of psychology, whether in the West or in the East. It has often been noted that psychology of the immediate biological family—father, mother, and children—as developed by Freud in his book *Group Psychology and Analysis of the Ego,* offers a useful clue to the structure of the religious life and of religious concepts. The deity, for example, is usually conceived, in the West, as a paternal figure to whom male devotees direct their filial attention. There is, however, a need for a balancing emphasis upon femininity, as in the cult of female figures of divine or near-divine status. In religious orders there are brothers, sisters, mothers superior, and so forth. The devotional life is organized in some ways around the themes of love and fear as they occur in the family. It has been noted in the same connection that this central role of the biological family does not appear to any great extent in the religions and philosophies of Asia. On the contrary, personal deities are seldom of absolute authority. Rather, they are secondary to vast, impersonal laws and principles, and when they appear, none of them has absolute power over the rest. There is, moreover, a group responsibility; so to speak, a social life, social authority, a precedence pattern in the Pantheon. The Pantheon of personal deities is in itself only a part of a vast schema of cosmic forces, many of which are semi-personal or wholly impersonal.

Now the question arises whether we might not properly assume a corresponding kind of religious philosophy as we turn to India, China, and Japan, where there is not a sharp separation of the biological or nuclear family from the extended family. These societies possess a rich system of brother-sister-aunt-uncle-grandparent-and-cousin relationships in the extended family. Such institutions give rise to philosophical and psychological systems much less sharply anchored upon individual existence, and upon the individual love and fear directed to a personal cosmic monarch. We might, in fact, expect to find in these Asian societies, with their extended-family systems, psychologies much less highly individualized, with less sharply defined individual personalities and status competition one with another.

The issue cannot be neatly resolved by historical data. Yet it is of interest to note that with the development of the family and caste system in India, there is the development of a psychology of caste, and of clan, in which individuality is hardly ever mentioned. It is rather extraordinary that we do not even have names for most of the Indian philosophers (whereas among the Greeks scores of philosophers' names are known). Every now and then an Indian philosopher with great force of character manages to battle against a great tradition and assert his name, but then for centuries his followers remain unspecified. Duty to father and mother, to husband and wife, is indeed constantly emphasized, but if one looks more closely, one finds that these are aspects of broader and more complicated social responsibilities. Both in the philosophy and in the great epic poems of India, the law of the extended family and the nation takes precedence over personal obligations. Indeed, the great Ram himself, who gave up a kingdom at his father's behest, and his devoted wife Sita, who clings to him rather than yielding to various supernatural claims and counter-pressures, are quite evidently carrying out their duty to a cosmic scheme. The point must not be pressed too far. But it looks as if the loneliness of the individual religious practitioner who follows the Upanishads or the ways of yoga is freeing himself from a social system as well as from a world of woe, and that he is doing this in retreat from all human relationships. He does not look for a reunion with the divine beyond the grave, as do both Christian and Moslem worshippers; rather, he is pursuing a process by which his own severe, pure, and eternal individuality will be set free in order to be absorbed ultimately into the nameless, but perfect, bliss which is available for those whose social existence has been purified and stripped bare, down to the ultimate pure reality of a selfhood which is no longer an individual self but only a divine spark.

When Buddhism, as a representative of a highly evolved Indian system of thought, was imported into China, it took with it very little of this mystical cultivation of the individual, but a great deal of the sense of social responsibility which Buddha's ethical teaching had established. It was partly because Buddhism often taught absorption in the eternal that some of the emperors were afraid of it, and it was precisely because Buddhism also taught responsibility to the social group that it finally fitted quite well into the ethical system—the system of family, group, and state relationships which was dominant in China. Neither in China nor in India, however, did a psychological system arise which dealt concretely with the specific problems of specific husbands, wives, fathers, children, as was characteristic of the Judeo-Christian applied psychology of the West.

To a considerable degree this held also for Japan, in which likewise the extended family is dominant. It is well known that from the time of the Samurai (the great warriors of the medieval period) onward the Japanese have cultivated selfless devotion to the extended family, the nation, and the Emperor as its personification. But it should be noted that this is merely a highly refined form of the doctrine of consecration and self-control (*bushido*) which in other forms had dominated the cultural, military, and political life of the Japanese.

Throughout this seven-league-boots procession that we have just made through the psychologies of India, China, and Japan, is the problem of individuality, certainly a primary problem for the Western world, fundamental in Western European and American thought for the last two hundred years, and central in a thousand social and political discussions of the relation of the individual's life to the fulfillments and sacrifices that are involved in group living. It may be that the mass and class problems of the Asian civilizations had relatively little place for the psychology of individuality because of the essential structure of family, clan, class, and state. Perhaps these issues will become more clear and concrete as one works through, at greater depth, the material selected above from the psychologies of India, China, and Japan.

If one allows oneself to characterize in broad strokes the major differences between Asian psychology and European psychology, it is probable that the Asian approaches will seem "pessimistic" as far as the realization of a sound mind and a good life is concerned. At least, in striking contrast to the Greek belief in the vitality, beauty, and rightness of body and soul, and despite much asceticism and unworldliness in both traditions, the West offers a gusty and lusty belief in the possibility of realizing, through wisdom or common sense, some modicum of happiness here below. The Asian psychological approach is rather consistently skeptical of this. Whether we take the disparagement of the body and of the world as we find it in the Upanishads, or the retreat into an inner discipline as expressed in the Bhagavad-Gita and in yoga, or the belief that a middle course, involving Buddha's noble eightfold way, must lead one into a loss of individuality, a state of nirvana, we seem to find very little genuine faith that life is really good. We must proceed now to make some exceptions and clarifications.

First of all, we are dealing with philosophers, not with middle-level mentalities or with common people. It is the priestly caste and the warrior-caste-turned-philosopher that speak to us from ancient India. It is the disillusioned prince, Gautama, who speaks to the masses. The masses are actually reached in this way, masses comprising both men of princely birth and bearing and men of the humblest walks of life. The message of despair, as far as the here-and-now is concerned, is rather consistently brought out. One may indeed rightly object, as Professor Hsu has plainly shown, indicating that most psychology and ethics in China were concerned with a practical, common-sense achievement of a way of growing, learning, thinking, and living that would make this life good. Moreover, we shall have to admit that the distinction we are trying to make holds for the *psychologies* of Europe and Asia. We are talking about optimistic and pessimistic *psychologies*; we cannot really assess the whole temper of whole peoples. But, up to a point, the receptiveness of China and Japan to Buddhism has its own symptomatic meaning. Despite the cheery mood of much Chinese literature and proverbial good sense, there can surely be no doubt that Buddhism made its way in China through the sort of otherworldliness that we have described, joining forces with the otherworldliness of Taoism. Perhaps a stronger case can be made for basic faith in life on the part of the more psychologically minded of the Buddhists in Japan, especially those of the Zen sect.

And here, we think, we find ourselves facing a deeper issue than the sheer question of the optimism or pessimism of European and Asian psychologies. We face the question whether there is actually a system of psychology in Asia which has a place for *human fulfillment in this world*. Stated in this way, it seems quite clear that there is very little place for this approach in the Asian systems. One can indeed refer to the bliss achieved by yoga and by Zen, but as we have already noted, there is a certain "double-talk" about these references to bliss, since it is the annihilation of affective states which is said to bring bliss, and one wonders if some double-talk is not fundamental to this whole psychological thesis. Indeed, there is no systematic cultivation of a life of happiness. The aims in psychological discipline are negative; that is, they are directed to getting rid of the overwhelming misery, suffering, and frustration which is conceived to lie in the very nature of human existence.

By virtue of this sharp contrast between the ocean of distress and the tiny droplet of serenity or bliss, one might very well refer to the enormous importance attached, in the Asian world, to self-control, to discipline, and to the limitation of immediate gratifications. One would expect—and indeed one finds—an apotheosis of self-control disciplines.

This prompts us to look more closely and see whether self-control is not actually more than a purely negative form of self-realization. The language of the mystics, whether in Hinduism, Buddhism, or Taoism, suggests that there was widespread realization, among disciplined adepts, of states of real joy or bliss. These experiences seem to have involved, on the one hand, enormous emotional investment in the world as a whole, a state of sublime identification with the cosmos of the sort called by Richard Bucke *cosmic consciousness*; or states of deep abrogation of individual competitiveness in favor of a loss of selfhood. Cosmic consciousness and loss of selfhood may, in some individuals, be identical, and in other individuals be different aspects of a general change in "state of consciousness," involving a reduction of striving and conflict.

So perhaps we should say that the Asian psychologies throughout their history have sought two chief positive goals: (1) a sense of the goodness of the ultimate timeless and limitless universe; and (2) on the other hand a sense of the unlimited ecstasy that could be found within a self which is freed of personal strivings. Again, we have stated these two doctrines in such a way as to suggest that they tend to coalesce; indeed, in most of Asian psychology they are, in fact, one: The goal is freedom from individual frustration and suffering, a process possible only when the battle of self against non-self is given up and cosmic order reigns within as it does without.

This is not a logical, orderly, scientific doctrine about human nature. It is a way of looking at human life which has developed among countless thinkers over great eons of time, over much of the earth's surface. It would be of interest and importance to the West even if it were limited to Asia; but it is not limited to Asia. In other volumes to follow, we shall attempt to show how quite different goals and means toward these goals have been developed by men of other cultures and other ways of understanding.

Another broad difference between Oriental and Occidental psychology seems to us to lie in method; specifically, in the way to seek psychological truth. One may either *seek diligently* and in travail the nature of psychological reality, or one may simply keep one's eyes open for it and *let it come* as it will. There are exceptions to be noted, but it will be apparent that, in the Upanishads and in yoga, a long and arduous *discipline* has to be pursued. The discipline of Buddha, though simple and of a common-sense variety, led on quickly throughout the East to the cultivation of a higher discipline having much in common with the Hindu methods. But whether we study it in Southern or Southeastern Asia, or in China or Japan, such discipline involves enormous feats of prolonged self-control. This notion of discipline appears particularly clearly in the interactions of systems within China, where, for example, the sage Confucius looks everywhere, under every stone, behind every star, so to speak, for "the Way," and Lao-tzu gently rebukes him for not finding it; and it appears in ancient and modern Zen in Japan in the form of a cultivation of that special state of mind, *satori*, in which one can *really* observe reality and self. Psychology that is worth anything is conceived to be very hard work.

But that is just one approach to psychology. It is, of course, true that the early Greek philosophers and the Church Fathers and Renaissance philosophers who followed them likewise had their discipline. In the marketplace, however, the Greeks *played with ideas*; they toyed with observations of self and the world. Whimsy and paradox played a large part in their thinking. Aristophanes was as much of their spirit as was Euripides. Often, as the Greeks said, "the god" breathes the ideas into one's understanding; just as, later on, the Christian deity, or an archangel serving Him, brought a message in a dream, and "sudden inspiration" became the hallmark of genius.

One of the differences between the sudden inspiration of Buddha and the sudden inspiration of Archimedes lies at least partly in the fact that Buddha had been seeking *within*, and seeking very hard indeed, while Archimedes was seeking *without*. It might, at first sight, appear that Oriental psychology is, from the beginning, predestined to look for *inner* realities; and Western psychology for *outer* realities. This will not, however, wholly solve our problem. As we have already seen, the otherworldliness or spirituality or mysticism of India is not truly parallel to any such trend in China or Japan. Chinese and Japanese life is rich in scientific and technical achievement, and Western psychology through much of its history is as introspective, as inclined to turn inward, as is the Oriental. No, the real distinction does not lie in inwardness or in outwardness, but in the conception of orderly discipline and training, guiding one into the recesses where true psychological reality can be directly observed—as contrasted with the rather matter-of-fact way of the West, well phrased by Thomas Hobbes when he asked the reader, when doubting what the author has to say, to "consider, if he also find not the same in himself." It would not take a British reader ten years of discipline to find out whether his own internal world was like that of Hobbes. When we teach Hobbes, our students accept or reject him on the first confrontation.

No, the Oriental psychologist carries his laboratory within him. It is the world of the spirit which he believes he can slowly learn to observe more and more accurately. He may, "sitting under the bo tree," have a great revelation; but in Buddha's case it came after years of strenuous seeking; and the first thing he did among his followers was to explain in detail and set up for them a discipline which, over the years and centuries, became more and more exacting, orderly, systematic. There was, in the foothills of Bihar, in northeastern India, a huge Buddhist university in which all knowledge was systematically portrayed, as it was shortly thereafter in the great monastic schools of Cluny and the other medieval academic centers of the West. But the force of the Buddhist tradition lies in *very arduous self-examination*, whereas the force of the Western educational tradition lay in training in *direct observation* and in the authority handed on from the past which taught one where to look. It did not lie in the training of mind and heart, as it did in the East; rather, it lay in training in the acceptance of what appeared to direct observation. The one thing of which Hinduism was afraid—direct outer observation, as full of illusion—was the thing in which Western intellectual history has excelled. So, after three centuries of observation of the outer world in a form which we know as science, we are coming around to a psychology which uses knowledge of the external world—physics and physiology—as a primary clue to the methods most suitable for the study of the world within.

Thus, paradoxically, we come through physiological relaxation or through the chemist's gift of many new drugs to the cultivation of those extraordinary states of altered awareness, cosmic consciousness, or depersonalization, which had been known, and indeed directly cultivated, for eons of time in the East. Instead of twenty years of discipline, it may take only a few hours or days of preparation—physiological and psychological—to prepare a person for the "unutterable revelations" which come from specially induced mystical states. The basic human nature which is tapped, displayed, or distorted, or whatever you believe happens during such conditions, is apparently much the same in the East and in the West, but the East has made these special states, so far from immediate, everyday, palpable reality, something to be *sought*; the West hands them to the aspirant or the casual inquirer as a gift from biological chemistry.

This is not to prejudge what kinds of psychology can best be learned in what parts of the world, and by what methods. "East is East, and West is West," and the two are coming together very fast indeed.

VI

Psychology's Future

In his recent volume *Design of Cities,* Edmund Bacon wrote: "We are in danger of losing one of the most important concepts of mankind, that the future is what we make it." As if to resist this possibility, several serious-minded professionals have undertaken not prophecy or prediction but a thoughtful consideration of alternative futures from among present expectations. Notable among these students of the future is Daniel Bell, eminent sociologist and chairman of the American Academy of Arts and Letters Commission on the Year 2000; Bertrand de Jouvenel, director of the *Futuribles* project in Paris; and Michael Young and Mark Abrams, chairmen of the Committee on the Next Thirty Years of the English Social Science Research Council. Psychologists in the United States have also begun to consider the future of their science and profession.

After reviewing psychology's progress and status in various countries, it is interesting now to consider its future possibilities. In Part VI three articles speculate about psychology's future trends and goals. The authors make no attempt to assume the role of seers or prophets. They are not writing science fiction. Instead, these psychologists provide a thoughtful assessment of present-day psychology and of currently identifiable trends as well as extrapolations based on these trends.

In the first selection, by means of a fantasy-like presentation, Henry Murray anticipates the judgment that will be made of contemporary psychologists in the future for their rigid dedication to systems, their insufficient concern with the humanistic aspects of their science, and their failure to promote peace and develop creative and humane solutions for the world's ills.

On the basis of a survey of ten topics, the second selection delineates the specific subject areas and methods that may be expected to develop and expand by the end of the 20th century. Here the author, Gardner Murphy, reminds psychologists of their responsibility to develop a psychology that embraces all men. He cautions that they will have to learn "how to look inside and how to look outside."

In the third paper, which is a kind of corollary to the second, Uriel G. Foa and Jim Turner examine Murphy's anticipation of the emergence of two new directions in psychology. These directions are "the merging of the study of overt behavior with the observation of internal states" and "the analysis of the integration of components into organized wholes or the investigation of structures." Foa and Turner venture the prediction that psychology will increasingly "go structural" in the years ahead.

All these authors seem to suggest that psychology will follow a steady course of scientific progress. Yet each admonishes contemporary psychologists to pursue and broaden their humane and humanistic objectives.

Prospect for Psychology:
A vision of the future, as reconstructed after one encounter with the hallucinogenic drug psilocybin

Henry A. Murray

Henry A. Murray, professor emeritus of clinical psychology at Harvard University, is distinguished for his contributions in theory and practice to psychology's understanding of man and his world. After undergraduate study in history at Harvard, he obtained a medical degree from Columbia University and a Ph.D. in biochemistry from Cambridge University in England. During the 1920s, under the influence of Carl Jung, Murray transferred his allegiance from medicine and biochemistry to psychology and psychoanalysis. Returning to Harvard in 1927, he assisted Morton Prince in establishing the Harvard Psychological Clinic, of which he became director in 1928. During World War II Murray developed various ingenious assessment procedures and researches for the Office of Strategic Services. His many achievements, which won for him the American Psychological Association Distinguished Scientific Award in 1961, include *The Thematic Apperception Test* (with C.D. Morgan, 1935) and *Explorations in Personality* (with staff, 1938) and *Personality in Nature, Society, and Culture* (with C. Kluckhohn, 1948). Murray's approach to the psychology of personality has been humanistic, holistic, and strongly psychoanalytic in its stress on the unconscious.

The following selection is adapted from an address Murray delivered in 1961 at the International Congress of Applied Psychology in Copenhagen. The theme is one that recurs in his writings—namely, that psychology should strive to solve the world's ills and to promote peace among nations. If it fails to do so, it will be indicted by future generations. The message Murray gives here is directly presented in his *Autobiography* (1967), in which he says:

> Peace must be insured by a world government of an unprecedented type, which would never be established or never last without a radical transformation of ethnocentric sentiments and values on both sides of our divided world; and a transformation of this nature would never occur without some degree of synthesis of the best features of the two opposing cultural systems; and this would not take place creatively except in sight of an unprecedented vision and conception of world relationship and fellowship, a kind of superordinate natural religion, or mythologized philosophy.

I shall skip the first, startling 30 minutes of my trance—the stabbing cortical sensations; the hailstorm of brightly colored

Henry A. Murray, Prospect for psychology. *Science*, 1962, **136**, 483-488. Reprinted by permission of the author and the American Association for the Advancement of Science. © 1962 by the American Association for the Advancement of Science.

particles, filaments, and figures; the kaleidoscope of celestial mosaics at the antipodes of mind; the rush of archetypes—and simply say that, after witnessing the birth in the Near East of the religions that shaped the souls of Western men and women, and after passing down the centuries to the agitations and enigmas of our own day, I found myself on the edge of a dark wood overlooking an existential waste of desolate absurdities with the straight way lost. Then, to my astonishment, I saw, floating down in my direction, an angel clothed in a cloud as white as wool. His countenance was as the sun in his zenith, beaming with encouragement to every benign form of life. In these features he reminded me so strongly of my cherished friend Edgar Tranekjaer-Rasmussen (1) that, out of my lonely state, I would have hugged him if it had not been for the inhibiting awareness of his far-superior, winged status in the hierarchy of being.

"This evening I am to be your Virgil," the angel said, "your appointed guide for the night hours of your journey into future time. Come with me. Over there is the forest path by which we must descend into the abyss of pain and woe and retributive justice."

As we proceeded in the semidarkness the angel informed me that the year was 1985 and that the long-dreaded Great Enormity had been perpetrated as predicted. Barely 6 months before, a biological, chemical, and nuclear war between the U.S.S.R. and the United States had been started inadvertently—by the push of a button during a small group's momentary panic caused by a slight misunderstanding—and concluded within a fortnight, leaving the essential structures of both countries leveled to the ground, their vital centers obliterated or paralyzed, their atmospheres polluted. Demoralized, isolated remnants of both populations, reduced to a molelike existence underground, were now preparing amid the wreckage to defend themselves with gas against invading forces, from China in the one case, from South America in the other.

"We are approaching the subterranean courthouse of posterity," announced the angel, "where those accused of responsibility for the Great Enormity—or of irresponsibility—are being tried before the gods, of whom there is a multiplicity, I should say, in case you have not heard the news. On trial this evening is a host of academic psychologists of all breeds and nationalities."

In a minute the two of us were entering a crowded underground cavern, constructed like the Colosseum, all parts of which were preternaturally illuminated. The tiers of seats that constituted the sides of the amphitheater were arranged in sections, each of which, the angel pointed out, was occupied by a different denomination of psychologists. At the opposite end of the oval arena, on a raised platform, was a long judges' bench behind which sat a row of unmistakable divinities. One of these bore a striking resemblance to Aphrodite and another to Dionysius, but the majority were essentially androgynous. I was informed that all of them had recently been created in man's image as visible representors of the major determinants of human personality, society, and history. Attracted by a masked figure that sat near the center of the bench, I was told that that was Alphaomega, the influential and often-propitiated god of Chance, whose unpredictable operations could result in either good or evil fortune. The angel informed me that several pagan deities, after a period of sincere repentance and character reformation, had been admitted to this high court and named anew, but that most of the more imperious deities of antiquity had been rejected— Zeus for juvenile delinquency, Jehovah for narcissism and delusions of infallibility, Allah for ferocity. Sitting at desks on both sides of the broad open space in front of the supreme court bench were the lawyers with their consulting sages. I recognized Buddha, Confucius, Moses, Thomas Aquinas, and a dozen more, engaged in whispered conversations with each other. One moody isolate was obviously Kierkegaard. As we took our seats, Socrates, attorney for the prosecution, was about to terminate his indictment of psychology.

INDICTMENT OF PSYCHOLOGY

"And now, divine judiciary," he said, "as I approach the slippery task of summing up my argument, I am assailed by the mutterings of sundry doubts. I have much fear of erring. To appraise the activities and the retailed wares of these most learned and industrious psychologists is a perilous and presumptuous undertaking for an untutored, rusty man like me. And yet, were I to permit cowardice to silence the voice of my indwelling daemon, ye gods and ancient sages would rise up in judgment to denounce me as a traitor to what light I have received from you, as one who would buy smiles from men at the price of sinning against conscience—against you, oh Va! [Here Socrates punctuated his speech with a deferential bow to one of the chief jurists.] Va, supreme arbiter of the better and the worse, who can discern differences, imperceptible to ordinary mortals, between fine gradations of beauty, love, and truthfulness; and of sinning against you, immortal Co, god of creativity in nature and in man.

"And so, ye gods, because I dread your odium more than anything I can name, I shall go on, despite my qualms, and inquire whether these most eminent psychologists did anything or endeavored to do anything which might luckily have modified the course of events that finally brought about the Great Enormity? When the world's dire strait called for the full investment of rational imaginations, did or did not these privileged professionals remain aloof, virtually indifferent to man's fate? Did they, or did they not, behave as if they were quite satisfied to be superfluous, if not frivolous? Had they, or had they not, acquired any knowledge, or were they, or were they not, seeking any knowledge which might have served in any way to stop the instinct-driven rulers of this earth from pursuing their fatal foreign policies or to help them reach a more creative and humane solution of the world's ills instead of letting loose the fury which at this moment—A.D. 1985—seems to be heading toward the termination of millions of years of evolution?

"As you have surely noted, revered justices, I am an inept fumbler in the mansions of the social sciences, and, though I shall have to use it, correctly or incorrectly, from now on, I have no stomach for their lingo, so obnoxious to a Greek. But, in spite of these impediments and others, I shall perform the duty with which I have been charged to the best of my ability.

"If we were to state, for short, that the crux of the world's dilemma consists of a conflict between two different ideologies, thesis and antithesis, represented by two blocs of power-oriented social units, would not a miniature paradigm, or analogy, of this condition—one susceptible to direct and detailed psychological investigation—have to include at least two interacting hostile personalities, each astringently attached to a contrasting set of social values or religion? If the answer is yes, I should like to ask what proportion of psychologists were observing and conceptualizing on the basis of two or more conflicting personalities, each operating as a directed system of beliefs, emotions, wants, and higher mental processes? Did, or did not, a goodly number of extremely intellectual psychologists, insisting on the utmost scientific rigor, shun the complexities of personality and, in search of higher pecking status, plant their minds in biology, physiology, statistics, symbolic logic, or methodology per se? And, among those academic psychologists who observed and tested persons, did, or did not, a rather large percentage conceive of personality as a galaxy of abstractions in a vacuum—a mere bag of traits, a profile of scores on questionnaires, a compound of factors without referents, or, perhaps some elaborate formulation of a conflict between oedipal hate and fear of punishment—giving little indication, in any case, of how the person would proceed, and with what outcome, in a vehement transaction, let us say here, with a specified type of ideological antagonist?

"I have been told that a large number of more statistically oriented American psychologists—social psychologists you might call them—constructed their propositions wholly in terms of the conforming majority of the population studied. If this is true, did, or did not, the conformists who confirmed their theories (and therefore behaved lawfully in the scientific sense) become equated in the minds of these psychologists with what was functionally right and proper? Since their results relegated to limbo the responses of the better-than-average members of the population mixed with the responses of the worse-than-average, did not the publication of these results reinforce, with the authority of science, the complacence of mediocracy? Did, or did not, these psychologists conceive of any better standard of values than was provided by the relatively well adjusted, happy exemplifiers of the so-called 'dominant' culture patterns of their country?

"And here, divine jurists," said Socrates with special emphasis, "comes the crucial question, which my daemon is impelling me to ask, harsh though it may seem: Did the psychologists see or fail to see that the dominant majority in pretty nearly every sovereign state had been rendered obsolete, in certain critical respects, by the discovery of genocidal weapons? Suddenly the old rules of evolution had been drastically revised. Were, or were not, the psychologists aware of this? And, if aware, did they, or did they not, bring their minds and hearts to bear on the problem of specifying what kinds of personalities would be fit to govern the nations of both blocs under these harrowing new conditions, as well as what kinds of men and women would be fit to support fit governments?

"To discover in what ways unfit personalities can become fit, could or could not psychologists have studied relevant transformations in depth of a few self-converted persons? The psychologists' models of a human being were various and ingeniously contrived—an electronic mechanism for the processing of symbolic information; an empty animal reacting in a standard cage; a self-centered, solipsistic atom in a social void; and a dozen other imaginal concoctions amazing to an old Athenian. An elegant sideshow, I would hazard, of cleverly contrived freaks. But if you, divine jurists, could ever bring yourselves to look any one of these models in the eye, would you, I wonder, be convinced that man is worthy of survival, or, if not worthy in his present state, capable of becoming worthy? Were, or were not, a majority of clinical psychologists—Western, not Soviet psychologists—so attracted by odors of decay, by neurotic illness, degradation, criminality, and whatnot, that they were blinded to all else? And did not the constant advertisement of their brilliantly analyzed cases of psychological decrepitude only serve to generate, through imitation, more of the same thing? In short, immortal judges, would you, or would you not, declare that quite a few psychologists—with no terminology at all to represent better-than-average personalities—added what influence they had to the general trend of denigration which reduced man's image of himself to the point of no revival, stripping it of genuine potentiality for creative change, the only ground there was for hope that people could do anything but what they actually did do? This brings me to the end of my queries as to possible explanations of the non-entity of psychology outside the minds of its own practitioners. With these I rest my case."

At this point Yu, one of the jurists—god of charity and forgiveness—intervened. "Socrates," he said, "all you have done so far is to decry the all-too-human darkness in the minds of these distinguished scientists. Are you not capable of kindling a little light? What would *you* have done?

MINIATURE WORLD MODEL

"Oh," exclaimed Socrates, "I foresaw, in dread, that one of you venerable deities would challenge me precisely on this point, and, after consulting with myself, I discovered that the senescence of my faculties had rendered me incapable of complying with your imperative request. Instead, I have a little parable to offer—the idle fancy of an aging cortex—which begins with a miniature world model that is quite close to the personal experience of every one of these admirable psychologists, and also so compact that it lies within their sphere of feasible investigation. For this model, the scope of concern is not the world at large but a single, purely hypothetical department of psychology marked by an ongoing, bitter competition between two contrasting scientific ideologies represented by two blocs of faculty members, each with its ambitious, rivalrous, charismatic theorist-leader. One competing ideational system is derived from Existentialism and the other from Behaviorism. The two systems, the two faculty blocs, and the two prime protagonists are competing for the minds of the uncommitted students as well as for power and prestige, the directorship of the department.

"In due course, the two ideological protagonists, Asa and Bede by name, become involved in an overheated argument which ends in a sworn compact to settle their differences in the morning with nuclear weapons. There is no law against dueling in this area, and since each theorist has nerves of iron, the death of both is certain. Moreover, since the members of each bloc feel that the grandeur of their theory demands that they too defend it with their lives, the elimination of the whole department is inevitable.

"Here, in a nutshell, is the problem which faces the psychologist—in this instance a visiting Danish scholar whose scientific curiosity and prudence have kept him securely in the role of a non-participant observer. What can he do? First, do as he was trained to do: produce a flock of promising hypothesis. If he applies method 27 to Asa and Bede, the existing high level of belligerent emotions will be lowered; and if he uses method 39, under conditions of lowered tension, Asa and Bede will agree to a postponement of the duel, and so forth and so on. But suppose the psychologist's entire structure of smartly conceived maneuvers collapses at the very start, when private talks with Asa and then with Bede unambiguously reveal that the whole pride system—the ego ideal—of each of them is glued to the conviction that his particular ideology is the complete, perfect, ultimate, and saving truth, and also glued to the moral imperative that a man must be prepared to kill or be killed whenever the survival or expansion of the authentic truth is endangered by the falsehoods or heresies of others. Asa and Bede are not deterred from the duel because each is supremely confident that he is quicker on the trigger and can kill the other before the other can discharge his weapon.

"The situation is clearly beyond remedy, and the visiting scholar, realizing that all his bright hypotheses have been invalidated, stumbles back to his room in a state of such abysmal melancholy that he turns to psilocybin for relief. Within an hour, Eureka! He has had a vision that engenders hope, and although it is long past midnight, he rushes out, calls on a few of his foreign student friends, gets them to dress up in the semblance of constables, and then at dawn, disguised as a sheriff, he conducts them to the selected spot outside the city limits. They reach it just in time to inform the two protagonists, with an ample show of authority, that a law against dueling was signed on the previous day and that if any man is alive after the shooting, he, the sheriff, will hang that man from the nearest oak tree. Faced by the absolute certainty of death, Asa and Bede, after a small hemming-and-hawing summit conference, agree to call off their war and return to the city with their two blocs of allies."

At this point Socrates, as if talking to himself, queried: "Is there no hint here of the power and advantage of world government?

"The parable ends with the staunch friendship of Asa and Bede, and with their joint production of a grand synthesis—an experiential-behavioral system of psychology—which integrates the inner and the outer aspect of a personality in action. Both Asa and Bede acknowledge their indebtedness to the Danish scholar, without whose beneficent intervention they would never have reached their present peak of solid satisfaction, justified in each of them by his proved capacity to understand and to encompass an ideology that is opposite to his own. As for the young Dane, his energies have been spent from first to last in recording and conceptualizing the stages of affectional and intellectual transformation experienced by Asa and Bede as they progressed from a monocentric to a dycentric pride-and-value system. The final climax of the fable comes with the Danish psychologist's publication of a generative book of postulates, theorems, and graphic illustrations which represent the validated way to a solution of ideological antagonisms, a book which promises to mark a turning point in the history of interpersonal and inter-ideational relations."

Socrates's whole oration—his charges against psychology and his concluding mythical narrative—had been delivered in the gentlest fashion, words dropping from his mouth as leaves from trees. His benign manner was such as to intensify the guilt aroused in me by my awareness that his accusations were, in large part, applicable to me. As this estimable philosopher took his seat, the defense attorney—none other than the formidable Aristotle, I was glad to see—came forward and immediately commenced his argument, pacing back and forth before the judges' bench with measured gestures.

IN DEFENSE OF PSYCHOLOGY

"Honored deities," he said, "I trust you have not been deceived by the wiles of Socrates, his seductive way of mixing fact and fiction, comic and tragic flavors. I myself shall rely on simple, referential language to convince you first that this generally wise old man has been unjust in overlooking the tender age of psychology as science, still in its adolesence in the years preceding the Great Enormity. Look at the giant strides it took from the days at the turn of the century when its sphere was virtually restricted to the sensations and perceptions of healthy, educated, adult European males.

"Second, I shall show that Socrates has little understanding of the differentiated modes of science-making, of the garnering of data, here and there, particle by particle. He is attentive only to the overarching generalist who struts on the stage at some timely moment to devour and digest the spread-out produce of the toil and talent of numberless devoted specialists. Academic psychology was approaching but had not reached the timely moment for a great, integrative generalist. Give this young science 20 years more and you shall witness, I predict, the emergence of a creative thinker of the first order—a Newton, Darwin, Marx, Frazer, Freud, Pavlov, Jung, Einstein, or Niels Bohr.

"You might suppose, honored jurists," continued Aristotle, "that these psychologists were a bit retarded in their growth; and I must confess that occasionally in private I have thought that they would have moved more surely toward their destined goal if they had been less patronizing toward me and toward other anticipators of some of their recently vaunted concepts. Quite a few of them, I noted, failed to heed my irrefutable affirmation that it is the mark of an educated man to know the degree of precision—precision of observation and of statement—that is most appropriate to each stage in the development of each realm of knowledge. In this sense, many psychologists, mostly American, were not educated, in so far as their zeal to approximate the technical perfection of the more exact sciences led them away from the phenomena which psychologists, and only psychologists, are expected to study and to elucidate by the fittest scientific means. Their tolerance of uncertainty was too low," said Aristotle with finality.

"I shall persuade you, however, that this methodological compulsion was a necessary expedient in effecting the emancipation of their discipline from the enclosing husk of one or another brand of idealistic or speculative philosophy. Give psychology another 40 years and you shall see one great embracement and the extinction of all separate schools. Monocentric schools, as Socrates has suggested in his preferred mythical mode of speech, are symptoms of adolescence. Medicine has no schools.

"The last and more agreeable part of my task will be to prove by reference to works and names how close psychology had come to an impressive status in the house of intellect, not only by way of its excellent technology but because of the genuine importance of its ordered knowledge."

Then Aristotle, starting with the first part of his announced plan of defense, proceeded systematically and logically, step by step, to annul the validity of each of Socrates's accusations. Though his performance was in no respect spectacular, the evidence he marshaled in our behalf was so copious, and his presentation was so lucid and concise, that within less than 30 minutes my guilt had turned to pride. This pride in my profession soared to even greater heights when Aristotle came to the last part of his oration, in which he made it apparent, by pointing to specific researchers and results, that Socrates had not read the literature of the four decades preceding 1985.

Aristotle's masterful exposition of psychology's achievements was followed by a short, inaudible debate among the gods. They had been visibly impressed by the great Stagirite's facts and figures, and I had no twinge of apprehension in regard to the decision that was on the lips of Va, the chief justice, when he stood up and faced the tiers of psychologists on trial. Unspeakable, then, was my dismay when, in one shocking sentence, he prescribed for all of us a period of purgatorial probation!

Upon the pronouncement of this verdict, the smoke of our collective shame swirled upward. The atmosphere became too dense for sight, and in a second I was elsewhere, wrapped in utter darkness without angelic guidance. Then, before my passive eyes there passed a startling succession of horrendous scenes: a bottomless abyss of fire and brimstone out of which emerged the notorious beast of the Apocalypse; then thunder, lightning, and a hurricane of deafening explosions; then a great expanse of scorched earth strewn with rubble and cadavers; and finally, a colossal earthquake which swallowed up the residues of all the wrecked creations of centuries of human toil and faith, all the damning evidences of man's inhumanity to man.

Suddenly the turmoil and the clamor ceased, and in a moment out of the pervading stillness of the night came the voice of the lark, the flush of Eos along the horizon in the East, and I found myself standing by the side of a clear stream next to another shadowy, winged figure, younger than the first angel but no less mellow, whose all-comprehending eyes and roguish twinkle were so reminiscent of my crony Gerhard Nielsen (2) that my leaden spirits were transmuted by his alchemy into a golden state of cheerfulness.

A NEW PSYCHOLOGY

"The year is 2085 and we're in Denmark, the most civilized country of our time," announced my new guide. "I might as well inform you right away that war is a thing of the past. Like cannibalism and dueling it is no more than an occasional fantasy in the minds of a few psychopaths excluded from the seats of government. After your last encounter with the future in 1985, just 100 years ago, a rapid succession of devastating wars, initiated by power-drunk dictators, finally brought the surviving members of your species to their senses. Taking to heart, at long last, what had been written on the wall in 1945, this saving remnant of humanity built, out of desperation, dread, grief, pity, love, and hope, a new Ark of the Covenant, devoutly dedicated, with solemn rites and pledges, to the unity of all mankind."

Then eyeing me with kindliness, the angel said: "Since I know you are incurably naive when it comes to political science, I shall not describe the scope and structure of the unique supranational organization that was set up to insure the peaceful settlement of disputes. Even in your day, rationality had concluded that some form of world government was necessary—government, by definition, being the only class of institution empowered to suppress violence. But in almost every country rationality was emasculated by monocentric nationalism—the lust for profits, power, and prestige— and by ideological fixations, coupled with pernicious anemia of the imagination. Anemia of the imagination dangerously reduced the capacity of people and their rulers to carry out, in their minds, long-span, vividly-envisioned trial-and-error experiments and to learn in this way that a reorientation of their aims and strategems was essential to survival and the making of a better world. And so humanity had to learn as animals learn, by tangible and irrevocable suffering and injuries, the dire consequences of aggression in an age of absolutely lethal weapons.

"Unutterable agony! But fortunately today's world can be most thankful that not all that agony was fruitless. For out of it came the curing concept of holocentrism for all nations—each for all and all for each—in place of the lawless monocentrisms of some 60 sovereign states bristling with pride. Another emergent concept was that of synthesism—the mutual embracement of two opposites—as of prime value at certain timely moments. For instance, in your day it was apparent that peoples of all societies would eventually demand and gain a fitting degree of *both* economic equality (guaranteed by some type of socialism or central regulation) and political equality (some type of representative government with certain guaranteed forms of freedom). Rationally viewed, it was simply a question of what degree of each of these desirable conditions was most fitting at a given historic stage of each society. But rationality—the possibility of arriving at just estimates through free discussions of ideological fundamentals in a calm, even-handed, and imaginative way—was canceled by the importunate fervor of the Apocalyptic myth which sharply dichotomizes all mankind into the virtuous and the vicious. To the people of 2085, who reverence and cheer creative syntheses whenever these are feasible and promising, the most virtuous individuals are those who actively participate in conclusive ideo- logical embracement, and so this country of Denmark, as well as other countries, enjoys a just and satisfying measure of planned economy, equality, liberty, and fraternity, not to speak of another *magnum bonum,* freedom from the plague of commercial advertising.

"At first," the angel said, "people were strongly bent toward holocentrism and synthesism as a consequence of having witnessed and experienced, on their own flesh and in their pulses, the horrors of the 21st-century warfare. But since each generation of children from then on would be a fresh swarm of savages, potential killers of their own kind, the formidable task assigned to the social sciences in 2035 was that of designing a system of practices of child rearing, education, and self-development which, under favorable conditions, would produce generations of adult personalities who would prove progressively more fit, emotionally and intellectually, to live and (if called upon) to govern in a world capable of producing genocidal weapons. Within 5 years these scientists—mostly psychologists and sociologists—came out with their first, provisional version of a program based on a sophisticated learning theory which stressed the efficacy of exemplars, or models. Later reconstructions of this program resulted in a document of the first magnitude.

"Psychologists had always been able to agree quite well about negative values, about what was wrong (such as crime), below normal (such as neurosis), or obnoxious (such as prejudice and authoritarianism), but never before had they been able or inclined to agree about positive values outside their own profession, about what was genuinely good or right, *above* normal, excellent, or admirable. This was none of their business, they had invariably insisted. But this time they knew for sure that they were backed against the wall and must fight for life itself with saving, creative concepts. They bowed to the dictum that science is for man, not man for science, and that if civilization should collapse again, science would collapse with it, and the human species might ignominiously perish from the earth. The only evaluative assumption which these psychologists had explicitly to put their minds to was this: that the best possible reciprocities between nations and between individuals (in friendships and in marriages) were of paramount importance, or, conceptually speaking, that creative holocentrism for the societies of the world, and creative dycentrism for men and women, were more desirable than arrogant, rivalrous, and hate-filled monocentrisms.

"The humanistic psychology which was constructed with these

two major orientations constantly in view is not a closed, logically deduced system of abstract values for adult intellectuals but an open, largely empirical, though partly ideal, developmental psychology which sets forth varieties of values for each stage of personological growth, for each sex, for each characterological type, and for each vocation.

"This psychology is ordered," explained the angel, "by the notion of three successive phases in the life of an individual and, by analogy, in the history of a civilization: the phase of childhood, marked by dependency, awe, and submission to authority; the phase of adolescence, marked by independency, egocentricity, and rebellion; and the phase of maturity, marked by interdependency, dycentricity, and creative reciprocities. This last is the phase that is enjoyably exemplified by the adults of this era. From this achieved position they can clearly see in retrospect that many Western people, especially Americans, in the years before the Great Enormity (children or grandchildren of the generation that gave the *coup de grâce* to all previously venerated sources and bases of authority—ecclesiastical, political, parental, and rational—in other words, many Americans of your time) were reveling blindly and irresponsibly in the transient sensations, half-baked pleasures, and senseless poses of inflated adolescent egotism. Since the young children of this new world are not deprived of an initial, preparatory period of firm and benevolent parental governance and tutelage, they can enter the phase of adolescence with characters of enough base for them to pursue some meaningful course of action with a heartening degree of genuine (not spurious) self-sufficiency and with a few implanted values to rebel against in the name of something better. All the self-centeredness, the self-pity and strident self-assertions, the worship of powerful machines, of quantities of matter, of bigness, height, and speed, all the dazzling vulgarities and other sorts of hollow grandiosities so prevalent in your mid-century are regarded in today's world as more or less natural and tolerable eruptions of adolescence. But whenever dispositions of this nature are manifested by anybody over 25, they become the target of searing ridicule and scorn. Adults of this society prize quality above quantity, particularly the quality of their interpersonal relationships—marriages and friendships."

I could see a suburb of Copenhagen straight ahead of us as the angel declared with emphasis: "To understand how these seemingly miraculous metamorphoses of human nature were accomplished, anybody of your vintage would have to read, thoroughly and sympathetically, the world testament of these people. This testament, which is based on the humanistic psychology I spoke of, consists of a periodically revised collection of chapters—passages of prose and poetry by Eastern and Western authors, a few of whom were trained in your profession. There are excerpts, for example, from the writings of a Danish psychologist of your day named Erik Erikson. The testament eloquently represents the substantial core of their religion, a very deep and complicated matter, difficult to expound.

"Of special interest to you," the angel said, "would be the story of the vehement refusal, then the unconcealed reluctance, then the halfhearted willingness, and finally the eagerness of psychologists to contribute in some way to the composition of this testament. You would be surprised to hear how their initial, stubborn opposition to the very idea of a religion was gradually dispelled as they approached the dawning certainty, with no residual distrust, that a natural, not a supernatural, religion was intended (one with only entities and forces *within* the order of nature to be symbolized and commemorated), that the underlying propositions of this religion would be tested by their fruits and hence would be as susceptible as scientific theories to refutation and revision, and that the whole endeavor called for extensions rather than suppressions of their creativeness.

"The psychologists took their next stand on the ground that they and other educated, disillusioned people could get along as well—if not better—without religion. For them, science had displaced religion. That this was not so for every intellectual became apparent to these psychologists after some of them had been challenged by a virtual epidemic of existential emptiness, such as you, my friend, observed after World War II, when scores of agitated or spiritless young men avowed that there was no theme for them to live by, except the theme that they were

> Grovellers between faith and doubt
> the sun and north star lost, and compass out,
> the heart's weak engine all but stopped ...

[Conrad Aiken]

It became apparent that in the psyches of these sufferers—among whom were poets and artists of the first rank—the lights of all traditional religions had flickered and gone out, and no existing political ideology had drawing power. These disaffected, alienated souls, in a state of spiritual deficiency which no consumer goods could remedy, seemed to be waiting for a Second Coming without a ray of hope that it would ever come.

"The psychologists' final objection," the angel said, "was to the use of the sacred words *testament* and *religion* to designate the work-in-progress—a compilation of visions and ideas some of which were being composed and recomposed, with the aid of consciousness, in the deeps of anonymous creative men and women. The psychologists were told that they, of course, were free to use any less pretentious terms that suited them. But when the essence of the published testament eventually became, in the estimation of the world, a matter of superordinate, ultimate concern, their antipathies to the word *religion* dwindled. Having witnessed the fatal consequences of deifying nationalism, the sage composers of this new religion saw that above the separate sovereignties of states there must be a firmly implanted and respected representation of humanity's profoundest moral intuitions, a *world* superego.

"Another reason for calling the testament a religious document is that its purpose is to generate and sustain interior emotional transformations—from anxiety to serenity, for instance, from hate to love, or from envy to magnanimity—all of which are impalpable experiences which cannot be veritably described or effectively induced by the conceptual language of science, philosophy, or political ideologies. The engendering of deep subjective changes calls for graphic models, mythic parables, emotive metaphors, archetypal symbols, personifications—in short, narrative and poetic speech, as in the Bible. The myths and symbols of this new religion have already supplied artists of all stamps with enough suggestiveness in depth to last them for two centuries.

"And in this connection," continued the angel, "I should tell you that the religion of this new world is marked by numerous efficacious rites and festivals which might be described, in your old language, as ways of cheering, checking, channeling, and controlling the wildest dispositions of the id. We shall soon be in the city, where you will be enlightened as well as entertained by a spectacular religious festival which was suggested a number of years ago by a young psychologist. It has been shown that the amazing decline in the incidence of discontent, criminality, and psychosis can be attributed in large measure to the cathartic efficacy of mythic festivals such as the one which is going on today. For this is Bacchanalian week, during which everyone reverses roles. At the university, for example, you will hear students, with masks and costumes concealing their identities, lecturing to their professors and telling them exactly what they think of them; and later, in the public square you will witness a ritual enactment of the death and recreation of the Kingship."

As we were entering the city of Copenhagen, the angel embarked on a strange, disjointed discourse about the riddles and mysteries of this new religion. But I could not follow him at all, and, being left behind with my own thoughts, I suddenly woke up and rubbed my eyes. The trance was ended.

NOTES

1. Edgar Tranekjaer-Rasmussen was president of the International Congress of Applied Psychology.
2. Gerhard Nielsen was president of the congress.

Psychology in the Year 2000
Gardner Murphy

Gardner Murphy is a versatile psychologist with interests in personality, social psychology, and the history of psychology. In the following article, first delivered at the Wayne State University Centennial Symposium in Detroit, Michigan, in 1968, Murphy predicts what psychology will be in the year 2000. His predictions cover ten categories: psychophysiology, internal scanning, confrontation of the unconscious world, voluntary control, nameless states, parapsychology, psychology's relations to biology, psychology's relations to the social sciences, psychology's development of new methods, and, lastly, psychology's concern with the human predicament. In the next few decades, says Murphy, there will be an urgent need to develop cross-cultural and cross-national communication so that a psychology that is "common human" may emerge with a "human enough point of view to speak for all kinds of human beings."

Our profound ambivalence about human futures, and our hopes and fears regarding the possibility of intelligent planning for the future, appears in a charming phrase of Sir George Thomson. Regarding the role of science in planning for new potentialities within the human germ cell, he says that the likelihood of genetic improvements is about like the probability of improving a statue by spraying it with machine gun bullets. Instantly, however, he catches himself up in the remark that with the electron microscope, the localization of individual genes is already very close. One dares not be overbold for fear the critics will laugh, while actually the science fiction, and the casual predictions of scientists for the last hundred years or so, have been much too modest—in fact, much too myopic—as to what actually can be achieved. The best guide here is a systematic and reasonable extrapolation from identifiable trends and, at the same time, a cautious but systematic utilization of the principle of emergence in which new realities constantly come into

Gardner Murphy, Psychology in the year 2000. *American Psychologist*, 1969, **24**, 523-530. Reprinted by permission of the author and the American Psychological Association.

being, not through the extrapolation of separate curves, but through specific interaction processes. Many of these new emergents are known in metallurgy, in embryology, and in the field of psychology. Some of them have to do with new perceptual and conceptual wholes as shown in countless studies of music and of painting; some of them have to do with dyadic or group patterns that come into existence when new relationships are achieved, for the first time, as shown in the dynamic leadership patterns of Lewin, White, and Lippitt. In a symposium like the present one, an ultracautious note may indeed *sound* like science, but only like the plodding science of Sir Francis Bacon's *Novum Organum,* not the creative science that indeed has remade the world, and is remaking the world through the extravagant inventiveness of a Planck and an Einstein. In this spirit, I shall attempt some predictions that, I believe, are just as likely to prove shallow and banal as to prove ultimately extravagant and exotic.

The 10 topics which I shall attempt to survey are extrapolations based upon *(a)* the current extraordinary development of *psychophysiology; (b)* together with such psychophysiology, the new possibilities of *internal scanning,* in the discovery of the inner human world; the renewed capacity to *observe, with full objectivity, a great deal that has long been regarded as hopelessly subjective; (c)* herewith, the direct *confrontation of the unconscious world* that merges into, and is isomorphic with, the world of physiology; *(d)* following these discoveries, the development of *voluntary control over the inner world,* such as scientists previously never dared to dream; *(e)* a new definition of a wide variety of nameless states, *psychological states for which there are no good names,* including feeling states, cognitive states, and volitional states, upon which human destiny almost literally may depend, with resulting understanding of those profound alterations in states of consciousness, well known to the East, regarding which Western man usually has expressed doubt or scorn; *(f)* together with these, the objective exploration of the vast sphere of *parapsychology,* at the edges of which science is nibbling, but so far has failed massively to invade; *(g)* a fresh *reconsideration of the relations of psychology to the biological sciences,* especially genetics; *(h)* a renewed *consideration of psychology in relation to the social sciences,* notably in the new science of social ecology, entailing cross-cultural collaboration of cross-cultural realities; *(i)* a note on the way in which changes in research *methods* alter all these basic concepts; *(j)* finally, a consideration, in all these terms, of the nature of the *human predicament* to which expanding science, which I am describing, may make a serious and indeed a crucial contribution.

PSYCHOPHYSIOLOGY

First, then, as to psychophysiology. Partly as a result of new concepts of the wholeness, the integrity, of the living system, as voiced for example by Sir Charles Sherrington in the *Integrative Action of the Nervous System,* and partly as a result of the sheer power of the research tools that have been developed, psychophysiology has become a dramatically new science in recent decades. Problems of specialization and subspecialization of tissues, as within the mammalian cerebral cortex, have assumed astonishing forms with Penfield's discovery of specific memory localization, with various techniques for studying the electronic functional realities inside the individual nerve cell, with X-ray studies of lattices, and with fine localization of sensory and motor function through implanted electrodes. Both the cruder spot localizations, earlier used in the study of the aphasias, and also the extreme equipotentiality concepts, based largely on extirpation studies, have yielded to a dialectical reconsideration of both local and general aspects of functioning, and with an extraordinary directness of application to the world of immediate experience. Donald Hebb's brilliant breakthrough in the study of sensory deprivation has helped scientists to think of the amazing possibilities of sensory enrichment. One can no longer speak of sensory deprivation or sensory enrichment without thinking, in the manner of David Krech, about the biochemistry and physiology of the mammalian cortex, as profoundly affected by very early postnatal experience. One begins to see, quite literally, the likelihood, in the next few decades, of a thoroughgoing isomorphism of physiological process and psychological process right across the board. Biochemical and neurophysiological progress has been so astonishing in the last few years that psychologists may look quite confidently for a rapidly advancing series of discoveries related specifically to the different kinds of human experience, essentially the sensory, the imaginal, the conceptual, the affective, and indeed certain types of experience that have never been analyzed finely enough to name. Psychopharmacology, long considered to be limited to the specific effects of toxins, is rapidly taking on the form of a powerful organist having at his command banks upon banks of keys, and hundreds of stops, calling into existence an incredible gamut of new experiences.

INTERNAL SCANNING

Following from, or upon, this concurrent study of psychophysiology and biochemistry on the one hand, and the phenomenal world of immediate experience and function on the other hand, psychologists will be drawn, as in a vortex, into the rich field of the study of internal scanning. By this I mean, first, the process by which delicate messages from the striped musculature can be identified more accurately as our subjects carry out reflex or skilled movements. Like a tea taster or a wine sampler, the subject, in several laboratories today, recognizes quickly the kinesthetic messages in different magnitude from different muscles. Specific muscular activities are experienced kinesthetically at the same time he sees on the panel the electronic evidence of what is occurring in specific muscle groups, so that he learns to identify and name them. He is learning, in the same way, to recognize on the panel many other messages that come from organs that are under autonomic control. One may think of the studies by the U.S.S.R. scientists, Bykov and Lisina, relating to proprioceptive and interoceptive conditioning.

But the work will soon move further along. Giving the subject feedback on a panel that shows him what specific internal activities are going on, he can be taught to make more and more refined differentiation within the inner world. His searching, his sweeping, his scanning, and his identifying of the different components from the proprioceptive world, as identical or isomorphic with the same messages from the exteroceptive world on the panel or conveyed to him through tones, give him more and more information as to the rich system of internal messages that have previously been nearly a blur, so precise that he can begin to play the instrument himself. The ancient prejudice that exteroceptive information has a kind of place in the reality world, which is lacking for the other sensory functions, has begun to collapse. A rich variety of internal messages has exactly the same possibility of cross-checking, consensual validation, as has held for sight, hearing, and touch. It is hard to set any limits. Something is known about discriminability when working with teas and wines, or even two-point thresholds on the finger tip, but these studies have never been pushed to their true physiological limits. Nor is it known how they are affected by a variety of parameters, anatomical distribution of receptors and afferent fibers, which in the past have never been sufficiently important to investigate; but today they are being seen in terms of individuality—an individuality based upon heredity, growth, and the learning process. A whole internal world is awaiting discovery.

CONFRONTATION OF THE UNCONSCIOUS WORLD

Third, this internal world, as Gregory Razran has pointed out, would include the entire world of the "observable unconscious," the world of psychologically meaningful, but hitherto not directly observable, processes discovered by Freud and his followers. More and more it appears to be the same world as that which anthropologists, playwrights, poets, and prophets have often enjoined without knowing, in any scientific sense, what they were doing.

But it is one thing to observe the separate components, of course, and another thing to study creatively how they can be put together into new and emergent wholes. Both Arnheim, in *Art and Visual Perception,* and Freud, in *The Interpretation of Dreams,* have applied some of the first informative steps regarding the synthesis, the creative reorganization, of a world that offers vast possibilities. Literally there are hundreds of experiences waiting patiently to be discovered through experimentation. It will not be just the clinicians and the "encounter" groups that will discover them; such discoveries will soon yield rich new harvests to general experimental psychology. I might remind you that while Chaucer, 600 years ago, had only a few words for colors, there are today some thousands of color terms, mostly representing *new* colors that have evolved in the last century as a result of industrial chemistry—colors that do not appear in any rainbow, natural sunset, or natural color schema. There are not only the stock experiences that human beings have by virtue of their anatomical equipment and their physiological capacity as human beings, but thousands of newly created colors. There also are many new kinds of inner experiences, ranging from the effects of new foods, drugs, smogs, exercise, fatigue, strain, anxiety, and ecstasy—scores upon scores of new kinds and shades of inner experience. Of course, many of the new methods may involve risks, and many of them will come under some sort of social control. Whether it will be control by a wise and humane Federal agency, or by public opinion, no present reliable clues are extant.

Inner responses include those called affective and impulsive states, and the vast range of expressions of mood and temperament used in the aesthetic world and in the personal world generally. There are new worlds just waiting; and they will not have to wait very long. Experimental methods for the study of differentiation are developing; for example, experiments in the Soviet Union proved that two-point thresholds within the body, say from the gastric mucosa, can be measured. It is believable that as such differentiations are carried out by classical psychophysical methods, experimenters may first identify a very large range of internal messages and, second, may learn how to integrate them in thousands of new ways.

VOLUNTARY CONTROL

Fourth, insofar as these new messages can be differentiated, tagged, and named, they apparently can be brought under voluntary control. A wide array of new possibilities exists, for example, in Hefferline's study of rapid acquisition of operant control over slight movements that are effective in cutting out a disagreeable hum spoiling music at the time. That is, individuals who could differentiate at all, could also learn, even though unwittingly, to bring in or shut out particular messages. Other laboratories are now continuing what Hefferline started. It appears to be a very refined, delicate, and far-below-threshold type of activity that can bring in an astonishing range of experimentally prepared visual and auditory material. Soviet work on voluntary control of cardiovascular processes appears to concur with what Robert Malmo has reported in Montreal. There are studies of bladder and of capillary control, using panel feedback techniques, strongly suggesting that the autonomically controlled organs are capable of being brought rapidly into the same sphere of voluntary control as that which obtains for the striped muscle responses. Within the next decade or two certainly a very significant control of cardiovascular and gastrointestinal responses may be anticipated, not only with immediate clinical values in bringing in or shutting out various classes of bodily information, but with the deeper scientific value of giving a much wider view of what the human potentialities for such inner experience and such inner control may be. Wenger and Bagchi studied adepts in yoga in various ashrams in India, while Anand and his collaborators pushed their studies further. The keen interest of Indian investigators in putting to experimental tests the classical yoga sutras of Patanjali means not only cross-national research collaboration but, what is more important, the serious awakening of Western psychologists to the fact that experiences treasured and cultivated on the other side of the globe may be as worthy of investigation as those encountered in Detroit, Cambridge, or Topeka.

Last, but by no means least, the process of directly observing one's own electroencephalogram, notably one's own alpha, was developed by Joe Kamiya at Langley Porter and independently by Barbara Brown at the Sepulveda Veterans Administration Hospital. With Kamiya, a 400-cycle tone is activated by the individual's own alpha rhythm, so the subject given the task of increasing the amount of alpha he is exhibiting can rapidly learn, through the feedback that this tone gives him, to bring this under his control. Soon he is turning on or turning off his own alpha. Apparently alpha is not the only rhythm that he can control. There are staggering possibilities both for the understanding of the nature of central nervous system control by the organized central nervous system itself in the form that is called voluntary, but likewise a vast area of further implications for the understanding of the isomorphic relation between a variety of subjective states that accompany the alpha and the exteroceptive patterns that are seen when observing the visual tracing or hearing an appropriate tone. While the clinical applications are important, it is this larger vision of learning to control the brain rhythms themselves that is likely to mean most to the scientist oriented to the year 2000.

NAMELESS STATES

Fifth, while neither Kamiya, nor anyone else, so far as I know, has published the implications that these new methods have for the study of whole new areas of experience only dimly describable today, it is highly probable that before the year 2000 there will be both identification of many kinds of phenomenological states that are anchored upon particular types of EEGs, and the invention of appropriate *names,* appropriate language to describe the newly identified and newly integrated components. I am thinking particularly of cognitive states, conceptualizing states, creative states that may, while retaining all their charm and all their majesty, become far more describable, controllable, and achievable.

PARAPSYCHOLOGY

Sixth, it is characteristic of science at any given period to cultivate the belief that it has a rather well-integrated system into which new observations can fit. While it is at many points open-ended, with really fuzzy edges, there would be chaos indeed if scientists relinquished their passion for a unified field of science. Suppose science was an archipelago of little, spotty, factual details, with no possibility of an implied closed system, an ocean bed unifying all the little islands that appear at the surface level. There is very good psychological reason why science, as it grows, takes on the conservative, the resistive character that is apparent. Under these conditions it is hardly surprising that there is some restlessness, or even resistance, when talking about the discovery of kinds of experience about which nothing has been known. Of course, there are many good reasons, in polite society, why people do not know too much about their insides. These have to do with delicate and complex systems of human expression, some related very broadly to love, some related very broadly to destructiveness, but a great many others that almost every human individual encounters, but does not really want at this time to communicate on a massive basis. I do not anticipate very much actual interference with science on this count, but I do think one must be honest in admitting that this quest of the inside will entail not only triumphs but occasional acrimonious encounters.

While saying this I must add that the resistance toward types of human communication, which presently are not understood, has shown the same attributes. One can understand very clearly that natural fear of scientists that their whole tough labor would be disturbed if they should admit perceptual, memoric, affective, or volitional processes that now are not explainable in terms of the basic biochemical and biophysical realities of human conduct. Even the thought elements that the Würzburg School brought into Wundt's psychological system led to much hostility. Today more serious difficulties are being dealt with as the study of *parapsychology* moves into more systematic experimental form. Most of the data, when closely observed, are like the perceptual and affective data already known, but appear to occur under conditions in which the time and space parameters are unfamiliar. For example, in several recent studies, the telepathic phenomena occur when sender and receiver are separated by very long distances; and while the data can be described psychologically without any mystery, a physical difficulty is encountered because how to conceptualize energies that could carry over these long distances is not known. In other words, the difficulty is at the level of physics, not at the level of psychology. Psychologists may be a little bewildered when they encounter modern physicists who take these phenomena in stride; in fact, take them very much more seriously than psychologists do, saying, as physicists, that they are no longer bound by the types of Newtonian energy distribution, inverse square laws, etc., with which scientists used to regard themselves as tightly bound. In the same way, new physical conceptions regarding the nature of time seem to remove a large part of the trouble that appears in precognition experiments, in which a randomly determined target order of stimulus materials can be foreseen by certain subjects. I think that with the computer methods that are now coming into use, and with the progressive rigidity in experimental controls, psychologists probably will witness a period of slow, but definite, erosion of the blandly exclusive attitude that has offered itself as the only appropriate scientific attitude in this field. The data from parapsychology will be almost certainly in harmony with general psychological principles, and will be assimilated rather easily within the systematic framework of psychology as a science when once the imagined appropriateness of Newtonian physics is put aside, and modern physics replaces it.

PSYCHOLOGY AND BIOLOGY

As I turn to genetics, I would venture to predict a period of massive reorientation of psychology to the biological roots of which it used to boast. The very substance of growth, of motivation, of the learning process, and indeed of most of the basic realities with which the modern evolutionary psychology will have to cope, are provided by the DNA-RNA system; the elements of field physics as they are known in the embryology of Spemann and Weiss; the intricacies of polygenic determination of structure and function; and the broad recognition that individuality in tissue systems, as described by Roger Williams, rewrites the psychology of individual differences in astonishing terms. These genetic terms, of course, will be held by some to be fatalistic, as indicating the genetically given limitations upon all human endeavor. But in two respects these discoveries will be most encouraging: *(a)* It will be realized that individuality always applies to the growth *potential,* which can be utterly different when a new environmental situation is supplied. An example is the discovery of the Mendelian basis of the phenylpyruvic type of mental defect that has nevertheless yielded, to a large degree, to a carefully prepared diet. In other words, that which was genetically determined was controllable. Through respect for the genetics of human individuality, how to become better environmentalists will be understood. *(b)* As Sir George Thomson's statement, quoted earlier, implied, scientific insight is moving rapidly to a point such that the electron microscope can greatly aid in studies of the internal organization of individual cells. This, together with some control of mutations and a great deal of control of selective breeding and the application of the principles of population genetics, makes it likely that, within a few generations, to a considerable degree, some of the most abhorrent threats to human development may be eliminated. In anticipating the year 2100 or 2500, biologists could talk quite rationally about not only the prevention of deterioration, but plans for the actual long-range improvement of genetic potentials.

PSYCHOLOGY AND SOCIAL SCIENCE

But the biological sciences do not have the whole exigent message. There is equal need for big gains in the social sciences, especially in the development of a social ecology. Ecology has been the most neglected aspect, I think, of the entire behavior field. The experimental psychologist may control, say, a $10 \times 10 \times 10$ foot area, and, with enormous and devoted attention to detail, think of everything that is in that space at a given time. Organisms, however, have life histories in segments of space time about which a fair amount is known if they are hatched or born in the laboratory. But if not, the higher they are in the phylogenetic tree, the more likely they are to bring more from their past into the laboratory. Mark May used to say that the American sophomore, from whom are derived findings from humanity at large, was expected to "park his culture outside." Only the regions of time and space that are involved in the experiment are observed, ignoring the whole vast area from which the individual organism comes.

The needed studies of ecological organization are vastly more complex than anybody has imagined so far. The maps that Roger Barker has drawn of a Kansas town, and the lists of situational pressures that Saul Sells has devised as a preparation for space travel, will be only a tiny sampling of that vast conception of past and present environmental totalities that Egon Brunswik asked scientists to imagine. It will be a genetics that is oriented to a systematic and scientific science of ecology that will really give new field clues to human behavior. By field clues I hope to suggest the modalities of interaction between the edge of the organism and the edge of the environment, such that a complete and real fusion is created. I mean the kind of thing that is involved in interaction between the visual centers in the brain, the retina, the external light source, the laboratory conditions, personalities of the experimenters, the laboratory tradition, and laboratory culture, all of which must be considered when a person sees an inkblot or a social scene enacted before him. There must be whole organisms and whole environments to be studied for the sake of the modalities of reciprocity that develop between them. Psychologists began to learn from Lewin, as earlier they began to learn from Clerk-Maxwell, how to think in field terms; but they really have not done much of the sort on a scale demanded by present knowledge. The subspecialization has driven them more and more from organs to tissues, from tissues to cells, from cells to molecules, from molecules to atoms, from atoms to microparticles. All this specialization is, of course, absolutely necessary. The job of seeing psychological function, however, in combined biological and cultural terms is mostly a promissory note with as yet very little backing.

Because of its rarity, I shall mention the example of audiogenic seizures in mice, which Benson Ginzburg showed to have a not too complex Mendelian basis. But some of the mice that were expected to have convulsions and die had no convulsions, or had convulsions but did not die. He then attacked the problem from the pharmacological viewpoint and, in terms of biochemistry, found a way to buffer the lethal effects of the genes. Allow me a free analogy in the field of human ecology: What will happen when one finds a human environment of space-time-sensory enrichment, maternal warmth, generous and skillful experimental reinforcement that will allow a poorly endowed, frightened, aggressive ghetto child to develop into full humanness? This is exactly the type of experiment now being launched at several outposts of research on disadvantaged children. Before long thought in terms of biology versus the social sciences will cease; an ecological science will be developed so rich and so concrete that it will articulate closely with the new biology of individual growth.

And if psychologists mean quite seriously that man, as man, is richly intertwined with his ecology, it follows that the psychology of the next two decades will depend enormously upon the discovery of new forms of cross-cultural, cross-national communication. Indeed, it follows that unless there is very broad cross-national communication and action, there will be no human race to investigate. It will not do for American psychology, now having about 92% of the world's psychological personnel and about 92% of its published communications, to undertake a bland and supposedly disinterested study of the rest of the world in order that the wise and productive science, which they represent, can convey appropriate knowledge to those struggling along in less enlightened paths of endeavor. The study of the human predicament can come from a human race familiar with the method of science, but a human race speaking many tongues, regarding many values, and holding different convictions about the meaning of life sooner or later will have to consult all that is human. There are a few living today who will still be alive in the year 2000, if there is a year 2000; and I hope they will still be battling the problem of developing a sufficiently coherent, human enough point of view to speak for all kinds of human beings. This will mean that the genetic and ecological progress that I am describing will have actually helped toward a psychology that is common human, that entails not only a study of all human beings, but a study by trained and devoted individuals within all human groups. Following the

American habit of delivering "State of the Union" messages, the Secretary-General of the United Nations has been asked to report on the "state of the human race." I personally do not understand why governments, and indeed professional psychologists, as well, are almost wholly ignoring the challenge to study directly the possibilities of achieving an international and intercultural plan for world order. Aiming at this goal, it is conceivable that there will be worldwide human modalities of investigation like those already existing in astronomy and in medicine, but oriented to the behavioral sciences. And it is even possible that they will be oriented not only to the behaviors as such, but toward the deep inner humanness that I have tried to describe as an object of study. This, in relation to the dyadic and group problems of the behavior sciences, may give both insight and control over the more destructive tendencies, and may utilize the common human aspiration to live not only more safely and a little more comfortably, but also a little more creatively and a great deal more humanly.

THE ROLE OF METHOD

You have noted that new discoveries in the field of psychology, and, I believe, in all scientific fields, are largely the children of new *methods.* Consider what the compound microscope did to histology, what X-rays did for the diagnostic procedure, and what the puzzle box, the maze, the Skinner box have done in the development and documentation of seminal scientific theories. I am raising these issues not simply to welcome the computer to our side, as a new brother, but to ask one final question. Psychologists can, as A.H. Maslow has pointed out, strip down the study of man to those methods common to the other sciences that do not deal with man; they can assume that the human sciences can best do their job by leaving humanness out. There is, however, another possibility. They might conceivably find that science can become big enough to develop fully human methods oriented to the complete panoply of human problems, that empathy, "tlc," rich dyadic methods of communication between subjects and experimenters, through patience, discipline, and imagination, might give them in the year 2000 a science more competent to deal with all the discoverable aspects of human nature.

But a still more basic problem of method relates to the way in which they try to hook together the data from laboratory, from clinic, from field observation, from home, from neighborhood, and from observation of human gatherings in schools, churches, juries, parliamentary bodies. On the one hand, they have neglected the use of laboratories, and today they are beginning to discover a more suitable laboratory approach to a wide variety of spontaneous human situations. They are discovering that inventive experimentalists can do even better work in free human situations than they can in the classical, highly planned, settings. But now I am referring mainly to the manner in which the experimental method does its work. Long ago, psychologists established for themselves the impossible task of creating a psychology through intensive observation of those phenomena that occur under controlled laboratory conditions, and then systematizing a psychology based solely on such findings. They tried to set up physics and chemistry, sometimes the biological sciences of genetics, embryology, and physiology, as models. Belatedly they have discovered that beautiful scientific structures, such as that of modern geology, with only slight use of experimental method, can be developed through the integration of many types of observations, short-term and long-term, outdoors and indoors, pinpointed or extravagantly blown up to cosmic proportions. The geologist uses experimental methods, but he uses them in the total context of his work. It is mother earth, not her fingernails, that interests him. Psychology, which attempted to pinpoint its existence in the nineteenth-century terms of Weber and Fechner, is now beginning a great awakening, a sort of Rip Van Winkle awakening; for we are discovering, and will discover more fully in the next few decades, the vast dimensions in which a mature psychology can be conceived. It will make even more use of experimental method than it does at present. But the experiments will be suggested, and the techniques controlled, rather largely by the broad perception of the nature of the human animal in his whole ecological setting. The observational systems that will develop cannot be categorized by any one word that is now known. The word *experimental* is a fine word, but it will have to be replaced by something much more systematic. Even the developmental approach will mean something quite new when conceived in the kind of general systems terms, the kind of life science terms, that I am trying to suggest. Mathematical models certainly will both benefit and be benefited by the transitions that I am suggesting; and, of course, the engineering skills, already so important in psychophysiology, will become even more important.

I think psychologists will have to admit that many of this era will be unable to see the promised land that begins to be sketched out. Psychologists who will be extant in the year 2000 will have to be smarter than the psychologists today, as well as enormously better trained—I might add, enormously more *broadly* trained—than the subspecialized people turned out today. The blade of the modern mind is sharpened until it breaks, and we damn the blade instead of asking the metallurgist to develop tools from which sharp weapons can be prepared that, while still unscathed, can cut through the hard inscrutable rock of man's basic resistance to discovering his own nature.

THE HUMAN PREDICAMENT

The year 2000 can come, and the twenty-first century can offer less terror and more joy, but only if psychologists have learned both *how to look inside* and *how to look outside;* how to recognize the reciprocities of inner and outer, through methods that are as far ranging and as deeply human as is the human stuff that is being studied.

Psychology in the Year 2000: Going Structural?
Uriel G. Foa
Jim L. Turner

Uriel G. Foa received his D.Jur. degree from the University of Parma, Italy, in 1939 and his Ph.D. from the Hebrew University in Jerusalem in 1948. In addition to teaching, he served as Executive Director of the Israel Institute of Applied Social Research. In 1965 he accepted a visiting professorship at the University of Illinois. Currently he is at the University of Missouri. Foa has written several articles on personality structure and on the development and cross-cultural aspects of role behavior. In the following selection he and his colleague, Jim L. Turner, attempt to provoke discussion about the trends and goals of psychology in the remaining years of the 20th century.

Predictions regarding the future development of psychology may connote more than an engaging exercise in prophecy and science fiction. Such diversions provide an appropriate occasion for an assessment of present trends and an opportunity for evaluating their extrapolation in terms of scientific goals. The stimulating, thoughtful, and well-informed essay recently provided by Gardner Murphy (1969) is a case in point. Murphy appraises and extrapolates from current significant developments to offer his predictions regarding the state of psychology in the year 2000. The viewpoint he obtains suggests that psychology will advance by extending at its periphery with a corresponding diminution in its traditional core of subject matter. With neurophysiology surging on one side, social sciences on the other, and the guerrillas of parapsychology undermining traditional concepts of our science, the area of psychology proper may become quite narrow: perhaps not much more than the conditioning of internal functions monitored by the advancing physiologists. This rather dreary circumscribed extrapolation of current trends is tempered and a more optimistic forecast warranted when Murphy

Uriel G. Foa and Jim L. Turner, Psychology in the year 2000: Going structural? *American Psychologist*, 1970, **25**, 244-247. Reprinted by permission of the authors and the American Psychological Association.

The preparation of this article was supported, in part, by Grant GS-2904 from the National Science Foundation.

anticipates the emergence of two new directions. One of these involves the merging of the study of overt behavior with the observation of internal states. The second concerns the analysis of the integration of components into organized wholes, or the investigation of structures.[1] These two developments are given brief attenuated consideration in Murphy's article. Since, however, it is these specific points that appear to define the difference between an optimistic and a pessimistic forecast of future psychology's scope as an independent discipline, the remainder of this note is directed toward a more detailed consideration of these two notions.

INTEGRATION OF BEHAVIORISM AND PSYCHOPHYSIOLOGY

Behaviorism emerged as a reaction to a psychology of unobservable internal states. This situation is changing rapidly now as the study of the relationship between overt behavior and internal states becomes increasingly feasible (Pribram, 1966). It is unlikely that the internal and external systems will be found to map one-to-one, as this is not what usually occurs between homologous systems. In language, for example, different words may have the same meaning, and words often have more than one meaning, so that one-to-one mapping of words and meaning does not always occur. The ambiguity is usually resolved when a word is seen in the context of an organized whole, a sentence. Therefore, appropriate study of the relationship among such complex systems requires first knowledge about the organization of each system and then mapping rules for linking each level to the other.

The task of relating behavior to psychophysiological states may thus be facilitated by studying the structure of behavior, a problem paradoxically but persistently ignored by behaviorists. This increased sophistication in identifying the alternative mappings of the same overt behavior will enhance the scientific respectability of investigations oriented toward a more ambitious destination than the mere cataloguing of response contingencies.

---

[1] A structure can be conceived as a pattern of interrelationship among the variables belonging to a set, in a space of stated coordinates.

It may also turn out that the relationship between psychophysiological states and overt behavior is mediated by the categorization of such behavior in the cognitive structure of the subject. Studies like those of Ekman and his co-workers (Ekman, 1965, 1969; Ekman, Von Cranach, Exeline, & Schefler, 1969) exploring the meaning of facial expression and other overt, but not necessarily verbal, behavior are likely to aid in the eventual understanding of this relationship. A recent article by Duncan (1969) reviews the burgeoning area of nonverbal communication and suggests some intriguing insights into the structural implications of such studies.

FROM SINGLE VARIABLES TO ORGANIZED WHOLES

Realizing the difficulty of mapping one-to-one isolated variables from different domains may lead to a growing interest in the investigation of the structure of each domain. Learning experimentalists then may find unsuspected value in their notions of stimulus and response generalization and discrimination, as avenues to structural exploration. Students of cognition, on the other hand, will probably abandon such expansive notions as cognitive complexity in favor of more detailed and specific structural models. This will involve identification of basic components and of the way these elements combine to produce interrelated patterns of variables. There is already some evidence suggesting that the structural units will not be behavioral classes but more elementary components which, in turn, combine to produce behaviors. The work of Luria (1966), on disturbances of higher mental functions in the presence of local brain lesions, indicates that more than one brain activity is involved in any given behavior while a given activity participates in several behaviors. For example, a complex activity like handwriting may be impaired in a distinct characteristic manner which is associated with the location of the lesion. Such components as spelling, distortion of the letters, and directionality (i.e., writing on a line from left to right) will be variously affected depending on the localization of the cerebral lesions. Where a handwriting component such as directionality is impaired we may also expect to find this component impaired in other domains of behavior. Social direction (e.g., differentiation between what one does to self and what one does to other) is one example of a behavior that would be defective because of disturbances in the directionality component. Similar notions may be applied to the study of basic sensory functions. Employing a visual discrimination task, Iversen (1969) has found that monkeys with posterior intratemporal lesions show impairment of pattern discrimination but perform as well as normal monkeys in color discrimination. These observations suggest that elementary components of behavior may well become identified and associated with specific brain activities and states. It follows that the relationship among different behavioral classes will be seen as a function of their underlying elementary components, each of which exerts selective influences on a number of seemingly disparate behavioral variables. Support for this hypothesis will decrease interest in the investigation of one or a few variables in favor of the study of organized wholes.

STRUCTURAL DYNAMICS

The identification of cognitive wholes will raise the problem of their dynamics, that is, the way structures modify in development or under specific experimental conditions. Longitudinal studies of cognitive structures at different ages, from infancy to adulthood and senescence, may reveal how the structural pattern becomes progressively more differentiated as one approaches maturity and then changes again in old age. The structure of the adult may well turn out to be a counterpart of the institutional structure of the social system, acquired in childhood through imitation and the differential reinforcement patterns of significant others. Conditions that facilitate or hinder learning of the societal structure will become open to investigation. It might be that under certain conditions defective learning will occur leading to deviance in the acquired structure. Different kinds of emotional, interpersonal, and intellectual disturbances may be found to correspond to specific deviance patterns. It will then become possible to devise preventive and curative treatments geared to each type of deviance in the structure. Experimental work on structure changes and longitudinal studies of structure growth will provide the knowledge required for devising specific remedial and preventive methods. The realization that culture can be seen as a complex learning program will lead on one hand to the study of structural differences among cultures, and on the other hand to a profound change in the approach to learning experiments. Reinforcement schedules as presently conceived typically bear little relationship to such manifold variation as cultural patterns. Hence the difficulty of applying laboratory findings to life problems, beyond the operant conditioning of specific responses.

Reinforcement schedules of the future will be conceived as minicultures—models of some areas in the organizational pattern of a given culture at large. A beginning in this direction is found in the work of Solomon (1964). On the other hand, Rescorla (1967), in describing the appropriate schedule for control groups in conditioning experiments, has already provided a model of a nonculture or an environment where nothing is contingent on anything else.

Learning studies relating experimental contingencies to cognitive structure will enable us to follow the spreading of effect through the structure and will explore the possibility of experimentally changing cognitive patterns. These field and experimental investigations of structural dynamics may lead to a unified psychological theory relating personality to culture and integrating experimental and developmental concepts with clinical problems and notions. A tentative but somewhat fuller discussion of the integrative role of cognitive structure is given elsewhere (Foa & Foa, 1970).

CURRENT WORK ON STRUCTURES

The notion of structure, or organized whole, has deep roots in the evolution of contemporary psychology. Freud's (1949) personality structures of id, ego, and superego, Lewin's (1936) topological spaces, and Piaget's (1952) schemata are all essentially oriented toward providing structural models for psychological processes and behavioral events. The notion of structure is also prominent in the anthropological work of Lévi-Strauss (1963) and Goodenough (1967), as well as in studies of linguistics (Chomsky, 1957; McNeill, 1966). A review of the notion of structure in psychology has been . provided recently by Mucchielli (1966).

Specific structural models, with varying degrees of empirical support, have been proposed for intellect (Guilford, 1967), interpersonal behavior (Foa, 1962; Rinn, 1965), emotions (Plutchik, 1962; Schlosberg, 1954), roles (Foa, 1966), a social institution (Foa, Triandis, & Katz, 1966), resources (Foa & Foa, 1970), and for task groups (Fiedler, 1967). The work of Shepard (1962) has provided the foundations for a variety of methods to determine the empirical configuration of a set of variables; Mukherjee (in press) has pioneered in the development of statistical tests for structural hypotheses, and structural dynamics have been discussed by Foa (1968).

In spite of these advances, structural work in psychology has failed thus far to generate the same excitement and commitment as that evidenced in other sciences where pursuit of the structure of the atom and the discovery of the double helix structure of DNA have completely remodeled scientific thought in their respective areas. Moreover, there has been some reluctance to recognize that specification of psychological components is likely to be as complex in construction and as revolutionary in consequence as the notion of structure has been in nuclear physics and in genetics.

CONCLUSION

Predicting the future of any science is a hazardous avocation. The revolutionary nature of scientific progress as well as the difficulty of transcending one's own interests and proclivities contribute heavily to the mortality rate of such endeavors. Perhaps the major justification for perpetuating these so frequently ill-fated fancies is that one hopes, in so doing, to urge a dialogue that offers a perspective from which to examine, if not to guide, the continuing elaboration of psychology's goals as a science.

The prediction is ventured that substantive and methodological progress will be toward an increasing interest in the study of psychological structures. This focus on the organized components of behavior appears indeed appropriate for integrating a variety of diverse subdisciplines into a framework that is uniquely psychological in orientation. Nevertheless psychology of the year 2000 might turn out to be quite different from the prediction attempted here. Even so, there remains a clear need for a continuing development of concepts and theories specific to psychology rather than reliance on the progress of neighboring disciplines. This autonomous, but not unrelated, growth will enable psychology not only to benefit more from the advances of other sciences but, what is more important, also to contribute its full and unique share to the understanding of man, his society, and its problems.

Finally, my hope is that the present corollary to Murphy's article will stimulate further discussion of the trends and goals of psychology in the last decades of the twentieth century.

REFERENCES

Chomsky, N. *Syntactic structures.* The Hague: Mouton, 1957.

Duncan, S. D., Jr. Nonverbal communication. *Psychological Bulletin,* 1969, **72,** 118-137.

Ekman, P. Communication through non-verbal behavior: A source of information about an interpersonal relationship. In S. S. Tomkins & C. E. Izard (Eds.), *Affect, cognition, and personality.* New York: Springer, 1965.

Ekman, P. Pan-cultural elements in facial display of emotion. *Science,* 1969, **164,** 86-88.

Ekman, P., Von Cranach, M., Exeline, R., & Schefler, A. Nonverbal communication. Symposium presented at the XIX International Congress of Psychology, London, August 1969.

Fiedler, F. E. *A theory of leadership effectiveness.* New York: McGraw-Hill, 1967.

Foa, U. G. The structure of interpersonal behavior in the dyad. In J. Criswell, H. Solomon, & P. Suppes (Eds.), *Mathematical methods in small group processes.* Stanford: Stanford University Press, 1962.

Foa, U. G. Perception of behavior in reciprocal roles: The ringex model. *Psychological Monographs,* 1966, **80**(15, Whole No. 623).

Foa, U. G. Three kinds of behavioral changes. *Psychological Bulletin,* 1968, **70,** 460-473.

Foa, U. G., & Foa, E. B. Resource exchange: Toward a structural theory of interpersonal communication. In A. W. Siegman & B. Pope (Eds.), *Studies in dyadic communication.* Long Island City, N.Y.: Pergamon Press, 1970.

Foa, U. G., Triandis, H. C., & Katz, E. W. Cross-cultural invariance in the differentiation and organization of family roles. *Journal of Personality and Social Psychology,* 1966, 4, 316-327.

Freud, S. *An outline of psychoanalysis.* New York: Norton, 1949.

Goodenough, W. H. Componential analysis. *Science,* 1967, **156,** 1203-1209.

Guilford, J. P. *The nature of human intelligence.* New York: McGraw-Hill, 1967.

Iversen, S. D. The contribution of the ventral temporal lobe to visual analysis in the monkey. Paper delivered at the XIX International Congress of Psychology, London, August 1969.

Lévi-Strauss, C. *Structural anthropology.* New York: Basic Books, 1963.

Lewin, K. *Principles of topological psychology.* New York: McGraw-Hill, 1936.

Luria, A. R. *Higher cortical functions in man.* New York: Basic Books, 1966.

McNeill, D. Developmental psycholinguistics. In F. Smith & G. A. Miller (Eds.), *The genesis of language.* Cambridge: M.I.T. Press, 1966.

Mucchielli, R. *Introduction à la psychologie structurelle.* (Psychologie et Sciences Humaines.) Brussels: Dessart, 1966.

Mukherjee, B. N. Illustration of a class of patterned covariance matrices in psychological data and tests of hypotheses associated with these patterns. *British Journal of Mathematical and Statistical Psychology*, 1970, in press.

Murphy, G. Psychology in the year 2000. *American Psychologist*, 1969, **24**, 523-530.

Piaget, J. *The origins of intelligence in children.* New York: International Universities Press, 1952.

Plutchik, R. *The emotions: Facts, theories and a new model.* New York: Random House, 1962

Pribram, K. H. Some dimensions of remembering: Steps toward a neuropsychological model of memory. In J. Gaito (Ed.), *Macromolecules and behavior.* New York: Academic Press, 1966.

Rescorla, R. A. Pavlovian conditioning and its proper control procedures. *Psychological Review*, 1967, **74**, 71-80.

Rinn, J. L. Structure of phenomenal domains. *Psychological Review*, 1965, **72**, 445-466.

Schlosberg, H. Three dimensions of emotion. *Psychological Review*, 1954, **61**, 81-88.

Shepard, R. N. The analysis of proximities: Multidimensional scaling with an unknown distance function. *Psychometrika*, 1962, **27**, 125-140, 140-219.

Solomon, R. L. Punishment. *American Psychologist*, 1964, **19**, 239-253.

Author Index

Subject Index